Fire and Grace

Fire and Grace

The Life of Rose Pastor Stokes

Arthur Zipser and Pearl Zipser

The University of Georgia Press

Athens and London

© 1989 by the University of Georgia Press
Athens, Georgia 30602   All rights reserved
Designed by Mary Mendell   Set in Galliard
The paper in this book meets the guidelines for
permanence and durability of the Committee on
Production Guidelines for Book Longevity of the
Council on Library Resources.
Printed in the United States of America
93 92 91 90 89   5   4   3   2   1
Library of Congress Cataloging in Publication Data
Zipser, Arthur, 1909–
Fire and grace: the life of Rose Pastor Stokes / by
Arthur Zipser and Pearl Zipser.
p. cm.   Bibliography: p.   Includes index
ISBN 0-8203-1133-2 (alk. paper)
1. Stokes, Rose Pastor, 1879–1933. 2. Feminists—
United States—Biography. 3. Socialists—United
States—Biography. I. Zipser, Pearl. II.
Title.   HQ1413.S69Z56   1989   305.4'2'0924—
dc19   [B]   88-31707 CIP

Unless credited otherwise, photographs in this book
are from the collection of John M. Whitcomb and
are used with permission.

British Library Cataloging in Publication Data
available

To David and his children,
Karl and Nina

TO A ROSE

In Bloom at Cedar Lodge, July 29, 1904

She comes: a breeze, a bird, a song,
  A laughter and a prayer,
  A thrill of sweet prophetic air,
A gleam the cedar boughs among, —
  And she—our Rose—is here.

Olive Tilford Dargan to Rose Harriet Pastor

Contents

Preface

The title of *Fire and Grace* is taken from a letter to Rose Pastor Stokes by the Reverend Albert Rhys Williams. He was describing the qualities she projected in her public speaking. The same words, we were to find, described her personality and character.

We had friends who had been friends and colleagues of Rose Stokes. (Very few of them survive today.) We recall occasional references to her name over the years, usually with some anecdote and a brief characterization: "She was dynamic"; "She was a fascinating person"; "She was beautiful."

And, in her time, she was famous. Over the period 1905 to 1925 she was as famous as any woman in the world. She was more famous than her partners in struggle, including Emma Goldman, Helen Keller, Elizabeth Gurley Flynn, and Margaret Sanger, all of whom have already been subjects of biographies. Until now Rose Stokes has been relegated to a footnote, almost dropped out of history. She is mentioned in many histories of labor and feminist struggles but is rarely accorded more than a sentence or two, often inaccurate.

Rose was a Russian-Polish Jewish immigrant, impoverished and with just a few years of formal education. In Cleveland she was a "factory girl" for twelve years until in a surprising leap she came to New York as an assistant editor of the English page of the *Jewish Daily News*.

Some two years later she became the bride of a son of one of the wealthiest banking families in New York society, a man who could brag—not that he was inclined to do so—of three university degrees and a family history dating to early colonial times. The Pastor–Stokes union received newspaper coverage not surpassed in the twentieth century, not even by the union of Duke Edward and Mrs. Simpson. It was a Cinderella story of a Jewish girl who married a Christian millionaire. A year later the Stokeses joined the Socialist party. These events were highly newsworthy, and the press of 1905–6 did them full journalistic justice.

Rose Pastor Stokes soon demonstrated that she was more than just the wife of a well-to-do man. Her sparkling personality and, above all, her oratory, driven by a bright mind and a golden tongue, enabled her to play an important role, especially before World War I, in political propaganda, in labor strikes and struggles, and in feminist campaigns such as the fight for suffrage and birth control. She did not hesitate to turn from socialism to feminism and vice versa to further the cause of women's rights. And in her limited free time she wrote plays, prose, and poems. Though she easily made the transition from underclass to upper class, she retained an allegiance to the working class under conditions that proved far from easy.

Rose began a lasting and intense friendship with Olive Tilford Dargan at the same time she pledged her engagement to James Graham Phelps Stokes. Dargan was a southern regional poet and folklorist and—as Fielding Burke—a regional novelist. Rose's last words of love and pain were to Olive Dargan.

Rose Pastor Stokes was a controversial woman in thought, lifestyle, and politics. She wanted to record the meaning of her life in her autobiography. Because of a devastating illness, she left it unfinished, hoping that a respected friend and admirer would complete it. But that work was never done.

We are not completing Rose's autobiography. Ours is a biography of one of the most prominent women of this century. Our hope is to rescue from undeserved obscurity a popular feminist heroine of only yesterday and to place her in her historical setting.

Acknowledgments

W e owe thanks to our old friends, now deceased, Elizabeth Gurley Flynn, William Z. Foster, and Will Weinstone, for their anecdotes about Rose Pastor Stokes that first stirred our interest in the subject of this book. And we give a hearty thanks to Herbert Aptheker, whose confidence in our book and whose assistance helped steer it to publication.

Most helpful was a man previously unknown to us who responded to an "Authors' Query" in the *New York Times*. This was John M. Whitcomb of Dedham, Massachusetts, who had known Rose Pastor Stokes when he was a child. After World War II he developed a curiosity about her which led him to collect her papers and to interview—in person and by mail and telephone—her friends and relatives. Whitcomb generously furnished us with useful documents, letters, and photographs. He was also instrumental in the acquisition by the Sterling Library of Yale University of its important collection of such materials. Yale also has papers of Anna Strunsky Walling and V. J. Jerome.

The Tamiment Collection of the Bobst Library at New York University has an impressive holding of Rose Pastor Stokes papers acquired from Anne Kaplan Williams Feinberg and a collection of papers of Eugene Victor Debs, which includes many letters between Debs and Stokes. Dorothy Swanson, the vastly knowledgeable head of the Tamiment, was extremely cooperative in making the library available to us. Peter Filardo and others of her staff were also most helpful. We were helped, too, by Bobst's Fales Library.

Anne Feinberg never refused to see us, but her family conditions never made it possible either. We are grateful to her, one of the few surviving friends of Rose Pastor Stokes, for information she provided in several phone conversations. Rosalyn Baxandall was also cooperative in supplying helpful materials.

Thomas Stokes, a great-nephew of Rose's husband, Graham, was very helpful, and he opened the door for us (literally) to the home of Lettice Stokes, widow of Graham, who gave us a guided tour of the Stokeses' townhouse and helped us in a friendly way.

Cedric Belfrage, a British subject, a onetime editor of the *National Guardian,* now living in exile in Mexico, was kind enough to send us more than two dozen letters exchanged by Rose Pastor Stokes and Olive Dargan. He had received them from V. J. Jerome in 1940 in anticipation of writing a biography of Rose Pastor Stokes. World War II precluded that project.

We made good use of the vast resources of the New York Public Library, especially its rich collection of newspapers and its general, genealogy, and Jewish divisions.

The papers of James Graham Phelps Stokes are in the archival collections of the Butler Library at Columbia University, where we also found the letters of Rose's friends Lillian Wald and Lincoln Steffens.

Materials in the National Archives were useful, particularly in relation to Rose's prosecution starting in 1918 and for Bureau of Investigation surveillance reports and investigative files plus what are known as the Old German Files. The YIVO Institute in New York graciously supplied its microfilm of the *Jewish Daily News* and other useful items. The Lilly Library at Indiana University supplied a number of letters from Rose to Upton Sinclair. Elinor Langer kindly found several letters for us in the Adelaide Schulkind Frank collection in the Schlesinger Library at Radcliffe College. We had helpful correspondence with the State Historical Society of Wisconsin, the American Jewish Archives in Cincinnati, the Jewish Community Federation in Cleveland, and the Friends of the Historical Library at Swarthmore. We received valuable materials from the labor history archives and the Walter P. Reuther Library at Wayne State University. We also found help at the Library of Congress and some small libraries on Cape Cod, notably at Falmouth and Orleans. The University Settlement and the Educational Alliance, both in New York, provided us with histories of their respective institutions. The International Tracing Service in Arolsen, West Germany, replied to a query. The Pack Memorial and Buncombe libraries of Asheville, North Carolina, and the University of Virginia Library, Charlottesville, helped regarding Olive Tilford Dargan.

A number of individuals replied to our inquiries or volunteered information: Lester Cole (one of the "Hollywood Ten"), Joan Dawson (whose grandmother worked with RPS), Mary V. Dearborn (biographer of Anzia Yezierska), Candace Falk (Emma Goldman specialist), Dr. Daisy Fletcher (collateral relative of RPS), Dee Garrison (biographer of Mary Heaton Vorse), Fred Jerome (son of V. J. Jerome), Harvey Klehr (Emory University professor), Edith Linsky (whose mother worked in a factory with RPS), Norman Markowitz (history professor, Rutgers University), Mrs. Bernard Pastor (widow of Rose's half-brother), Richard Pastor (nephew of RPS), Junius Scales (who knew Olive Tilford Dargan), Edith Segal (who knew RPS in the 1920s), Ida Cohen Selavan (of the American Jewish Archives), David Soibelman (reporter who covered a 1923 speech by RPS), Isaac Newton Phelps Stokes (father of Thomas), Chris Warwin (son of Jerry Warwin), Jerry Warwin (son of V. J. Jerome), Mrs. Bertram D. Wolfe (widow of a 1920s colleague of RPS), and Lester Zwick (whose mother worked with RPS in the 1890s).

We thank them and all others who may have been omitted from this list because of imperfect record-keeping. We also proclaim them innocent of any of the flaws of this book for which we alone take the blame.

The Cub Reporter

When Rose Harriet Pastor arrived in New York City in 1903, brushing the tobacco dust of a Cleveland cigar factory from her clothing, two social movements that were soon to claim her allegiance were approaching their heydays. One of these was the newly formed Socialist party of America. The other was feminism with its prime issue, woman suffrage.

The Socialist party at its founding convention in 1901 had debated a list of twelve immediate demands, one of which was woman suffrage.[1] The flagging suffrage question was to be revived around 1906 by the energetic Harriot Stanton Blatch, who added the indispensable force of working women to the traditionally genteel suffrage movement.

Neither of these issues—socialism and suffrage—was on the mind of Rose Pastor as she made her way into the teeming ghetto of the Lower East Side of Manhattan. After twelve years as a factory worker she was to become a journalist on the *Jewish Daily News (Yiddisches Tageblatt)*. She must instantly become knowledgeable about the East Side and its counterparts in Brooklyn, the Bronx, and elsewhere.

For the most part her subject matter was parochial. When she had been on the job for about half a year, for example, she had to answer the question, Should a Jewish woman marry a Christian man? The question was a staple of the popular Jewish press around the turn of the century.[2] In the August 12, 1903, issue of the *Jewish Daily News* a letter by a poor, anxious, lovesick, eighteen-year-old who signed herself "B.C." appeared on the English-language page:

> My dear Zelda . . . I am in love with a Christian young man who is two years older than myself. He loves me too, and he wants to marry me but my father objects. My father says that a Jewess should marry a

Jew. I call my father old-fashioned. . . . My lover is a tall man. He has blue eyes, black hair, and a blond mustache. My lover is a nice looking man. . . . People say that my father is a clever man, but I think that if a man objects to a mingling of Jew and Christian he cannot be very clever. What would you advise me to do—marry my Christian lover or listen to my father?

Despite her youth, Zelda knew how to guide Jewish maidens facing the perils of the New World along lines approved by the editors of her paper and most of its adult readers. She answered "B.C." in one of her frequent columns of advice and uplift, a department titled "Just Between Ourselves, Girls." Under the heading of "Twixt Passion and Conscience" she told "B.C.":

I do not intend to advise you. I do not think you need my advice. If you had decided to marry a Christian . . . if you had thought your father was wrong to object, you would not have asked my advice. It is because you know it would be wrong to marry him; it is because . . . you know your father has lived years and years before you saw the light, and is a sensible man, far more sensible than you, perhaps, can ever hope to be; and because you know in your soul your father objects to such a marriage because he wants to save you from misery and from moral death—you know all this in the depths of your heart in spite of what you are trying to fool yourself into believing—and that is why you write and ask for advice.

My dear, my advice to you would be superfluous. *I know that you will not marry a Christian.*

Zelda continued with another five hundred words of chiding and admonition. We do not know anything of the troubled "B.C." But we know that the pseudonymous Zelda was Rose Harriet Pastor and that she was twenty-four years old, five feet five inches tall, weighed 108 pounds, and had a massive pile of reddish hair. We also know that within the next two years she would have occasion to rethink her position on marriage between Jew and gentile.

Rose Pastor's stories, sketches, verses, comments, interviews, and columns filled an impressive amount of space on the *Tageblatt's* large-format English page. She certainly must have earned every penny of the $15 a week that was her starting salary. That sum barely sufficed to meet her obligations as the principal support of a houseful of her siblings and her mother.

Rose Harriet Pastor's advice to "her girls" followed a conservative line that could have been laid down by the grandmothers of her audience of young ghetto-bred women. Her answer to "B.C." was reinforced the next day in the "Voice of the Ghetto" column (a regular feature of the English page), which invoked the Bible to affirm that it was God's will "that Jewish blood should be unmixed with non-Jewish blood."

Her judgments in matters of religion, Zionism, courtship, marriage, literature, and labor relations conformed to the outlook of the older men who were the editors of the *Tageblatt*. It is not surprising that as she matured, broadened her experience, and became increasingly radicalized she felt obliged to change her mind on almost every question about which she exhorted her readers with such aplomb in her first year as a Jewish journalist.

In an article on October 25, 1903, Zelda sternly admonished "all you factory girls": "Love your work. . . . The girl who hates her work is one too many for any employer . . . the girl who hates her work invariably hates her employer and foolishly holds him accountable for all the misery of the masses." One may wonder at the high level of didacticism and the low level of class consciousness Rose displayed in this message to her readers—but only if we take too seriously her own record of her early manifestations of worker partisanship. Allowing for the self-serving factor that creeps unbidden into memoirs, she had reached no great depth of class consciousness when she joined the Socialist party in 1901, seeking social contact as much as anything else. Her membership soon lapsed. About the same time she joined the Zionists and the Friendly Society. Working for a conservative journal, even on the radicalized East Side, she was no easy convert to socialism.

Socialist men, according to Zelda, could be as wicked and dangerous to a woman's virtue as any other men. "Dinah" wrote to Zelda that she found herself "strangely influenced" by a young man. "He makes love to me and talks 'Socialism' to me." He spurns marriage and "almost persuades [me]" that "free love is the only bond that should unite two ideal human beings." "Leave him!" cries Zelda. "There is no Socialist, who is also an honest man, who would not marry the woman he truly loves." There are socialists who are moral and whose hearts are filled with love and tolerance, Zelda acknowledges. But, she goes on, "The Socialists who are found within certain East Side cafes . . . the farther distance a girl puts between herself and them the better for her."³ Rose Pastor had been in New York for some eleven months when she issued this caveat, based, no doubt, on her own experience of East Side café society.

The Lower East Side cafés attracted clientele according to their intellectual preferences. "It is each to his own. The Socialist has his chosen headquarters, the chess crank his, the music lover his, and so right down the line," wrote Rose Pastor's editor, A. H. Fromenson. And the use of the male pronoun did not exclude females. Where denunciation of government is loudest, "there you find women!"

> One wishes he could write these women down more gently. But to none would gentle words sound more strange than to the women of the radical "parlor," who listen to the strongest language, and loudest voices, nor fail to make themselves heard in the heat of the discussion. . . . If they are not the objects of fine courtesies and considerateness, they do not miss them. The stern realities of life, the terrible disappointments of the thwarted ambitions, the struggle for existence—all these have conspired to rob them of the finer attributes of womanhood.⁴

Though Zelda's column was supposed to be just between her and the "girls," young men read it too. One signing himself "Yankel" urged her to "teach your girls to think." Zelda obliged by asserting: "All girls are what they read. Ask any girl you have never met before what she reads and, if she answers truthfully you will know her heart and soul. . . . With our free circulating libraries what excuse is there, other than ignorance, for any girl who reads the crazy phantasies from the imbecile brains of Laura Jean Libbey." This challenging observation brought a flood of mail from young women urging Zelda to recommend some "good books." In reply she prescribed for girls under sixteen any book by Louisa M. Alcott. They might also try Charles Dickens (especially *David Copperfield*) and George Eliot's *The Mill on the Floss* and *Daniel Deronda*. Highly recommended was George Aguilar's *Vale of Cedars*, a book that makes one "proud to be a Jewess." Charlotte Brontë's *Jane Eyre* made the list, and Zelda added a strong endorsement of biographies of "great men and women including those of Brontë and Alcott." At the same time she warned against "listening to the voice of illicit love and yielding to that which God and man have stamped as wrong."[5]

Another letter from a young man, signing himself "Victim," says that the attractive girl he recently met and to whom he had become engaged is suffering from "a nervous disorder." What should he do? The answer: If the disorder is one that can be cured by a few years of a husband's loving care, he should not worry. But if it is epilepsy, "Even public opinion will cry out: 'You must not marry her!' "[6]

Rose Harriet Pastor had her say on the *Tageblatt*'s English page under several guises—sometimes as an anonymous conductor of the "Observer" column; sometimes as a writer of aphorisms as R.H.P. She wrote short stories and poems under her own name. One senses that the *Tageblatt* ran something of a journalistic sweatshop at 185 East Broadway amid the many more conventional sweatshops that kept the sewing machines whirring in the surrounding tenements. At any rate, Rose was later to complain that while working there she had no time to read or think.

But surely she had more time for reading and thinking as a junior editor of the *Jewish Daily News* than she had had as the fastest cigarmaker in Cleveland, Ohio. The Lower East Side ghetto into whose life she had been instantly and intimately plunged was not only an area of crushing poverty but one of resistance and aspiration. "Culture" was promoted by the settlement houses, but immigrant gurus also made their contributions, keeping alive the transplanted intellectual ferment of the *shtetl* and the czarist Pale while coping with the new language and new ideas of the adopted environment of the ghetto.

Rose Pastor's poems appeared from time to time on the *Tageblatt*'s English page. They were simple in form and content. For example, in the Labor Day issue of 1903 we find a poem of four stanzas, "No Sabbath." The last stanza reads:

World! Thou resteth not nor knoweth quiet,
    Soul and body suffreth quick decay;
Tired thou art, because thou hast no Sabbath;
    Oh, world grown weary! Keep the Sabbath day.

A few weeks later she paid tribute to three active leaders of the Zionist movement—Theodore Herzl, Max Simon Nordan, and Israel Zangwill—

in two stanzas and a chorus, designed to be sung to the tune of "Marching through Georgia." She called it "Marching to Zion." The chorus went:

Hurrah! hurrah! we hail the noble three;
Hurrah! hurrah! the men who'll make us free—
'Twill be Herzl, Nordan, Zangwill who'll be leading you and me
When we are marching to Zion.[7]

A few years later, with the helpful criticism of talented friends, she would acquire more sophistication in technique and subject matter. But in her first years on the *Jewish Daily News* her verse evidently appealed to her readers and editors.

When Rose arrived in New York the new subway was carrying passengers northward from City Hall. Several elevated railways (the El), converted from steam to electric power, rattled uptown from the Battery, veering on curves to within arm's reach of tenement windows, canceling the privacy of lower-floor dwellers. Main streets—East Broadway, Grand, Delancey— were clogged with horsecars and electric cars, with pushcarts and horse-drawn wagons. An occasional horseless carriage attracted attention. In summer vendors sold "snowballs" made of shaved ice and flavored before the buyer's eyes with vividly colored, poisonous-looking syrups. In winter vendors pushed wood-burning ovens through the streets offering baked sweet potatoes, the fast food of the day. Rose kept a watchful and protective eye on the poor people who were her journalistic constituency. The harsh life of the Lower East Side streets, tenements, and waterfront, where sailing vessels vied with steam, was frequently the subject of her sharp vignettes.

One of her stories received considerable publicity. In it she alleged the inhuman treatment of an old man who had been found helpless among the ashcans close to the East River front. Rose Pastor's story asserted that a policeman's dilatory handling of this pathetic creature had been responsi-ble for his death of pneumonia at Gouverneur Hospital. A stern old police inspector by the name of Max F. Schmittberger investigated the case to determine whether the policeman should face charges. Rose and the doc-tor who rode the ambulance the fateful night were summoned to appear at the inspector's office. Both women were surprisingly young. The doctor was Emily Dunning, the first woman doctor in New York to perform the function of an ambulance physician, riding to the site of accidents and illnesses in the horse-drawn vehicle that was standard for the time. The appointment of young Dr. Dunning to the role of ambulance surgeon was so sensational that in April 1902, when she got the assignment, some newspapers proclaimed the news in extra editions.

Dr. Dunning, however, did not support Rose's account. The man had been taken to the hospital as speedily as possible on that fearsomely cold night. According to the doctor, she, her driver, and the policeman had done their best. Hunger and cold had already devastated the old man. In the hospital he shortly succumbed to pneumonia. No charges were preferred.[8]

The daily life and death on the East Side, the color and the drabness, the fragrance and the stench, the blooming geraniums in the windowbox and the garbage and horse droppings in the street furnished generations of authors with material: novels by Abraham Cahan, Anzia Yezierska, and Meredith Tax; biography-fiction by Michael Gold and Samuel Ornitz; plays by Clifford Odets; nonfiction by Irving Howe and Ande Manners—sufficient to satisfy anyone's quest for fact and nostalgia. This was the world in which Rose Harriet Pastor had stepped in 1903.

Rose made an easy transition from the dusty factories where she had toiled monotonously for twelve years to the editorial rooms of a daily newspaper and the teeming life outside the red brick building that housed it. Her new job brought her in touch with Jewish writers and actors. She soon came to know Eliakum Zunser, the novelist and poet who, like her, came from Russian Poland. Around him was a circle, including his talented sons. In this group, and others like it that enlivened clubrooms and dingy cafés, a wider world opened up to the ghetto newcomer.

Rose's many duties at the *Yiddishes Tageblatt* included outside assignments and interviews. From the summer into autumn of 1903 Rose Pastor did several interviews and articles dealing with the settlement houses that flourished on the Lower East Side. These institutions were generally modeled on the pattern of Jane Addams's Chicago Hull House. Affluent do-gooders and social workers lived in the settlement houses and tried to "uplift" downtrodden slum dwellers. The settlement houses varied in style, facilities, and services. They offered lectures and musical programs. They taught English and some vocational skills. Though they reached out to all generations, they proved to be most attractive to the young and unmarried. Many of them, adapting to changing times and changing constituencies, exist to the present day. The settlement house movement which Jane Addams fostered in Chicago about 1890 was a humanitarian institution, and it engaged the social ardor of many educated people. Although Addams was guided by her own interpretation of Christian activism, there was no requirement that a settlement engage in overt religious activity or be either pro- or antisocialist.[9]

Katherine Kish Sklar points out that Hull House's uniqueness lay in its "community of women reformers giving women the opportunity to realize the full potential of their collective power to sustain their own institution." It provided assistance to the needy, and it was in the forefront to obtain beneficial legislation for the working population in the community. Sklar states that "their power encountered limits created more in response to their class specifics than to their gender-specific reform efforts."[10]

Through her work on the paper Rose Pastor was knowledgeable about settlement houses on the Lower East Side, but her first personal involvement with the movement occurred when she was asked to substitute for the regular counselor of girls at the Educational Alliance in the summer of 1903. The Educational Alliance, still in existence today, was founded in 1889 by a committee of affluent, German, uptown, Jewish businessmen including such well-known persons as Louis Marshall, Joseph Schiff, and Isidore Straus. They were embarrassed by the lifestyle of the immigrants on the Lower East Side. They saw them as "barbarians, 'Orientals,' and 'outlandish,' because of their dress, adherence to Orthodox Judaism and Yiddish-speaking." They felt duty-bound to help these mostly Eastern European immigrants. The settlement, though nominally nonsectarian, promoted a Jewish culture. It served as an educational and cultural center. It emphasized teaching the English language and was the first to establish summer camps for children.[11] The success of the English and cultural classes led to the inclusion of such classes in the program of the city Board of Education.

In July 1903 Rose interviewed Lillian D. Wald, head of the Henry Street Settlement. In addition to the usual activities, the Henry Street Settlement maintained a visiting nurse service that helped meet the needs of a community notoriously deficient in health care services. During the interview Rose brought up the question that interested Jewish parents of the area and consequently was of interest to the *Tageblatt:* a concern had been expressed that the settlements might subvert the religious loyalties of the young Jews who frequented them. Were they a device to convert these youth to Christianity? Wald assured Pastor that they were not. She defined her settlement as a "renaissance of democracy." Rose assured her readers that "Miss Wald is loved by all who come in contact with her."[12]

No fears of undermining Jewish faith need have been felt about the Educational Alliance. Its ideology has been described as secularized Judaism—though that too might have worried orthodox parents. But when Rose reported on an investigation of the Jacob Riis Settlement in August 1903 her heading read "Mothers Beware!" and she warned that "children must be kept away from its Christianizing influence."

"The University Settlement, founded on the Lower East Side in 1886 was the first such settlement . . . in the United States and the second in the world," wrote Jeffrey Scheuer. It retained a more neutral bias and aimed "to provide a place where people could come for social and recreational activity, for advice, assistance or learning." Concern about Christianizing influence must surely have agitated Rose Pastor when she went on July 13 to interview the leading light of the University Settlement, located, then as now, on Eldridge Street at Rivington. Like all the other Lower East Side settlements, it was within easy walking distance of the *Tageblatt* office. Prominent, affluent, uptown gentiles supported and operated the settlement located at a crossroad of the Jewish community.[13]

Fromenson, her supervisor, was training Pastor to conduct interviews, but she had resisted the University Settlement assignment because she disagreed with Fromenson's mode of conducting the interview. Fromenson's threat to dismiss her ended the argument.

On her reluctant way to the settlement house, Pastor encountered a friend, Edward King, who was on his way to deliver a lecture at the Educational Alliance. She urged him to accompany her to the University Settlement. She must have used the persuasive eloquence for which she later became famous. King never got to his lecture. At the University Settlement it was Edward King who got the subject to talk while an enchanted Rose mostly listened and looked.

The interview was with James Graham Phelps Stokes, a prominent scion of a prominent family. The occasion was one of those electric moments often depicted in romantic novels, films, and TV soap operas when boy meets girl. Pastor saw a "very tall, slender young man who both in features and in general appearance was so like the young Abe Lincoln and so full of sympathy for the poor." Stokes was asked: "What do you think of Judaizing the settlements?" He replied: "Just what I would think of Christianizing the settlements. Sectarian work belongs to the churches and the synagogues. . . . For no settlement can be sectarian without being to some degree class-conscious, and class-consciousness is not desirable in a democracy. I am a Christian: but my faith is something that is between my God and me." All this was duly recorded by the interviewer. When the interview was over, the tall, young Lincoln looked down benignly on the young reporter-editor-columnist and asked if he might read the interview before it was published. She sent it to him. Evidently dazzled by the brilliant, good-looking, good-hearted, very rich Mr. Stokes, Rose wrote earnestly of her impression of him:

> Mr. Stokes is a deep, strong thinker. His youthful face "takes" by virtue of its frank, earnest and kind expression. One glance at his face and you feel that Mr. Stokes loves humanity for its own sake and as he speaks on with the sincerity which is the keynote of his character, you feel how the whole heart and soul of the man is filled with "welt schmerz." You feel that . . . he "has sown his black young curls with bleaching cares of half a million men, already." Mr. Stokes is very tall, and, I believe six feet of the most thorough democracy. A thoroughbred gentleman, a scholar and a son of a millionaire he is a man of the common people, even as Lincoln was. . . . He does not flaunt his democracy in one's face, but when his democracy is mentioned to him, he appears as glad as a child told by an appreciative parent "you have been a good boy today."[14]

At the office Pastor's fellow editors teased her mercilessly. They told her Stokes would never want to see her again after such a public display of fulsomeness. She was out when Graham came to the office, evidently to see Pastor, ostensibly to return the article. Her fellow editors told Rose that Graham had said her article was "punk." It ran as some twenty-odd column inches of earnest prose in the *Jewish Daily News* on Sunday, July 19, 1903.

That same summer Rose's mother and some of the children came to New York from Cleveland and Rose took a flat for all of them on Madison Street, on a block teeming with the bustling life of the Lower East Side. By contrast, the Stokes family lived in their mansion on Madison Avenue at East 37th Street on Murray Hill next to the mansion of banker J. Pierpont Morgan. The physical distance between Madison Street and Madison Avenue—a matter of several miles—symbolizes the distance in social status between the Stokes and Pastor families.

II

The Immigrants

Augustowo in Suwalki, northeast of Warsaw, was not an invention of Sholom Aleichim like his celebrated Kasrilevka. But the factual Augustowo must have had something in common with the mythical *shtetl* of Aleichim's imagination. At the very least they shared the problem of marrying off daughters.

Rose Harriet Pastor's mother, Hindl, also called Hannah, born in 1860, was the daughter of Robert Lewin, a fisherman. She was called the "straw girl" because she was fair-haired, fair-skinned, straight, and slender. At age seventeen she was deeply but secretly in love with a young Polish fisherman who was in love with her and wanted to marry her. Unlike the Lewins, the young fisherman was not Jewish—a fatal flaw in his pedigree.

At that time and place daughters did not marry—they were married off. Robert Lewin had chosen for his daughter the learned bootmaker Jacob Wieslander, who had a son, Samuel, by a previous marriage. At the hour set for the wedding of Hindl and Jacob, the bride was not at the *shul*. She was in her father's fishing hut, dressed in worn homespun, disheveled. Her father found her and slapped her. Her weeping mother hastily dressed her. She was literally carried to the marriage canopy.

A daughter, Rose Harriet, was born about two years later, on July 18, 1879. Rose put it this way: "I slipped into the world while my mother was on her knees scrubbing the floor." The marriage did not long survive the birth of Rose Harriet Wieslander. Some biographers say that the marriage was dissolved by the death of Jacob Wieslander, but this is disproved by Rose's own account of her meeting with her father in New York in 1903. Jacob went to America not later than 1882, leaving behind his wife, his son Sam, and his daughter Rose. By the time he left, Rose's mother had already gone back to her parents. After much pleading by members of Hindl's family, Jacob Wieslander, in New York, granted his wife a divorce. Hindl yearned to marry her Polish lover, but she was bound by tradition not to marry outside the faith and in defiance of her father's command.

Sam was cared for by his paternal grandmother and sometimes by Hindl and became a playmate of Rose. Eventually, he too arrived in America. In New York he followed the trade of a gentleman's tailor, a maker of custom clothes, but he did not prosper.

Augustowo apparently did not have much to hold its Jewish sons and daughters. Hindl Lewin Wieslander had three older brothers who lived in Germany. The fisherman Lewin had been able to provide musical training for these sons, but education was not for female children. Hindl and little Roselie, now three years old, crossed the border at Koenigsburg and spent three months in Germany visiting the brothers, known in the family as the Three Nightingales. They had become fairly affluent as a result of their musical talents. Each was a cantor in a synagogue. Vocal ability ran in the family. Hindl had a fine voice for the folk music of her youth, and Rose's speaking voice was by all accounts extraordinary.

After some time in Germany, Rose and her mother moved to London. Rose never saw the Three Nightingales again. In London she met her mother's brother Solomon and his wife, Esther. Rose called this uncle the "fourth nightingale." Uncle Solomon toiled as a shoemaker, eking out an existence threatened by the machines that were driving out the hand craftsmen. Rose and her mother were taken in by Hindl's only sister, Sarah, who had four children. Rose played with them and with other children in a "grey courtyard." She recalled them as a group "robbed of childhood. . . . When we played we played solemnly, not joyfully . . . we sang without gladness."

Rose was entered in the Chicksand Street School, known for its iron discipline. She proved to be an obedient scholar, and the teacher "took kindly" to her. One day, however, while the teacher was presenting a lesson on "The Spider and the Fly," Rose absently drew caricatures. One of her efforts amused her so much that she laughed aloud and couldn't stop. Her helpless, convulsive laughter set the other children to laughing until the whole class was affected. Punishment was called for. "Come hither, come hither my pretty fly," said the teacher. She tried to smite Rose's palm with a ruler, but the child snatched her hand away. When she tried again, Rose locked both hands behind her back. The infuriated teacher grabbed one of her hands and beat her on the knuckles. Her hand was disabled for weeks, and the scars were permanent. Rose ran home and told Aunt Sarah, who went to the school and sharply slapped the teacher.

Years later Rose could realize that both teacher and child were victims of a cruel system. But at the time she refused to return to the school on Chicksand Street. For a while her education consisted of playing in Whitechapel Road, a busy thoroughfare traversed by an omnibus line. She delighted in picking up discarded bus slips, each of which had on its back a four-line verse ending in the word "Sapolio," the most heavily advertised soap product of its day. From these quatrain jingles Rose learned the concepts of meter and rhyme. Eventually the devoted Aunt Sarah moved her menage close to a new Jewish free school, the Bell Lane School, where her niece registered as Rose Rosenthal, a subterfuge to make her eligible as a local resident.

When Rose was nine years old her mother again considered matrimony. Hindl's father made the journey from Poland to meet the intended groom. He vetoed the match on the grounds that the prospective husband smoked on the Sabbath. Hindl, obedient but unhappy, broke the engagement. Her father died soon after returning to Poland and Hindl soon had another suitor, another desecrator of the Sabbath. But now there was no father to thwart her.

Aunt Sarah's home was a lively place, filled with talk and song. The talk was of religion and work in the shops. Rose's mind registered "notions" derived from the stimulating chatter: "There is no heaven elsewhere. . . . Earth will be heaven, someday! . . . We'll live in peace and justice with one another. And will learn to live on and on and on! There will be no dying. Great men will learn the secret and we'll live without end—here on earth." Protest against the harsh conditions of life underlaid the heady talk in Sarah's kitchen, but there was no talk of action. Rose understood little of the grievances of the poor or the distinctions between poverty and wealth. All she knew was that "the rich ride in carriages and look unhappy, and the poor ride in none and look miserable. I never had a childhood. I was always a woman."[1]

While Sarah took care of the house, Hindl worked in a shop. One day the boss whitewashed the windows because he thought the young women workers looked outside too much. This incident aroused the workers as long hours and low wages had not done. Hindl Wieslander was to organize and lead a successful one-week strike for the single demand: "Clear the windows!"

Hindl's new lover, soon to be her husband, was Israel Pastor. Pastor was to prove a willing but unstable provider, a venturesome *luftmensch* who never found success, though he tried. Eventually he abandoned the family, but Rose never wrote an unkind word about him. He was a charmer, "tall, broad-shouldered, young, reddish-brown hair, brown eyes, bristling mustache, arched eyebrows." His wife and stepdaughter loved him. Pastor had come from Yassy, Romania, bringing another language into the multilingual household in which Yiddish must have been the lingua franca. His uncle's death made him heir to a modest legacy, which he returned to Romania briefly to claim, then came back to London to claim his beloved Hindl.

Pastor put most of his tiny fortune into a plate glass business with a partner who proved to be a scoundrel. He broke with the partner and gave up the glass business. The family then moved to a small house in Black Lion's Yard—London had no lack of colorfully named places for the poor—where they lived downstairs and converted an upstairs room into a workshop. Here Israel Pastor set up a cap "factory" with the help of a single workman, Abraham. Abraham was already seriously ill of tuberculosis and soon died. The kindly Israel continued to send money to Abraham's widow—but not for long, for the cap business failed.

Fortune now beckoned Israel Pastor in far-off Buenos Aires, and he left to seek it there. Rose and Hindl, who was in an early stage of pregnancy, moved to Red Lion Court. Hindl took in a lodger and turned to home industry, making black satin bows for shoes, to survive until Israel could send for her. Rose had to help. She was not yet ten years old when she dropped out of school. Her role in the production process was to pick up the raw materials at the shoe factory, return the finished products, and help with finishing at home.

For a while she found other work at night on the stage of the Princess Theatre in Whitechapel, where the appeal of her bright red hair may have helped her to this brief career. She delighted in the pretty theatrical costumes she was required to wear while she spoke her few lines in a pageant-play with a message: "Any child may grow up to be Lord Mayor of London."[2]

Rose had little time for play. On Saturday morning she might slip away to hear the hurdy-gurdy man, or to read over and over again her only book, Charles Lamb's *Tales from Shakespeare,* or to visit the Salvation Army to sing

Rescue the perishing, care for the dying.
Jesus is merciful, Jesus will save.

Of course, she had no idea what salvation meant and not the foggiest notion of who Jesus was.

One day she observed the May Day celebration at Hyde Park. She did not understand this either, but she was impressed because on the way home the bus conductor gave out free transfers in honor of the occasion. She had witnessed the first European observance of May 1.

By the time Israel Pastor returned from South America his son Maurice was six months old. Pastor had failed to make his fortune in Buenos Aires. But times were hard in London too, and soon he was off again, this time to North America, where fate took him to Cleveland. Four months later he sent money for the family to join him.

After eleven years in the Old World, during which she remembered being hungry most of the time, Rose looked forward eagerly to a new life in the New World. But getting there was not pleasant because the Pastors traveled in steerage. After two days at sea the vessel started taking on water and had to put into Antwerp for repairs. For two days the passengers were lodged in a rooming house while the ship's hull was patched. Then, after three miserable weeks at sea, the ship arrived at New York and the immigrants were delivered to Castle Garden, where "huddled masses yearning to be free" were processed before the opening of Ellis Island in 1892.

No one met them in New York, and they had no money for the journey to Cleveland. Officials put them on a train to Philadelphia, where a boardinghouse for immigrants was their first home in America. After a week Israel Pastor sent money to take them on the final stretch of the journey to Cleveland.

The family reunion was joyous. The three-room flat in a two-story frame structure on Liberal Street delighted Rose. Its floor was covered with gaily patterned linoleum. The kitchen stove warmed the flat despite the chill of the autumn day. There were beds, chairs, and a kitchen table covered with oilcloth. There was even a clock. And there were Israel and Hindl (who, in America, anglicized her name to Anna), young people happily in love.

In the 1880s most Jewish emigrants from eastern Europe settled in New York City, but by 1890 many thousands had preceded the Pastors to Cleveland. From 1800 until 1880 a relatively small trickle of Jews from middle Europe had arrived in that city. Many had prospered; some had brought their fortunes with them. The newcomers after 1880 found a ghetto prepared for them in the areas around Broadway, Woodland Avenue, and Orange Avenue. Liberal Street, one block long, which ended with a left turn into Cherry Street, was in the heart of the downtown ghetto when the Pastors arrived. (It is no longer on the Cleveland map; it may have been absorbed into one of the numbered streets in the downtown East Twenties.)[3]

The Jews of Cleveland were engaged in a number of occupations, but the needle trades, which dominated the immigrant working scene in New York, were less important in the Cleveland economy. The small sweatshops that oppressed so many New York Jews were present but did not predominate. Substantial modern factories were more characteristic.

About a third of the Jewish immigrants became peddlers or junk dealers. Others were employed as cigarmakers.[4] There was an important distinction between those whose skills made it possible for them to create the upper-scale finished, shaped, and banded cigars and the less skilled who turned out the lowly stogie. The skilled cigarmakers had the protection of a craft union; the stogie makers were not eligible for membership in that union.

Israel Pastor was a junkman who patrolled the streets with a horse and wagon scavenging for bits of metal that could be recycled. Folklore has it that this humble calling always led to fortune. The steel mills of Ohio must have been insatiable in their need for scrap iron, but Pastor did not become rich. In 1895, five years after he arrived in the United States, his name appears for the first time in the Cleveland city directory, which lists his occupation as "scrap iron." He was still living on Liberal Street and certainly no tycoon.[5]

The family received bad news about the bright little flat in Cleveland. They were told that the furnishings had been purchased on time and still had to be paid for. The proceeds of Pastor's one-horse enterprise had sustained him, but now there were three more mouths to feed. Rose's formal schooling had ended in London and was never to be resumed. At age eleven she must join the vast army of wage slaves. Two days after her arrival in Cleveland, she started work in a cigar factory.

With only brief periods at other work, Rose Harriet Pastor remained a cigarmaker for twelve years. The factories varied in size, but the operations performed by the workers and the conditions in which they worked were the same as in Rose's first job. Two flights up in a large loft building she pushed open a large metal door and was immediately conscious of the suffocating tobacco dust. At workbenches "the bodies of the workers moved in short, sharp rhythms as the arms rolled dark brown sticks on a board, or cut dark brown leaves into patterned pieces or chopped the ends of the sticks with a small cutting tool."[6]

It was three weeks before Rose was paid for her work. The first weeks constituted a training period without pay. The next six weeks were at half pay. Her first paid week yielded seventy-seven cents. Wages were paid on a piecework basis, and as her skill increased she was able to earn $4, $5, and $6 a week, sometimes more. The speed required to earn $6 could not be maintained steadily.

Her stepfather's earnings as a bottom-level entrepreneur were erratic. He might earn from $2 to $3.50 in a day. But some days he earned nothing, and other days he sustained net losses.

After almost a year at her first shop, Rose went to work in a "buckeye." Buckeye is a nickname for a resident of Ohio and used to describe a small cigar factory in a private home—a cigar sweatshop. Here Rose worked on and off for six years. The factory consisted of three small rooms with twelve benches. Working with Rose were the boss's four sons and two daughters, a few other relations, and a boy and another girl. As the boss prospered, the operation was moved to a loft building and he was re- garded in the circle of stogie makers as a big manufacturer. He acquired a large home, and his children acquired education and culture. One son graduated from Yale and became a lawyer in Cleveland.

A younger son, Zelig, became the unwitting object of Rose's affection. In her thirteenth year she fell in love with "this homely lad." The affair never progressed; over a period of six years the two had only three conver- sations. In the first he said, apropos of nothing, "So, you like noodle pudding?" She said, "Yes," and ran away in confusion. The next occa- sion—about a year and a half later, he asked her what time it was. She was thrilled. The third occasion must have made less of an impression for Rose could not remember it.[7]

Zelig's older brother, whose relationship with Rose was not impeded by a young girl's crush, was important in Rose's life because he suggested that she obtain a card at the public library. A property owner had to sign the application, and he got his father to sign it. He recommended *Les Miserables* and by this simple act opened up to Rose the world of literature—a world of which, except for Lamb's *Tales,* she had hitherto been completely unaware. Her library card also began the process of self-education that was to prepare her for her next career. The gaslight burned far into the night as Rose earnestly read book after book.

Rose worked at Feder Brothers, Baer Brothers, and other establishments. Conditions were generally the same in all. When she took the job at the buckeye, which Rose called B's, the boss gave her a pep talk. "Here one does not play," he cautioned her. "One hustles." The warning was unnecessary. "Youth and want" drove her flying fingers. She was impelled "to race till she broke." As her skill mounted and her work became automatic Rose became the boss's "pride," as he put it. Her speed sped up the others. It did not occur to her then that the boss was using her to set the pace.[8]

New burdens fell on Rose's shoulders when her brother Robert Emmanuel was born about 1892. The child was sick for eight months, and then Lillian, her first sister, came along—together with the financial crisis of 1893. With half a dozen people to be cared for on the earnings of Rose and the faltering Israel, Rose added a night job at another buckeye to her steady job. She also helped her mother care for the flat.

The economic depression in 1893 further reduced Israel Pastor's unstable income. He often missed meals at home, partaking instead of the free lunches offered in saloons. Anna explained to Rose that he bought a beer to get the lunch and so relieve the situation at home. Sentimental songs, bathetic melodramas, and parodic comic turns have dealt with the consequences of Pastor's remedy for domestic poverty. Anna and Rose felt only love and sympathy for him, but one night he came home drunk, turned angrily on his wife and stepdaughter, and struck Rose for "calling him names." She had exclaimed, shocked, that he was drunk. It was the beginning of his downward slide. Of the events that ensued, Rose wrote, "I cannot tell of them now. There are some things in the lives of workers that cannot be told. We have no words to tell them, even to each other in secret."[9]

A boarder had been taken into the crowded flat for the pittance he could add to the Pastors' income, but Israel created scenes that made the man's life miserable and he moved out. Then the Pastors had to move to another flat, also on Liberal Street, this time with a shed behind for the horse and wagon. To provide the necessary rent deposit Rose had to ask for an advance on her wages. The boss lent her $10 accompanied by a moralistic lecture on the perils of improvidence. Israel Pastor made a new start and tried to give up liquor. Anna told Rose that he had "a heart of gold," an opinion Rose always held.

But the weight of Israel's responsibilities and his inability to solve his economic problems resulted in erratic behavior. When Rose was about sixteen, Israel left home without notice to the family. Anna feared he had been hurt, but she was helpless to find him. After several months, he returned. Intervals of unexplained absence occurred several times during the next few years until the day, after the turn of the century, when he left and was never seen or heard from again. His goings and comings were recorded in the births of his children.

It would have taken a miracle to sustain so many lives on Rose's income, which never exceeded $15 a week. The miracle took the form of help at some critical periods from Cleveland's charities, which cared for some of the children in orphanages.

Even in the paternalistic environment of a small family-owned business, grievances occurred. Workers were fined for "spoiled" cigars—most of which was the result of poor tobacco—which had to be rerolled; complaints were ineffectual and after too many complaints the worker was fired; as a last straw, the rate of pay was reduced. A strike took place over one pay reduction at Rose's factory, just two weeks after Israel had left the family for the first time. The instigator was Lyoti, a relative of the boss and Rose's "loyal friend." On several occasions he proposed marriage to her. But Rose, in love with Zelig, declined. The strike lasted about ten days. The "men returned in triumph . . . the boss yielded to their demands. For the women their only gain was that they now felt stronger and were less timid."[10]

Unlike the cigar factories that employed Hispanic workers, the stogie factories had no lector or reader to break the relative silence of the plant. Cigarmaking used no machinery. The few automatic movements in rolling and trimming a stogie were done in a silence broken by chatter and singing. Rose's friend Lyoti was a fine tenor and knowledgeable about music. Rose, too, was a popular singer in the shop.

Of the twelve years that Rose Harriet Pastor worked in Cleveland cigar factories, six were spent in the buckeye, the shop Rose called B's. At her mother's urging she tried a shirtwaist factory once, the L. and N. Gross

Co. Her mother feared that constant exposure to tobacco dust would impair her health, and years later there was no doubt that it had done so. But Rose found the din of the sewing machines intolerable. "If the effluvia of the tobacco dust was an evil the unceasing roar of the machines which made speech with a fellow worker impossible, that drowned out the sound of singing and swallowed one up in tidal waves of incredible noise was a greater evil." She was driven to tears each evening after a day's work in the whir and roar of the garment factory. After two months, she went back to rolling cigars.[11]

Some time after this experience she made another attempt to escape the dust and the monotony of simple, repetitive operations endlessly performed. She had lost her speed, which meant that her earnings declined perilously. "Try as I would I could not make my hitherto remarkably swift fingers do more than creep over my work." She left the stogie factory and got a job in Block's Department Store on Ontario Street. She was not driven to tears by this experience. But she could not cope with standing on her feet all day—on Saturdays until 10 P.M. After ten months she went back again to cigarmaking.[12]

One of Rose's friends in the cigar factories was Sarah Ernstein, also born in Russia and an immigrant to Cleveland when she was fourteen. She and the other children in her family were promptly enrolled in the stogie factories. Ernstein did not know Rose later in life, but she told her children that Rose was a person of "beauty and character" and that "it was obvious" she would not stay long at cigarmaking. But Rose stayed much longer than Sarah Ernstein, who was married at eighteen and left the stogie shop. Some years later word drifted back to Cleveland from New York that Rose had married a young man (a goy, no less, creating a minor scandal), a wealthy man. She became "the envy of her co-workers."[13]

It would have been impossible by 1901 for any worker with ten years of factory experience not to have heard something of Marxism and socialism. Nat, a worker at B's, had introduced Rose to Karl Marx as well as to Percy Bysshe Shelley. She read what was offered her. It did not bring about any miraculous conversion, but it did plant a seed. Nat told her that "poverty and misery, and insecurity are not things that a cruel God put into the world to punish us for our sins. Poverty and all its evils can be abolished, and the workers will someday abolish them through Socialism."[14] Rose found this a stunning idea.

About the beginning of the twentieth century a "suction machine" had been introduced into the manufacture of inexpensive cigars and had been adopted by some of the larger companies in the industry (the "cigar trust"). The device increased the productivity of the individual cigarmaker manyfold. Workers were needed to learn how to operate the machines. A foreman named Young, who had been at Baer Brothers when Rose Pastor worked there, was hired by the cigar trust to start up its Cleveland factory. He remembered Rose's skill and energy and brought her in to learn the new machinery and train others in its operation. At a munificent $15 a week she was soon put in charge of an entire floor.

The plant was running smoothly when Weiss, vice-president of the trust, came to Cleveland to make an inspection. One morning a few days after Weiss's arrival, Rose came to work but was barred by the building superintendent from going to her floor. "I'm sorry, Miss Pastor," he told her, "but you can't go up to the suction room any more. Mr. Weiss was here. He opened your desk and he found a book—." Rose was stunned but realized that he had found Emile Vandervelde's *Collectivism and Industrial Revolution,* issued by Charles Kerr's cooperative socialist publishing house in Chicago in 1901.[15]

Rose was demoted to the ranks. Working at the bench, she was back to earning $6 to $7 a week by dint of maximum effort. The experience did not alienate her from her budding interest in socialist ideas. Rather, it stimulated her growing class consciousness so that when a young fellow worker asked her why she didn't join the newly formed Socialist party her only question was "How?"

Eugene Victor Debs ran as a Socialist in the presidential election of 1900, but the party was not formally organized until 1901. Rose probably joined in 1902, for when she received her Red Card at the Ontario Street headquarters the factional arguments that had delayed the consolidation of the party from 1900 to 1901 were still raging. Rose was puzzled and put off by the seemingly violent conflict within the party. Max Hayes, a member of the International Typographical Union, who in 1913 made an impressive run as opponent to Samuel Gompers for president of the American Federation of Labor (AFL), was the bright star of the party in Cleveland.

Nobody in the local party took any pains to acquaint Rose Harriet Pastor with the meaning of the shrill discussions in the clubroom and what they had to do with socialism. Moreover, the books on socialism that had been loaned to her—certainly including Vandervelde's *Collectivism,* which had cost her job—were not for beginners in the study of Marxism. She soon drifted out of the party, and it was about five years, and under very different circumstances, before she came back.

Simon, a distant cousin of Rose, migrated to Cleveland. Rose found this young needle trades worker attractive, and soon they were discussing matrimony. Simon promised Rose that "when you are my wife you will wear silks and jewels." Rose refused the generous offer, saying, "I am a socialist and I don't wear jewels." Nevertheless, Simon persisted and gave Rose the traditional ring. But Rose got word that Simon was "infatuated" with another girl. In a stormy denunciation scene Rose returned the ring. He pressed it on her, but she refused. Simon married soon after—not the object of his infatuation—and acquired a sweatshop.[16]

Before she finally left the stogie industry, Rose joined some of the radical workers in an attempt to organize several factories. They made progress and hired a little hall. They applied to the Cigar Makers Union—Samuel Gompers's union—but it accepted skilled male workers only, those who from filler, binder, and wrapper created the carefully molded product. The aspiring union of men and women whose principal skill was the speed with which they rolled tobacco into the stick called a stogie did not survive the rebuff by the AFL craft union.

Rose Pastor began to exhibit her interest in poetry under the patronage of the prosperous members of the Ladies Friendly Club, an organization subsidized by well-to-do women of Cleveland which provided young working women with opportunities for recreation. The services the club provided sometimes took the form of entertainments with performances by members and leaders. Rose was invited to be part of an evening program that attracted two hundred persons and inaugurated the club's new auditorium. She delivered a passionate recitation of Edwin Markham's "The Man with the Hoe" with its revolutionary message of the rising of the downtrodden. The shocked ladies of the Friendly Club quizzed Rose about "Man with the Hoe"—where did she get it? Why did she learn it? Didn't she know it depicted an oppressed French peasantry, not free American farmers? Rose answered by explaining her own experience of the travails of American workers, pouring out the protest she held within her. The women were appalled by her tale of a fatherless family and of children placed in orphanages. How was it possible to live on $6 dollars a week? The answer: "Sickness, semi-starvation, despair." She received a flurry of attention. "They kept an eye on us for a season or two," says Rose. They sent milk for the children and a handed-down coat for her.[17]

In 1901 the family was living on Sterling Avenue. The youngest of Israel and Anna's children, Flora, was born in 1902. A neighbor gave them her copies of the *Jewish Daily News*. Each issue of the paper featured an English-language page, and Rose was beguiled by the editor's constant plea to readers for letters to be printed there, including letters from factory workers. On July 16, 1901, Rose Harriet Pastor posted a bantering letter to the editor, which in due course appeared on the *Tageblatt*'s English page. In addition, the editor sent a letter to Rose in his own hand urging her to tell him more about herself, the shop, and her home life. This exchange of correspondence led to her being invited to contribute regularly, especially in the form of "talks to girls." The first thrill of seeing her work in print was reinforced by the payment of $2 that the paper sent her for each piece she submitted. She developed a lively correspondence with the English page editor, A. H. Fromenson, who one day made the journey to Cleveland to visit with his interesting contributor. After that, the correspondence took on a more ardent tone and there was talk of marriage.

The dynamism, the as yet unfocused energy, and the underused leadership ability of Rose Pastor were not fully tapped by the Friendly Club and her writing for the Jewish press. In 1902, when the Cleveland Zionist organization Bnai Zion established a young women's branch called Roses of Zion, Rose Pastor became its president. After a while she had to stop contributing to the *Tageblatt*. She had written on time borrowed from necessary sleep, and her health would not sustain the burden of writing on top of eleven to twelve hours of physical toil.

By this time Rose, writing under her pen name of Zelda, had developed a following among the paper's readers, especially young women. Hundreds of letters asked the editors, "What has become of Zelda?" The editors, prompted by the eager Fromenson, invited Rose to come to New York to write for the English page and assist its editor. The salary was to be $15 per week. Rose was delighted by this wonderful turn of events, and her mother joyfully danced around the kitchen. The mother had to be assured repeatedly that Rose would soon bring her and the children to New York. Early in 1903 Rose left to take up her new work. Within a few months Anna

Pastor and some of the children joined Rose in New York. But $15 a week stretched just so far. As late as January 1905, Flora and some of the older children still spent time in institutions or other foster care.

A. H. Fromenson, who had wooed Rose Harriet Pastor on a whirlwind trip to Cleveland, who had courted her in sweet-talking letters, and who was to be her immediate boss at the *Jewish Daily News,* had promised to meet her at the train on her arrival in New York City. Fromenson, whose unreliability in such niceties was soon to be further demonstrated, did not show up. Rose, not a greenhorn anymore, made her way via the streetcar to 185 East Broadway, across the street from the soon-to-be-opened Seward Park. When Rose found her new boss at the paper's editorial rooms, she asked him whether he was Mr. Fromenson, a formality he had cautioned her to observe. In the same bland manner he inquired whether she might be Miss Pastor, then told her to "report tomorrow morning."

Temporary lodging for Rose was provided at the home of Belle Sapiro, Fromenson's secretary, where she was made welcome. The accommodations at the Sapiros' were of a kind Rose was accustomed to—crowded with children. Mrs. Sapiro treated Rose with maternal solicitude, but Rose was obliged to sleep with Belle and Belle's sister Bess, three in a bed.

The Sapiros were not reticent about asking questions about her background. Rose acknowledged that she had already met Fromenson. "And," said Belle Sapiro, "did he tell you about other women?" "Yes," lied the stunned Rose, "everything." "But did he tell about . . . the one he's been engaged to for eight years?" Belle persisted. "Everybody knows it but you!" The next day, January 23, 1903, she started work. She was assigned her very own desk and was broken in by the English page editor. She realized she "must associate with the editor but decided to associate little with the man."[18] It was not easy to adjust to this uncomfortable and unhappy situation. Fromenson did not make it any easier for her, harassing her with his advances despite her rebuffs. Those first days were sad and lonely.

Her life was soon brightened by the friendship she made with Miriam Shomer, a nineteen-year-old frequent contributor to the *Jewish Daily News.* The young women were delighted when they met each other at the newspaper's office. Miriam, whose father was a popular Yiddish novelist, invited Rose to her house for a Friday evening, when they usually had company. Rose became a frequent guest at Miriam's house and was thus in a position to meet the intelligentsia of the Lower East Side.

"At the time our acquaintance began," Miriam Shomer has written, "Miss Pastor was about five years older than I and could not therefore completely bare her heart before me. But in our silent evenings together, in the Jackson Street Park, or sometimes on the river bank sitting between the posts of the Market Street pier, she would say enough for me to sense her suffering. Quietly we spoke, quietly we sang old English ballads and quietly she wiped away her tears."[19]

Her sadness was also relieved by Israel Zevin, the "hunchbacked humorist" on the staff of the *Jewish Daily News*, who wrote under the name of Tashrak. Zevin fell in love with Rose. She admired him and appreciated his friendship and good humor. When Rose's mother moved to New York with some of the children, Zevin agreed to share the Pastor apartment, thereby helping with the rent and keeping close to his beloved.

The work that was piled on the new writer may have helped take her mind off her disappointment: she launched into Zelda's "Just Between Ourselves, Girls"; she pinch-hit on the "Observer" column with sketches of the East Side; she wrote articles and verse under her own name and published original aphorisms under the "Ethics and Dustpan" head. Looking back, Rose acknowledged that her material was "dominated by the traditional viewpoint."[20]

Rose found it easy to be friendly with fellow staff members. Her favorite, Zevin, was the brightest of the lot. He was something of a socialist and cynical about newspaper corruption. He told her about the "publicity hounds" among the rabbis and "socialites" of the East Side. A freelance writer named Imber, who styled himself "the poet of the Zionists," was a frequent visitor at the *Jewish Daily News* and was well liked by the editors. His visits became more frequent after Rose Pastor started to work there. But he was an alcoholic and Rose was a teetotaler who was repelled by his drinking habits. One night she found him lying under a street lamp on Grand Street. She got him up and steered him to a safe haven. Imber later died of his addiction.

Rose Pastor got a taste of settlement work the same summer that Graham Stokes came into her life. She substituted for one of the regular group leaders at the Educational Alliance on East Broadway, just down the street from the offices of the *Jewish Daily News* and the *Forward* in a neighborhood dense with *shadchans* (Jewish marriage brokers).

By the time the regular group leader returned to work, Rose had endeared herself to the girls, who refused to let her leave. One of these young women was the bright and attractive Sonya Levien ("blue eyes, black hair"), whose tears of protest helped keep Rose at the alliance that summer of 1903. Sonya Levien later did secretarial work for Rose Pastor Stokes and became an editor of *Metropolitan* magazine and a writer for the silent films. Her self-devised spelling of her real name Levine helped make her name memorable. Rose and Sonya became long-term friends.[21]

Rose also had a visitor at the paper who came only twice. He performed a seemingly self-appointed mission—to inform her of the whereabouts of her natural father, Jacob Wieslander, "the learned shoemaker." The visitor, who identified himself only as "a countryman of yours," was acquainted with Rose's half-brother, Sam Wieslander. Rose had met Sam once in Cleveland. She went to the tiny shop where Jacob worked on nearby Scammel Street. Without identifying herself, she told him she had met his daughter Rose and son Sam in Cleveland. Jacob said he had lost track of Sam. It was a deeply emotional moment for Rose, who covered her confusion by having the heel of her shoe repaired—"price 15 cents, while you wait." A week later the mysterious stranger came to the paper again. This time he told her that Jacob had left New York for Denver. The explanation was that "he realized that you were Hindl's daughter and he was afraid you might make demands on him." Rose never saw her father again. She believed her half-brother Sam had died in the West, but he actually died in New York in 1929 of tuberculosis.[22]

III

The Engagement

The future husband of Rose Pastor, James Graham Phelps Stokes, was a member of one of New York City's "great families." This distinction was certified when the family headed by Anson Phelps Stokes was included in Ward McAllister's "Four Hundred," the number that would comfortably fit into Mrs. William Astor's ballroom. They were the cream of "society"; all others were the milk, not to speak of the curds and whey.[1]

The men of the Stokes family were generally burdened with four names of which the first was mere decoration. Graham's younger brother Isaac Newton, for example, was called Newton, commemorating his maternal grandfather. Graham's first name commemorated his paternal grandfather, James Boulter Stokes. The Phelps honored Graham's mother. His father's brother, William Earl Dodge Stokes, did honor to the Dodges, business partners of the Phelpses and Stokeses. Graham's sister Caroline, who married his friend Robert Hunter, named their son Phelps Stokes Hunter. The given names in this family-conscious group came out of a small pool and were recycled from generation to generation.

The family of Graham Phelps Stokes was respected and respectable and furnished little scandal for the lively press of the day. Its doings were frequently mentioned in the newspapers but mostly in connection with business, politics, philanthropy, and religion. In so large a family, however, there were exceptions. A ripple was caused by the marriage of Graham's oldest sister, Sarah Maria, in 1890. As was not uncommon at that time, both inside and outside the novels of Henry James, this American heiress married a baron, a Scotsman, Hugh C. G. G. Halkett. There was another ripple when, about 1905, she divorced him.

What flamboyance was to be found among the Stokeses was almost monopolized by Graham's uncle, his father's brother William Earl Dodge Stokes,[2] who in 1895 married Rita Hernandez de Alba de Acosta, who has been described as "a beautiful Cuban heiress." In making this marriage, he seems to have waived his oft-expressed loathing for foreigners; or perhaps his divorce from the heiress in 1900 caused this antipathy. Gaining possession of the couple's son, who had been in the mother's custody, was said to have cost Earl Dodge Stokes a million dollars. He married again in 1911. In that year he was involved in a contretemps with two "chorus girls" in the course of which "he was shot and painfully wounded." In the early 1920s his suit for divorce and the countersuits furnished reams of copy for the newly established tabloids.

James Graham Phelps Stokes's great-grandfather Thomas Stokes came to New York City from London near the end of the eighteenth century and became a merchant. Graham's mother, Helen Louisa Phelps, was descended from George Phelps, who came to Dorchester, Massachusetts, from England about 1630. Graham's great-grandfather had founded the mercantile establishment of Phelps, Dodge and Company. At age twenty-three Anson Phelps Stokes, Graham's father, became a partner in this family enterprise in which he had gone to work straight from elementary school. Later, Anson, with his father and father-in-law, became a banker and built a reputation as an expert on foreign exchange and currency matters. Then he turned to real estate and the construction of office buildings in lower Manhattan. In Ansonia, Connecticut, named for one of his forebears, he was an official of the Ansonia Clock Company.

In addition to his many business interests, Anson Phelps Stokes maintained a lively participation in public service. He was active in the causes of civil service reform, currency reform, bimetalism, and free trade, along with anti-imperialism. He was a founder of the Metropolitan Museum of Art and a collector of art and books. He had a fine library of Americana. He was also an outdoorsman, a yachtsman who sailed his own schooner, and a horseman who lost a leg in a riding accident in 1898.

Housing presented no problem despite a family of nine children. The Stokeses spent time in a massive brownstone mansion on Madison Avenue, the spacious Brick House at Noroton, Connecticut, and a summer home at Lenox, Massachusetts. For more rugged vacations there was the camp at Upper St. Regis Lake in the Adirondacks, where roughing it was done elegantly. Anson Phelps Stokes and his wife were very rich.

Olivia Egleston Phelps Stokes and Caroline Phelps Stokes, two of Anson's sisters, were also very wealthy. Though they did not engage in trade or other remunerative callings, they must have invested their inheritances very prudently for they spent much of their fortunes on numerous religious and charitable works without noticeably impairing their own circumstances. The sisters, who grew up in "an atmosphere pervaded by evangelical Protestant piety, missionary zeal, and good works," were presumably implementing the intentions of their father and grandfathers, who viewed their acquired wealth "as a stewardship or trust to be invested in the conquest of sin and pursuit of Christian perfection on earth." Their mother was fanatically religious and an abolitionist.[3]

Grandfather Anson Green Phelps was president of the New York Colonization Society and helped establish the republic of Liberia, whose first president was a visitor in the Stokes home during Olivia's and Caroline's childhood. Olivia and Caroline, Graham's unmarried aunts, gave liberally to enhance vocational education for southern blacks at Tuskegee Institute. The sisters' most enduring philanthropy was the founding of the Phelps-Stokes Fund to give money to serve the causes of American Indians, Afro-Americans, and New York slum residents.[4]

James Graham Phelps Stokes was born in New York City on March 18, 1872. As they did for his brothers, his parents provided him with a fine education: a Ph.B. from Yale's Sheffield Science School in 1892 and an M.D. at Columbia University's College of Physicians and Surgeons in 1896, followed by a year of graduate work in political science at Columbia University. He never practiced medicine and, though his studies at Yale may have helped in managing his mining properties, his political science study proved more directly useful to his life interest than the rest of his schooling.[5]

Graham served in the New York National Guard from 1899 to 1901. During the Spanish-American War, 1898–99, he was a private in the U.S. Army cavalry but did not serve overseas. During this time his father was active in the Anti-Imperialist League, a group of substantial citizens (including the grandfather of Adlai Stevenson) who opposed U.S. intervention in the Philippines. In September 1900 Anson delivered an address at Cooper Union, "Is American Imperialism Inconsistent with American Principle?" at a meeting sponsored by the Anti-Imperialist League. As president of the National Association of Anti-Imperialist Clubs he appeared with the Democratic candidate for president, William Jennings Bryan, at Madison Square Garden in the same year.[6]

Political involvement and social consciousness, modified by the possession of great wealth, were a tradition in the Phelps Stokes family back to
its British-American founders. Graham's older brother, Isaac Newton, an
architect, was interested in the design and development of low-cost housing for the poor. More consistent in practicing a humanitarian spirit was a
sister, Helen Olivia, who, like Graham, became a socialist—a somewhat
more staunch one than her brother.[7]

James Graham Phelps Stokes never became as deeply and publicly involved in business as did his father. If the father could be described as a
banker, Graham might be called a publicist, a role defined by his frequent
serious articles on public affairs and his frequent, sometimes pompous,
letters to the editors of various journals. Graham maintained an office in
his father's business headquarters at 100 William Street in the financial
district of Manhattan.[8] At various times he was president of such firms as
the Nevada Company, the Phelps Stokes Corporation, Austin Mining
Company, and Nevada Central Railroad Company and vice-president of
the State Bank of Nevada. Almost every year he made at least one railroad
trip west to survey his interests there. Nevertheless, his involvement in
these principal sources of his income was not so deep or so burdensome as
to prevent his giving major time to politics and social welfare.

There is no doubt that James Graham Phelps Stokes was a very serious
young man and that he shared the sense of responsibility owing to his
privileged social position that was felt by his unmarried aunts, his grandmother Caroline Phelps Stokes, and his sister Helen. He shared, in an
informal way, the piety of his mother, Helen Louisa. He moved from university to social work in the YMCA, in Hartley House, and finally in the
University Settlement where Rose Pastor met him in 1903. In 1904, with
Thomas L. Watson, the eminent populist, he tried to revive the People's
party of 1896. In 1905 he joined William Randolph Hearst and other candidates of the Municipal Ownership League for local office.

It hardly needs to be mentioned that no worlds could have been further
apart than those inhabited by Rose Harriet Pastor and James Graham
Phelps Stokes when she and that highly eligible bachelor began to take an
interest in each other.

There was a lively intellectual atmosphere on the top floor of the University Settlement house, where the highly educated, mostly rich, young social workers had their residence, dining, and club rooms.[9] It was a world

apart from the lower floors of the building, where the regular settlement house functions were carried out among the denizens of the surrounding ghettoized slum. This separation between leaders and led was not the goal they were aiming for, which was the outreach of the privileged to the downtrodden. But the separation was real.

Graham invited Rose to tea in the exclusive clubhouse on the settlement's top floor, and she was exposed to the heady talk that went on there. She received more invitations, including an exciting Thanksgiving celebration on the top floor, where Rose found herself in the midst of "learned gentlemen and brilliant ladies"—professors, publicists, doctors, lawyers, scientists, educators, and scholars. Rose was intimidated into silence by this impressive congregation. If she had been required to speak she would have blurted out: "Ladies and gentlemen—there need not be poverty anymore." But she would not have been able to give thoughtful reasons "for the faith that was in me." It was different on the lower floors with "the girls." There Rose "talked freely and eloquently. They were like me. Their homes were like my home."[10]

But Rose's education was being enhanced by the systematic study of sociology, especially as expounded in the books of the radicals' favorite, Lester F. Ward, a wise, self-taught son of the poor. It was also enhanced by the battle of ideas that she witnessed—and gingerly took part in—on the settlement's top floor. Here she began to meet the rich mix of people—not just the mix of rich people—that typified her associations to the end of her life.

It was at the settlement that she met such people as Margaret ("Lilette") Wein, who was later the wife of Marcel Cachin, a communist deputy in the French chamber. She met Algernon Lee, a leading socialist, and Leonard Abbott, a leading anarchist. She met Emma Goldman, notorious if only for her association with Alexander Berkman, the would-be assassin of Henry Clay Frick.[11]

Rose was impressed by the Russian aristocrat Madame Katherine Breshkovskaia, who told her she had learned English in a Russian prison and was returning to Russia to help the revolution. Breshkovskaia, a libertarian rebel who later fell out with the Bolsheviks, was affectionately known as Babushka—the Little Grandmother of the Russian Revolution.

Rose also met the wealthy J. B. and June Barrows and their daughter Mabel. The Barrowses were presenting a series of Greek plays in which June Barrows appeared. They owned a summer retreat, Cedar Lodge, on

Lake Memphremagog in Quebec province. In the summer of 1904 Graham was invited to be a guest there. The invitation was extended to Rose as well, and Graham arranged to have Louise Lockwood of the settlement house invited too, possibly in the role of chaperon.

That summer the Pastors were living on Webster Avenue in the Bronx in a ghetto considered nicer than the one downtown. Graham was a caller there. On Rose's twenty-fifth birthday he was invited to supper. Years later Graham reminded her: "When you gave me a glass of milk, bread and butter, an egg and a banana you were so simple and so solemn about it." Rose mused on this reminder: "To me to have food enough was 'party' enough. How vast was the distance between our two worlds."[12]

Anna Pastor encouraged her daughter to go to Cedar Lodge, and the faithful friend Zevin said he would lend her money for the fare. It was an overnight trip, and her companions would ordinarily have occupied Pullman space. This was beyond Rose's means so they sat up all night in the coach.

Life at Cedar Lodge was a romp, a fairly mindless one in Rose's judgment, a way of life she was not used to. One might suppose that Rose would have welcomed this carefree vacation, but, as she remembered it twenty-five years later, she seems to have taken, and retained, a dour view of it.

But there were good memories, too. One of the guests was Olive Tilford Dargan, in whom Rose Harriet Pastor discovered a kindred spirit. As with Graham, the backgrounds of Rose and Olive could not have been more different. Olive, who was about ten years older than Rose, was born on a Kentucky farm. Her parents were poorly paid country schoolteachers with a love of books and a respect for learning. By the time Olive Tilford was fourteen she was herself a teacher in a one-room schoolhouse near Warm Springs, Arkansas. She attended Peabody College on a scholarship and then worked and saved to study at Radcliffe. In 1898 she married the poet Pegram Dargan.[13]

Olive Dargan was a talented writer. Her work included the difficult medium of verse drama. Her *Semiramis and Other Plays* was published the year she met Rose. This meeting was the beginning of an affectionate relationship that endured until Rose's death. Both women had known hardship and struggle.

Cedar Lodge occupied the top, slopes, and bottom of a hill. When Rose sprained her ankle near the bottom, the nonpracticing medic Graham

Stokes made a splint; crutches were sent for from Quebec City; and sleeping quarters were devised for Rose in a summerhouse near the bottom of the hill. Olive slept on a cot beside her. Confined for a while to the summerhouse, Rose spent much of her time reading, and Graham spent much time reading to her of Buddha's life and telling her about his own life—his youth, college years, and study of medicine "because he wanted to help the people." He spoke of his belief that "all diseases have their roots in social causes." He left home to live in the settlement to learn about "social ills and to help to destroy them." The enchanted Rose likened him to the young Buddha Siddartha, who had also left his home. In Rose's words: "I sat in worship of him." There was time in the peace of Cedar Lodge to speak of his future, which included Rose. The understanding arrived at was that they were engaged and that the engagement was to be a secret from everyone except Rose's mother.[14]

In April 1905, when the news of the impending marriage was publicly acknowledged, Graham Stokes told a reporter: "We have never mentioned such a thing as an engagement between us. There has been no formal engagement as the world calls it. We are one. . . . To call ourselves engaged would be to belittle our relations. . . . An engagement implies two persons. We are already one."[15]

From Cedar Lodge Rose and Graham went with some of the vacationers for a brief visit to the Adirondack retreat of John and Prestonia Martin, a Fabian couple, where Rose apparently resisted the beckoning outdoors to play chess with Charles Sprague Smith, the head of Cooper Union. Finally, with Maud Younger and Kellogg Durland, friends from the University Settlement, she headed back to work in New York. Graham joined his parents and other family members at the Stokeses' Adirondack camp.

Despite the pledge of secrecy, rumors reached Graham's aunts Olivia and Caroline about his attentions to an "Israelitish maiden." A family conference may have resulted. In any case, it was arranged for his aunts to take Graham to Mexico "to provide a change of scene." If the romantic literature of that period is to be believed, it was not uncommon for well-to-do maidens to be taken abroad to keep them out of the clutches of ne'er-do-well adventurers. The results of this expedient are reported to have been mixed. In the case of James Graham Phelps Stokes, thirty-two years old, six feet three inches tall, and with an established record of independence, the efforts of his aunts were foredoomed to failure. Olivia and Caroline

Phelps later became friendly to Graham's "Jewess," as did most of the large immediate family.

Whether or not Rose and Graham had plighted their troth at Cedar Lodge, whether or not they were "spiritually one," the matter eventually had to be reported to his mother—and Graham undertook to do so in a letter in March 1905. The Stokeses—father Anson, mother Helen Louisa, and sister Mildred—were on an extended tour of Europe and North Africa when Graham's letter reached them. Anticipating a question he knew he must deal with, Graham wrote: "Despite her Jewish origin she is as Christlike a Christian as I ever knew—I don't know where to find another Christian who is truer to the teachings of her Master. . . . Prior to two years ago, Rose . . . was a 'stogie girl' in a cigar factory in Cleveland. But her thoughts became so beautiful and her influence so great that she was called to New York to become assistant to one of the editors of the Jewish Daily News." From Tunis, Graham's parents sent a cable: "We most sincerely congratulate you and wish you all joy and happiness. Give our love to Rose."[16] There are no newspaper records or letters to verify the response of Anna Pastor to her daughter's friendship with and engagement to James Graham Phelps Stokes.

Many immigrant Jews lost some of their religious fervor—assuming they had any—after leaving their homelands. Some became slack in their observance of the rituals; some forsook Orthodoxy for the Conservative branch; some—especially Germans—adopted the Reform synagogues. Some were content to observe only the major holidays. There is no evidence of how thoroughly Anna Pastor observed her religion. But one may assume that, as a person who in her teens had yearned for wedlock with a gentile fisherman, she took a kindly view of her Roselie's passion for Graham. As we know, she aided and abetted the trip to Cedar Lodge in Canada, and she surely must have been dazzled by the prospect of a union between her impoverished daughter and a very wealthy man—especially one whose only flaw was his religious heritage. As for Rose, she was in love from her first close-up view of her future husband, and he with her. There is no need to speculate that she was motivated by a "quest for respectability" or a "lust for gold." It was love, no more, no less.

A talkative cable company employee must have tipped off the *New York Sun,* for about the time Graham's mother's cable was delivered a reporter checked the rumor of an engagement by telephone and was sternly warned by Graham that he would sue for libel if the paper dared print such a statement. The couple had not planned a formal announcement for another couple of weeks, but on April 5 Graham held a press conference in his settlement house quarters and told all.[17] He said they would be married in mid-July. He told the press that a few weeks earlier Rose had left her job at the newspaper to work full time at the settlement, but she had interrupted her work there to go back to her trade of cigarmaker in one of the largest shops in the city so as to get in touch with the people again.

Rose did not stay long at cigarmaking this time. Her hands swelled, and the work was too much for her. She quit on April 6, the day the papers carried the story of her engagement. Though she had taken the job under an assumed name, she was recognized after the evening papers came out, and as she left the shop she received a hearty round of applause that embarrassed her. Within a few days the Cigar Makers Union, which had never considered her eligible for membership when she was a Cleveland "stogie girl," invited her to join. She did and then took an honorable withdrawal card which she carried proudly for the next twenty years at least.[18]

A couple of months later Rose and Graham paid a surprise visit to a membership meeting of the Cigar Makers Union—a "friendly call," as they described it. This local accepted women as members and some of those present had worked with Rose. Responding to a request to speak, she described the poor working conditions she had found in shops in Cleveland and New York and spoke of the burden borne by women with large families who had to work in factories, citing one case she knew of in which mother, father, two children, and grandmother worked together.

Graham was also asked to speak and expressed his approval of trade unionism, though he deplored the quarreling he had found among union men. "I believe in a spirit of charity—exercised by union men not only toward one another but toward their employers as well." Some unionists would not have approved of every word of this generous statement. Nevertheless, both he and Rose were warmly applauded—the women waving their handkerchiefs—and the entire assembly rose as the visitors departed.[19]

Within a few days after the announcement of the engagement, its Cinderella–Prince Charming aspect would become the main point of interest in the feature stories that proliferated. But the headlines when the story first broke focused mainly on the religious issue: "J. G. P. Stokes to Wed a Jewess" (*New York Sun*); "J. G. P. Stokes to Wed Young Jewess" (*New York Times*); "Proud of Ghetto Bride" (*Philadelphia Record*).

When Rose's stern injunction to "B.C." in the August 13, 1903, *Jewish Daily News,* in which she admonished the young woman not to marry a Christian, was mentioned, she responded in words that are hard to reconcile with her former language. She told a reporter: "I advised a Jewish girl . . . against marrying a Christian, but that was not as some say because I am opposed to inter-marriage. It was simply because it was obvious that the girl did not love the man . . . and I was always opposed to loveless marriages." Then, on somewhat firmer ground, she added: "For instance I spoke approvingly of Israel Zangwill's marriage to a gentile girl, Elizabeth Ayrton."[20]

Graham asked the *Times* to correct two errors that were circulating. One was that his family opposed the match. Not so, said Graham: his family had received the news with the "utmost cordiality and delight." The second was that there was a difference in religious belief between the two lovers. Again not so, said Graham: "She is a Jewess as the apostles were Jews—a Christian by faith."[21]

Graham had already dealt with the religious question in his first letter to his mother regarding Rose. He was pleased now to be able to send her press clippings that she would surely find reassuring:

> It is surprising what an outpouring of public approval has been occasioned by my announcement. The entire press, both Christian and Jewish, varies from friendly to enthusiastic. Even the most bitter Jewish opponents of Christianizing influences have written most enthusiastically sending congratulations and felicitations.
>
> Rose is a very devout Christian . . . I have never met a nobler or truer Christian woman. . . . In spirit we have been married for so long that the formal ceremony seems of less importance than usual. I don't believe that in the sight of God the ceremony will make us more truly one than we are already . . . Rose is a very wonderful woman, darling mother, and I am very devoutly and profoundly grateful that she is in the world and so close to me.[22]

A friend of Rose and Graham, Edna McCaughtry, a magazine writer and settlement worker, told a reporter that "Rose Pastor is above any religion or creed. Humanity is her religion." In McCaughtry's opinion,

"Mr. Stokes is a gem without a flaw and Rose Pastor is a Rose without a flaw."[23]

The Stokes family's acceptance of Rose Harriet Pastor was verified by the Reverend Anson Phelps Stokes, Graham's brother, secretary of Yale University: "Miss Pastor is an ideal woman, loving, true, tender hearted, gentle and intellectual. She is a noble woman and has done noble work. The family is very much pleased with the match. It is an ideal one in all respects."[24]

New York's many newspapers vied with each other for news and feature material about Rose Pastor. The evening papers, the *World,* the *Journal,* the *Telegram,* and the *Sun,* in particular, carried stories about her, all of them favorable. One paper carried an interview with the woman with whom, a little over two years before, Rose had slept three in a bed—the former Belle Sapiro, who had married her boss, Abraham Sarasohn, one of the owners of the *Jewish Daily News.* The Sarasohns remained friends of Rose for many years. Belle Sarasohn told a reporter: "One of the most beautiful traits of Rose Harriet Pastor was the way she would sacrifice herself for the sake of others. It was not unusual for her to stop as she walked along the street at night and help a drunken man out of the gutter or rescue a woman under the influence of liquor . . . lead the poor creature to her home or a lodging and bathe her feverish forehead. . . . She was doing what she could for humanity and she cared little for the consequences in the minds of others."[25]

In the next fifteen years Rose would receive a great many sincere tributes to her "goodness," her "nobility," and her readiness to "sacrifice herself for others." She would receive scores of letters praising her fine qualities, and they would come from close friends as well as strangers who had never been closer to her than the distance between audience and a speaker's platform.

In time, the principal focus of her good deeds and good intentions would shift from the random stray to society as a whole. The one-to-one act of kindness and helpfulness would yield to a principled belief that the evils of society stemmed from the system itself and could be remedied only by changing the system.

In the early months of 1905 the industrious New York press turned Rose Harriet Pastor into an instant celebrity, and the feature syndicates made that celebrity national. The Hearst syndicate sent out a full-page eight-column mat, the entire page enclosed by a simulated rococo picture frame, decorated with plump seraphim, headed "New York's Most Interesting Romance." The florid art that accompanies the text is in tune with the prose it encloses, which seems to be a synthesis of some previously published material. Featured at the top, in twenty-four-point type, is a quote from J. G. Phelps Stokes: "My love for this woman whom I will make my wife is so holy and pure that the marriage ceremony is needed only to legalize a union that has existed between ourselves since the beginning." And Rose Pastor was quoted: "Marriage will merely give legal sanction to a spiritual life that has always made us one."[26]

According to the conventions of the year 1905, the words *holy, pure,* and *spiritual* meant that the relationship, however ardent it may have been, was chaste. It took many years of the wear and tear of married life to bring this extraterrestrial romance down to the realm of earth.

The *Evening Journal* republished a fine piece by Rose Harriet Pastor, "An Airshaft Tragedy," described as a "Pathetic Story of N.Y. Ghetto by Millionaire Stokes's Bride-to-be." It carried a sidebar headed: "People of the Ghetto / Says Millionaire J. G. Phelps Stokes / Equal 'Four Hundred' / 'Only Lack Opportunity,' Says Fiance of Ghetto Girl."[27]

On April 11 the *Evening World* began a five-part series by the "'Genius of the Ghetto', the fiancee of Mr. J. G. Phelps Stokes, 'the woman Zangwill.'" The same day the *Evening Telegram* carried a full page of pictures and text chronicling the meeting of Rose Pastor and Graham Stokes, their love affair, her work, and the forthcoming marriage. Stokes, who was active in prison reform circles, was quoted as saying that prison life is the chief source of crime.[28]

The popular columnist Ella Wheeler Wilcox presented her young women readers with a moral lesson. She warned poor working women not to draw the lessons that the fiction they read, notably the works of Mrs. Southworth and of Laura Jean Libbey, suggested. She wrote, "It was not destiny which took Miss Pastor out of the cigar factory—it was her overwhelming desire to help her fellow toilers and to find a larger sphere of usefulness in the world. . . . All the great spirits of good who hover about this earth seeking the unselfish came to her assistance and helped to further her wishes." Nor was it "her mere physical charms which won her the love of her wealthy fiance." "It was this unworldly, unmercenary and unselfish quality in her nature" that "brought her the happiness she so desires." Wilcox offered the hovering "spirits of good" in place of Libbey's luck, destiny, and physical appeal—fictions "which turn the heads of hundreds of poor girls."[29] Wilcox may have exaggerated about the "spirits," but her certification of Rose's "unworldly, unmercenary and unselfish" qualities was certainly merited.

Probably the soberest and most accurate estimate, amid the general hysteria of the commercial press, was that of James H. Hamilton, head worker of the University Settlement:

> The engagement is not as sensational as it appears. While it is true that Miss Pastor at one time earned her living by rolling cigars, it is simply a case where a worthy young woman did not reach her proper sphere until fate had ordained that she should. She is by no means a child of the streets.
>
> Temperamentally Mr. Stokes and Miss Pastor have everything in common. While her education has been limited her capabilities are large. She has gained culture rapidly in the few years during which she has been in touch with cultured persons.[30]

The physical appearance of the fiancée of J. G. Phelps Stokes was commented on in a number of press items. Many persons who knew Rose Pastor in later years commented on her beauty, and those who wrote about or spoke of her years after her death used that term in remembering her. In 1905, however, the popular press, not generally conservative in describing its heroines, was somewhat reserved in describing Rose Harriet Pastor. The *World* proclaimed in a headline: "Her Face Though Not Pretty Reflects the Beauty of Her Mind" and called her the "Young Genius of the Ghetto."[31]

The *Herald* declared, "She is not beautiful, but there is that in her face which attracts and holds attention and interest as beauty would not. Her hair is the most striking . . . auburn and full of waves and light." Her hair has also been described as "flaxen." Others noted her piles of "copper colored hair," and *Harper's Bazaar* said, "She might have been the model for Rossetti's Beatrice or for the quiet and dreamy maidens in Burne-Jones's drawings." This dreamy quality that was often mentioned contrasted with the impression of a dynamic and poised character whose personality made a strong impression on all beholders.[32]

If the writer from *Harper's Bazaar* found something of a Burne-Jones maiden in Rose, an item Rose clipped and saved by an unidentified female reporter for an unidentified paper saw a bit of Burne-Jones in Graham:

"Temperamentally, J. G. Phelps Stokes is a dreamer. He was fore-ordained to be a socialist or a poet, or, perhaps, a lover. Tall and thin, of the Burne-Jones type, he is a bundle of nerves and earnest convictions."

Sir Edward Burne-Jones did not contribute to Rose's image of her "Graemie." Her first impression of a democratic Abraham Lincoln remained. At the very time the great engagement story was breaking in the press, Graham Stokes spoke for the Municipal Ownership League from the platform of Cooper Union and Rose recalled that it was from this very platform that Lincoln had launched his 1860 campaign for the presidency. Graham was the young Lincoln, without the beard.

For some, Pastor's looks and Stokes's wealth were second in importance to the religious views of the affianced couple. Graham was happy to report to his mother late in April that a "prominent Jew in Milwaukee" had told him that "the Jewish press throughout the entire country had been publishing the best sort of comment about the forthcoming marriage."[33]

There were Jews, however, who dissented from this rosy opinion. An editorial in the *Hebrew Standard* (reprinted in the *New York Times* and other papers) declared: "The cristological influence the young millionaire and his newly Christianized bride will exert on our children with whom they come in contact will be distinctly harmful. They are Jewish children. . . . Notwithstanding the statement that all work the gentleman in question will do on the east side will be of a non-sectarian character we find that he is . . . doing distinctly Christian work on the east side . . . and to this we strenuously object."[34]

The people of the Lower East Side rendered a split verdict on the approaching marriage. In general, the younger group rejoiced at what they saw as "the most wonderful romance the East Side had ever known." Rose was indeed one of them, and many had known her. The older group generally disapproved. They remembered that she had worked on a Jewish newspaper and had written of her disapproval of just such a marriage as she was about to enter.

Chief Rabbi J. Widrewilz expressed his disapproval of the marriage, though he acknowledged that he was unacquainted with Rose Pastor and "had no opportunity of ascertaining her character." Even a year and a half later, Rabbi H. Pereira Mendes of the Spanish Synagogue in New York objected when Rose Pastor Stokes appeared before the Sisterhood in Temple Emanu-El: "That our religion will be merged into Christianity if intermarriage be encouraged, all loyal Hebrews will declare. Mrs. Stokes's marriage is her own private affair. But she must remain a private in the army of workers, so far as Jewish interests are concerned. She should not be promoted or brought forward, or honored in the slightest way in connection with Jewish work, by us who call ourselves Jews or Jewesses."[35]

The religious issue eventually died down. References to Rose as a Jewess faded out, but allusions to her as the wife of a millionaire endured beyond the marriage. During their twenty years of wedded life, Rose and Graham did not practice any doctrinal religion. They would have agreed with William E. Alberts: "Religion does not mean worshipping what the Prophets did but doing what the Prophets worshipped." And they would have agreed with the Chartist Abram Hanson, who denounced those who "preached Christ and a crust, passive obedience and non-resistance" and favored "those who preached Christ and a full belly, Christ and a well-clothed back—Christ and a good house to live in—Christ and universal suffrage."[36]

Graham told reporters, "This is an affair of the soul . . . has been so since the beginning." And Rose told them: "I have no ambition to be rich. . . . Our thoughts are above all this."[37] Graham Stokes and Rose Pastor were involved in a love match. If Rose's personal appeal had dazzled Graham at first sight and if Graham represented to Rose a dazzling pile of gold, they both had other qualities that reinforced and dominated their more obvious charms and augured well for a successful marriage.

Three weeks after the announcement of their betrothal, Graham was away on a business trip and his lady wrote to her "Darling Graemie": "It is now 11 pm and I am longing for you, dear darling Saint! I am yearning for the touch of your hand on my head and the wonderful peace of your presence. . . . God bless and keep you, Soul of my Soul! and bring you back safe and well to me and to those others who love and need you. Lovingly and reverentially, Your Rose."[38]

And Graham, conscious of a "wonderful peace," wrote to his mother: "I know of no one who has the qualification which Jesus asked in larger measure than has Rose. . . . Dear Mother, I am very fond of Rose, a wonderful peace fills my soul as seems in itself to prove the divine. . . . We shall be glad to have Anson marry us if he will, but have not yet asked him. He might find it impracticable to omit 'obey.' . . . If so we shall have to be married by someone else."[39]

A week later Graham wrote at length to his brother Anson Phelps

Stokes, explaining in theological detail why he and Rose insisted that the word *obey* be omitted from the marriage ritual: "It would be impossible for a clear-seeing moral being to consciously pledge obedience to any other authority than the dictates of its own soul. . . . To us it seems that the pledge to love (or to love and cherish) one another always is sufficient. . . . Was it not Jesus himself who said that 'love is the fulfilling of the law'?"[40] Anson raised no objections. In 1903 he had married Caroline Green Mitchell, described as an heiress to millions. Hence he might feel awkward explaining to his flock the matter of the camel and the eye of the needle, but he readily agreed to omit *obey*.[41]

Plans went ahead for the wedding to take place at the Brick House, the Stokes country home at Noroton, Connecticut, on Rose's twenty-sixth birthday, July 18, 1905. Rose now began to meet her future in-laws. Graham's sisters Helen and Ethel were helpful during the premarital shopping, guiding Rose across the threshold of shops she had never ventured into before. Rose met the family when she attended the wedding of Graham's Uncle James in mid-April to a young woman of direct Puritan descent, Florence Chesterfield, distantly related to the Phelps and Whitney families. This marriage conformed so well to the expected mold that it attracted no undue media attention.[42]

Rose received a full-scale introduction to her legion of relatives-to-be when she went, early in the summer, to stay at the Brick House. What she saw there made her weep. She had not intended to exchange her old world for such richness, and in some respects she did not do so. She wept to see "a corps of workers making a paradise for the few," and she identified with the "helpless," the "gardeners, servants, the stablemen, the mechanics."[43] Her marriage brought about many changes in her style of life, most of which made her more comfortable in the ways that only money can. She had told Graham that he would be coming to her world, not she to his. What ensued was an earnest attempt, ultimately disastrous, to synthesize both. But Rose's commitment to the working class and the poor never flagged—and eventually returned her to their ranks.

IV

Matrimony:
Rags to Riches

Lthe heat record in New York City for July 18 was broken in 1905 when the mercury reached 96 degrees.[1] On that day two hundred passengers, dressed in the best they owned or could rent, alighted at Stamford from the 10:28 train from New York and made their way to St. Luke's Church at Noroton. They were friends of Rose Pastor and Graham Stokes. Another two hundred guests also found room inside the church where the couple was joined in wedlock by the rector, assisted in the ceremony by the groom's brother, the Reverend Anson Stokes, Jr., secretary of Yale and rector of St. Paul's Episcopal Church, New Haven.

The men who had come up from the Lower East Side wore frock coats and high hats, despite the heat, while their "wealthy brethren," as one paper called them, "thought summer clothing more appropriate to a morning wedding." It was recorded that despite the different dress styles of the respective groups, the celebration of the joyous occasion was marked by the easy merging of the socially distinct parties.[2]

One day at the Educational Alliance, Rose Pastor had excitedly told Miriam Shomer and Hattie Mayer that she was about to "make history." "I am going to be married to the millionaire Stokes," she revealed. "Riches and poverty, Jew and Christian will be united. Here is an indication of the new era." "I went to her wedding," wrote Shomer, almost fifty years after the event. "On Grand Central Station, where the wedding guests assembled, we began to realize that Rose's dream . . . would come to grief." Shomer had little evidence for her expectations. Rose's aunt, she says, was at the wedding and caught the 10:28 train. She was in silk and spangles, hardly the right attire for a summer morning wedding. "The

Stokes family and scores of friends . . . looked contemptuously at Rose's dressed-up relatives."[3] We prefer the *Times* view that "the socially distinct parties" merged easily on the "joyous occasion." And the marriage was remarkably smooth and successful for many years. The problems that eventually arose had nothing to do with wealth, poverty, religion, or family snobbery.

Following the ceremony, carriages and autos ferried the guests to Brick House for a wedding breakfast, which included champagne. Rose did not drink alcohol, even with bubbles in it, and lighthearted assurances that the glass contained only ginger ale did not entrap her.

The wedding day seems to have been an auspicious beginning in the attempt to bridge the two worlds of Pastor and Stokes. The Stokes ambience prevailed, of course; the occasion was one that only great wealth could provide. But the matron of honor was Flora Mayor (Mrs. Henry Raugh), a friend of Rose's from Cleveland. Mrs. Sapiro, who had sheltered Rose in her first days in New York, and her daughter Bess were there, but not Belle Sapiro Sarasohn, who was home caring for her new baby. Sonya Levien was there, of course.[4] Charles Zunser, son of the honored Yiddish poet Eliakum Zunser—the "People's Bard"—was present with his fiancée, Miriam Shomer, on his arm. But Rose's journalist friend Harry Debrest declined—he was against mixed marriages.[5] In an ecumenical gesture, the bride wore a cross for her wedding.

There was much goodwill in the whole event, but it foretold the inevitable: despite the earnest wishes of both Rose and Graham, his world would prevail in the material circumstances of their life together. Rose staunchly sought to overcome the seductiveness of this situation by devoting herself unsparingly to the interests of the working class. This was "her class," she believed, if only because she had invested the years of her youth in it.

The wedding trip was a leisurely motorcar tour of part of Europe. Mother Stokes dispatched her Packard and a chauffeur-mechanic to meet the honeymooners' vessel in Liverpool. The newlyweds occupied a comfortable but not luxurious stateroom aboard the SS *Cedric,* which sailed the morning after the wedding. They would return in October. They tried to avoid the press. A couple of young women friends of Rose from the Lower East Side were the only ones to see the couple off. A diligent reporter noted that "Mrs. Stokes wore a white shirt waist, a gray walking skirt, and a wide-brimmed straw hat, with a big black ostrich feather."[6]

She must have been wearing much the same outfit when the Packard drove up to Black Lion's Yard, where Rose had spent part of her girlhood. She wanted to revisit some of these early scenes and to show them to Graham to help him understand her origins. But when they came to the courtyard, she realized the women were waiting for her. She could not confront them with all the panoplies of her new station—the car, the well-made clothes, the magnificent ostrich plume. She reentered the car and drove away.[7]

They went to see Aunt Esther and Uncle Solomon Lewin. Rose got Graham to agree to pay their fare to New York, and they came over later that year. Solomon Lewin died in 1906. Graham declined, however, to pay the passage for Aunt Sarah and Uncle Sam.[8]

From London Graham wrote to his mother to tell of their meeting in Scotland with Helena Frank, with whom Rose had carried on a correspondence though they had never met before. Rose and Helena were later to collaborate in translating poems of Morris Rosenfeld from Yiddish to English. Helena Frank was a niece of the Duke of Westminster. Graham told his mother: "Mr. Frank [Helena's father] spoke to me of the influence which Rose had had upon his daughter, and the meaning of Rose's friendship to her touched me very deeply."[9]

Their sturdy Packard took them to Scotland, Paris, Geneva, Budapest, the south of Italy, and many places in between.

Rose was glad to be home when they walked down the gangplank in New York. Home was a flat on the Lower East Side, as she had insisted when their life together was being planned. They had thought three rooms would be enough, but on June 16, 1905, Graham signed a lease for six rooms and bath on the seventh (top) floor of 47–49 Norfolk Street at the corner of Grand. This was nine blocks east of the sinister-sounding Bowery, notorious for its population of derelicts. The monthly rent was $38.[10] This figure, which sounds absurdly low today, was in the high range at that time and for that place. The house was sturdily built and was far superior to the surrounding tenements. It was one of the few residences in the community to boast an elevator. The surrounding area was mostly filled with five-story walk-ups, four flats and two hall toilets on each floor. Baths were taken in the kitchen wash tub with water heated on the coal range. Great blocks of such buildings may still be found on New York's Lower East Side. Somewhat modernized to meet legal requirements, they are badly deteriorated by age and neglect.

The Stokes apartment was furnished with dark, heavy, comfortable pieces such as were favored by the late Victorians. Graham had a bulky rolltop desk in the library; Rose had a trim flat-top desk and a massive upright piano in the living room.[11]

Returning to work for Graham meant reporting to the office at 100 William Street, which served the several western mining and railroad interests he controlled. Though the press had proclaimed Graham Stokes a millionaire, he denied that his fortune put him in that exalted state. Graham's father and most of his brothers had offices at 100 William Street. Perhaps certain functions of the various enterprises in which the family members were involved were handled by a joint staff; otherwise it is hard to understand how Graham was able to be absent on a long wedding trip and seemingly neglect his business.

For Rose, getting down to work meant writing, which was in demand by a number of publications, and answering piles of mail that had accumulated while she was abroad. To help her whittle down this mass, she engaged Sonya Levien as a secretary. One early writing chore was to review an anonymous novel, *The Long Day,* an account of a working girl's life in New York City on the Lower East Side. Its author, Rose was sure, had lived the life it described. It bore "the stamp of reality." The editors of the *Independent* judged, reasonably enough, that this was a subject Rose Pastor Stokes was an expert on.[12] Her expertise was also evident in an article she contributed to the scholarly *Annals of the American Academy of Political and Social Science* titled "The Condition of Working Women from the Working Woman's Viewpoint."[13]

There was housework, too, of course. Rose tried to keep it simple. She spurned the luxury of fine linen napkins and the burden of laundering them by using a novelty of the day—paper napkins imported from Japan and available at one hundred for twenty cents. The janitress of the apartment house could be hired to lend a hand on heavy cleaning days. Rose's cooking sometimes produced disastrous results, and she depended heavily on canned goods.[14]

In a well-intended but fatuous attempt to involve Rose in a socially acceptable form of charitable activity, her sister-in-law Ethel (Mrs. John Sherman Hoyt) took her to meetings of a flower club, which, Rose found, placed flower boxes in the windows of the poor and sent the no longer fresh bouquets of the rich to the poor in hospitals. Rose soon dropped out of the flower club.[15]

In this early period of their married life Rose and Graham became disenchanted with settlement work and came to the conclusion "that it was helping the poor in order to keep them in their place." The settlement house approach was "like pouring water through a sieve." Rose thought of the coldness with which she was received as a "charity lady" by an Italian family, although when she gave them her name they drew her warmly into the flat saying, "Oh, yes—you too were a worker."[16]

Having made their break with the settlement house, they became interested in workers' organizations. They attended socialist meetings and lectures and meetings of the Women's Trade Union League. They went to meetings at City Hall at which citizens might speak on pending matters. Graham might have spent much of his time at City Hall if his candidacy for president of the Board of Aldermen had been successful. He and publisher William Randolph Hearst, who ran for mayor, were candidates of the Municipal Ownership League, which, though defeated, made a strong showing. In fact, there is little doubt that the unscrupulous Hearst did defeat the Democrat, George B. McClellan, but Tammany boss Charles F. Murphy reversed this embarrassment by throwing thousands of Hearst ballots into the East River and by other devices that proved him bound to be the winner in a contest of the unscrupulous. The rather unworldly Graham Stokes emerged untainted from this battle between rascals.[17]

Rose now began in earnest her life in two worlds, which became a remarkably successful effort over some twenty years to serve the working class while subsisting in the upper-class milieu. At a luncheon she attended at the home of Mr. and Mrs. Henry Siegel, rich manufacturers, the other guests included Mr. and Mrs. Hearst and the Protestant Episcopal Bishop Henry Potter, one of New York City's leading clergymen.[18] On another level there was Lillian Wald, whose Henry Street Settlement was nearby Norfolk and Grand Street. Graham wrote to Wald in November—there was no telephone in the Stokes flat—inviting her to "drop in to lunch or supper with us almost any day. . . . We live in a very primitive fashion and so should appreciate it if you would drop in in a similarly primitive and informal way."[19]

The Stokes family's interest in "Negro improvement" brought about Rose's first visit to the South. The occasion for the visit was the celebration of the twenty-fifth anniversary of the Tuskegee Institute in Alabama and the opening of a new Carnegie Library in Atlanta, Georgia. Graham Stokes was on the Tuskegee Board of Directors. His aunts Caroline and

Olivia were liberal donors to the institute, and Graham had been invited to speak at the anniversary celebration. Rose was to meet many of the rich and powerful on this southern trip. One of the more distinguished among them was Charles William Eliot, president of Harvard University, whom Rose met on the southbound train. He knew of Rose's background as a factory worker and delivered his own impressions of such labor, but when he questioned her about it he would not permit her to reply. She got up and walked away from him.

Mr. and Mrs. Andrew Carnegie were also aboard the train, as was Henry Clay Frick, chairman of Carnegie's steel company. Frick had survived an assassination attempt by Alexander Berkman in 1892. Rose had slightly better luck with Carnegie than with Eliot. Carnegie, a self-made tycoon, gave lectures on "success," which, generalizing from his own experience, he attributed to "Patriotism, Personality, and Perseverance" each with a capital "P." He said to Rose confidentially, "Don't tell anyone, but I don't believe in God."[20]

The separate waiting rooms for blacks and whites in the Atlanta railroad station horrified Rose. It was her first encounter with Jim Crow. She wanted to sit in the black waiting room. Graham begged her not to. But when at the luncheon celebrating the opening of the library a speaker declared that "dogs and Negroes are not allowed in this building," Rose walked out and Graham left with her.

Soon after the trip to Tuskegee, Rose and Graham went to Nevada to attend to his mining and railroad interests. They had planned to visit San Francisco, but the fire and earthquake of April 18, 1906, intervened. They went to Pasadena instead and while there attended a May First meeting. The persuasive eloquence of the socialist speaker, J. Stitt Wilson, gave them much to think about. On the way home to New York, Graham said to a pensive Rose, "What is it, Roselie—Socialism?" He told her that if he stayed with the Municipal Ownership League he would be nominated for governor of New York State—but he chose socialism with Rose. On August 1 they both applied for membership in the Socialist party and were promptly accepted.[21]

Although their decision to join the Socialist party had been prompted by J. Stitt Wilson, for whose inspiration they were grateful, Wilson seems to have been equally impressed by his two recruits. He wrote to Rose: "My very dear Comrade—I would gladly address you in more expressive and less conventional terms. For somehow you were a great inspiration to me—not for anything you said—not for any deed performed nor for any service rendered. But surely for the sacred atmosphere of your presence as of one who felt and knew."[22]

The Stokes couple joined the Socialist party about a month after moving into a new house on Caritas Island, just off Wallacks Point in Stamford, Connecticut. Within a couple of years, Caritas became a social focus and political way station for Rose's and Graham's relatives, friends, and assortment of acquaintances. Visitors prized the honor, as many of them saw it, of an invitation to Caritas. Performers, poets, and politicians—the latter in shades of pink to red—were in constant passage to and from the island, declaiming, reciting, and arguing. Since some individuals could be classified in two or even three of the above categories, they were likely to express themselves accordingly. Mothers came with newborn babies to give the children a fresh-air start in life. On May 3, 1907, the child of Olive and Pegram Dargan was born, died, and buried on the island within a twenty-four-hour span.[23]

The three-acre island abounded in daisies as well as wild roses, purple asters, goldenrod, and sumac. A bit of lawn was in front of the house, some rock at the shore side, a tiny beach, and then the waters of Long Island Sound ten miles across to Long Island. A wooden bridge led from the mainland to Caritas, and from the bridge flounder and snappers could be caught at high tide. A sandy road led the few yards up to the house (two stories and an attic), which could also be approached by a little path through a bit of woodland. Travel time via either route was about one minute.

The house, designed by Graham's brother, the architect Isaac Newton Phelps Stokes, was shingled outside. Inside it was lined with plain boards with a soft, gentle grain. Most of the fourteen rooms were small, but the central living room was spacious. It had a big fireplace with a splendid hearthstone, set two steps below the floor level. The menage proved unmanageable without servants.

One marvels at the patience and good nature manifested by Graham the first summer at Caritas, for he was not surrounded by the circle of artists and thinkers who in the following years constantly made the pilgrimage to the island. In 1906 the island was inhabited by a flock of Pastors, Anna and five of her children; a sixth child was Sara, Rose's typist, who, though seventeen years old, sought to be treated like a child and went up to bed with the rest of them at eight o'clock. Even Israel Zevin, Rose's friend at the *Jewish Daily News,* was there, as a companion to her mother.

It was a new world for Rose Pastor Stokes. She learned to swim that summer and to go far out on the Sound in one of the small sailboats—there were five of them that would accommodate two or three persons—for unproductive attempts at deep-sea fishing.

Caritas means *charity* in Latin. Rose chose the name whimsically. The island was a wedding gift from Graham's mother, and so was the house that was built for them. Mother Stokes's largesse did not end there. In August Graham wrote to "My Dear Mother" thanking her "for the check which was duly received, and for the promise of another one to come later." Graham and his mother did not, however, see eye to eye on social questions, as he gently but firmly told her in a letter from the Norfolk Street flat to the Madison Avenue mansion in December 1906: "Indeed, darling Mother, I never questioned or doubted your devotion to study as you saw it, nor have I been unaware of an immense amount that you have done and still do to help the victims of wrong. . . . But I have doubted whether you recognize the injustice of the system which provides you with your great income at the expense of theirs; and whether you recognize the relation between this system and the terribly widespread suffering which you endeavor so earnestly to relieve."[24]

At about the same time that Graham was writing this stern but patient message to his mother, Rose was writing at great length to her friend Helena Frank in Scotland. The letter, which answered Helena's questions about Caritas Island, also tried to describe Rose's emotional response to her new environment:

> Can you think, dear friend, what all this meant to me who had but yesterday come out of the abyss for the first time in my whole life! And the joy of the children and the rest of my mother—and to Zevin, and another one or two occasional friends. God is surely good! . . . My Beloved and I are so grateful.
>
> That is the pause in the summer when one can rest and gather strength and inspiration for the work that lies before. For through it all we do not, cannot forget the suffering world. Injustice of Capitalism; misery of wage-slavery—and again the fight! Socialism! . . . A great, glorious fight. The only thing worth living for in these inspiring days.

In the same letter Rose admitted that she had not yet started on the translation of Morris Rosenfeld's working-class poems. She hoped that Helena, her collaborator, was not anxious. "Last summer in the spare moments there was the house to get settled in. Next summer I hope to work on them. Tell me if you are anxious. [More than six years were to pass before the translations were ready for the press.] I am sending you Mrs. [Olive] Dargan's book. Rolfe, Shakespeare's great editor, says of it: I have seen nothing in the same line from any English or American pen for twenty-five years or more, at all equal to it. It is admirable in every way."[25]

Rose's letter to Helena Frank failed to mention Maxim Gorky's visit to Caritas in 1906. He was one of the first of many prominent political and artistic figures who would make that pilgrimage. Gorky came to the United States with the dual purpose of raising funds for the Russian revolutionists and lobbying against a proposed U.S. loan to the czar. His mission received warm support from the liberal and radical intelligentsia. Mark Twain, Jane Addams, and Finley Peter Dunne were among a large committee of prominent persons who sponsored the fund-raising committee. Robert Hunter, the Stokeses' brother-in-law, sponsored a fund-raising dinner at the intellectual Club A, to which the cognoscenti flocked. The press lionized Gorky and his "young charming wife" and hailed their arrival on April 10.[26]

But after the *New York World* broke the news on the front page on April 14 that the charming Madame Andreyena, who accompanied Gorky, was not his wife, most of his support, including that of Mark Twain, dissolved. Gorky was turned away from three hotels in one night, and he and his small party were on the sidewalks of New York at 4 A.M. when they were given shelter by the John Martins on Staten Island. The wealthy Martins, friends of Rose and Graham, also provided Gorky's little group with a home in the Adirondacks, where he did much of his writing of the celebrated novel *Mother*. Gorky visited Rose and Graham at Caritas on July 4. Communication was aided by the presence of the socialist (and sociological) writers Leroy and Miriam Scott. Mrs. Scott, who wrote as Miriam Finn, was born in Russia and did the interpreting.

Within a year or so, the Scotts moved to a small house on Caritas, as did William English Walling and his wife, Anna Strunsky, forming, if not a socialist circle a socialist triangle on the island. "Thus," as one writer has pointed out, "three wealthy WASPs of impeccable social standing were living on a tiny New England island with their wives, all Jewish women born in Russia."[27]

Late in 1909 a headline announced: "Stokes plans a Utopia—Will Establish Colony of Social Workers Near Connecticut Home." The story deflated the hyperbole. Graham had bought nine acres adjoining Caritas Island. "Mrs. Stokes and I feel that it would be more congenial for us to have as neighbors people whom we know and are in sympathy with us. . . . It is not a colony we are establishing but just a gathering together of congenial people engaged in the same work."[28]

Although Rose Pastor Stokes was new to the Socialist party and had spent her short time in it mostly in writing and in settling into her island home, she had already learned the lesson of a socialist activist that the "glorious fight" is conducted at various levels: the ultimate revolutionary goal—socialism—is linked to the struggle to meet immediate demands—reform.

Hence on December 14, 1906, Rose Stokes was to be found in New York's City Hall, a short streetcar ride from Grand at Norfolk. At City Hall Rose "voiced the East Side's bitter protest against the dilapidated disease-breeding horse cars . . . and in an impassioned plea urged the Aldermen to adopt an ordinance prohibiting the operation of horse cars in the future."[29] She told the city fathers: "You gentlemen don't realize what they suffer on the East Side. They can't protest. They don't know what to do. Some of them don't even know you exist. If they wanted to protest they couldn't spare the time to come here. But they feel these conditions deeply, and they are learning."[30]

From Norfolk Street Rose could see the rugged new Williamsburg Bridge, opened in 1903. It carried streetcars, elevated trains, horse-drawn vehicles, and pedestrians. It afforded a pleasant walk in favorable weather and attracted many residents at its East Side and Brooklyn ends. Rose thought there should be more benches on the walkway and wrote to the Department of Bridges, which promised to place one hundred more benches on the bridge "if they get a release from the State Prison from which benches must be purchased."[31]

Concerned with benches and horsecars, Rose Pastor Stokes was at entrance level as a socialist activist. From this parochial beginning she was soon to advance to national scope.

The Socialist party of America (SP) was formed essentially by the merger of the small Social Democratic party with a split-off segment of the older

Socialist Labor party in a process that began in late 1899 and ended in a unity convention at Indianapolis in late July 1901. The party was entering its heyday when Rose and Graham joined it in 1906.

Rose was recruited into the SP on the basis of its general and long-range program—its revolutionary goal of socialism rather than its program of immediate demands such as equal rights for women. Some of the women who had preceded her into the party—and no other party at that time welcomed women as the Socialists did—had already found that women members were not accorded full rights and recognition. Some had become organizers and held official positions, but the dominant male leadership failed to understand the need for activity to overcome the disadvantaged position of women in American society. Neither the 1901 nor 1904 conventions did much more than offer "a formal declaration demanding equal civil and political rights for men and women."[32] Eight women delegates and 120 men had attended the first convention. In 1908 there were 20 women delegates, and Socialist women were publishing a monthly journal titled *Socialist Woman*.

There is no doubt that in its day the SP took the most advanced theoretical position on the "woman question" of any political party, but in practice it was a man's party, which made it difficult for women to gain leadership or even a voice. Few men recognized the special oppression endured by women in the general economic and social system which Socialists opposed as an issue requiring immediate struggle. Most held the view that when socialism had been achieved and men were able to obtain the high wages and independence that would allow them to give women what they needed, most of women's problems would be solved. Women's needs, therefore, could—in fact, must—wait.

Some Socialist women were also persuaded by this line of thought. As good Socialists, they did not consider equal rights for women as separate from the general "labor question" under capitalism. Moreover, as Ira Kipnis states: "By 1908 the male superiority complex of the Socialist Party apparently had increased considerably. Although the party platform demanded complete political and economic equality for women, equality was to come as a gift presented by man to woman out of his infinite generosity."[33]

Nevertheless, women felt they had good reasons for being SP members. They recorded these reasons in *Socialist Woman*, founded by Josephine Koneko in 1907 and published in Chicago. In a series on why women should be Socialists, Mrs. E. H. Thomas, state secretary of the Wisconsin SP, stated: "Women, as mothers of the race are 'dealers in futures' . . . the mother who should save her son from the life of a wage slave and her daughter from the more dreadful fate . . . should throw herself into the only cause that can make equal opportunities for all children of the human race." May Wood Simons asserted, "Every woman should be a Socialist because it means her economic and political freedom. She can never better her condition until she has both the ballot and is free from wage bondage."[34]

By 1909 the *Socialist Woman* had become the *Progressive Woman,* but it remained a staunch advocate of socialism. In the March issue Lida Parce declared: "No mere reform can reach the roots of the evil of sex subjection. Only revolution . . . will do the work. Two things are essential to this revolution: the socialization of industry . . . and the ballot, which will enable her to remove those special and artificial disabilities which have been placed on her by male legislation."[35]

The women Socialists felt frustrated by the party's failure to give appropriate attention to their special problems. They even considered and then rejected forming a Socialist party of their own. Instead they created scores of women's clubs from coast to coast, mainly to spread propaganda and education and to reach women outside the party. They sought to attract working women, housewives, and women who stayed home while their husbands attended SP meetings.

Writing in the *Socialist Woman,* Eugene Victor Debs paid tribute to Mrs. Grace Brewer, a tribute no doubt well deserved and certainly well intended: "She is one of those who work for the cause . . . merging herself in it, and may her tribe be much more numerous. Mrs. Brewer is a splendid example of what a woman can do in the way of giving her thought and energy and capabilities to the Socialist movement while at the same time"—and here the great Debs showed that he too tended to see Socialist woman through the kitchen window—"maintaining an ideal home adorned with all the graces and amenities of home life."[36]

Debs spoke before the Christian Socialist Fellowship in early June 1908 on the subject "Women and Their Struggle under the System." Rose Pastor Stokes, by then a veteran of almost two years in the SP, attended the lecture with Florence Kelley (Wischnewetsky). Kelley was so moved by Debs's talk that she turned to Rose and said tearfully: "I am ashamed to be out of the Socialist Party that has a man like that at the head. I'll take out

my membership for him tomorrow."[37] From this anecdote one may learn
with some surprise that Florence Kelley, who had long been an adherent of
the socialist movement in America, who corresponded with Friedrich Engels, and, in 1885, translated into English the American edition of Engels's
The Condition of the Working Class in England, did not join the Socialist
party until 1908.

The pages of the *Socialist Woman* (1907–9), and after 1909 the *Progressive
Woman*, regularly featured reports popularizing active Socialist women.
The cover would carry a picture of the featured woman, and inside
would be a story and a biographical sketch. Rose Pastor Stokes received
this honor in the October 1907 issue. The lead story quotes from an article
in the magazine *Woman* in which the interviewer describes Rose as "a tall,
slender, young woman . . . with a pallid complexion, a face framed with a
glory of rippling, brown hair, and lighted by leaf-brown eyes in which is
the most spiritual expression I have ever seen in a living face; it is like that
in the pictures of Joan of Arc and St. Cecelia." The strong impression of
Rose recorded by this interviewer is in its intensity and much of its detail
identical with the record we have of her encounters with scores of other
individuals over the next ten years. "What women most lack," she told the
reporter, "is opportunity. When they have opportunity and grasp it, they
will be the greatest of the world's forces. They will be even more than men,
because they have greater spiritual and stronger moral fiber than men."[38]

Rose was again on the cover of *Progressive Woman* in February 1910. The
caption describes Rose as a "Socialist Writer and Speaker." This issue was
the "Dramatic and Literary Number," and Rose Pastor Stokes is listed
among "Magazine Writers and Artists Who Are Socialists."[39]

Though most of Rose's working hours were devoted to writing, she had
become well known as a Socialist speaker in the Northeast and frequently
shared a platform with Graham. There is a legend that people who came to
hear this famous couple generally dozed peacefully through the husband's
prepared remarks only to be roused to spirited response by the extempo-
raneous eloquence of the wife.

Rose was nominated as a delegate to the 1908 SP convention, but she
was not involved with the internal policies of the organization. With the
exception of the William D. (Big Bill) Haywood case in 1912, she remained
aloof from the ideological conflicts that enlivened SP life. In later years
she would regret her lack of attention to such matters and recognize that
her indifference to them had made her subject to the views of the educated

and influential men in whose circle she moved. Graham, who was elected to the National Executive Committee in 1908, did involve himself in inner-party battles.[40]

Socialist Woman addressed a ringing admonition to the SP convention of 1908:

> Mere theoretical recognition will not suffice. We demand of you strong, practical action. We demand that the SP shall institute an active campaign in behalf of obtaining the ballot for women. We demand above all things that the SP shall pay more attention than it has paid . . . to the organization of women within our own ranks and that the main object of such organization shall be the bringing about of a national working woman's movement, to offset the narrow-minded viewpoint of the bourgeois women who do not and cannot fully present the working woman's side of the question.
>
> Let us remember, comrades, that as surely as there is a class struggle, there is also a sex struggle, and that the working woman has a double burden of her sex; that she is doubly exploited as a worker and as a woman.[41]

This appeal is poignant, but it ignores the triple exploitation of the black woman, and it takes too narrow a view in focusing on the working woman to the total exclusion of women of other classes who also suffered discrimination.

John Spargo, a prominent ideologist of the SP, used the pages of the *International Socialist Review,* the intellectual journal of the socialist left wing, to polemicize against the party's negligence in addressing the woman question: "The goal of freedom can never be attained by a master sex dragging a subject sex behind it. . . . It is essential that our stand for sex equality be made . . . a real, vital and earnest part of our faith and our struggle. . . . Harsh as it may sound, I say that we have consistently and deliberately ignored the woman's side of the program."[42]

A few months later, in June 1908, with twenty women delegates present, the convention met. The agitation by the women and Spargo led to resolutions elevating the role of women in the party and advancing party agitation and organization among women generally. A Woman's Committee was set up; a full-time paid organizer for women's work was appointed; consideration was given to addressing women's problems; and it was resolved that suffrage was to be recognized as an issue and discussed in all

Socialist locals. In 1910 Lena Morrow Lewis was elected to the National Executive Committee, and in 1912 Kate Richards O'Hare, one of the more prominent of the SP women leaders, was placed on the National Executive Committee. The 1908 convention, though not the millennium, was an important milestone for women in the socialist movement.

V

In the Movement

Stitt Wilson's rhetoric may have propelled Rose and Graham Stokes into the Socialist party of America in 1906, but there is no doubt that they had been headed in that direction before their marriage. Graham had read a pamphlet published by the Ruskin Club of Oakland, California, in 1904 and underscored a passage that read: "Every Christian who understands and earnestly accepts the teaching of his Master is at heart a Socialist."[1] But Graham never joined the structured Christian socialist movement. In 1907 Ellis E. Carr, editor of the *Christian Socialist*, urged him and his "noble wife" to subscribe to that magazine. But Graham replied, "My wife and I do not believe that any other movement affords us such large opportunities for useful service . . . as the Socialist Party movement itself."[2]

Even before he had joined the party, Graham called a conference at the Stokeses' Noroton home to discuss "rapidly growing evils." Informal discussions were held on economic and social conditions.[3] Morris Hillquit, who was present at the gathering, recalled that Graham

> was a physician by training but not by profession, had traveled widely, and had spent years in social and philanthropic work and developed radical political leanings. . . . He was ascetic in appearance and habits and deeply earnest in his convictions, whatever they happened to be. About half a year earlier he had married Rose Pastor Stokes, a Jewish factory worker of rare charm, who in the aristocratic surroundings of the Noroton "Brick House" looked and acted more to the manner born than almost any other member of the assembly.[4]

Perhaps the most newsworthy result of the Noroton conference was its conversion, though only temporarily, of Medill Paterson to socialism. By

1912 Paterson was a former socialist and therefore qualified to found and publish the *New York Daily News* in 1919.

James Graham Phelps Stokes had shown his active interest in socialism in the spring of 1905, when Upton Sinclair, soon to write *The Jungle*, conceived the idea of a society for promoting the discussion of socialist ideas on college campuses and among alumni. Sinclair recruited George Strobell, an affluent socialist, to help him establish the new society. They assembled a prestigious group to issue a call for a founding conference.[5] The call went out on June 4, 1905, over the signatures of James Graham Phelps Stokes, Thomas Wentworth Higginson, Charlotte Perkins Gilman, Clarence S. Darrow, William English Walling, Leonard D. Abbott, Jack London, Upton Sinclair, and a few others.[6]

On September 12 the Intercollegiate Socialist Society (ISS) was formed. Stokes was on his wedding trip when the meeting was held, but he was elected one of the three vice-presidents; the others were Owen R. Lovejoy and George Strobell. Jack London was president until 1907, when Graham succeeded him; he held the post until he resigned from the society in 1918. Florence Kelley was first vice-president for a while. Besides Graham, two other members of the Stokes clan were on the executive committee, Robert Hunter and Helen P. Stokes. Another member of the executive committee was Mary R. Sanford, Helen Stokes's housemate.

Not all of the founders and officers of the ISS were Socialist party members, though several of them joined later. The purpose of the ISS, as stated in the call, was to promote "an intelligent interest in socialism among college men and women graduate and undergraduate, through the formation of study clubs in the colleges and universities and the encouraging of . . . an interest in socialism among the men and women of the country."[7] Harry W. Laidler, a student at Wesleyan—the only student among the ISS officers—became organizational secretary, a full-time post which he held for decades. Success came in time, and until it did funds contributed by George Strobell and Rufus W. Weeks, a vice-president of the New York Life Insurance Company, sustained the organization.

Starting in 1913 Rose Pastor Stokes undertook extensive speaking tours for the society and became its most prominent and effective ambassador. But as early as 1908 Rose spoke at Barnard College to the Columbia University chapter of the ISS. Her speech provoked a protest from Ralph M. Easley, chairman of the executive council of the National Civic Federation, which for a generation or more maintained an "unholy alliance" with the

American Federation of Labor.[8] In a letter to Nicholas Murray Butler, president of Columbia University, Easley complained that he noticed that "Mrs. Phelps Stokes made quite a hit at Barnard last night." He asked for a speaker in rebuttal. William T. Brewster, dean of Barnard, advised the Barnard club to get faculty approval of outside speakers in the future.

Rose Pastor Stokes's life in the cigar factories may have predisposed her to illness and exhaustion. She was often plagued by upper respiratory problems. Although she was usually energetic and quick, she was frequently obliged to halt her public speaking briefly to gather strength to continue. Her activity was always at a higher level than could be long sustained.

Olive Tilford Dargan, whom Rose had met in Canada on the fateful trip that sealed the love affair between Rose and Graham, was probably the first to express worry about Rose's health. Dargan loved Rose dearly, as is clear from a (slightly tardy) message she sent to Caritas on the occasion of Rose's twenty-seventh birthday, which was also her first wedding anniversary:

> You are forever my Rose—I am always your Olive. I am happy dreaming of you on the eighteenth—of all that the year must have brought of promise and vision—of all that the years will bring of bloom and achievement. Then the picture of yourself the first hour I knew you . . . of my dream like a sweet rebuke. For even then the harvest of true, young years was in your eyes. . . . The rest is heart's pride—such as the glow I felt when I chanced one day upon a eulogistic comment on one of your talks. . . . Are you writing any [poems] now, dear poet-heart, or doing better—living all your poems? Always your sister—Olive.

There was a ten-year difference in the ages of Rose and Olive, and Olive found in Rose the epitome of youthfulness. She worried over her young friend and when a letter came from Rose saying she was tired, Olive responded vehemently:

> Rose, Darling: I see, I feel that you are very tired. You have used your life-capital all your days instead of the "interest" and sometime you must stop for breath and rest. Couldn't it be now, or must you wait—as I did—until you can go no farther and fall. Ever since the beautiful love came to you I have had a dream of you resting for one—two—

three—years in some nook of England or Germany or sweet South France with your husband, studying the things that you want to tell and teach. . . .

Dear Rose, precious Rose, you are one in 10,000. Don't waste yourself as though we can find another Rose any day. You are so young. It strikes to my heart to think of you making a mistake so early and halting perhaps the rest of the way you should tread so buoyantly. It is not reaction from this summer and busy enthusiasm, but the overwork of years and years that you are beginning to feel. But I must stop—before I annoy you—for no matter what I say and think, you only know what you can do and must do.[9]

Olive lived at this time in Almond, North Carolina, with her husband, Pegram Dargan. "There is beauty here, and I love it—and here's my heart's best," she wrote, "but I long for a bit of rest on your island—seeing no one, not even, Rose perhaps, on some of the days. But the dream, I fear must end with the longing." Rose called Olive her "most precious friend," and Olive visited at Caritas more than once. "Olive would come and share all my personal thoughts as well as my social hopes," she wrote. "I can't get rid of my bourgeois background," Olive would say, "but depend on my love and my understanding—always, always." "They have never failed me," Rose commented.[10]

The *Concise Dictionary of American Biography* lists Rose Pastor Stokes's profession as "Agitator." In a time of great agitators, she was one of the greatest and certainly one of the best known. Among her contemporaries were such noted platform speakers as Elizabeth Gurley Flynn, William Jennings Bryan, Kate Richards O'Hare, and Eugene V. Debs. Until Graham drastically curtailed his public speaking and Rose sharply increased hers around 1913, the Stokeses were a popular team on the socialist lecture circuit.

Robert Hunter, who had been a pillar of the University Settlement, announced his intention to withdraw from settlement work and join the Socialist party on January 17, 1907. A few days later, Rose and Graham Stokes announced in an interview held in their Norfolk Street kitchen that they too were withdrawing from settlement work.[11]

The change in their focus from the world of the settlement house to that of the socialist movement did not mean a cessation of all contact and sympathy with the settlement houses and their goals. They retained, for example, a friendly relationship with Lillian Wald and made financial contributions to her Henry Street Settlement.

The Stokeses, and socialists in general, were not the only critics of the settlement houses. Jane Addams, for example, invited attack from both Right and Left. In presidential elections she supported the chauvinist Theodore Roosevelt against Woodrow Wilson in 1912 and the "pacifist" Wilson against Charles Evans Hughes in 1916. In 1928 she endorsed Herbert Hoover against Alfred E. Smith. In 1932 she endorsed the conservative Hoover against Franklin D. Roosevelt.

The extreme of antiradicalism is evident in the declaration after World War I of General Henry J. Reilly: "I tell you if things continue to go as they have recently in Washington we can expect to see Jane Addams President and William Z. Foster [leader of the 1919 steel strike] Secretary of War."[12]

In joining the Socialist party, Rose and Graham were dedicating themselves to a cause. They now saw settlement houses as impediments along the revolutionary road and thus competitors for the minds and hearts of workers and the poor, diverting their attention from the need for fundamental change in the mode of production and the nature of the state.

Their announcement followed their attendance at a Syracuse University alumni dinner at which Chancellor John Day defended the corporations, attacked the unions, and denounced the ten thousand saloons frequented by workers between the Battery and Harlem. Graham took the floor to rebut the chancellor's remarks and explained that workers went to saloons because their home conditions were so miserable. Day had spoken vaguely of the need for "big men" and "big industry." Graham agreed on the need for "big men" but deplored the devotion of such men to the accumulation of wealth rather than to the service of the people. In somewhat elitist language he said that in the future "the largest men will be among the most devoted servants of the people," a primitive socialist reply to the chancellor's primitive defense of capitalism.[13]

In their kitchen interview the Stokeses emphasized that they had withdrawn from settlement work and private charity and would be giving up their Lower East Side apartment as soon as they found a place that afforded them the quiet they needed for writing. They were planning to devote themselves to education, by which they must have meant writing and public speaking. One newspaper reported: "Asserting they were more fervent Socialists than ever J. G. Phelps Stokes and his wife . . . admitted yesterday they have entirely given up settlement work, and that the future for them would be years of toil to arouse in others the spirit of Socialism. Stokes termed his work 'applied Christianity.' " Rose was more specific. She told a reporter: "The rich are blind to the fact that a donation to charity or philanthropy can serve no real good purpose so long as an un-just social system remains, which legalizes the taking of great wealth by the idle. The oppressed are blind to the fact that settlements, churches, and the like can do little good so long as there remains the injustice inherent in the industrial system which makes and keeps people poor." In the Norfolk Street kitchen interview Graham reported: "My wife and I just returned from a ten-day trip to Pennsylvania, where we spoke every evening. Here in New York and vicinity we are upon the platform three or four nights a week regularly."[14]

There is no doubt the name *Stokes* opened doors for them that would ordinarily have been closed to a card-carrying Socialist. At first, Graham's was the magic name, but after a while it was Rose's. Years later Rose quoted Oscar Wilde's remark about Frank Harris: "Frank has been invited to all the great houses in London—once," remarking by way of analogy about the many organizations that invited the Stokeses to speak, thinking them merely "noted settlement workers." When they spoke about so-cialism, they were rarely invited a second time.[15]

A few days after the announcement that they had discontinued the set-tlement work in which they had been conspicuously involved, they spoke at the Baptist Church of the Redeemer in Brooklyn on the subject of ap-plied Christianity. "Many of the best known residents of Flatbush" came to hear them. A reporter said: "If there were those who were attracted to the meeting by curiosity to see the son of a great and wealthy family and the young woman who had lived and worked on the East Side . . . pre-ceding her marriage to Mr. Stokes, their feeling soon must have deepened into sympathetic interest and finally turned to admiration. . . . There was nothing new in their message, but it unquestionably was attractively pre-sented. This was especially true of Mrs. Stokes." The Reverend A. W. Holladay, who preceded them on the program, spoke of the value of "practical Christianity" in business life. Graham Stokes took higher ground when he declared that "the teachings of Jesus did not enter into the affairs of today" and that "business was conducted on the theory of smashing one's rival." A provocative question from the floor led Graham to describe the way he disposed of his personal wealth: "I support myself by my own earnings. . . . My unearned increment I devote to the causes in which I am interested, especially Socialism. For instance, I get dividends from my real estate purchased years and years ago. If I could turn these dividends over to their rightful owners, I should do so, but that is now obviously impossible. If I were to distribute them among all those who earn them for me each man would get just one-fortieth of one per cent. Therefore, I have to do the best I can with them by applying them to the purposes I have described."[16]

Graham had given this explanation before and would give it again. If one concedes that there was truth in his denial that he was a millionaire, one may yet be reluctant to concede that his dividend income came solely from real estate unless that term includes the mining properties he controlled in the Far West and the ninety-seven-mile-long Nevada Central Railroad. In addition to an income which most of his contemporaries might have envied, he benefited from the largesse of his mother, who provided Caritas Island and, a few years later, a modest townhouse in Greenwich Village as well as cash gifts. In spite of his disclaimers, whenever James Graham Phelps Stokes was mentioned in the press, which was often, he was identified as "the Millionaire Socialist." Similarly, Rose Pastor Stokes was identified as "wife of the Millionaire Socialist."

The modest labors Graham performed at 100 William Street and the trips to supervise his western properties were the principal extent of his productive toil. The couple never lived lavishly, but they lived on a scale that could hardly have been supported by the dollar value Graham placed on his labor. He eventually wearied of being quizzed about the seeming irreconcilability of his socialism and his wealth. When a reporter mentioned the subject in 1912, Graham answered that he did not intend to distribute his holdings among the poor in an effort to emancipate people from wage slavery. He did not believe alms-giving would bring about emancipation.[17] Rose told an interviewer: "Mr. Stokes devotes every cent of his unearned income to Socialism. The money which . . . he earns, and it's not as great as many think, we use for living."[18]

When Rose and Graham Stokes addressed a meeting in Milwaukee in July 1907, they were joined by another "millionaire socialist," William Bross Lloyd. In the city that beer made famous the three spoke to over a thousand people whom a summer shower had driven into the pavilion of Pabst Park. The speakers had to make themselves heard over the noise of sideshow barkers and waiters rushing beer to the thirsty. A reporter noted: "On one occasion Mrs. Stokes had to stop short because of the continuous tooting of a miniature locomotive whistle." Nevertheless, "the intense earnestness of Mr. Stokes made a profound impression." Graham was reported as being "tall and dark after the Lincoln type, his dark deep set eyes flashed with the arguments he enunciated, and his gestures betokened a high-strung temperament." Graham predicted that the socialist revolution would be accomplished "without bloodshed." The Socialist party was not doctrinaire, and this comfortable assurance did not breach the party line though many of its members would not have agreed. Rose sounded a less controversial note when she told the crowd that "there is no question that the salvation of the poor man must come through poor men."[19]

A year later Rose elaborated her views on the point Graham had dealt with. She told a reporter, "Never has the world been riper for Socialism. Never have the capitalist classes feared the truth more. In every country of the world discontent is growing. . . . This is the new rebellion—the rebellion that will be fought with the ballot if possible—as it is our right that it should be—but with the bullet if necessary. . . . I cannot see that we can win with the ballot alone. I wish that I could."[20]

During the summer of 1907 Rose and Graham gave up their Norfolk Street apartment but not their base in that deprived community. Though they were now commuters from Madison Avenue and from Connecticut, they were to be found on the Lower East Side early in 1908 actively supporting a strike against rent increases. Later in the year Graham ran for political office in that district, and Rose stumped for him.[21]

In the meantime there was some surcease from toil: they were in Cairo on March 5 and were still abroad on May 1. In July they were at Stamford, Connecticut, and Rose, who was gaining self-confidence and was as ready as her husband to play the publicist, gave an interview to a *New York Times* reporter which produced the headline "Calls Roosevelt Ignorant."

President Theodore Roosevelt stirred Rose's indignation by statements he made while resting at his home at Oyster Bay, Long Island. He repeated a not very original view he had expressed on more than one previous occasion. "He is truly ignorant," said Rose, "concerning the principles of the most vital questions of our day." She went on:

> A friend said to me only a few moments ago: Mr. Roosevelt on the subject of Socialism is the most ignorant man in the country. That

> Mr. Roosevelt still tags on to Socialism the "dividing up" theory, the stalest of all stale theories regarding Socialism, proves that there can be few people in the country more ignorant concerning the theory than he is. . . . The next step forward in line with economic development is the assumption of ownership and the control by the people of our highly organized industries.
>
> If Mr. Roosevelt wishes to abuse Socialism, he must learn what Socialism is.[22]

Though Rose and Graham had moved away from the hurly-burly of Grand Street—and its atmosphere redolent of decaying garbage and fresh horse droppings—to escape the noise pollution that hampered their thinking and writing, their political roots were still there. In July 1908 came a call to Graham to run for assemblyman from the Eighth Assembly District on the Socialist party ticket.[23]

The Eighth Assembly District was the turf of the East Side's shining Socialist star Jacob Panken, a perennial candidate in that community for any office. Panken was later to be rewarded for his persistence with a municipal judgeship, which gave him prestige in that teeming area, especially among its Jewish majority, Socialist or not.

In 1908, however, it seemed worthwhile to make use of Graham Stokes's prominence, which had been so vastly enhanced by his marriage to a Jewish immigrant. A *New York Times* interviewer said in 1910: "Mr. Stokes is the hero of our greatest social romance, a figure in the one marriage of recent years that has come nearer than any other to demonstrating the ideal of universal brotherhood."[24] Rose, of course, could not run for office—not because she was Jewish or an immigrant but because she was a woman.

Panken deferred to Stokes, whose nomination in the strong Socialist district was made unanimous despite some concern that the voters might be put off by a millionaire who spent much of his time at his country home. Given the choice between Grand Street and Caritas Island, one may easily understand why the Stokeses preferred Caritas, a three-acre chip of woods and rocks barely severed from the mainland of suburban Stamford, washed by the waters of Long Island Sound, within easy commuting distance of New York. The Stokes mansion on Madison Avenue furnished a legal residence qualifying Graham for political office in the city.

The simple hospitality of the lord and lady of Caritas, a modest manor but a charming one, brought frequent visitors. The only problem if, unlike Rockwell Kent, you did not own a horse, was getting there from the station, and that could be done by hailing a hack at fifty cents per passenger.

When there were no visitors, Rose and Graham never lacked conversation and companionship once the Wallings and the Scotts had joined them as tenants on Caritas, forming an insular sextet of affluent socialist intellectuals.

From Caritas Rose wrote one day to the poet Edwin Markham inquiring about one Katherine Kennedy. In the half decade Rose had been in New York, she had made a friend of Markham just as she and Graham had done with a large coterie of the socialist intelligentsia. She had come a long way from the day she had electrified the Ladies Friendly Society of Cleveland with her impassioned recitation of Markham's "The Man with the Hoe." Writing from Landing, New Jersey, in August 1908, Markham addressed Rose as "Comrade in the Labor Struggle." Regarding Kennedy he said:

> For years she has been a leader in the Christian Science Church, and has been looked on by many as the proper successor to Mrs. [Mary Baker] Eddy. But some months ago she was led to see that there was a Social Problem which her church does not reach. The upshot of it all is that she is reading Socialism, and she has concluded to join her fortunes with this new enthusiasm of humanity. One of her first requests of me was to make her acquainted with you.
>
> Mrs. Kennedy is a strong character, and she would be a force in any cause which she might espouse upon the platform.
>
> Please bear my affectionate regards to your noble husband, whom I greatly honor.
>
> Ever Yours, Edwin Markham.[25]

Rose Stokes and Katherine Kennedy must soon have become acquainted, for Rose wrote Graham a few weeks later that Kennedy was "not an old woman—only 32 and looks 18." Rose had faith that Kennedy would help their cause. Perhaps Graham was away on one of his periodic business trips when Rose wrote him about Kennedy as an addendum in a political/love letter from Caritas on a stormy day in August. "Darling," she writes,

We are all safe and cozy in the little house. But I am not "safe" Beloved. I am out in the storm with the homeless and wandering—the men and women we so often see huddled together on the benches in the public squares and drifting down the stream of human life in our own crowded streets. . . . Oh, my love! I am with them in their place so often that half my vitality I believe is spent in the crucial spiritual agony that I endure thereby. . . .

Oh! what a wonderful cause we are working for, My Precious! What a lifting of loads there will be when our cause triumphs. That is the joyous thought! that some day all our striving, all our straining will gain for the world that peace that passeth understanding. For I know it shall come in wonderful Peace to the World, darling, and we shall have done our share.[26]

It was this message, ardently expressed in a letter to her husband, that people responded to when they heard it—in suitably modified form—from the platform.

Rose Pastor Stokes was introduced to the rough forum of street-corner speaking when Graham ran for assemblyman in the fall of 1908. She also spoke from indoor platforms, fire escapes, and the tailboards of wagons. It was common opinion that Mrs. Stokes was a good speaker. Besides, she knew the district in which Graham was running and the people from whom he sought preference. Her energetic support was expected to bring him many votes, though not enough to elect him. Perhaps it was not the year for a Socialist or for a millionaire Socialist, or perhaps Tammany Hall, the New York County Democratic machine, gave Graham Stokes a short count. If Socialists could prevail anywhere, it was on the Lower East Side. They made Jacob Panken a judge, they put Meyer London in Congress in 1914, and they helped send five men to the state assembly in Albany and two aldermen to City Hall in 1920.

Rose's preoccupation with Graham's campaign did not preclude her attention to other Socialist activity. She attended a special banquet on October 4 that had been arranged by the New York Socialist party leaders to honor Eugene Victor Debs. The guest of honor was too exhausted to appear, but the inevitable fund appeal was made. It must have been unusually effective for Rose Pastor Stokes "climbed on top of her table and dramatically took off her jewels and tossed them in the contribution box.

From her rostrum she pleaded with other women to do the same. Some other ladies leaped upon their tables and gave their baubles to the cause."[27]

If Debs, who was running for president, was too exhausted to attend this event, perhaps his stumping for Graham had helped tire him: "Rutgers Square was crowded with enthusiastic Socialists spurred on by the coming of Debs. . . . J. G. Phelps Stokes, the millionaire socialist, and his wife who was Miss Rose Harriet Pastor, a cigar factory girl, were speaking from their open barouche. . . . At the close of the meeting the hearers had become so enthused that they unhitched the horses from the barouche and, taking the pole themselves, drew Mr. and Mrs. Stokes around the square several times amid shouts for Debs and Stokes."[28] This must have been a unique experience for a couple of East Side Socialists.

Before and after the elections Rose and Graham scurried about the Northeast filling speaking commitments. In October Rose went to Trenton, New Jersey, to speak at a Sunday Socialist party meeting at the State Theatre. She sent word that she wanted "all the working women of Trenton to be present. . . . She will have a special message for them."[29] Her December lecture to the Sorosis, the progressive women's club of Patchogue, Long Island, had no special message for working women, of whom there were few in Patchogue at that time. Both the sisters and the brothers heeded the call of Sorosis and came to hear Rose. The *Brooklyn Times* reported:

> Probably nothing could have compelled more respect for so little understood a problem as Socialism than the temperate and at times, the sweet-tempered tone of Mrs. Stokes during an address of nearly two hours.
>
> Without doubt many who "came to scoff remained to pray" and when questions were asked and when, later, the "legal fraternity" actually cross-examined the speaker right and left, the same sweet temper; the same unruffled responses; the same sincerity that permeated her whole bearing, won the admiration of even her sharpest cross-examiners.[30]

The meetings kept Rose and Graham busy as the year 1908 drew to a close—Elizabeth, New Jersey; a demonstration by the unemployed at Cooper Union; the Twentieth Century Club in New York City; a debate at the Economic Club in Boston in which Graham Stokes confronted President Eliot of Harvard; and a meeting at which Graham spoke to an audience of one thousand in New Haven while Rose was silenced by a cold.

While Graham held forth in New Haven's Steinert Hall, his brother the Reverend Anson Phelps Stokes, Jr., was preaching a sermon in St. Paul's Church in the same city. A heckler asked Graham: "Why don't you give some of your money to the Church?" Graham replied that he thought "the Church does more harm than good sometimes." In the formal question period Graham was asked: "Haven't you a brother in the Church?" Graham replied quickly: "Yes, and I am glad of it . . . because he may be able to do some good. Different men have different temperaments and he may do some good in the Church."[31]

In August 1907 Rose Pastor Stokes made a brief return to journalism when she agreed to conduct an "advice" column for the *Jewish Daily Forward,* then under the editorship of Abraham Cahan. The *Forward* was a socialist paper in the Yiddish language, published down the street from her former employer, the *Jewish Daily News.* Her counsel to the lovelorn and to their mothers was syndicated by the *Forward* and picked up by the *Boston American* and the *New York Journal* of the Hearst press.

In November 1908 Rose undertook to conduct a "women's department" (nowadays called a "family page") for the *New York Call.* This was the principal daily newspaper of the socialist movement, regarded generally as the all but official organ of the Socialist party. The women's department was a weekly half page or so of articles, editorials, letters, and poems. Under Rose's editorship it was not sufficiently distinct from the rest of the paper because, in tune with her interests, it emphasized working-class matters as a whole rather than matters pertaining specifically to women such as suffrage, women's liberation, and day care for the children of working parents. By March 1909 Rose was relieved of her *Call* assignment. The paper's editor, John Block, installed his wife, Anita, as women's department editor, a post she held for several years.

The Stokeses now had time for a two-week stay at Palm Beach. Amid the conspicuous consumers in that playground of the rich Rose felt a predictable ambivalence. She despised the affluent idlers in that sun-stricken enclave, and she loathed the pleasure domes that catered to the whims of the superaffluent. But she found "the sun and the silence are healing. . . . The silences and the roar of the breakers. . . . It is inexpressibly restful and my bronchitis seems hourly better. The sun, the balmy air . . . I can't tell you of the renewed astonishment I feel every hour at the healing of it all."

They were visiting Graham's parents and stayed at their cottage. "This corner," she said, "is not the typical Palm Beach. Palm Beach is really the two huge hotels—the Breakers, and the Royal Poinciana," which were full of wealthy idlers. "I have already trod on idle toes. I confronted one of these idle women with the facts of exploitation—and saw the light in her eyes grow as hard as the precious stones she wore."[32] After this restful, healing interlude there was the train trip north, interrupted at Jacksonville and Baltimore for meetings.

In 1909 there occurred a struggle within the Socialist party similar to those that had broken out from time to time since the difficult labor of founding the party in 1900–1901. The 1909 contretemps was by no means the last or the worst. Inner-party struggle generally resulted from the existence of a Left, Right, and Center in the organization. Although the factions were unstructured and did not resemble the factions that troubled the Communist party in the 1920s, they were identifiable to those who busied themselves with inner-party matters.

A small group of party activists, led by A. M. Simons, editor of the *Chicago Daily Socialist,* set out to capture the party by conspiratorial means. In November 1909 Simons sent a letter to William English Walling in which he projected the formation of a labor party to bring the Socialists closer to the American Federation of Labor and to end the hostility between the party and the federation. Walling was not then a party member; he joined the following year. Simons may have been attracted to him because Walling had written in a magazine article that the labor and socialist movements must ultimately merge. But if Simons thought that meant Walling was sympathetic to Simons's scheme he was wrong, for Walling believed that merger should come only when the Socialist party had gained sufficient strength among the workers, farmers, and intellectuals. In addressing Walling, Simons was acting conspiratorially. After Walling revealed the scheme and charged him with plotting—together with such prominent Socialists as Victor Berger, Morris Hillquit, Robert Hunter, and John Spargo—to take over the party and convert it into a labor party, a full-fledged inner-party fracas broke out.[33]

The main body of the SP left wing was generally hostile to the American Federation of Labor, which at that time and for many years after took a nonpartisan approach to politics. It was expressed essentially by the slogan: "Reward our friends; punish our enemies." Since the AFL was principally a federation of the craft unions of the skilled, it held aloof, with few

exceptions, from industrial unionism; it sought to restrict the availability
of craft workers by means of high initiation fees, long apprenticeship periods, and racist exclusivity. It paid no attention to migrant workers and
little to women.

A few weeks before the Pastor-Stokes wedding, the Industrial Workers
of the World—also known as the IWW and the Wobblies—was formed in
Chicago. Its aim was to create One Big Union. It sought to rival the AFL
with none of the latter's deficiencies. It scored a number of triumphs but
never achieved a numerous or stable membership, though it exists ves-
tigially to this day.

When it was founded, such labor stalwarts as "Big Bill" Haywood of the
Western Federation of Miners, Eugene Victor Debs of the Socialist party,
Daniel De Leon of the Socialist Labor party (SLP), "Mother" Mary
Jones of the United Mine Workers, Lucy Parsons, widow of Albert Par-
sons, a martyr of the 1886 Haymarket Affair, and Father Thomas J. Hag-
gerty, a Texas parish priest, were among those on the founders' platform.
Elizabeth Gurley Flynn joined in 1906 at age sixteen.

The IWW was classified as a syndicalist organization: it assumed that
the working class would eventually transform itself through the One Big
Union into the inevitable socialist society to come. Most of its founders
were members of the SP or SLP. The IWW and the AFL were under-
standably at odds with each other. In the SP there were many who favored
one over the other, or both, or neither.[34]

Rose Pastor Stokes was drawn into this battle despite the involvement,
on opposite sides, of her brother-in-law Robert Hunter and her friend
(and Caritas neighbor) William English Walling. It was not typical for her
to participate in inner-party struggles. She was usually content to leave
such conflicts to the self-confident male politicians who surrounded her.
When World War I came and positions had to be examined and reex-
amined, she realized she had made a mistake over the years by not paying
more attention to inner-party matters. Dedicated as she was to work in the
field—the aspect of the work she loved best—she tended to leave party
affairs to Graham and the highly educated coterie of which he was a part.
She stood in awe of the formidable intellectual group in which her husband was so firmly rooted.

Debs spoke up against the Simons "plot," and so did both Stokeses.
Rose said it was "nothing but a desire to get into office. . . . Since we
cannot win the entire A.F.L. to the revolutionary position, these comrades

think it would be an advantage to come down to the narrow positions of the A.F.L." Though the Simons group was rebuffed on its immediate proposals, the controversy dramatized the tensions that were usually present in the SP between a principled revolutionary element and a controlling leadership leaning to a class collaboration outlook.[35]

Graham and Rose generally sided at this time with the amorphous left wing of the party, the side on which Debs could usually be found. Graham was critical of the electoral policy of the Cincinnati Socialist party in 1910, and he said as much in a letter. He was, after all, a member of the National Executive Committee and thus could be presumed to be a guardian of party policies. He cited the example of the Wisconsin organization: "The election in Milwaukee [Victor Berger's stronghold] was won largely by appeals to the smaller capitalists to vote the Socialist ticket 'as a protest against the trusts.'" This, said Graham, was not the party line. But he did not want to criticize them "because they had worked so hard."[36]

Operating as they did in the political limelight, Rose and Graham never lacked for issues to confront and political chores to do. Malicious government policies and bumbling police could be relied on to provide the stimuli for their constant activism when all else failed—and that seldom happened. One typical event concerned Emma Goldman. Although Goldman was an anarchist, she coexisted peacefully with many SP members. Her doings, or what she was charged with doing, frequently gave her newspaper coverage, if not a trip to jail, even when what she did was innocent. Nothing that Emma Goldman was capable of doing could have been more innocent than her standard lecture on Henrik Ibsen's plays, but her attempt to deliver this lecture in New Jersey made certain policemen angry, and they dispersed her audience. This audience held a number of persons of wealth and position who were not used to being dispersed and who were outraged by this crude act of censorship. One such person was Alden Freeman, a man who is not usually counted among the "millionaire socialists" but who must certainly have deserved that distinction. Freeman was a socialist. His father, Joel Francis Freeman, was the treasurer of the Standard Oil Company.

Alden Freeman was an ardent admirer of Emma Goldman's lectures on Russian drama and on the works of Ibsen. As he wrote to the newspapers, he had once enjoyed the lectures in the "company of a high official of the New York Life Insurance Company," probably Rufus W. Weeks. Freeman organized a meeting for Goldman at a hall in swanky East Orange, New

Jersey, the site of his estate. But the local police would not permit it. Free-man then organized a meeting in a large barn on his estate, and Goldman finally delivered her lecture to an overflow crowd.

By this time the chain of events had generated a Free Speech Commit-tee, which sponsored a meeting of two thousand persons at Cooper Union in New York. The roster of members of the Free Speech Committee in-cluded, among others, Eugene V. Debs, Clarence Darrow, William En-glish Walling, Anna Strunsky Walling, J. G. Phelps Stokes, and Rose Pas-tor Stokes—a list that became almost standard for such an event.[37]

Soon after the Cooper Union meeting Elizabeth Gurley Flynn de-scribed to Rose a police attack that broke up a meeting in Stamford, Con-necticut. Flynn wrote urging Rose to speak there at a protest meeting under the auspices of the Free Speech League. The police chief had said, "You may have the right to speak," Elizabeth reported indignantly, "but we have the power to stop you."[38]

During 1909 and 1910, at about the time that Alden Freeman was carry-ing on his well-organized, well-financed, somewhat genteel campaign in the East, the Industrial Workers of the World were carrying on their dog-ged fights for free speech in the Northwest. When they were barred from speaking on street corners—the only forum they could afford—they fol-lowed one another onto the soapbox as one after the other was arrested. They filled the jails and sent out calls to Wobblies everywhere to grab a freight and ride to Seattle, Spokane, or wherever and replenish the pool of volunteers facing certain arrest. A pregnant Elizabeth Gurley Flynn, nineteen years old, answered the call and ended up in the inevitable cell.

When the Stokeses were at their townhouse at 88 Grove Street in Greenwich Village, they were a short walk from most of their activities—a few blocks from Cooper Union to the east and from Union Square and the Labor Temple to the north. The Lower East Side and the City Hall were easily reached by public transportation. The Stokeses eventually ac-quired a small automobile, but in Stamford they sometimes got around on a motorcycle, Graham in the driver's seat and Rose in a ladylike sidecar. When they were in a minor accident, it was reported that they "prefer this vehicle to the capitalistic motor car."[39]

On May 31, 1909, they were at the Hotel Brevoort in one of the least raffish parts of Greenwich Village to attend the fifteenth annual dinner meeting of the Whitman Fellowship. Graham's name appeared in a head-line on this usually sedate and routine occasion ("Stokes Rouses Whitmanites") by chiding his brothers and sisters of the fellowship. In his speech he told them he objected to the ideals of the organization because there was too much concern for "beauty." He reminded his audience of the condition of the unemployed and of the capitalists, whom he blamed for their plight. If the fellowship supported the old system, it was better dead, he said. And he feared that the organization was supporting the system. Others on the list of speakers, remarkably radical considering the aesthetic bent of the fellowship, were Emma Goldman and Rose Pastor Stokes. Mrs. Stokes told her fellow dinner guests that she admired Walt Whitman because he was not afraid to express his thoughts in the face of bitter opposition and because he refused to be bound by conventions.[40]

Earlier on the same day the Stokeses had attended another event, of more importance than they could have foreseen. It was the conference that led to the founding of the National Association for the Advancement of Colored People (NAACP). In 1909 an especially gruesome lynching occurred in Springfield, Illinois. The city's identification with the memory of Abraham Lincoln helped render the incident so outrageous that William English Walling was moved to take action in protest.

Walling, soon to be a Socialist party member, was brought up in the South and had a conscientious antipathy to racism. The Socialist party had no special planks in its program to advance the immediate interests of blacks. It offered only ultimate socialism and little present remedy. This negligence was exacerbated by the overt racism of some of its leaders; Victor Berger, one of the most prominent, wrote "there can be no doubt that the negroes and the mulattoes constitute a lower race."[41]

Walling's initiative brought together a group of liberals in meetings at his home, including Charles E. Russell, a "millionaire socialist." Joining in these preliminary sessions were a number of the black intelligentsia led by William Edward Burghardt Du Bois, who was beginning his long and brilliant career. Monroe Trotter and Ida B. Wells held aloof from Walling's initiatives because they mistrusted white leadership. In July 1905 Du Bois had rallied twenty-nine black leaders to a meeting in Fort Erie, Canada, where they formed the Niagara Movement. The founders had in common a rejection of the leadership of Booker T. Washington and an insistence on an end to segregation. They demanded full social, economic, and political equality for black people.

On May 31, 1909, at the United Charities Building in New York, Du Bois, Walling, and their associates brought together three hundred persons, black and white, all distinguished in various fields of intellectual and economic endeavor. Not all who were invited agreed to attend. Among those who did not were Booker T. Washington of Tuskegee, Seth Low of Columbia University, and Andrew Carnegie. The Stokeses were among those present, as were Charles Edward Russell, John Bassett of Smith College, and a group from Columbia University which included Livingston Farrand, John Dewey, William T. Brewster, and H. R. Seligman. Judge Wendell Phillips Stadford was also present. An impressive contingent of women leaders attended, several of whom were socialists. Among them were Anna S. Walling, Ann Garland Spencer, Leonora O'Reilly, Miriam Finn Scott, Fanny G. Villard, Madeline Doty, and Mary W. Ovington.

The conference moved to Cooper Union for an evening session and concluded the next day with an undertaking to raise $5 million for "Negro uplift." The National Association for the Advancement of Colored People was born out of this meeting. W. E. B. Du Bois and most of his Niagara Movement leadership joined the new organization, and most of the Niagara members were absorbed without a formal merger. In 1910 Du Bois became director of publications and research of the NAACP and was a founder and editor of the *Crisis,* the NAACP journal.[42]

Rose did not become active in the NAACP, but Graham remained in it for several years. When the *Crisis,* a six-page pamphlet, was published in 1911 to promote the forthcoming (June 1911) first issue of the journal of the same name, it included a testimonial from J. G. Phelps Stokes.

VI

On the Picket Line

Caritas Island must have been a mag-
ical place—or was it the charm of the
extraordinarily vital woman who presided over it that made such an im-
pact on those who visited there? In September 1909 Anne, wife of Horace
Traubel, went from Caritas back to the drab precincts in which she lived in
Camden, New Jersey. There she wrote a letter full of love for Rose and
Caritas. The letter indicates that Anne had a brief but ardent crush on
Rose. Such crushes are documented in a number of letters Rose received.
Some men, some women, some husbands and wives together were smit-
ten after hearing her on the platform or hosting her overnight on one of
her speaking tours. Anne Traubel's adoration of Rose is perhaps the best
documented, both in its intensity and its brevity, for the letter avowing her
love was enclosed with a second that already indicated a cooling—but not
a coldness:

> Dearest Rose: I am still walking in the dream of Caritas . . . I want
> you to be here. There is nothing beautiful to offer you—not so much
> as a resting place when you are work weary and except as this vital
> thing I touch you with—that touches me from you again, transmutes
> the plainest, least comfortable spot into a place of heart's desire, I
> could not ask you to come.
>
> Why is it that the image of a life mostly etched out by anxiety,
> sorrow, grief is after all a beautiful result; not disastrous, not bitter
> even but tender and lovely with creative power springing from it as
> other Gods spring from Jove's head? I don't know why I think, I don't
> know quite how it is, but this I do know: it is this perception which
> gives me to be free to your love and frees my love to you.

I first saw you four years ago. I touched you this summer and found you in divine ways never to lose you—never to lose you, never to say good-bye. Wherever I am I shall be coming toward you. If you lift your eyes you may see me now on My Rock listening to the voice of the sea among the stones. What is the moon path for? Every night I will travel that road for your dear sake, my Rose, and wait for you on the wave-washed rock called

—Anne's

This must not have been an easy letter to write, and Anne did not find it easy to mail. She held it until October 5. In the meantime a letter came from Rose. It probably did not encourage Anne to send her sweet, sad, loving message, for she held it two more days, then enclosed it with a merely friendly note saying: "I hesitate to send it now, I am sending it as I think there is enough living moisture in it to keep it unfaded still." The letter then turns to trivial matters. A last paragraph asks: "How is Kathleen Kent?" And a last sentence wanders from the moon path to ask: "Have you caught a striped bass yet?"[1]

Kathleen Kent was Mrs. Rockwell Kent. The young Kents, recently married, had spent the summer of 1909 on Monhegan Island, Maine. He had been industriously painting the headlands, the gulleys, the surf, and the woods of the island, thus beginning an identification with Monhegan that put the island on the aesthetic map. As the summer came to an end it was time for Rockwell Kent III to be born, and Kathleen and Rockwell accepted an invitation to move into the Stokes place on Caritas. "We were received with open arms," wrote Kent, "and we were no sooner established in the separate quarters that the big Stokes house afford than we entered into doing our part, and thereby lightening theirs, in the household's very simple way of life. . . . Before September came to a close we were settled on Caritas Island as though we had grown there."[2]

Rockwell Kent now had to go to a job in the city. To assist in his daily commuting to Grand Central Terminal, he stabled his horse, Kitty, in the Stokeses' unused garage. At seven o'clock each morning he would gallop two or three miles to the railroad station. He put Kitty in a nearby livery stable, caught his train, and promptly at nine o'clock walked into the offices of the architectural firm where he was employed. At seven in the evening he would be back at Caritas.

With punctuality equal to his father's, little Rockwell III was delivered in a small private hospital in New York City and a few days later the happy threesome was reinstalled at Caritas. The father wrote:

> The baby was a source of great delight to Rose for she and Graham, ardently though they desired a child, had not been blessed. "The trouble is," said Horace Traubel, a frequent visitor on Caritas, "they don't know how to go about it." And it is true that they were as spiritually disembodied and generally impractical a pair as one might ever meet. If they had known how to make a baby, what in the world would they have done with it when it came? How, even would they have done for themselves about the house but for what order and system Kathleen was permitted to bring to household affairs, and the completely unskilled, heavy-duty services of a young Bulgarian peasant woman who plodded, bare-footed, about her daily chores? But she, at any rate, knew how babies were made—even, one might conclude, without the services of a lover. For certainly no man showed up to claim it. But what difference did that make to Rose and Graham, God Bless them! Immaculate conception or otherwise, it was a baby and was welcome. And I have no doubt whatever that they made that child and its mother their responsibility as long as they might be in need. But you know it is not easy to live with other people. It is not necessarily, if ever, a question of one being right and the other, consequently, wrong. If you like order, you dislike disorder; and if you incline to a sort of free and easy neglect of dust and dishes, the incessant tidiers-up are apt to prove annoying. But although in that Caritas Island household different inclinations were evident, we aimed to please and our good hosts to like us. So all went well.[3]

Rockwell Kent met scores of the Stokeses' friends at Caritas. Rose Strunsky; Leonard Abbott, editor of the *Literary Digest;* and Horace Traubel were his favorites. Traubel was the devoted friend of Walt Whitman, an editor and publisher, and a writer in the liberal literary monthly, the *Conservator.*

Kent met lawyers, journalists, social workers, politicians. Most of these people were socialist intellectuals, unquestionably devoted "to the advancement of their Cause for mankind's sake." But it bothered Kent that these men and women "were inclined to view that Cause as . . . a separate activity to which such work as painting pictures, writing music and the arts in general were not only secondary but unrelated." He considered Abbott and Traubel to be exceptions. He empathized with Traubel, who was strongly influenced by Walt Whitman and who based his criticisms of the arts on "a people's art, a widely comprehensible and democratic art."[4]

Sometime after the Kents had moved from Caritas, another mother and child came to visit. The child was Fred Flynn, the ten-week-old son of Elizabeth Gurley Flynn. Gurley Flynn was twenty years old when she came to Caritas. She was seventeen when she married J. A. (Jack) Jones, an exuberant Wobbly, an ore miner on the Mesabi Range, a vigorous man in his early thirties. Elizabeth and Jones met in December 1907 and were married in January 1908. Elizabeth gave birth prematurely to a boy later that year, when she and Jack were living in a back room in a Chicago flat. The child, John Vincent, died within twelve hours. By the time Fred Flynn was born, Jack and Elizabeth had separated. Jack, wishing to remarry, divorced Elizabeth in 1920. She had been living with Carlo Tresca for six years. They separated in 1925.

Baby Fred was born on May 19, 1910. The summer weather came on early, and June and July were hot. The doctor who looked after Elizabeth and Fred was the brother of a Caritas resident, Anna Strunsky Walling. Rose Pastor Stokes heard about the stifling and crowded conditions of the Flynns' Bronx apartment where Gurley Flynn and her baby were uncomfortably and unhealthfully situated. For about ten weeks she established them, says Elizabeth, "in a large downstairs room and bath all to myself, next to a spacious library. I sat outdoors in the sun reading a great deal with the baby asleep in a basket. Many interesting people came there. I recall Horace Traubel and Shaemus O'Sheel, then a budding young poet. There I first met Ella Reeve ["Mother"] Bloor, who was the Socialist Party organizer for Connecticut."[5]

Horace Traubel's lighthearted explanation for the childlessness of Rose and Graham is no answer to a question that must have aroused some curiosity among those who knew them and even some of the general public. There is no record that sheds a glimmer of light on this subject. Was one or both of them infertile? While Emma Goldman was writing sexually explicit letters to her lover, the newly married Rose was writing to her husband that she longed for his pat on her head. Graham said no more than that he missed her.

Both of the Stokeses came from large families. Graham's mother bore nine children, a burden to be sure but a burden lightened by all the help money could pay for. Anna Pastor had seven children, and Rose had a hand in every aspect of their nurture, including earning their keep. It may be that she had had her fill. If so, she knew how to prevent pregnancy.

The Socialist party was enjoying its heyday in 1912. Its presidential candidate, Eugene Victor Debs, received 900,000 votes, and in April it had more than 135,000 members. It counted 1,200 officeholders in 340 cities, and 79 of these were mayors in 24 states. But by June 1913 membership was down to about 81,000, largely because of the clash between Left and Right, which took place at the Indianapolis convention of the Socialist party in May 1912.[6]

Around the time of the convention the IWW, with support from the left wing of the SP, had been engaged in great struggles, including the Lawrence, Massachusetts, textile strike, the related murder frame-ups of Wobbly leaders Joseph Ettor and Arturo Giovannitti, and a campaign for free speech in San Diego. The Right, in the effort to make the party mainly an electoral machine, found grounds for undercutting these Wobbly battles. "Big Bill" Haywood, the IWW leader, who was a member of the SP National Executive Committee and a delegate to the convention, was its special target. The Right sought to make sabotage a major issue. The Left was maneuvered into defending it, though the definition was ambiguous, ranging from damaging machinery to a workers' slowdown—a "walking in wooden shoes"—*sabots* in French.

The convention passed an amendment to the constitution calling for expulsion of any member who advocated sabotage. Before many months passed Haywood was accused of such advocacy and was removed from the executive committee by referendum. Haywood took the next step himself—he resigned from the Socialist party. When Haywood left the party thousands of left-leaning members followed him out. Thousands of right-wingers also left but for a different reason: the candidacy of Woodrow Wilson and his election in 1912 gave many of the reformists in the party a new rallying point—Wilson's liberal platform, which he projected with beguiling rhetoric. Graham Stokes, a member of the National Executive Committee, opposed the right-wing drive on Haywood. Others associated with him in this losing cause included Walter Lippmann, Max Eastman,

Margaret Sanger, Osmond K. Fraenkel, William English Walling, and Louis Boudin.[7]

In September 1912 Rose Stokes wrote to her friend Anna Walling expressing her distress at what was happening to her party and of the "dissensions" that "make the day of fulfillment seem far, far off." The dissension "indicates a lack of vision—a lack of basic fundamental knowledge among a very, very considerable number of those who call themselves Socialists—upon whom so many depend for light and representation in the coming revolution." But Rose saw an advantage in the departure of the "reformers" from the party: "They flocked to it only because there was no other 'reform' party in the field." Without them, the Socialists "will find it easier to carry on more clear-cut revolutionary propaganda."[8]

Rose apparently identified herself with the left wing of the Socialist party though not in any factional sense. Just as she did not, despite her feminist activity, consider herself a feminist "as such,"[9] so she did not think of herself as a leftist as such. Her instincts led her to align her activity with the interests of the class in which she had been raised while enjoying the advantages acquired through her marriage. When in time she found herself veering from the proletarian pole, she made the necessary course corrections. When she could no longer contain her political body within the integument of her elite married condition, she returned to the condition in which she had been nurtured.

She was scornful of her socialist brother-in-law Robert Hunter, who had made a niche for himself in the movement through his talents as a writer, speaker, and ideologist and who fought on the wrong side, as she saw it, in the Haywood case. "He was always impeccably dressed and manicured." He had a large farm and a comfortable house at Noroton Heights, the wealthy area where his wife's family had an estate. He had a love for the comforts of a country gentleman. He moved to Berkeley, California, says Rose, and became an "expert gentleman golfer and thus was lost to the Socialist movement."[10]

In 1912 Graham ran for the office of mayor of Stamford. His Republican opponent was Gutzon Borglum, the artist, sculptor, and publicity hound. At a meeting at which both spoke, Borglum, after hearing Graham, said that he did not think his own program was in any way superior to what Graham had propounded. This comment could hardly have pleased either the more rock-bound Republicans or the more hard-core Socialists in the audience. In any case, the election became moot for Graham Stokes when his eligibility was challenged on technical grounds and he withdrew. Borglum lost to a Democrat.[11]

Rose never heeded the plea of her friend Olive to curb her activity and guard her health. She spoke on socialism in a variety of forums, even to the Daughters of the American Revolution (DAR) and the Women's Christian Temperance Union. "Come and tell us about Socialism," the DAR requested, pointing out that "in 'free' and 'democratic' America, any working girl can marry a millionaire." Rose recorded her feelings about speaking to these groups:

> There were Comrades who argued against our speaking before these non-working class organizations: "No use bringing the message of Socialism to its logical enemies," they said. "Beside they are only curious about you, or they want the publicity you can bring them." But experience taught me the value of accepting these invitations. Many came out of curiosity, but remained to listen, and that was important. Moreover, they often stayed to take sides. As a rule these bodies were controlled by wealthy bosses and landlords of the town—or their paid servants and retainers; but many workers and poor farmers, or people of the lower middle class, attended the meetings. The question our meetings raised—that of Socialism versus Capitalism—clarified the class struggle for those present.

Despite a history of intermittent bronchial attacks, Rose retained an enthusiasm for platform speaking and liked to think she never tired. No doubt her zeal enabled her to push herself further than prudent care of her health would have allowed. She especially liked talking to people on a one-to-one basis after a meeting. Graham had no patience for this and would urge her to cut these postmeeting discussions short. Years later she realized that "he loved the people in theory only; that there was no personal warmth in him for them. Often I thought I detected a look of contempt as he looked upon some members of my class."[12]

Public speaking claimed more of her time than any other activity over a period of some fifteen years, and there is ample evidence that she excelled at it. One small-town journalist wrote that "Mrs. Stokes is one of the most eloquent women speakers in the world today. She is full of fire and enthusiasm."[13]

A big city writer was assigned to interview Rose in connection with the

1909–10 shirtwaist workers' strike, and he came away from the assignment no less impressed than his suburban colleague. He was asked by a worker: "Why are you so anxious to write up Rose Pastor Stokes? There are other brilliant socialists." "I don't know," he replied, "but everyone always wants to read about Rose Pastor Stokes." He decided that "in manner she is absolutely unaffected. . . . She is intangible, elusive, charming—she is perfect. . . . A woman as Shaw describes his most vital heroine, to make men dream."[14]

From 1906 to 1910 Rose "spoke at organization meetings for the Women's Trade Union League, she helped in organizing new workers in a variety of trades and attended meetings of the Executive Board of the WTUL."[15] The Women's Trade Union League (WTUL) was founded in 1903 in Boston by a group of women trade unionists and educated middle-class women including social workers. It had been resolved at the start that the Executive Board would have a majority of women unionists and a minority of earnest sympathizers. This goal was not achieved until 1907. The league sought to solve three basic problems facing American working women: unionization, education of the unions to the need for bringing in women members, and aid in the formation of new unions of women workers.

The WTUL was never officially part of the AFL, but its stated aim was to assist in organizing women, preferably into affiliates of the federation. The AFL accepted this goal politely but gave the WTUL scant encouragement and even placed obstacles in its way. The league did succeed in setting up some unions and was effective in picketing, raising funds, and running relief kitchens and welfare functions. Mainly it mobilized public opinion and publicized the need for improving the conditions of working women. It provided social activities to brighten their drab lives and carried the union message to women workers, especially in such trades as clothing, textiles, laundry, millinery, and gloves. Rose Schneiderman of the cap makers was probably the outstanding working-class figure in the WTUL, and Margaret Dreier Robins was outstanding among the women of independent means.[16]

Starting in 1909 Rose was active in some of the most hard-fought strikes of the period in the garment, hotel and restaurant, and textile industries. All these strikes involved women. In the strike of the shirtwaist workers, which started late in 1909, the women workers were a pronounced majority of the participants. The strike started with a suddenness that took both workers and bosses by surprise. A meeting had been called, sponsored jointly by

Local 25 of the International Ladies Garment Workers Union and the WTUL, to be held at Cooper Union on November 22. The hall was filled, mostly with Yiddish-speaking young women. Other smaller halls on the Lower East Side were also filled. The meeting had been called to discuss the intolerable conditions and wages under which these women—immigrants or daughters of immigrants—were forced to work by their employers— immigrants or sons of immigrants. On the platform were Mary Dreier, president of the WTUL, and union leaders, all men, right on up to Samuel Gompers himself. The restless women heard one speaker after another tell them how poorly off they were—a matter on which they were themselves the greatest authorities. Despite the militant-sounding rhetoric in Yiddish and English hurled from the platform, no one proposed action.

Finally, a young woman who had already taken blows for her efforts to organize her shop, left her seat and walked down the aisle to the platform. She was Clara Lemlich, already known to many of the workers for the efforts she had shown and the beatings she had suffered in the organization drive. She demanded the floor. There were cries of "Let her speak," and she was lifted onto the platform. Lemlich, in furious Yiddish, said there had been enough talk, it was time for action. She called for a general strike. The assembly echoed her call with "Strike! Strike!" In a scene that could have been written by Clifford Odets, the union leaders were spurred to action, the strike was ordered by unanimous voice vote, and a solemn oath was taken not to capitulate. Soon the word was carried to the other meeting rooms and the strike was on under the leadership of Local 25, ILGWU.[17]

The manufacturers were outraged at the effrontery of their mostly youthful, mostly female workers. Before long they announced their own intentions: they would hire strikebreakers for as "long as it takes to break the strike." Almost thirty thousand workers walked out.[18]

The police responded with force against the pickets. Fighting back in an organized way, the union called for a protest march on City Hall to begin with a rally at Bowery and Rivington streets. Rose Pastor Stokes was the principal speaker. Ten thousand strikers and supporters answered the call. As they marched down the Bowery under the El they displayed banners with such slogans as: "Fifty-two Hours a Week," "Peaceful Picketing Is the Right of Every Woman," and "The Police Are for Our Protection, Not for Our Abuse." When the marchers reached City Hall, about a mile from where they started, a delegation presented Mayor McClellan with resolutions "to overthrow the tyranny of the police interfering with the strikers' pickets."[19]

The demonstration had some effect. An employer complained to a reporter that Rose Pastor Stokes, who had been picketing his shop, "now goes to her picketing duty with an escort of from one to three policemen."[20]

The Women's Trade Union League gave the strikers full support. The WTUL had some members with the know-how and the financial means to get certain things done. One of them was Mrs. O. H. P. Belmont. As Philip S. Foner describes it, "Alva Belmont hired the Hippodrome and invited leading suffragists and trade unionists to speak. An audience of eight thousand, including suffragists, trade unionists, Socialists, and even anarchists, applauded wildly as Reverend John Howard Melish of Brooklyn, Socialist organizer and lecturer; Anna Howard Shaw, Methodist preacher, National American Women's Suffrage Association; pleaded for justice for the shirtwaist strikers."[21]

Alva Belmont was for some years a stalwart supporter of women's labor struggles, of woman suffrage, and of the birth control movement. The shirtwaist workers, the poorest of the working poor, attracted the sympathy of their well-to-do sisters, notably Anne Morgan, the niece of banker J. Pierpont Morgan. The strikers' dogged and courageous picketing reinforced by the backing of sympathizers began to crack the ranks of the shirtwaist manufacturers. By December 12, 240 employers had settled with the union.[22]

But the large manufacturers held out. It was a bitter winter, and the strikers suffered miserably from hunger, cold, beatings, and jailings. The toughest of the employers offered to settle on December 23, granting some concessions on wages and hours but refusing the union shop. The workers rejected the offer. Eventually they were worn down by their suffering. The strike ended on February 15. Important gains had been made: working hours had been reduced from sixty to fifty-two per week, overtime was paid at time and a half, and other small gains were made—and the strikers had made a lasting contribution to the building of the powerful International Ladies Garment Workers Union (ILGWU).[23]

In the so-called waiters' strike of 1912 Rose was even more involved than she had been with the shirtwaist makers. In the latter case she was an active sympathizer; in the case of the waiters she was part of the leadership, a member of the strike committee.

The strike also involved cooks, oystermen, dishwashers, busmen, and bartenders. As it spread to upstairs and downstairs departments of hotels it was joined by scrubwomen, firemen, porters, and bellhops. All were assembled in an industrial union in a city where such unions as existed were, with the exception of the semi-industrial ILGWU, craft unions. The hard-fought strike lasted for seven weeks and, if for no other reason, is notable for introducing mass picketing to the city of New York.

At noon on May 7, 1912, a well-dressed young man strode into the Hotel Belmont dining room across the street from Grand Central Terminal and (literally) blew the whistle. It was the signal for 150 waiters to take off their white aprons and march directly out of the dining room onto the picket line. Kitchen employees followed. Similar scenes were taking place in other hotels and eating places. On the first day three thousand hotel and restaurant workers struck. At the end of two weeks almost eighteen thousand were out.

This uprising, this slave rebellion, this unexpected revolt of one of the most exploited strata of service workers, stunned the employers, their patrons, the press, and the conservative International Union of Hotel and Restaurant Employees (HRE). The HRE, an American Federation of Labor affiliate, had never extended its organization to the sculleries of the restaurants or the housekeeping departments of hotels and had hardly made a dent in its claimed jurisdiction of waiters and cooks.

The IWW, flushed with its success among the lowly unskilled and semi-skilled textile workers of Lawrence, Massachusetts, now came to the big city and dared to lead a strike of some of the city's most maltreated employees. The Wobblies brought with them their policies of rank-and-file participation besides their novel tactic of mass picketing. Though the strike caught almost everyone by surprise, it had been carefully prepared by leaders of the IWW and the hitherto unheard-of Hotel Workers Industrial Union.

The luxury hotels and restaurants were principally affected by the strike. Patrons were outraged to realize that the obsequious automatons in dark suits and white aprons from whom they had instinctively relied for unquestioning service and faithful attention had turned out to be human beings capable of fighting for their rights.

Hotel employees put in ten to fourteen hours a day—when they didn't work eighteen. Chambermaids, scrubwomen, and laundry workers had to sleep in vile accommodations so as to be available at all hours. For this the boss pocketed "rent money."

Cooks were paid as little as $30 a month. Busmen, pot cleaners, and pantryhands got $20; bellhops, scrubwomen, and chambermaids, from $12 to $18; waiters, $25. They were fed, of course, but the food has been described as "trimmings, refuse, leavings unclean and unwholesome. . . . Everywhere the ordinary bill of fare is hash and stew—so the boss may use up the scrapings and leavings from the plates of the patrons. . . . Coffee in 'Help's Hall' is usually brewed from yesterday's grounds. Tea is an infusion of willow leaves." Another grievance was the system of fines and breakage charges. One waiter reported a flat charge of a $1.50 per month for breakage whether or not any occurred. "When we really break something we pay another fine." There was a twenty-five-cent charge for dropping a spoon or forgetting a napkin and a dollar for smiling in the dining room.[24]

The IWW sent in some of its most fiery orators to spur the strikers. Veterans of the Lawrence strike such as Arturo Giovannitti and Joseph Ettor spoke frequently. The official history of the Hotel and Restaurant Employees Union refers to other speakers, naming Inez Haynes Mill-holland and Rose Pastor Stokes, as "parlor socialists . . . feminists out of the upper crust of New York Society." Rose, of course, was hardly a socialist of the parlor and, though a feminist, not of the upper crust.[25]

The strikers were kept in a constant state of alert by an endless meeting at the strike hall, conveniently located at Bryant Hall, under the El on Sixth Avenue and 42nd Street, across the street from Bryant Park, within easy walking distance of many struck hotels. Workers dropping in at the hall were sure to hear speakers reporting the latest developments and urging solidarity. Union headquarters was at the top of a ramshackle building at 77 West 44th Street, also near Sixth Avenue, where Rose worked on the executive committee and handled press relations when she was not in the field.

She was the principal speaker at a mass meeting of the striking workers held at the Amsterdam Opera House on May 19. "Mrs. Stokes Berates Hotel Proprietors," said a press account. Rose read from a letter a friend of hers had received from a hotel manager. She said it showed the attitude of the "master class": "I see that Mrs. Stokes intends to befriend the IWW. If she knew what a contemptible crowd they were she would not have anything to do with them. They are the most low-lived people in the world. They thieve alone and when they organize they thieve together." Rose turned to the crowd, which filled the hall: "Wouldn't you think," she said, "that he was thinking about Wall street?" The audience applauded, and they applauded again when she told them proudly that she was a Socialist.[26]

The strike was having its problems. Early in June the strikers, who had already had to cope with police violence and harassing arrests, had also to face hired thugs and Pinkerton guards. President Eliot of Harvard encouraged "college-boy scabs." The press was hostile. Efforts to get the chambermaids, whose grievances were also on the union's agenda, to join the strike were not successful.

The second week of June, New York's upper crust, with Mayor McClellan leading the way, enthusiastically welcomed a visiting fleet of German war vessels. Members of the social elite vied with each other to entertain the naval officers. The supreme event in the rivalry to capture the attention of these enchanting navigators—who five years later would be the arch-enemy—was the official dinner for the honored visitors, presided over by the mayor and held in the dining room of the Waldorf Astoria, at taxpayers' expense, on June 10.

The strike worried the mayor, who feared that the well-planned event would be disrupted by a well-timed walkout of the waiters. But such a disruption proved to be beyond the reach of the union. The union did produce a mass picket line at the hotel, driving the mayor into a fury and causing some nervous moments for arriving guests. Ninety-six pickets were arrested and carried off to jail in a fleet of paddy wagons.[27]

The hotel keepers announced that they would "voluntarily" grant some of the strikers' demands but made no offer for the busmen, bellhops, and chambermaids. Secretary Jacob Bloechlinger of the industrial union spurned the offer for this reason and because it did not include recognition of the union.[28]

On June 16 the press reported that additional hotels had been affected by the strike. Nevertheless, the strike was winding down. The union attorney, Charles Recht, wrote to Rose Stokes at the union headquarters: "Dear Madame: The number of sincere friends you have made during the present waiters' strike . . . is impossible to imagine. All over the country every hotel worker heralds you as a saviour. . . . There is not one that is not carried by your eloquent appeal and that is not ready to stay out till you tell them to go back and you are the spiritual leader of this struggle against the bosses." Recht thought nevertheless that the strike should be ended on the basis of limited concessions with a view toward keeping the union intact and striking for further gains at the next opportune moment.[29]

By the third week in June an organized retreat seemed advisable, and Rose suggested that the strikers return to work. They at first rejected this idea by a vote of 1,381 to 426 and on June 22 Rose withdrew from active participation on the executive committee "because I believe in majority rule." But three days later, on a second vote, the strikers resolved to return to work. Rose told the *Times* that it was "a mistake to suppose that nothing was gained. . . . Nearly every hotel and restaurant involved had granted marked concessions in wages . . . fining and revenant systems have been abolished." Though the union had not been recognized, it had moved into "permanent new headquarters on West 38th Street."[30]

The next day the *Times* declared editorially that Stokes was wrong if she thought the paper considered the strike a failure. "As a result of the strike the conditions of payment and service in many establishments have been measureably improved."[31]

The waiters' strike had personal repercussions for Rose, some of which she was not fully aware until 1918.

She had a relative in the business, William Earl Dodge Stokes, the brother of Anson Stokes, Graham's father. This very rich uncle, whose principal sources of income were his extensive real estate holdings and his profitable horse-breeding farm in Kentucky, was the owner of the Ansonia Hotel, which occupies the entire Broadway block from 73rd to 74th streets. He was against the strike, he was against foreigners, and, for both those reasons, he was against Rose Stokes, his niece by marriage.

By June 24 W. E. D. Stokes had learned that the strike was about over. He had also heard, and believed, the absurd rumor that Graham was prepared to donate $6 million to the strikers. Stokes wrote to Rose:

> You have upset the minds of thousands of waiters, buses and cooks who came here from distant lands, some, perhaps with the honest intention of becoming good American citizens. You have made them dissatisfied, unhappy and caused them to lose their positions, while their wives and innocent children go hungry and are in dire want. . . .

Had you succeeded, poor Graham would have lost his $6 million, that he was prepared to give the waiters . . . and then where would you and Graham be, if you had lost the $6 million? . . . My brother Anson, report has it, has so trusteed Graham, that he and you will have just enough to live on, that the principal goes to your children, if you have any. If not all goes to his other children outright.

A waiter who used to be here at the Ansonia called on me this morning and brought me a clipping from the *World*. It reads as follows: "America was for Americans. We are taxed to death to pay for the support of this worthless, rotten crowd. Take them home. . . ."

Now is your chance. Spend your $6 million in doing real good and save us from being further annoyed, and yourself made unhappy. . . . The sooner this country gets rid of this rotten trash the better for it. If the immigrant law were strictly carried out, and the principles of eugenics followed in this country, we would not have any of this trouble.[32]

Uncle Will's reference to Graham's $6 million is the only evidence from family papers that Graham may indeed have been literally a millionaire socialist. Of course, the rumor that he contemplated donating so large a sum to the waiters was promptly denied by Rose. It was preposterous for a number of reasons, not least of which is that Graham was parsimonious in his dealings with the movement. He was never lavish in his contributions, never even particularly generous. While Graham's aunts Olivia and Caroline were industriously involved in the labor of giving away their seemingly inexhaustible millions, Graham might donate $50 to the *New York Call* or the Intercollegiate Socialist Society (ISS).

The lifestyle of Rose and Graham was modest. They evidently had a secure income that was adequate for their relatively simple mode of life. Graham did not pursue wealth, nor did he throw money around. He and Rose lived at the level of the quiet well-to-do, not the conspicuously affluent. While Rose's occasional partner in struggle, the doughty suffragist Alva Vanderbilt Belmont could choose on any given night to sleep at her $3 million Fifth Avenue mansion or her $2 million cottage at Newport, or her Beacon Towers at Sands Point, or her fifteenth-century villa on the French Riviera, Rose and Graham had to be content with their fourteen-room place at Caritas or, later, their townhouse in Greenwich Village.

For several years, until they settled into the Village home, their New

York address was 230 Madison Avenue, the family mansion that sheltered Stokeses by the dozen. The family playgrounds were always available to them. In the winter they might retreat to Palm Beach (though they rarely did), and in other seasons there were the camp in the Adirondacks and a huge place in Lenox, Massachusetts. With a perversity based perhaps on a quirky health notion, they were at the Adirondack "cabin" in January 1911, where, defying an outside temperature ranging from 40 degrees below to 40 degrees above zero, Graham was recovering from illness. There, in the twilight hours, Rose would read to him from the poems of E. Carberry. Her "Comrade-lover," she wrote to Anna Walling, "is almost his old strong and happy self again."[33]

The death of Anson Phelps Stokes in June 1913 does not seem to have materially enhanced the circumstances of Graham Stokes. The press reported with some surprise that the Anson Stokes estate was in the neighborhood of a mere million dollars, rather than the $20 million that had, at the least, been expected. It may be supposed that the major part of his fortune had been distributed in anticipation of death.

Actually, Graham informed Rose in a letter after Anson Stokes's will had been probated, the estate came to $750,000 with a 10 percent share going to his widow and to each of the nine children. Graham told Rose that, as a result, their income would be reduced by $2,000 annually. We do not understand this reduction any more than we understand why this millionaire socialist should, in 1908, have asked his mother for a loan of "several hundred dollars," of which, he said, he was "desperately in need."[34]

Rose may have been kept on an allowance. Her independent earnings were small, derived from occasional articles or a speaker's honorarium from outside the orbit of "movement activities," and never permitted any significant accumulation.

In the interval between the end of the waiters' strike and the start of her next major strike effort, Rose found a strike going on at her very Caritas doorstep. The Kroeger Piano Factory, an early example of the runaway shop, had moved from New York City to Stamford. Most of its employees moved with it or commuted to their jobs. Forty of the one hundred employees of Kroeger went on strike for higher wages. On September 4 Rose addressed their meeting and urged them to "keep up the fight."[35]

The scolding Rose received from W. E. D. Stokes for having "upset the minds" of the hotel workers and for having made them "dissatisfied and unhappy"—as though they had not realized the misery of their condition until she brought it to their attention—did not intimidate Rose from further involvement in labor struggles. Nor did the uncle's opinion of immigrant foreigners—"rotten trash"—deter her from adopting the cause of precisely that stratum in her next major venture into strike activity.

For a while she had to take things a bit easy. "After the first Hotel Workers strike, in which I . . . worked as I should not sanely have done, I was ill for weeks and half invalid for months." She had chronic bronchitis. Years of work in the tobacco dust of the cigar factories may have made her prone to respiratory ailments, which could be exacerbated by heavy programs of oratory without the blessing of electronic amplification.[36]

On January 1, 1913, a new assault began on sweatshops and "sweatshop conditions" in the garment industry. Strikes broke out in the men's and women's branches, including whitegoods workers, kimono makers, shirtwaist makers, and others. The *New York Call* pointed out that "the local needle industries have been practically paralyzed by one of the most gigantic and general uprisings which Greater New York has ever witnessed."[37]

It was yet another battle, and one of the greatest, in the long, unending war to eliminate the sweatshop evil. Though the sweatshop was once thought to have been "eradicated," it was reported in October 1983 that in

immigrant neighborhoods around New York, a new industry has emerged in recent years. It is the sweatshop. . . .

After nearly being eradicated, thousands of new shops like these—garment factories disregarding labor laws and health and safety regulations—have in the last few years opened in New York. . . .

"These stinking little factories survive," said Sol C. Chaikin, president of the International Ladies Garment Workers Union. The workers, he said, are largely powerless immigrants, members of minority groups and women.[38]

This present-day description no doubt is also applicable to the sweatshop of the early decades of the twentieth century against which the garment workers of Rose Pastor Stokes's time did battle.

On January 6, 1913, Rose Pastor Stokes was in New York to "answer a call to serve on the strike committee of the S.P. to aid the garment workers." She was thus placed at a distance from actual leadership of the strike, but she instantly became fully involved as a supporter. The initial week was busy as Rose scurried about the city covering the rallies of various units of the garment workers' uprising.[39]

She was back at Caritas on January 7 after spending the night at 230 Madison Avenue and having supper there. "I must not foolishly waste my energy by neglecting to eat as I used to do almost constantly a couple of years ago." She arranged to return to New York to take part in the strike for an indefinite period. She had to bear in silence "poor Graham's laments at my leaving him alone on the Island. . . . He is very dependent on my presence and dreads the thought of my going into the strike without him, yet feels that he is not specially fitted for that kind of work in the movement—that he can be more useful in other directions—which is undoubtedly true. Yet he cannot protest at my participation because he recognizes my greater usefulness in such as the present struggle. As I left the house for the station he called after me, 'Deary, be careful! Don't get into trouble with the police.' "[40]

Friday, January 10, Rose showed no sign of wishing to spare herself. All day she toured the strike areas to get a close-up view of the situation. At 5 P.M. she met with the SP strike committee, which was preparing to open lunchrooms for the pickets. There were 110,000 workers out, and the number would grow to almost 150,000.

At 9 P.M. she was at the Brooklyn Labor Lyceum when a dramatic and disturbing incident occurred. A young woman arose, came to the platform, and began to read what she called an "address," attacking the strike and Rose. She challenged Rose to go out on the firing line herself and be clubbed by the police. It later developed that the incident had been set up and the address written by a reporter for the *Brooklyn Times,* who had promised the young worker to put her picture and a story on the front page of his paper.

At noon the next day Rose spoke to three thousand cutters, who were not striking for their own grievances but had gone out in support of the others. They were the "aristocracy," the most skilled craft among the garment makers. They could not readily be replaced and were therefore the key to a successful strike, assuming all the trades held fast. "The men wept and when I finished they applauded wildly."[41]

Rose had reported to the workers at Beethoven Hall about the episode the night before when the young striker—her name was Christina Volpe— had attempted her provocation. Now she told her listeners: "I don't have to go out on the picket lines, because I am living on the wealth you are creating—I wear good clothes and I belong to the idle class. But the time will come when I will have to go back to work again among you. It will come when all the wealth belongs to the men and women who create it. . . . But there was a time when I did have to work just as you do now. There was a time when I starved for want of food because of the lack of decent wages." As a newspaper described the scene, "Rose leaned far over the edge of the platform as she went on with her defense, her fingers pointing at the audience as if to rivet their attention. . . . At one point she nearly broke down and had to pause until she could control herself . . . when she concluded the strikers broke into prolonged cheering."[42]

Before the day was over, she had spoken to meetings of various groups of strikers starting at 2 P.M. with the young women whitegoods workers at the Labor Temple on 14th Street and then going to 319 Grand, 117 East Broadway, and 207 East Broadway, all on the Lower East Side. She was already tired when she addressed the whitegoods workers, and she felt a cold coming on. She noted in her diary, "I have rarely made so poor a speech." But the next day, a Sunday but not a day of rest, she spoke to a packed meeting of vest makers at Clinton Hall. "So many of them were bearded men upon whom the burdens of the world lay with a terrible patience." This time she thought her speech was "one of the most competent I have ever made."[43]

On January 13 Rose arrived at Union Square at 10 A.M., about two hours early for the speech she was to make at the reviewing stand that had been set up there. On that day "one of the greatest parades in the history of the city occurred, as thousands upon thousands . . . of strikers in the men's and boy's garment industry marched . . . to protest the brutality of police and hired thugs and to demonstrate their solidarity." She filled some of the time before her turn by visiting the nearby headquarters of the ILGWU, where John Dyche, secretary-treasurer, bluntly told Rose that "we don't want any talk of a revolutionary character and of One Big Union."[44]

Rose made her speech from the reviewing stand, then had a talk with the editor of the *Brooklyn Times* about his paper's provocation at the Brooklyn Labor Lyceum. At 3 P.M. she was interviewed by the magazine *Fair Play*, then at 8:30 she saw William (Billy) Hard, a prominent journalist whose beat was Washington, D.C. It was a fairly typical day. The next day was less typical; there was only one meeting. It was "a big, earnest, splendidly enthusiastic meeting of the buttonhole makers, the lowest paid workers in the garment industry." "I ache in every limb and my heart contracts with pain," she wrote in her diary. Then came another typical day. At 2 P.M. she spoke to the whitegoods workers in East Harlem; at 3 P.M. there was the tailors' meeting at Harlem Casino; at 4:30 the vest makers at the Comedy Theatre; and at 5:30 she attended the executive of the strike committee on East Broadway.

Rose would not participate in this round of the garment workers' struggles. After ten days of responding to every demand made upon her, she took to her bed "with high fever, sore lungs and a bad heart."[45]

The strike ended with a protocol of peace in mid-February, and by mid-March "every branch of the ladies' garment industry in . . . New York City had contractual relations with the ILGWU."[46] In April Rose, much improved in health, attended a dinner given by the Intercollegiate Socialist Society. She used this opportunity to denounce some terms of the protocol that had ended the great series of strikes in the garment industry. Rose focused her criticism on the compulsory arbitration clauses and the curbs on the right to strike. "If we withdraw that right for a week," said Rose, "it is a dangerous precedent." Rose Schneiderman of the WTUL and Elizabeth Dutcher, a social worker, defended the protocol. It was also defended by another dinner guest, Julius Henry Cohen, who had drafted the document. He accused Rose Pastor Stokes of "a lack of confidence in Socialism" and "a willingness to resort to violence."[47] This mixture of leftist and rightist rhetoric came from the counsel to the garment manufacturers' association.

VII

On the Campus

After Rose's brief, intense, and physically wearing involvement in the garment strike, she moved at a more reasonable pace for a while. In March 1913 another trip to Palm Beach contributed to her physical rehabilitation, though the weather was capriciously vile. Much of their short stay was spent aboard the *Scorpion,* a boat "Mother Stokes bought from young Mr. Vanderbilt in order that father might have 'something to cruise about in for the winter.'" They had hoped to navigate the small streams and the Everglades, but the yacht drew four and a half feet of water and could not sail out of the main channel. "Mr. Vanderbilt sold it to them saying he wanted to buy a bigger boat," Rose noted in her diary. "There is some suspicion he wanted to get rid of it because it drew too much water."[1]

Cruising along the coast from Palm Beach, they caught a sea trout, hauled in a "beautiful fish" that was "as strong as a horse," and hooked a thirty-five-pound channel bass while fighting off seasickness. After three days of lazy, often rainsoaked, cruising, they put in at the Clarendon Hotel in Seabreeze to await the arrival of Mother and Father Stokes, who were motoring up on the way to Orlando and were bemired by the rains.

Rose complained to her diary on March 20, 1913, that Graham "has been disagreeable most of the day." This complaint is a reminder that the married life of the Stokeses was not spared its moments of abrasiveness. Graham's crankiness began when Rose "ventured to interject a suggestion" while he was discussing a possible automobile trip with the man in charge at the hotel. "It is not customary to interrupt," Graham admonished his erring wife. Rose noted: "Now and often before, my interest in the subject doesn't count. Neither does he seem to realize that an interruption kindly caused and in good faith cannot be half so much a breach of good manners as an annoyed reproof in public. Sometimes my more cultured half is hard to understand. I said nothing, but took the reproof as seems best. Quarreling is unprofitable business when it isn't done in the spirit of fun." An invitation arrived this same day from "Baltimore comrades" to speak in their city on April 30. Rose suggested to Graham that they stop there on the way back to New York and give the talk a bit earlier than requested. He was "anything but pleased and seemed bored at the idea." Rose also suggested that they arrange to speak on socialism at Jacksonville on the evening they would be passing through that city, "taking advantage of an opportunity." The grouchy Graham replied, "We certainly have different notions of opportunity." On their first visit to Florida in 1908, the Stokes couple had appeared as speakers in Jacksonville and Baltimore.[2]

The year 1913 had begun with a whirl of activity and Rose's almost instant collapse. It would end with another whirl, somewhat more controlled and survivable, as Rose embarked on the first of several speaking tours for the Intercollegiate Socialist Society. But there were the quieter spells, and they could be savored either at 230 Madison Avenue or at Caritas. There was correspondence to be answered constantly, and there were poems, plays, and articles to be written.

Among the letters, which included a steady flow of appeals from strangers for financial assistance, were ones from her siblings. Her oldest brother, Maurice, now about twenty-two years old, was in the army. He thanked Rose for the check she had sent him for Christmas and added, "I have kept out of trouble . . . and I hope to stay out for the rest of my enlistment." This was not easy, for by Maurice's account, "a man gets into the guard house for every little false move he makes." Her brother Cecil, still in school, wrote: "I always bear in mind that I owe almost all to my darling mother and sister, for it is you and she who infuse me with the grand feeling known to all of us, Ambition." To "Meine liebe Cusine Rose" came a long letter in German from Berlin. It was from "Cusine Rose Goldstaub," evidently a relation of the Three Nightingales. And to "Darling Sister Rose" from "Your little Sister Lil" came information about Brother Mannie (Emmanuel), who had a wife and child and had just taken a flat. The rest of the letter expresses political opinions that Rose must have found pleasing.[3]

Opportunities for public speaking were not lacking in 1913. *Mother Earth,* Emma Goldman's anarchist monthly, was to celebrate its eighth anniversary with an "affair" on February 20, and Rose was asked to "say a few words for you are our comrade in spirit."⁴

Rose interrupted her quiet life at Caritas in mid-August to speak in the Ohio area where she had grown up. Besides Cleveland, she made well-publicized appearances at Peru, Portsmouth, and Columbus. Following her appearance at Portsmouth, a local paper reported: "Rose Pastor Stokes, wife of a New York millionaire, held a large crowd for nearly two hours in an impassionable [sic] speech . . . in behalf of the Socialist doctrines. Mrs. Stokes, together with her husband, are well known as the 'Millionaire Socialists.' . . . Probably the best woman orator that ever addressed a Portsmouth crowd. She presents quite a pleasing appearance in her neat modish dress."⁵

An incident at one of her next stops, Lima, Ohio, diverted attention from both the substance of her speech and the modishness of her dress. It seems that $90 disappeared from her hotel room, and the theft was traced to a young hotel employee. Rose refused to prosecute. The *Republican Gazette* quoted her as saying, "'I would rather lose the $90 than see the boy's life ruined. I would rather destroy the system that makes it needful or tempts him to steal.' Thus did Rose Pastor Stokes, socialist wife of J. G. Phelps Stokes, dismiss the theft of $90 from her room in the Lima House yesterday afternoon." Rose told the *Cleveland Leader* that "a man who will resort to robbery certainly needs money worse than I do."⁶ The story was picked up and widely circulated by the press services and generated several editorials that chided Mrs. Stokes for a generosity that not all readers would be able to afford.

Also in 1913 Rose Pastor Stokes became involved in the bitter strike of the Paterson, New Jersey, silk workers. This strike is well known in labor history if only for the spectacular pageant organized by John Reed and presented at Madison Square Garden with twelve hundred strikers acting out their lives.⁷

On December 27, 1913, the *Hoboken Socialist* published Rose's sentimental poem "Paterson." Reprinted in the *Mechanics Journal* in 1920, it was called a "labor classic" by the *Universal Jewish Encyclopedia,* and it inspired Lincoln Steffens in 1920 to refer to Rose Pastor Stokes as "the poet of the people."⁸ Agitprop drove Rose's pen. She is one of many writers who tested the truth of John Reed's lament that "the class struggle plays Hell with your poetry."⁹ With all her other work, Rose made time for her writing though not as much time as she would have liked. It was not easy to do, but it was easy on the throat and on the legs and should have been comparatively restful.

In September 1912 Rose told Anna Walling, then in Chicago, that she wanted to write "a play that will be a work of art for life's sake, and someday I know I shall succeed."[10] Rose worked on her plays in 1913 and in the years following, but in that year, in her most productive effort, she concluded the translation from Yiddish of Morris Rosenfeld's *The Song of Labor* in collaboration with Helena Frank. The collaboration had lagged since 1905. Its completion in 1913 resulted in publication in 1914 in England and by the Boston firm of Richard G. Badger in the United States and Canada. Rosenfeld's work was well known to Jewish intellectuals. It was popularized among literate Jewish factory workers and by Jewish bards in the Yiddish text. Rosenfeld was born in 1862 in the same Russian province as Rose Stokes. He emigrated to Amsterdam, then to London, then, in 1886, to New York. Nowhere did his labor as a tailor yield an adequate living. His poetry, which gave a voice to immigrant workers, appeared in various Jewish newspapers and brought him some fame but never enough money to provide more than a marginal existence.[11]

A letter to Rose from Miriam Bloch contained a review from a London publication that said: "These are the songs of the sweatshop by the famous and poor Jewish poet whose poem 'I Am a Millionaire of Tears' found so wide a public. Mrs. Rose Pastor Stokes and Miss Helena Frank have caught their spirit splendidly."[12]

Late in 1913 and in the three following years Rose Pastor Stokes undertook tours for the Intercollegiate Socialist Society which brought her to college campuses in the Midwest and throughout the East. Her years of lecturing had proved her ability to address a variety of audiences of all social classes. The 1913 ISS tour was her first systematic effort to bring her message to academia.

In July she made an appearance at the adult education resort at Chautauqua, New York. Chautauqua had evolved from a religious camp meeting in 1874 to a commercial lecture circuit by 1913, eventually giving the language a common noun for rural educational extension. Its main base remained near Lake Erie in upstate New York. In her speech at Chautauqua Rose Pastor Stokes sounded some of her favorite notes: she denounced institutional charity, argued that socialists do not believe in abolition of all private property but only abolition of private ownership of the means of production, and asserted that all men are not absolutely equal ("Socialists believe in equality of opportunity"). She deplored widespread unemployment and castigated the employers of child labor.[13] Two weeks later at the Manhattan Labor Lyceum she addressed a meeting of hoboes.

Chautauqua was not a college campus, but Rose's success there must have confirmed her suitability for the college circuit, even though her educational background did not come within the scope of ISS concentration on students, faculty, and alumni. She attended the three-day conference of the ISS held at the Whittier Guest House in Hampton, New Hampshire, in August, and the *Boston Post* considered her the principal speaker. Others were John Spargo, Graham Stokes, William English Walling, Ellen Hayes, Juliet Poyntz, and Agnes D. Warbasse.[14]

In 1913 volunteer lecturers for the ISS spoke to hundreds of meetings of its chapters or of the general public. The society's modest newsletter, the *Intercollegiate Socialist,* was transformed into an impressive quarterly journal. In the year 1913–14 the ISS added ten campus chapters to its fold for a total of sixty-one, in addition to twelve alumni chapters. The society published the names of some forty professors who endorsed its work, including Emily G. Balch, Charles A. Beard, and Charles Steinmetz. Among those who had lectured for it were Mayor John Purroy Mitchel of New York, Harriot Stanton Blatch, W. E. B. Du Bois, Max Eastman, Walter Lippmann, and John Reed. From this distinguished company, the *Intercollegiate Socialist* singled out Rose Pastor Stokes, who "alone addressed large groups of students in college chapels, economics classes and before ISS chapters in a score of colleges in New England and the Middle Atlantic States. Her efforts were attended with noteworthy success."[15]

With its audience limited to college campuses, alumni, and subscribers to its quarterly review, the ISS was reasonably successful, claiming to have chapters at seventy-five locations. An impressive number of important names were associated with the ISS from 1905 to 1920. Its best work was done by its speakers' bureau, which reached many campuses and beyond. Many of its adherents were intellectuals and among the financial upper crust of the socialist movement and writers of socialist books, such as Walling, Hunter, Simons, Hillquit, and Spargo. Their principal works were published not by the socialist publishing houses such as Charles E. Kerr but by such mainstream presses as Macmillan and Harper's.

In the 1910s there was much curiosity and considerable support on campuses for the message of the ISS. It was a time of social restlessness and apprehension because of the war and European revolutions. And, as in the more recent 1930s and 1960s, the campuses were alert. Economic conditions were generating competition among newly graduated college men and women, who were seeking employment in a market already—if only temporarily—oversupplied with candidates seeking entrance into professional jobs. A mood of social protest was apparent in the colleges.

The decision to send Rose to lecture on the campus circuit was made at the Hampton conference. On November 8 she began a ten-day trip; on the train for Providence, Rhode Island, feeling hungry, she scribbled a note to Graham regretting that they had left on a Central Park bench the remains of a bag of peanuts they had been feeding to the elephants that morning. In the evening she spoke to the Providence local of the Socialist party and the next day launched into her college tour with a talk at Brown University. It was an auspicious start because she succeeded in setting up a new ISS chapter.

In the next days she traveled from Rhode Island to Massachusetts to Connecticut and back to Massachusetts. She spoke in an economics class and at chapel exercises at Clark University and at the Agricultural College of Amherst, Massachusetts. She spoke at Simmons College and the American International College. She was respectfully received at Wesleyan, then doubled back to Agassiz House, Cambridge, where she spoke to a new Radcliffe ISS chapter. In Springfield she addressed an ISS alumni chapter. In Wellesley (as later at Vassar) she was barred from the campus by administrative command. But from Professor Ellen Hayes, an ISS stalwart at Wellesley, she received word that "Comrade Josephine Bowden of Springfield brings us a most enthusiastic account of your Springfield meeting."[16]

Harry W. Laidler, who ran the society on a day-to-day basis, was pleased with Rose's brief but intense foray into academia: "Your visit to the Northeast certainly was a splendid success and you have done us a world of good . . . I have received enthusiastic reports from all the chapters about your talks. . . . The society appreciates your willingness, not only to devote your time to the cause but to pay your own expenses."[17] Graham Stokes apparently was not pleased that she was paying her own expenses. He had pledged $50 to the ISS but informed the organization that he was deducting $25 to cover Rose's expenses on her lecture trip.[18]

Rose Pastor Stokes's talk at Wesleyan engaged the interest of Professor

Durant Drake of the Department of Ethics and Philosophy of Religion. He wrote to her immediately asking her to explain the difference between the ideas of H. G. Wells in his *New Worlds for Old* and those of Rose and Graham. He was concerned about this because he was "convinced that you must have or be going to have great powers of leadership in the Cause." Drake explained that he had "deep sympathy with the movement" but thought he could do more as a Bull Moose (referring to Theodore Roosevelt's Progressives). He urged her to outline how socialist changes could be brought about. "I fancy the general reception of your talks in such places as this would be—beautiful ideals but impracticable! Show them they can be worked out!" Drake also inveighed against those within the SP "who are trying to incite a class war." Rose replied so fully and promptly that Durant Drake felt apologetic for imposing on her time. But she did not make an instant convert. Professor Drake told her as gently as possible that "it is arrogant to limit socialism to the party of that name, just as one may be a prohibitionist without giving allegiance to the Prohibition party—as is my own case."[19]

The Intercollegiate Socialist Society conscientiously aimed "to project an intelligent interest in Socialism." In compliance with this principle, it would try to offer among its speakers individuals who would present the antisocialist position. But there was a problem: as the *Intercollegiate Socialist* lamented, "We have great difficulty in securing thoughtful and responsible speakers who are willing to go publicly on record as opponents of the Socialist ideals; this reluctance is due . . . to a dawning impression even among honest antagonists of Socialism that there is or may be, much good in the fundamentals of Socialism."[20]

In a break between ISS activities, Rose Pastor Stokes attended a conference of the American Museum of Safety held in New York December 10 to 12, 1913. The conference dealt with safety in the workplace, a perennial unsolved problem, and Rose was asked to speak on the subject "Willingness of Americans to Take Chances." Her theme was that the worker, not the boss, takes chances. A magazine reported: "Speaking from her experience as a working woman, Rose Pastor Stokes was followed intently as she scored the employer who introduced industrial efficiency and 'the speeding up system.' . . . What we call industrial efficiency is like tightening up the strings of a musical instrument until they snap."[21]

This busy year ended with the annual convention of the Intercollegiate Socialist Society. Even though Rose lived with the president, she was sent a letter on the organization's stationery asking her to make the collection speech at the public dinner that was to close the convention. The letter, dated December 19, asked her to make the appeal with the "grace and enthusiasm manifested" in her college tour. It was informally signed Aunt Mary, who was not Aunt Mary at all. She was Mary R. Sanford, who lived with Helen Stokes next door at 90 Grove Street. Both Mary and Helen were devoted to the ISS.[22]

The convention consisted of several sessions, each held at a different place. It began at Helen Stokes's studio, where the principal business meeting was held. There was talk of changing the ISS from an organization for the study of socialism to an outright socialist organization. Feisty young Alexander Trachtenberg, a postgraduate delegate from Yale, was vehemently opposed to linking the Socialist party and the ISS. The great majority of the sizable Yale chapter, he pointed out, did not belong to the SP. Paul Kannaday, another Yale delegate, disagreed. He thought the ISS should "show its colors." The convention took no action to change into an overtly political body.

Walter Lippmann (Harvard Class of 1910) thought that after graduation students should be interested in socialism but cautioned against jumping "hastily into a Socialist commonwealth. . . . Youthful enthusiasm leaps to the conclusion that as soon as they know something about socialism they know it all and they have only to tell everyone to make it universal. . . . If a movement is of use," Lippmann went on, "it must prepare for the struggle. . . . Unless this is done it will be impossible to contend . . . with the forces of progressivism and radicalism. We socialists do not have a monopoly of radical reforms." A biographer says: "What attracted Lippmann to socialism was not a fiery passion for justice and equality, as was the case with his friend John Reed, but an impatience with how badly society was managed."[23]

Mary Wood Daley (Wellesley Class of 1907) reported on the efforts of the young women at Wellesley to form an ISS chapter, but "the heads of the institution blocked every effort of the students to organize a club that would have for its subject the study of Socialism." Daley had requested the administration to give Rose Pastor Stokes permission to speak, but she was refused without any explanation. A representative of the prestigious German Social Democratic party attended the ISS convention, and plans were made to hold an international conference of students in

Austria in August 1914. The outbreak of the European war in July 1914 prevented this conference from taking place. A highlight of the ISS convention was a reception at the upper-class Finch School, whose headmistress, Jessica Finch, was a member of the ISS. It concluded with a dinner on December 20 at which the subject was suffrage and socialism. Rose Pastor Stokes was one of the speakers, but the most important one must have been Harriot Stanton Blatch, who had revived the militancy of the woman suffrage movement. Other speakers included Max Eastman and Freda Kirchwey. The last speaker was W. E. B. Du Bois, identified in one press account as "the negro poet," which, among many other things, he was.[24]

The quarterly *Intercollegiate Socialist* was launched at the convention and in its first year had among its contributors such notable writers as Howard Brubaker, J. Keir Hardie (British member of Parliament), Morris Hillquit, Florence Kelley, Karl Kautsky (the most prominent ideologist of the Socialist International), Jean Longuet (a French descendant of Karl Marx), Harry W. Laidler, Caro Lloyd Strobell, Ernest Poole, Juliet Poyntz, Professor Vida D. Scudder, A. M. Simons, John Spargo, Rose Pastor Stokes, William English Walling, and Sidney Webb (a British Fabian).

Rose Pastor Stokes never read her speeches from prepared drafts or even referred much to notes. Her oratorical style was not compatible with a fixed-text speech. She had a small repertoire of titles of which the most frequently used was "What the Socialists Want and Why They Want It," which could accommodate many different speeches. Speeches on certain subjects, of course, such as birth control, suffrage, war, peace, industrial safety, and capital punishment, had to be titled for the occasion. "What the Socialists Want" took different form and content depending on the character of the audience, the length of time allotted for her speech, the responsiveness of the group being addressed, and such variables as Rose's emotional state and health.

Rose was to speak at Bryn Mawr College early in February 1914, and perhaps that is why Scott Nearing wrote to her in early January, inviting her to enjoy the laissez-faire hospitality of the Nearings in Philadelphia: "We have a sleeping porch on our house facing the West. Come over as early as you can, go out there on the porch if you like, or lock yourself in my study, and no one will speak a word to you. You can even eat dinner alone if you like. At my house we do about as we please. If you prefer not to come early do not, but please feel welcome—so welcome that you will be able to do exactly as you please."[25]

Margaret Darkow handled the arrangements for Rose's appearance at Bryn Mawr. A letter from Rose to Graham after the event indicates that her speech may not have had the approval of the administration: "Mrs. [sic] Thomas was away and they did not know that I was to come. Someone will get into trouble, but I had a splendid meeting."[26] Darkow told Rose that the "Socialist class . . . were overjoyed to have you with us and to be able to speak to you. Most of all we were glad that you have interested in Socialism those who before were perfectly indifferent and ignorant." There were many who wanted to form a chapter of the ISS, but Miss Thomas would not permit it.[27]

At Rose's next stop, which was Dickinson College at Carlisle, her appearance had the approval of the president, Eugene A. Noble. An audience of several hundred in the Dickinson chapel heard a one-hour informal debate between Stokes and the dean of faculty on methods of obtaining possession of industry. Rose believed this issue would have to be decided by a majority of those concerned and only at the time it actually took place.

At Princeton on February 19 Rose gave her "What the Socialists Want" speech to an attentive audience of two hundred students and faculty and received an ovation.[28] A few days later she was in Boston again. On February 24 she spoke at the Technology Union of Massachusetts Institute of Technology. She drew one of the largest crowds that had ever gathered in the union, speaking under the auspices of the MIT Forum and the first woman ever to speak there. Her appearance at the Technology Union provoked a protest from unsympathetic students who moved that speakers be excluded during the noon hour so that suitable quiet might be preserved. The motion lost and was blasted by the college paper, which remarked that the speaker was very well received.

Departing from her ISS circuit, Rose addressed "a cultured and intelligent audience" in the Unitarian Church at Newton Centre, Massachusetts, on Sunday evening, February 22, 1914. Her message, as reported by a local weekly, was that "under Socialist rule the parasite at the top and the parasite at the bottom will be absorbed into the great producing mass, and there will be enough for all to comfortably maintain themselves." She held her audience from 7:30 to 11:00 P.M. "It was," said the paper, "a simple, forceful and at times thrilling recital of the need for and aims of Socialism by a very charming woman."[29]

A few days later Rose Stokes received a three-page letter on the letterhead of the chair of Christian theology of the Newton Theological Institution in which the signer, Richard M. Vaughn, expressed his sympathy with her "contribution of the social question" but felt that she had made a "grievous mistake" in asserting her "indifference to the flag as the symbol of our country." Rose replied at length expressing her gratitude for "the earnestness and kindliness of spirit" expressed in Vaughn's letter. She hoped for an opportunity for fuller discussion and pleaded that "the symbol, whether red, white and blue, or red only, must not be confused with the things it symbolizes."[30]

Rose spoke the following night at a non-ISS event in Lorimer Hall. The following day, she used the time riding on the train to draft a letter to the *Boston Post* to correct the paper's "inadequate report" of her speech:

> I did not say that "Catholics and Socialists cannot mix." Indeed . . . many Catholics are Socialists and members of the Socialist Party.
>
> In answer to a question "why is the church opposed to Socialism?" I said I believed the chief reason . . . to be the hold that the rich pewholders had upon the ministers. . . .
>
> In the Catholic Church, I said the opposition was logical—the Catholic Church is built upon the principle of absolute authority. The Socialist movement is built upon the principle of democracy. . . .
>
> The masses in the church, being themselves workers concerned with the problem of living, will in time be reached by Socialism.[31]

Rose would soon be on a swing through upstate New York. She and the ISS and some of the people at Vassar would have liked to launch this trip with a stop at Vassar, but it was not to be. The administration did not care to expose the young women in its custody, almost all of them daughters of the rich, to the message Stokes might bring. But at the home of political science professor White, on campus, a meeting was held at which Rose spoke on socialism. This was believed to be the first such meeting ever held at the college. Professor Mills of the Department of Economics tried to get permission for her to speak before his class, but it was not granted.

The first stop on Rose's upstate New York tour was Cornell University. The second was Hobart College in Geneva, which proved to be a high spot of her tour. That night she wrote to Graham: "I am still aglow with the beautiful welcome I got at Hobart College."[32]

Graham also got a letter from Lyman P. Powell, president of Hobart, which showed that her hearers felt the glow as well:

> Her singularly effective way of eliminating personalities and discussing the great central issue pleased the audience and made personal friends of mere acquaintances and of hundreds who knew her only by reputation. . . . She is an asset to the cause she represents which can scarcely be overestimated. . . .
>
> You ought to be very proud of Mrs. Stokes, as I know you are. It is so fine to see a woman think and speak about the big things of life and yet retain—as Mrs. Powell was saying after she left—all of the womanly charm without which no woman can be most highly efficient no matter how important the cause she represents.[33]

Rose received an even greater compliment from Foster Boswell of the Psychology and Education Department of Hobart in the form of a letter asking her opinion of a program for improving college education, with reference to the shaping of mind and character. Rose modestly deferred to academicians when it came to planning a course of study, but she felt that "character is best developed in the individual . . . who is inspired with big social ideals." At the end of the year Professor Boswell asked for her permission to quote from her letter to him concerning defects of college education.[34]

In Rochester she spoke before an economics class at the university in the morning, at the theological seminary in the afternoon, and at the men's club of the Rochester Temple in the evening. Then she went to Hamilton to speak at Colgate and over to Clinton to speak at Hamilton. She had left Rochester for Utica, there to catch the 4:37 P.M. train to Hamilton. The train took her to Earlville. From there it was several miles to Hamilton via a one-horse open sleigh.

On the way back to New York she stopped at Schenectady, where she spoke at the Mohawk Theatre to the People's Forum. Finally, still banned at Vassar, she spoke at a church in Poughkeepsie; many members of the Vassar faculty attended. The *Call* reported: "Mrs. Rose Pastor Stokes has just completed what is undoubtedly one of the most successful trips ever conducted under the auspices of the Intercollegiate Socialist Society. . . .

Mrs. Stokes is a wonderful lecturer. There is charm in her manner of speaking that makes a potent appeal to the hearer's heart; her clear, tense, lucid style, and the ring of fervent sincerity in her voice produce a profound impression upon an audience."[35]

After her return from the ISS tour, Rose's time was filled with the usual events: a talk at the Harlem Neighborhood Association, a showing at the Berkeley Theatre of her one-act play *The Saving of Martin Greer,* a speech to a synagogue men's club made up of wealthy antiunion clothing manufacturers, an ISS meeting at Carnegie Hall, where she shared the platform with Emile Vandervelde and his wife, prominent Belgian socialists. Rose was at the pier to greet the Vanderveldes on their arrival, and she must surely have told Vandervelde how possession of his book *Collectivism* had cost her her job some fifteen years before.

When Olive Dargan was in England in 1913, she wrote to Rose: "The Labour Party is called by real rebels 'the cow' because it is the cow on the line—the obstacle to the revolutionary locomotive. . . . I wish I could tell what is growing up in England, fast and furiously. Jim Larkin stayed here when he came for his meeting. He is big and splendid and loveable. . . . My darling sister, I wish I had you for one day."[36] Dargan came home late in the year to care for a Miss Whitney in Boston, evidently a paid job. Rose tried to spend some time with her there, but Olive's obligations to Miss Whitney made it a very poor visit. In March 1914, in New York, duty again interfered. But late in April these two blithe spirits left for England, leaving Pegram Dargan and Graham Stokes to their own devices. They were to overstay their leave. Olive took the blame. She assured Graham they had been living frugally: "We have lived very economically—board, lodging, laundry and fire—all covered by eighteen shillings a week. . . . Rose bought a hat because your mother was coming and her old one was somewhat shabby for the hotel. She paid only ten dollars and your mother thought it extremely becoming. That's our only extravagance."[37]

A few days later Rose wrote to Graham that she would be coming home on the *Ascania,* through Montreal (£ 11), and would take the train to New York ($25). She had visited Mother and Helen in London, and Mother had suggested that she come home with them on the *Carmania,* but Rose did not want to because she would be traveling second cabin into Boston and the newspapermen would think it was newsworthy, and "we want to avoid that." She had visited her old school, had entered the playground and heard the teachers through the open windows—"dear little old tin pan alley." Then she told Graham:

> I went to Red Lion Court today and wandered about the old places. In front of one of the tiny little shops stood a woman of about 50. . . . She asked what I was looking for. I told her I lived there many years ago. . . . Then she began to tell me of "another girl" . . . who "lived upstairs of that shop over there" who went to America and became a speaker. A "millionaire" heard her speak one day and fell in love with her right then and there. . . . "The papers told how they were coming over here . . . we cut out the pictures and watched and waited for them . . . and was already to give them a welcome. . . . One day as I stand here I sees a motor stop right out there at the end of the court and a lady and a gentleman in it and before I had time to run in and tell the others to come out she just waved her hand out as much as to say to him 'this is where I used to live' as if she was ashamed to show him and they drove away!"
>
> Wasn't it amazing? I felt like the man buried alive, going to Westminster to hear his own funeral sermon.[38]

A restless Graham had not yet received this letter when he wrote: "I have had no letter from you since your letter of the 20th which I received about five days ago. Five days seems an awfully long time to wait to hear from you—dear love of mine—dear Roselie. I can understand how hard it must be for you to be patient with me who means so earnestly to have you back again, but perhaps you can't understand how deep that meaning is and it's not a selfish meaning—no, dear love of mine, it's not!"[39]

Soon after this Rose was home and Olive was writing from England: "Your letter from steamer is here. . . . Your wings are unfurled for the great sail but no ocean that we know can divide us, precious friend. . . . I am glad Graham will hear the song that I miss. How good he has been! I shall never, never forget. Yours always and whatever."[40] Two months later Olive was at Rocky Point, North Carolina, taking care of Miss Whitney again.

The European war had started on July 28. Joanna F. Cooke, an active socialist and free-lance writer, wrote to Rose from Paris that she had seen the comrades and was sending *Humanité* and other papers. She wanted Patrick Quinlan's address. And she said if Germany were crushed "it will cost Europe dear."[41] Cooke evidently feared that the Socialist party of Germany would be destroyed.

Olive had her own response to the war: "I try not to think what you and Graham are suffering, but my mind comes back and whirls around and round the one thing. I have given up asking what I should or could have done. The Moving Finger has writ. But the future, O, my best friends! If I could see happiness coming to you out of it all! Graham has his pure glowing faith. He can find serenity at least. You suffer most perhaps, tossed now on these war waves. But he is great enough to enfold you and every throb of your heart."[42]

Throughout 1915 and 1916 Rose was deeply involved with the ISS. She was even asked to help in a campaign among Chinese students in cooperation with Sun Fo, son of Sun Yat Sen and the leader of some 850 Chinese at the University of California. A meeting was arranged by Professor G. H. Bristol, director of the summer session at Cornell, to set up an ISS chapter, but it was short-lived.

Caro Lloyd Strobell wrote to Rose in early 1915 that the New York chapter of the ISS "is getting up at rather short notice a meeting on February 17. . . . We are going to have John Reed and Madeline Z. Doty, and perhaps one or two other Socialists who have been in Europe since the outbreak of the war, tell us about the effect of the conflict on the revolutionary movement."[43]

Rose undertook an intensive ISS tour in mid-March 1915 beginning with a lecture at Temple University at 11 A.M. on March 15 and another at the University of Pennsylvania in the afternoon. The next night in Wilkes-Barre she addressed the alumni chapter and the Socialist party at the YMCA. On the seventeenth she lectured at the state college, on the eighteenth at Carnegie Institute of Technology at Pittsburgh, and on Friday, March 19, she was at the University of Cincinnati. When she arrived in Cincinnati, she found the university administration had banned her. She was, however, scheduled to speak on Saturday afternoon, booked by the Hamilton County Woman Suffrage Association. Her meeting opened the new hall of the Women's City Club.

The closing of the university's doors to her stirred much resentment. Many students were among the overflow audience of more than five hundred who showed up at the new hall for her lecture. She expressed indignation because she was refused the right to speak at the university. She declared that "the European War was brought about by capitalists and that when socialism prevails the end of war will have come. . . . Working people of today are much worse off than the chattel slaves in the days before the Civil War." (There were former slaves alive in 1915 who might have questioned that statement.) Years later, Rose spoke of the meeting and of her rejection by the university: "The authorities of Cincinnati College by opposing, provided us with a crowded hall outside the college." It was a "spirited meeting"—so spirited that she did not realize she was running a temperature of 102.6 degrees as a result of her old complaint, bronchitis. That night a sick Rose was on a train to New York. The eight lectures scheduled for the next six days would have to wait.[44]

There is no doubt that Rose Pastor Stokes's Socialist message made an impression on her college-trained audiences. Certainly socialism was not for all, but she stimulated thinking and even made some recruits. Though many news reports on her speaking were favorable, some were critical and were cautious about reporting favorably on socialism. These stories emphasized her manner, personality, intellectuality, and ability to present her material rather than the subject matter.

Following her breakdown in Cincinnati, Rose needed a short period of rest at 230 Madison Avenue and at Caritas Island. She then resumed her speaking with a pleasant session at the Woman's College of Brown University, where the dean had invited her to speak. And a difficult situation ended in satisfaction at the meeting at Syracuse University on April 20 when the intransigent Chancellor John Day yielded to the importunity of Rose Pastor Stokes. When it was proposed that Rose speak at Syracuse, Chancellor Day, a friend of John D. Rockefeller and defender of Standard Oil, uttered a stout "No." When this ban raised a stir, the chancellor reversed himself. He provided a large hall, and it was crowded with students, as well as faculty and friends, most of whom the chancellor helped to bring, and the chancellor himself. "At that meeting," Rose Pastor Stokes recalled, "we discussed not only Socialism but who controls Syracuse University."[45]

In the summer of 1915 Harry W. Laidler was a guest at Caritas, and he used his letter of thanks to involve Rose in work on the ISS convention and dinner to be held at the Rand School, September 4 to 6, to celebrate the organization's tenth anniversary. Rose would read George Bernard

Shaw's statement on suffrage. Her singing teacher, Laura Elliot, would sing, as would Rose.

In 1915 Rose was busy writing, fighting for Patrick Quinlan's release, battling for birth control, and, of course, attending meetings. Among the latter was one in the small town of Dover, New Jersey, which was advertised as follows:

> For the First and Only time, the Public will be
> able to listen to
> ROSE PASTOR STOKES
> Former Factory Girl, Student, Editor, Poet, and Eastside
> Settlement Worker, Who Won, Married and Converted one of
> America's Millionaires[46]

Rose Pastor Stokes clipped this ad from a Dover paper and wrote on it: "One of the disgusting ways in which comrades sometimes advertise my meetings—even now—ten years after my marriage!"

Early in 1916 she was engaged in correspondence with Kate Barnard, commissioner of charities in Oklahoma City, who wrote, "I am ready to Pay the Price Rose but I will never announce for Socialism until I see the way clear to work out my Plans for SUCCESS for the CAUSE. . . . I am sure you know by this time that I play no child's game and it would be perfectly futile for me to go down and take out a Red Card unless I can get the Message over."[47]

Rose's health was fragile in 1916, yet she achieved major accomplishments. She was in Philadelphia for a speech in January and stayed at the home of Nathalie B. Ells, who wrote to her: "I look upon you as my Godmother—for the words that led me into the paths of service and righteousness were first heard from your lips. . . . I am glad I shall have the privilege of giving you a little rest under my roof.[48]

Robert W. Dunn wrote from Laurence Hall, Yale: "Ray and I are so glad that we know you and your great ideals. We hope we may get more inspiration from your friendship . . . and that we do something for the cause in Yale and in the world."[49] Over a long lifetime Dunn served the cause as he saw it as head of Labor Research Association.

In a different vein, Evelyn Kessel wrote her from 88 Central Park West: "Next Saturday evening, the Twentieth—Virginia Gildersleeve, the Dean of Barnard and Charles Duvent the great French artist, Sir William Wiseman and Lady Wiseman—he is the English munitions expert—and Professor and Mrs. William Carpenter—the Provost from Columbia—will be here. I know that you like to meet intellectual people—and I know how much they like to meet you. So won't you and your husband come in about 9:30. We'd just love to see you both."[50]

Rose was off on a month-long ISS tour that began on March 5 at Cleveland, about the point where her 1915 tour had been aborted. This time she covered her whole route, which ranged broadly from campus engagements to Socialist party locals to a Town Club dinner and the Sisterhood of Temple Israel in St. Louis. Along the way she spoke in Illinois, Michigan, Missouri, and Ohio.

In April, soon after her return to New York, she was elected to the executive committee of the ISS and was requested to write a statement for a leaflet the organization was issuing. She wrote:

> I believe socialism to be one of the most vital influences in the world today, making for a clear understanding of modern conditions, and this regardless of one's attitude toward it. For a friend and foe alike a study of the movement makes for clearer vision. The college graduate who is suddenly projected into social-economic conditions he had not taken the trouble to understand, finds himself an educated nonentity instead of a conscious factor in progress—a drifter in the willy-nilly stream of Blind Evolution, instead of a master engineer in the stream of Conscious Direction.[51]

James Graham Phelps Stokes also remained involved in the movement. In his assured, elitist manner he told Professor F. H. Giddings of Columbia that "Socialism has hitherto appealed altogether too much to relatively inefficient and unpractical people, and altogether too little to men and women of initiative, efficiency and power," among whom he surely included himself.[52]

In August 1916 Graham found that the *Call* was importuning Rose to buy a new issue of *Call* bonds in a drive to provide more capital for the paper. He pointed out that he and Rose made regular sustaining donations to the *Call* and reminded the publisher that in 1908 Rose had purchased $1,250 worth of *Call* bonds that had not been redeemed. The tussle ended amicably in February 1917 in a letter addressed to Graham at 100 William

Street agreeing that Rose would get new bonds for the old and that no money need change hands.

In October Graham and Rose agreed to speak on the Lower East Side on behalf of Meyer London, the Socialist party's candidate for reelection to Congress. London was reelected, running against a single Democratic/Republican opponent in a district where Graham had been voted down or counted out in 1908.[53]

A few days later Graham sent a $5 bill (together with $25 for the election campaign expenses) to Socialist headquarters on Clinton Street. The $5 was for Harry Gold, a pushcart peddler who had been fined that amount for selling a sweet potato for a penny on Sunday. "If Harry Gold wants to thank anybody," wrote Graham, "let him thank the Socialist movement, which helps a man to see the injustice of imposing a relatively enormous fine on a poor peddler for selling a wholesome food on Sunday, when drug stores and refreshment counters are allowed to sell refreshments with impunity."[54]

The year was to end with a tour of the South, in some ways the most important of Rose's career as an ISS speaker and also, as it turned out, her last. A month or so before starting on her southbound trip Rose wrote to Nathalie Ells:

> I have been for long deeply impressed with the need of bringing the straight doctrine, as it were, to the young men and girls in the colleges. It is far better that the uncompromising principles be brought to them than that they should receive a milk and water brand of socialism. Presenting the principles to such men and women without compromise without at the same time creating bitter antagonism, requires a talent rarely found in the movement. It is a talent I think I possess, dear Comrade, and the movement in the colleges can utilize it with greater benefit to the movement as a whole, than the Party itself can, I believe. I feel sure that I have made many fervent and devoted comrades through my work for the InterCollegiate Socialist Society. Perhaps if I had devoted all that time and energy to Party platform work I would have made many more; but when you hear my basic reason for working chiefly, these last few years, for the I.S.S., you will understand why it pains and saddens me to think that my Comrades in the party think that I have deserted them, because I am

not working as much as formerly through Party channels. Here is the situation:

For the past several years I have not been as well able to stand long hard campaigns and speaking tours as, say, from the year 1906, when I joined the party for active work, and 1911. Those years, the first half of my ten in the Party, I felt I could remove mountains. Nothing was too difficult, no campaign so hard and trying, but that I could come through it stronger and more buoyant than at the start. Then something happened to my health, and I have not yet succeeded in recovering my old staying powers. I remember a party tour, during the early part of that period that nearly killed me, and I am using no figure of speech. This was months after I had heart-brokenly cancelled my engagement with the National Office to tour the Middle West. This was at the strict command of my doctor who then told me frankly that he did not think I could live if I took the trip at that time. I who had never thought of my body had to think of it, and think of it too as a sick body needing special care! . . . .

For many months I was useless for any public work. I took to writing. My first book, just published by Putnam's, "The Woman Who Wouldn't," is really the result of that desperate desire to create. I did not dare, if I hoped to do all the work in the world that I felt I ought to do—I did not dare speak at party mass-meetings, to working-class audiences. The emotional strain was too great. I had the opportunity the I.S.S. offered. I took it.[55]

Nathalie Ells tried to warn her against the arduous trip: "How deeply grieved I feel to know of your ill health, my dearest Comrade loveliest of women. . . . Comrade, try to realize and believe that you have already done enough for the cause—take care of yourself for you are a most unusually precious person. Few of us are blessed with so much charm and charm can win souls to our cause."[56]

Early in the year Rose had begun correspondence with friends at Goucher College and bit by bit the announced subject of her first talk of the southern tour was manipulated until, finally purged of socialism, it was announced as "The Activities of College Men and Women in Helping to Improve Labor Conditions." The meeting was held in a large hall, and Rose Pastor Stokes was introduced by the president, who was very cordial. But the college administration would not permit the young women to organize a study group. In the evening she had an informal discussion with the alumni chapter and recruited new members for it.

In Washington she spoke for the Socialist local at the public library. She commented, "I felt fit, had a crowded hall, gave a really good talk and managed the discussion to the delight of the entire audience." The next evening, at Howard University, she was tired, but her talk "was not utterly disappointing, as it aroused interest in the group," about one hundred altogether, under the auspices of the Social Science Club.[57]

She felt satisfied with her reception at Randolph Macon College, at Richmond College, at Wake Forest College, and especially at Chapel Hill, North Carolina. Professor Charles L. Raper wrote to Harry W. Laidler: "I am happy to say that she made a very profound impression here before the classes in Economics, before the Equal Suffrage League, and before the Y.M.C.A. She left the impression on many people that she has a very unusual capacity to think deeply and sympathetically and to express her convictions in a very capable way. We have had no one in Chapel Hill during my connection with it—that is, during the last sixteen years—who has left so fine an impression on the thought life."[58]

All went well until Columbia, South Carolina, where Professor J. Morse of the University of South Carolina led her through a series of meetings until, as he reported to the ISS in New York, she did "an impolitic thing": she formed an ISS chapter at Benedict, a "Colored" college.

Rose wrote to Laidler:

> If I were doing this work on my own "hook" I'd simply go ahead without seeking to be politic. . . .
>
> Yesterday I had five meetings. I began with Chapel at the U. of S.C., was whisked from there to a colored church meeting where I talked on the need of industrial organization as greater than the need of charity organization. . . . Then I was whisked away to Benedict College where I spoke at great length. Then organized, returning to the Morses' home at 3 o'clock. I took a hasty lunch as my meeting was at four in Flinn Hall. Threw myself on the bed for 15 minutes, then off again where my meeting (the one at Flinn Hall) lasted over two hours, then again home to brush up and rush off to the seven o'clock "lunch" of the "Social Workers," an earnest and influential group. I

talked there until ten-thirty. . . . All five meetings were, I think, very successful. Thurs I had spoken at eight meetings in Columbia . . . and yesterday five.[59]

But Professor Morse, who had arranged for her to speak at Benedict, was in despair when he learned that she had organized twenty-seven black students into an ISS chapter. "If it were known anywhere in the Southern Colleges that Negro Chapters in the South had been organized it would kill all effort and interest." Meeting a black on terms of social equality was unthinkable. "Should the ISS place Benedict College in the list on its letterhead it would be the end of all effort," said Morse. Rose wrote to Laidler: "I was appalled at this attitude. It is difficult for me to understand the feeling that exists. Of course, having been advised to speak there I naturally took the opportunity to organize too."[60]

She was not to have her way. In January President J. G. Phelps Stokes sent Harry W. Laidler a letter he had received from John Spargo which stated "that to organize negro chapters would make it quite impossible for us to work in the white colleges and set back the Socialist cause for many years."[61]

Graham and Rose exchanged many letters during the four weeks of her absence on tour. He planned to go to Baltimore to meet her: "It will sure be good to be with you again, dear Love." Two days later, he wrote, "Dear Roselie—five whole days have passed without a letter from you!" He had ordered something beautiful for the hall. He planned to have Thanksgiving dinner with Mother and Ethel and Mildred's family. He had trimmed the window box plants. On December 6 he wrote, "Only ten days now and we shall be together." The next day, "Of course, the money is considerable, but the usefulness of your trip has been so great that the money cost is nothing in comparison." He would ask the ISS to send her some more money.[62] And at last it was December 16 and they were together in Baltimore, where the Reverend Hogue had sponsored an Open Forum.

Finally, they were home. A few days later she received a letter from Elizabeth Gilmer of Baltimore: "We were very grateful to you for coming on. . . . The Rev. and Mrs. Mercer Johnston have been taking Christmas with us and we have been having many good talks on Socialism and kindred subjects. To me the appeal is how a Christian can help in the social movement which means so much to us."[63]

VIII

On the Feminist Front

I have never been a feminist as such. I have sympathized with the [feminist] movement only because I felt that the working woman was far backward in status and her political emancipation would help her to a clearer consciousness of her place in the social economic world."[1] These were the words Rose Pastor Stokes wrote from the hospital in Frankfurt, Germany, to her agent, Maxim Lieber, on April 17, 1933, just two and one-half months before her death. In this letter she explained her understanding of and responses to the women's struggle for independence and equal rights with the hope that Lieber would convey her rationale to Samuel Ornitz, who had agreed to complete her autobiography. Her letter was prompted by a script from Ornitz that a friend who was traveling from New York to Czechoslovakia had brought to her at the hospital. A copy of the script had also been sent to Lieber.

In this letter Rose quotes from Ornitz his conception, which she strongly rejects, of the character of her feminist responses. She implores Lieber to convey her thinking to Ornitz; she fears that he does not understand the meaning of her life and will betray her deepest feelings. She fears especially that he does not grasp her development "during those early years with Graham" when he states: "You accepted that masculine leadership of your husband, Spargo, Walling, et al. You did not question their masculine leadership, their masculine prerogative. . . . That was the point of view of the Victorian woman." Rose did not deny her response to the "masculinity" that surrounded her. She admits:

> I accepted their leadership, not from the point of view of their masculinity, but wholly from the point of view of their superior opportunities. I had one and one-half years of schooling. My husband and

these leaders . . . had every type of intellectual training, university and post graduate courses. They were men of great learning . . . had read much, infinitely much more than I had read in those specialized subjects in which we were interested. It was the difference of one with no opportunity to those with every opportunity to acquire learning. This very fact proves the poor state of consciousness at which I had at that time arrived. Had that been 1921 -22 -23 or -24 such an attitude on my part would have been wholly out of the question. In that lack of development lies the ancient danger: the worker deferred to the intellectual.[2]

In Rose's autobiography she analyzes her reaction to Graham, whose intellectuality she recognized and respected: "J.G. read much socialist theory . . . I being a worker with no schooling, looked up to J.G. in all matters theoretical."[3] Aware of her lack of education, Rose had a deep desire to learn. She did not see this as submission to "masculinity" but as her modest recognition of her lack of knowledge and her acceptance of the opportunity to learn—a stepping-stone to her future activities. Samuel Ornitz referred to her dependency on Graham and the learned men in his milieu as characteristic of the "Victorian woman" in submission to the male.

Ornitz's interpretation has much truth. Aspects of the "Victorian woman" are manifest in her early life. But this characterization does not fit her mature years.

Rose wrote to Lieber: "Please ask Ornitz to heave to the line as here given and not to make it a question of Victorianism but place it squarely . . . on the basis of those who have every opportunity and those who have little or none. That I escaped at all is due to many factors . . . which I have already written and which Sam Ornitz can further develop. Otherwise he will be completely off the track. [His] inclination is to make my life an appeal to the liberal woman and what he calls the articulates, that is liberal intellectuals, a rather paramount affair. It is not my wish."[4]

Ornitz's treatment of her must have shocked Rose because he had previously shown sympathy and had encouraged her to write about herself. In a letter to Rose at Grove Street in 1923, when she was beginning her autobiography, he declared: "Your fight for freedom should be the note of the book." In a letter as late as December 1, 1932, Ornitz wrote, "How I wish I could sit with you and talk about your book. You have such an important thing to say, perhaps the most important warning for both masses and intellectuals. . . . Make it a full book; make it warm, rich and vibrant as your nature. To me one of the most beautiful memories of my life is your voice, and I believe your book will be like it."[5]

In 1934, after her death, Earl Browder, then secretary of the Communist party, wrote to Ornitz asking him to complete Rose Pastor Stokes's auto-biography. Ornitz responded that he would no longer continue work on it; and he states: "I read her manuscript and quite agree with . . . others that the contents were unorganized, diffuse and suffered particularly from the bourgeois tradition of memoir writing . . . I was placed in a position of refusing . . . not only a dying woman . . . but a great revolutionary martyr."[6]

Some have suggested that Rose's fame derived mainly from the circumstances of her marriage. Irving Howe remarks: "The fiery socialist Rose Pastor Stokes became famous only after she married the millionaire, Graham Stokes; the idea of a red, Yiddish, Cinderella made its claim on the popular imagination as the idea of a brilliant rebel girl could not." James Weinstein notes that Rose Pastor Stokes met James Graham Stokes and "after marrying him became one of New York City's most prominent and exuberant Socialist women."[7]

Though these judgments bear some measure of truth, they do not do her justice. Her intellectual ability and unusual personality were recognized, yet her fame was still considered a result only of her marriage. But the *Jewish Daily News* brought her from Cleveland to its editorial staff. Her gifts had been displayed through her letters and poems. Her ability had already started her on a career before she met her husband.

As Rose often said, "opportunity" plays its role—"it is a matter of those that have 'opportunity' against those who have none"—"what women most lack is opportunity"—"we believe in equality of opportunity." She was not unaware that her fortunate marriage had given her an opportunity to realize her own potential.

One may agree with Ornitz that Rose's unfinished autobiography is "badly organized." And there is no doubt that, as a mature woman of fifty-four, she looked back and reflected on the happy and unhappy moments and incidents of her life. But this is neither "bourgeois" nor radical. She was not writing a diary but an analysis of her life.

Rose concluded her letter to Lieber with the words: "My life is chiefly a lesson to workers . . . and to women generally as well as workers. . . . It is a matter of those who have 'opportunity' against those who have little or none." And in a postscript to Ornitz, she wrote: "Dear Sam, Please, I urge you, keep these truths firmly in mind. You are quite right about the Stokes family struggling to absorb me into their class. But they never succeeded in weaving cocoons about me. I was already wary—even though not conscious as today."[8]

It was not unusual for women entering the socialist movement or joining the Socialist party to find themselves initially—and sometimes durably—subject to the ideas and will of a dominant husband. For example, Meta Schlichting Berger, wife of the redoubtable Socialist party leader Victor Berger, had to cope with this problem. Victor was thirteen years her senior and had been Meta's teacher in grammar school. By her own account, her husband, while he was courting her, set out to remake her "according to the pattern he thought a wife should be." Victor demanded that the young woman attend various political meetings. When she asked for explanations of matters she did not understand, he laughingly dismissed her as "a stupid goose."[9]

Rose's devotion to women's problems was not always related to socialist ideals. Nor did she work with women only through the Socialist party. She also associated with politically unrelated feminist groups and movements, drawn to them by women's issues and women's social position. One of the groups to which she belonged was Heterodoxy. In disguise it was the Luncheon Club, a quasi-secret group of women devoted to the principles of feminism.[10] Selected women were invited to join; it was not an open membership club. A note to Rose tells her, "You were today elected to our Luncheon Club, the Heterodoxy . . . there are no dues. Each one pays for her lunch which is 85 cents." It was signed by Marie Jenny Howe, initiator of the club,[11] a onetime minister of the Unitarian church. She resigned her church assignment when she married Frederick Howe, commissioner of emigration under President Wilson and later director of the People's Institute, which sponsored the Cooper Union meeting on feminism in 1914.[12]

There was also at this time another feminist group, the Liberal Club of Gramercy Park. Henrietta Rodman, a member of Heterodoxy, resigned from the Liberal Club because it refused to admit black women.[13]

Heterodoxy was for all women. It was a nothing group, yet an every-thing group. Its members were feminists without a platform. They rarely took a stand on any question. They were married, single, lesbian, virgin. Many retained their maiden names prefixed with "Miss." That they made their own sex choices, that they selected and followed their own careers, were symbols and realities of their independence. They were an eclectic group of intellectuals, professionals, actresses, teachers, novelists, poets, and journalists. They were not a workers' group, but they included one worker, Rose Pastor Stokes, as well as one professional revolutionist, Eliz-abeth Gurley Flynn. There was one black woman, Grace Nail Johnson, wife of one of the founders of the National Association for the Advance-ment of Colored People and herself an activist in that organization. There were no race, religious, or political restrictions. The political range was from the Daughters of the American Revolution (Dr. Sara Josephine Baker) to the Socialist party (Rose Pastor Stokes) to the Industrial Work-ers of the World (Elizabeth Gurley Flynn) and women with other political interests or none.[14]

To maintain secrecy and security, luncheons were held at different places—usually somewhere in Greenwich Village. Only members knew the address. With the permission of the club, a member could bring one guest. In her autobiography, Dr. Baker wrote that the reason for this se-crecy was that someone had advised the "secret police . . . to keep an eye on the club" because pacifists and radicals belonged to it. She comments that "perhaps it was the name that alarmed the spy chasers."[15]

Though the club did not take part in any political struggles, most mem-bers were active in some group of a political, labor, or social nature, and all may have been working for suffrage, for as Rheta Childe Dorr asked in her autobiography, "If militant Suffragism is not feminism then what is it?"[16]

Elizabeth Gurley Flynn remembered Heterodoxy fondly:

> It shunned publicity, but as its name implied had free and frank dis-cussions on all subjects. I was invited to join after my speech [there]. The speakers were always women, and included Helen Keller, Mar-garet Sanger, Mrs. Malmbery, the Finnish woman peace advocate, Bessie Beatty and Louise Bryant on their return from Russia, Mrs. Skeffington from Ireland and other interesting foreign visitors. The subjects mainly dealt with women and their accomplishments. All its

members were ardent suffragists, some were quite extreme feminists. All were people in their own right in many fields of endeavor. No one was there because her husband or father was famous.[17]

The luncheons were talk sessions with the subject decided on by the group. Speakers were invited to address the group or to read from their own writings. One speaker, the poet Amy Lowell, lectured on her theory of poetry and then read one of her poems. It was a sad poem as Dr. Baker reports, "so sad that Rose [Stokes] turned around and laid her head on her neighbor's shoulder and cried down her neck, sobbing an obligato to Miss Lowell's sonorous voice. The poetess stood it as long as she could and then: 'I'm through. They told me I was to be speaking to a group of intellectuals, realistic, tough-minded leaders in the women's world. Instead, I find a group that wants nothing but my most sentimental things. Good afternoon.' "[18]

A major event in feminist history took place at Cooper Union on February 17, 1914, when the People's Institute presented what the *Call* described as "the first feminist mass meeting in this part of the world."[19] Of the six women speakers including the chairperson, Marie Jenny Howe, four could be identified as Heterodoxy members. There were also six men speakers. The topic of the evening was "What Feminism Means to Me."

The New York *Times* headlined its report "Talk on Feminism Stirs Great Crowd." Rose Young, one of the speakers, said: "Feminism was some fight, some fate, and some fun. . . . To me feminism means that woman wants to develop her own womanhood. It means that she wants to push on to the finest, fullest, freest expression of herself. She wants to be an individual. When you mention individualism to some people, they immediately see a picture of original sin, but the freeing of the individuality of women does not mean original sin; it means the finding of her own soul." Frances Perkins, who some twenty years later would be Franklin Delano Roosevelt's secretary of labor, stated: "Feminism means revolution, and I am a revolutionist. I believe in revolution as a principle. It does good to everybody." Marie Jenny Howe said: "Feminism was the entire woman movement." Rose Pastor Stokes would have agreed. Marion B. Cothren stated: "The basis of feminism, the basis of suffragism, the basis of all of the modern movements making for progress, lies in the labor movement." Max Eastman, a liberal on the subject of women, said: "Feminism is the name for the newly discovered and highly surprising fact that it is just as important for women to be happy as a man."[20]

Another meeting on the same subject was held at Cooper Union on February 20, 1914. A different group of women spoke, but Marie Howe was again the chairperson. Rose Pastor Stokes may have missed these two exciting events. She was then busy with an ISS tour.

Heterodoxy as a club did not take part in any social or political movements, but many of the women were politically active—and not all of the same persuasion. The club maintained an open, tolerant attitude toward the political choices of its members. After the United States entered the European war, however, Rheta Dorr and Charlotte Gilman demanded the expulsion from Heterodoxy of Elizabeth Gurley Flynn and Rose Pastor Stokes because of their antiwar positions. Gilman and Dorr did not have their way. They then dropped out of Heterodoxy and Stokes and Flynn remained.[21]

Rose had been invited to join Heterodoxy in the early days of the club. In her later years, she was not always diligent in attending meetings, but letters to Rose from the club continued until about 1931, when Inez Haynes Irwin wrote her: "I cannot tell you how concerned Heterodoxy was when we learned . . . that you were so far away from us and that you were ill. Many times we have wondered where you were, what you were doing, and when you would come back to us."[22] Rose maintained contact with several of the Heterodoxy women until the end of her life.

In the early years of the twentieth century the most important woman's issue was suffrage. Woman's independence could never be fully achieved without the vote. But the suffrage movement, though adamant in its ultimate goal, was then in a state of confusion and disagreement. It had originated as an outgrowth of the abolitionist movement. After the Civil War, however, with the end of black chattel slavery, some suffragists, including Elizabeth Cady Stanton, opposed black suffrage as simply giving more men the vote. Middle-class to rich women could see only their own needs and aims. In their campaigns they generally excluded working women, who in any case would have felt socially unacceptable alongside their more affluent sisters.

As her biographer has written, "Although Elizabeth Cady Stanton identified herself as an abolitionist," when citizenship and the vote were proposed for black men, she asked: "Do you believe the African race is composed entirely of men?" Her attempt to involve working women in the suffrage movement was negligible. She and Susan B. Anthony "helped some local New York women to form a union," and she "often came to the defense of factory women . . . but Stanton's position evolved from Anthony's initiative."[23]

Susan B. Anthony understood the need to involve working women in the suffrage movement and in the fight for women's "natural rights." Her approach to wage-earning women, however, was inept: "On the one hand, she was clearly familiar with and sympathetic to their struggles and knew a good deal about the trade unions they had formed and the strikes they had waged. On the other hand, she understood them from the perspective of a middle-class woman, for whom work meant independence. She did not really understand the miserable ill-paid work that many of them faced."[24]

The organized suffragists concentrated mainly on the vote—a worthy cause but hardly to be gained without the support of women outside their upper-class groups. Barbara Deckhard, in her evaluation of them, asks: "Why did they concentrate only on the vote? Middle class women had already won the right to a higher education, provided the family could pay for it. They had also won new property rights . . . their immediate needs had been won. . . . From 1870 to 1910, the suffragists were remarkably unsuccessful. This was partly due to their own conservative tactics and racist, elitist positions, which alienated their potential allies." And many of these allies they did not want, notably blacks and working women. Eleanor Flexner notes that the period from "1869 to 1910 came to be known among suffragists as 'the doldrums'."[25]

In the late nineteenth century and the early years of the twentieth, the suffrage movement, though single-minded in its aim, faced confusion and disagreement in its ranks. Lack of aggressive leadership limited the ability of the suffragists to organize meaningful campaigns. After the death of Susan B. Anthony in 1906, Carrie Chapman Catt tried unsuccessfully to provide leadership.

Harriot Stanton Blatch, daughter of Elizabeth Cady Stanton, married an Englishman and spent twenty years in England. She was inspired by the English suffrage movement and its involvement with working women. She returned to the United States after the death of her husband and found that the suffrage movement was "completely in a rut in New

York . . . at the opening of the twentieth century." She felt that "a great change was called for in the method of attack by the reformers." She soon "began speaking before organizations of working women, girls' clubs and trade unions."[26]

Eventually she was able to gather a group of forty women for a meeting in January 1907 in a small rented room in lower Manhattan. "We all believed that suffrage propaganda must be made dramatic, that suffrage workers must be politically minded. We saw the need of drawing industrial women into the suffrage campaign and recognized that these women needed to be brought in contact, not with women of leisure, but with business and professional women who were also in the world earning their living. The result was the formation of the Equality League of Self Supporting Women, later called the Women's Political Union."[27] Blatch was troubled by the same issue that concerned the Socialist party. Both believed that the movement was in the hands of a middle-class group unaware of, or indifferent to, working women. This issue had alienated the SP from the established woman suffrage organizations and made the party distrustful of the women who were working to attain the vote. At the 1908 convention of the Socialist party, the importance of the vote for women was recognized. But Socialist women were not to join any suffragist movements; they were to work for the vote within their own party through their clubs and by writing, speaking, and other forms of propaganda.[28]

Not all women within the SP supported the party line. They worked for the vote inside and outside of the party. When in 1910 the WTUL initiated the Wage Earners Suffrage League "to reach the union women on the suffrage issue," Socialist women, Rose Pastor Stokes and Florence Kelley among them, took a more active part in organizing and working within the league. Leonora O'Reilly was chairperson and Clara Lemlich vice-chairperson.[29]

Of course, Socialist women had been involved in the suffrage movement before the Wage Earners Suffrage League was established. Ella Reeve Bloor recalled working in the suffrage movement in 1906–8 with Caro Lloyd Strobell, sister of Demarest Lloyd, and Mrs. Thomas Hepburn, mother of actress Katharine Hepburn. But Bloor found that "for most of the ladies the suffrage movement was a mere feminist fad." (She excluded Hepburn from this judgment.)[30]

Rose Pastor Stokes was an early recruit for Blatch. In March 1906 she and Graham occupied seats on the platform of Clinton Hall "at the mass meeting called by the presiding officer, Mrs. Harriot Blatch, to discuss the political rights of working women. He [JGPS] was the principal speaker of the evening. . . . The other speakers included Samuel Gompers, William Edlin, Rose Schneiderman, Harriot Stanton Blatch." This meeting took place a few months before the Stokeses joined the Socialist party.[31]

On October 17, 1906, a few months after they had joined the party, they both spoke at the thirty-eighth annual convention of the New York State Women's Suffrage Association. Here Rose stated that "the Socialist Party believes in equal suffrage and that if the party was in power tomorrow all women would have the ballot." On another occasion sometime later, Rose mistakenly claimed that the SP had advocated equal suffrage long before the suffrage movement, which was founded more than fifty years before the Socialist party.[32] Aware of the vile conditions under which women lived and worked, Rose recognized their needs and did not pose the two groups against each other. She understood the oppression of women as part of a total pattern of society that would be solved with the success of socialism, which possibly meant that suffrage too must wait for that elusive day. She spoke and lectured for suffrage organizations, but she accepted the limited, sectarian view of the Socialist party, which rejected the established suffrage organizations. This does not mean that the Socialist party—the only party that allowed women to be members—did not work for the vote for women. Barbara Deckard believes that "the Socialist Party helped greatly to make workers conscious of and sympathetic to women's suffrage."[33]

The *Woman's Who's Who (1914–1915)* says that Rose Pastor Stokes was "active for Suffrage through the Socialist Party."[34] Although Rose maintained the Socialist party's approach to suffrage, she must have wavered at times. As early as December 1909, for example, she told the shirtwaist strikers: "You should identify yourself with the Women's Suffrage movement. It is far more important for women to have a share in the making of the law by voting for those who make them than even winning of the strike."[35]

Alva Belmont, an ardent suffragist and president of the Political Equality Association, was also active in the strike. Some of the strikers wore suffrage buttons. Although the Women's Trade Union League had not yet organized the Wage Earners Suffrage League (WESL), it was already working with Blatch and other suffragists. The WESL was the real beginning of workers' involvement in suffrage.

From 1906 to 1917 Rose spoke on suffrage throughout the country at specially arranged lectures and on college campuses. She spoke at Socialist clubs and at women's social or suffrage clubs, as well as at men's clubs interested in suffrage. Her good friend George H. Strobell asked her to speak at the New Jersey Men's League for Women's Suffrage. She told that group that she believed "men would benefit when women vote."[36]

Following an interview with Rose, the *Springfield* (Ohio) *Daily Republican* reported that she "believed in suffrage but does not see it as a solution of the present problems of society . . . although those interested in it have noble ambitions. . . . It is superficial and only manages to touch the surface." The Boston Suffrage Association for Good Government importuned Rose Pastor Stokes: "If you will do us the honor to speak . . . we need your help in this conservative state of Massachusetts." And in October 1914 the Boston Equal Suffrage Association included her in a series of talks on suffrage.[37]

Around mid-1915 the Socialist party appears to have become more accepting of the suffrage movement. The *Call* opened its women's page to letters and articles on the subject and asked Rose to contribute. She wrote a letter that appeared in the *Call:* "I wish to call the readers' attention to the last of a series of lectures under the auspices of the Working Women's Protective Union . . . at the WTUL rooms . . . from my point of view, nothing may help women to better labor conditions through the ballot so much as working for and with labor's own political party, because I believe it to be the only party with a platform worthy the support of the working and humanity-loving women."[38]

Soon after the outbreak of the European war in 1914, Rose Pastor Stokes became a member of the Women's Peace party (WPP). She opposed the war and believed that women on the home front suffered as much as men on the war front. The WPP was a group of prestigious women—writers, liberals, and women of wealth. Among its members were Fanny G. Villard, Crystal Eastman, Mary Austin, Charlotte Perkins Gilman, Carrie Chapman Catt, Marie J. Howe, Lillian Wald, and many others known for their work in various women's rights movements. Some were socialists. The WPP was not limited by the political preference of women. Its program was antiwar, noninvolvement of the United States, and a democratically arbitrated peace. Association with such an organization was not, at the time Rose joined it, contradictory to her ideology. She believed that women of all categories of society should work together for peace. In February 1915 Rose and eight other women, including Carrie Chapman Catt, Lillian Wald, Marie J. Howe, Charlotte Perkins Gilman, and Anna Strunsky Walling, were elected honorary vice-chairpersons of the WPP.[39]

In December 1915 Rose presided at a meeting at Washington Irving High School sponsored by the Labor Forum. The subject was the Henry Ford Peace Ship project. Helen Keller, the main speaker, spoke against workers joining the army and said that only munitions makers and J. P. Morgan stood to gain: "I hold true patriotism to be the brotherhood and mutual service of all men." She advocated a general strike and called for the workers to form one "great worldwide union to gain true liberty and happiness." She received an overwhelming reception from the audience of two thousand and needed six policemen to escort her to her car through the friendly crowd.[40]

A letter from the WPP in March 1916 advised Rose of the work of the past year and that the "immediate danger" was that "military drill and militarist ideals will be put into the public schools." The WPP wished to organize against such an eventuality and to "nationally join hands with other organizations to withstand the prevailing militarist hysteria." Since funds were needed for this campaign, Rose was invited "to join us in a Finance Committee of One Hundred. (signed) Fanny G. Villard." When the World Court Congress was held at the Park Avenue Hotel in New York City on May 2, 3, and 4, 1916, Rose was a delegate from the WPP.[41]

Later in May Rose received a "Dear Comrade" letter from Emma Goldman. Goldman, Giovannitti, and others were meeting to work out an "anti-military manifesto. . . . We are very anxious to have you with us."[42] But some time after this the Stokeses made a sharp turn.

On December 17, 1916, the WPP asked Rose and Graham to speak at a New Year peace demonstration on December 31, 1916, at Washington Square. Other speakers would be Dudley Field Malone, an attorney, and Meyer London, the Socialist congressman. The letter was signed by Emily Balch, chairperson of the Joint Committee, and by Jane Addams and George Kirchwey, who were also on the Joint Committee. Rose and Graham were asked to "lend the weight of your influence to this popular demonstration to America's desire for speedy negotiations of a just and lasting peace." They refused to attend the demonstration. On December 28

Rose wrote to advise the WPP that "however much we love peace and hate war . . . our separate reasons are too many and require detailed discussion . . . perhaps someday we may get a chance to talk." Rose, who had devoted time, money, and energy to the peace movement, now made an about-face. On March 17, 1917, she sent her reasons and her farewell to the Women's Peace Party. They appeared in the *New York Times* the next day.[43]

One of the women's issues to which Rose devoted her energy and time was birth control. A political movement for its acceptance in the United States began in the second quarter of the nineteenth century; it blossomed forth as a feminist issue in the first quarter of the twentieth century. The term *birth control* was coined by Margaret Sanger. Birth control in the United States had to contend with censorship and suppression. Legally, the practice of birth control, or rather the dissemination of information on birth control, was forbidden under a federal law passed in 1873 and enforced eagerly through the persistent efforts of Anthony Comstock. Comstock was the founder of the Society for the Suppression of Vice in New York, and birth control was one of the "vices" he sought to suppress.

Birth control methods were known and practiced in all European countries. Even Queen Victoria, again pregnant in 1841, confided in a letter to her uncle, King Leopold of Belgium: "I think dearest uncle, you cannot really wish me to be the mama of a nombreuse famille, for I think you will see the great inconvenience a large family would be to us all, and particularly to the country, independent of the hardship and inconvenience to myself. Men never think, at least seldom think, what a hard task it is for us women to go through this very often."[44] Victoria went through it nine times. Frances Wright and Robert Dale Owen, social reformers, made the first statement on birth control in the United States in their *Free Enquirer* in 1829.[45] In 1877 in England Annie Besant and Charles Bradlaugh were tried for selling *The Fruits of Philosophy,* a pamphlet on contraceptive methods written in 1832 by Charles Knowlton, an American. The action for "corruption of youth" brought against Annie Besant was dropped for "faulty indictment."[46]

By 1912 Emma Goldman and Margaret Sanger had each started to work for birth control. Sanger published several articles in the *Call,* and Goldman was busy lecturing on the subject. Emma Goldman had been concerned with birth control as early as 1900, when she attended the Neo-Malthusian Conference in Paris, and birth control was one subject she included in her popular lectures. She did not discuss methods, however, unless "privately requested." She did not wish to tempt arrest. But even her less militant activity eventually led her to jail. Goldman does not credit her efforts or Sanger's as "pioneer work." She credits Moses Harmon, who served a three-year prison term; his daughter Lillian; Esra Heywood; Dr. Foote; and Foote's son Walker.[47]

Margaret Sanger, who had spent the year 1913 in Europe with her husband and children, returned to the United States and in March 1914 issued *The Woman Rebel*. Its slogan, taken from the Industrial Workers of the World, was "No Gods! No Masters!" The aim of the revolutionary newspaper was to give advice on "prevention of conception."[48]

The publication irritated Comstock, who got it barred from the mail as "lascivious." Sanger was arrested and faced a five-year jail term. To avoid prison, she left for Europe through Canada on a false passport. On October 4, 1915, she returned to the United States ready to face trial and continue her work in birth control.[49]

Women in the United States, however, had not stopped their work for birth control. Early in 1915 Mary Coffin Ware Dennett, an active suffragist, Clara Gruening Stillman, a socialite, and Anita Block, editor of the woman's page of the *Call,* started the National Birth Control League (NBCL). Rejecting defiance of the law as advocated by Margaret Sanger, the NBCL sought to legalize the dissemination of birth control information. It demanded "the repeal of all laws, national, state and local, which make it a criminal offense, principally by fine or imprisonment . . . to print, publish or impart information regarding the control of human offspring by artificial methods of preventing conception."[50] The NBCL sought to achieve its goal legally. Margaret Sanger sought also to change the law— by breaking it if necessary. Emma Goldman did not consider the law—she considered the issue; Rose Pastor Stokes considered both.

Sanger, according to James Wesley Reed, "understood that reform only came after birth control became a daily topic of conversation. . . . Margaret Sanger was able to provide thousands of women with contraceptive services without waiting for legislation."[51]

On November 19, 1915, Clara Stillman, aware of Rose's interest in birth control, asked her to join the NBCL and to become a member of the Executive Committee. Soon after that, Rose became the NBCL financial secretary.

Rose Pastor Stokes was not involved in the planning of any of the birth control organizations that were springing up, but they all asked her to become a member or to help in the work. Though each one of these groups had its own principles and methods, their aim was similar—legalization of the dissemination of birth control information. Rose chose to work in all birth control campaigns.

Her awareness of the need for controlling unwanted and unplanned births dated from well before this time. She knew of the fears of young women considering marriage and of the hardships they would face as working women, working wives, and working mothers. Growing up in the baby-filled home of Anna Pastor must have convinced Rose of the need to control the growth of a family. Her thinking on the subject was revealed in 1909, when she was one of four notables asked to write on a subject relating to birth control.

They were asked to contribute their thoughts to an article to be titled "Why Race Suicide with Advancing Civilization?" in answer to an article asking the cause of the "diminishing birth rate in America and other civilized lands," published in the *Arena* in December 1908. Besides Rose, those asked to answer the question were John Haynes Holmes, pastor of the Church of the Messiah, Helen Campbell, a popular writer on social and economic problems, and Joseph Lorren, a pseudonym. The four responses appeared in the February 1908 edition of the *Arena*.

Rose's answer was directed to the concerns of the working woman, indicating obliquely that such women did not have the facilities to control the birth of their children or their rearing. She said in part:

> Let us consider the hundreds of thousands of women rendered unfit for motherhood by the infirmities due to excessive hours of labor under conditions least conducive to physical health . . . also . . . those women who, forced by a starvation wage, sell their bodies under circumstances that make motherhood and the rearing of children impossible. . . .
>
> Our present system of industry, under which wealth is produced not primarily for social use but for private gain, is responsible for an immeasurably greater amount of race-suicide than any other factor; is, in fact, the basic cause for race-suicide, both as regards quality and quantity, and such destruction is wrought most widely, not among those parents who deliberately restrict the birth-rate, but among those helpless victims of our industrial system who are either denied

opportunities for family life or who, having large families, cannot rear their children to manhood and womanhood; and who are themselves prematurely exhausted and sink to early graves.[52]

When Margaret Sanger returned to the United States in October 1915, she needed money and help because she was still under indictment. She contacted the NBCL, but the meeting between her and Dennett was disagreeable and the NBCL refused to work with her. The overt reason was that the NBCL disapproved of Sanger's method of work. In her autobiography Sanger speaks of the NBCL as "law abiding. . . . They wanted to change the law."[53] Sanger had broken the law, but apparently there was also a personality conflict between the two women and antagonisms arose even though they had the same aims. Sanger's appeal to Dr. William J. Robinson, who was on the Medical Committee for Birth Control, was also rejected. He told her his committee was only in "embryo," but he sent her $10.[54] As time went on, the NBCL softened its attitude toward Sanger, and she became more conservative. But when the NBCL showed some inclination to work with her, she rebuffed its advances.

Margaret Sanger had made many changes in her life. Up to about 1914 she had been a member of the Socialist party, a member of the party's Women's Commission, and a contributor on the subject of birth control to the *Call*. In 1912 she worked on the children's exodus from Lawrence at the time of the strike in that city. When she returned from Europe in 1915, she had criticism of the birth control movements, and there was also criticism of her. But her contacts with Rose Pastor Stokes continued.

In the early part of 1916 Emma Goldman encountered difficulty with the law as a result of a talk that mentioned birth control. Leonard Abbott, an editor of *Current Literature*, president of a Free Speech League, and director of the anarchist Ferrer School, was an associate of Emma Goldman. He started a birth control committee specifically to protest Goldman's arrest. Another group, the Women's Committee of One Hundred, chaired by Mrs. Amos Pinchot, was initiated mainly to spread educational information about birth control and to give financial and moral support to Sanger. The Physician's Committee on Birth Control was not totally committed to any other group. Though approving of birth control, the committee questioned the legality and professionalism of groups made up of lay women.

Rose Pastor Stokes made her position toward these various organizations clear. She retained membership in or contact with all, including the physicians. She was accepted by the different organizations and called upon to work and speak. She was able to obtain assistance from physicians in many of her campaigns. She was not concerned about legality or petty personality conflicts but wished only to spread information on birth control.

A featured article in the *Louisville Herald* gave Rose's answer to the question, "Is it wrong to bring a child into the world?" She states: "Yes, I believe it is wrong . . . where sickness in the parent makes practically certain permanent weakness." She says that she is not a physician, but as "a student of social problems" she feels strongly about the issue. She felt that generally the children of the poor suffered the most. "We are really the criminals. We, collectively, have power to educate and are silent; power to legislate and are indifferent."[55]

Sanger's trial for misuse of the mail was set for January 18, 1916. William Sanger, her husband, was picked up by Comstock himself, who sent an agent to his studio to obtain a pamphlet. He was tried on September 15, 1915, and given a choice of thirty days in jail or a fine of $150. He chose the thirty days. Linda Gordon summarizes the legal problems of birth control advocates:

> Many activists were arrested and jailed for their birth-control activities—at least twenty besides Sanger on federal charges alone. Carlo Tresca, an Italian-American anarchist, was sentenced to a year and a day for advertising a book called *L'Arte di non fare i figli* ("The Art of Not Making Children") in his radical labor paper, *Il Martello*. (American Civil Liberties Union intervention got his sentence commuted after he served four months.) Emma Goldman was also jailed for giving out contraceptive information.
>
> There was, of course, class injustice in arrest, convictions and sentences. Jessie Ashley, Ida Rauh Eastman, Boston Hall, and Rose Pastor Stokes gave out birth-control pamphlets publicly at mass meetings at Carnegie Hall; although Ashley, Eastman and Hall were arrested, Stokes—a millionaire's wife—was not. Carl Rave, an IWW longshoreman, was jailed in San Mateo, California, for three months for selling Sanger's *Family Limitation*. He complained that Professor Holmes of the University of California (probably a eugenist) proclaimed the need for compulsory birth control on the front page of

the papers with impunity. Others took risks as abortionists, though none was prosecuted on such charges. In addition to Dr. Konikow in Boston these included Dr. Marie Equi in Portland, Oregon, a lesbian who later served ten months in San Quentin for making an anti-conscription speech during World War I.[56]

Having left the country without reporting to court on the day she was to be sentenced, Margaret Sanger looked forward to a long jail term. Her friends rallied to support her. John Reed, creative on all fronts, thought her upright character should be publicized. He suggested that she pose for a photograph with her two sons, that she dress modestly and assume an angelic pose. The resulting photograph portrayed pure motherhood. It was widely circulated.

Another set of friends, feminists and liberals, gathered at the home of Henrietta Rodman in Greenwich Village and planned a farewell dinner at the Hotel Brevoort for January 17, the eve of Sanger's court hearing. Rose was among the "feminists" and was selected as chairperson of the dinner. She worked diligently with this group, raised money, and obtained signatures on the petition for Sanger's release. Dr. Sigismund S. Goldwater circulated the petition and advised Rose that he could obtain about fifty signatures among physicians.

The dinner was attended by approximately two hundred professional and socially prominent persons. Speakers included Dr. Ira Wiles, member of the Board of Education, Dr. Goldwater, and Henrietta Rodman, who said Sanger had made mistakes but still she must be "protected." Present also to express her support was Mary Dennett. At the close of the meeting Rose suggested that as many of those present as possible attend the trial hearing on the following day. The court was crowded with Sanger supporters. But her case was postponed that morning and eventually dropped.

Emma Goldman, who for years had included birth control in her lectures, taking a theoretical rather than a practical approach, was now faced with jail, charged with "lecturing on a medical question." A protest meeting was held at Carnegie Hall, presided over by Leonard Abbott and attended by Dr. William J. Robinson and civil rights attorneys. John Reed and Margaret Sanger sent their protests.

On the eve of her trial, set for April 20, 1916, a dinner was arranged for her at the Hotel Brevoort. Rose spoke and then distributed birth control literature outside the hotel. Asked by a *New York Times* reporter why she so defied the law, Rose answered that she "wanted to do what Emma Goldman did." Rose was not arrested. Emma Goldman spent fifteen days in the workhouse, the alternative to payment of a $100 fine.

The *Herald* reported Rose's talk:

> I have come here prepared to do just what Emma Goldman did. I am not bidding for arrest and do not speak in a spirit of defiance. I want to do what Emma Goldman did. That I am a married woman and have social standing makes no difference. There is nothing brave about what I want to do. I am merely honoring the law by breaking it.
>
> Young girls have written to me asking advice about marrying on slender incomes. It makes no difference whether birth control is practiced on Fifth Avenue or Hester Street . . . I am not criticizing the eminently respectable. They were brought up that way.[57]

On April 23, 1916, Abbott, head of the Emma Goldman Defense Committee, advised Rose that the committee was preparing a second mass meeting at Carnegie Hall on May 5 to welcome Goldman on her release from prison. The committee wished Rose to be at the planning meeting because issues of procedure pertaining to the birth control movement would be discussed.

This meeting for Goldman was both a tremendous greeting and an expression of endorsement of her work for birth control by an audience of three thousand. The meeting was chaired by Max Eastman; Rose was on the list of speakers. Goldman was the last speaker. Rose announced that after the meeting she would distribute birth control information. A newspaper article reported: "Mrs. Stokes had just finished a speech and Emma Goldman was scheduled to be the next and last speaker when Mrs. Stokes announced 'as soon as Miss Goldman was finished, all those desiring pamphlets may march up to the stage and get them.' The Anarchist leader had not even finished her speech when a youth accepted Mrs. Stokes's invitation to mothers and wives. He sallied down the aisle, others followed and, as Miss Goldman ended, the audience surged forward."[58] The meeting was ended but pandemonium was just beginning. The *Herald* said that Rose was giving out "prescriptions for birth control. There was a riot. . . . Men did fancy scaling of seat and orchestra pit to reach the stage." Some of those who got to the stage first were probably college students. Rose declared that they were too young and would not give them the precious slips. She was mobbed until Arturo Giovannitti, who had "a frame like a bull wrestler," came to her aid.[59]

Rose was overpowered; surrounded by the audience, who for the first time thought they were free to obtain the information so long sought, she could not get off the stage. The *Times* reported that "the meeting was a demonstration to welcome Emma Goldman but Mrs. Stokes ran away with the meeting." Fights started before Rose was rescued and taken to a retiring room where she met her husband. No attempt was made to arrest her.[60]

But Rose was not happy with her immunity. Jessie Ashley, an attorney and a socialist active in the birth control movement, wrote to Rose: "They think you want to be arrested and they are loath to increase the notoriety of the b.c. propaganda. They think your trial would be as widely advertised as Margaret Sanger's or Emma Goldman's. In any case it seems to me to the advantage of all of us to keep you out of jail. While you are free you can go about doing your work, and yours is now more effective than Ida Rauh's or mine. After all, everyone knows there is injustice and we don't have to demonstrate that, that is not what we are trying to accomplish."[61]

A news service reported "Mrs. Stokes [was] Mobbed by Men after Birth Control Literature—Millionaire's Wife Distributes Pamphlets Similar to Those for Which Emma Goldman Was Sent to Jail." (Goldman was sent to jail for "illegally" discussing medical problems at a lecture, not for distributing pamphlets.)[62]

Goldman says that Rose Pastor Stokes, at the banquet at the Brevoort, was the first to distribute birth control information and that Rose "demonstrated direct action at the banquet. She announced that she had with her typewritten sheets containing information on contraception and that she was ready to hand them out to anyone who wanted them. The majority did. . . . The next Carnegie Hall meeting was held as a greeting upon my release. . . . It was again Rose Pastor Stokes who carried wishes into action. She distributed the leaflets on contraceptives from the platform of the famous hall."[63]

Not everyone appreciated Rose's devotion to the birth control movement. Members of Graham's family were among the dissenters who did not approve of the stir she had created at Carnegie Hall. The Reverend Anson Phelps Stokes, as spokesperson for the family, expressed their dismay at the events of May 5. He wrote to Rose:

That episode has been hard for all of us, but I realize that this is nothing in comparison with what you must have suffered, especially in trying to decide on what was your right course of conduct in this matter for the future . . . I can realize that there is room for honest difference of opinion—the cause is not advanced by defiance of law and its sworn upholders. . . . This is a democracy . . . consequently the machinery is available . . . to get changes in the laws brought about by legal means. . . . You have appeared . . . more than once in defense of strikers or speakers, arrested contrary to law and you should be defended for doing so . . . but in such cases in the future your word will lose influence, unless you express public regret for defying the police, or give a statement that you have been misquoted.[64]

Rose replied:

My deliberate running counter to the vicious law that keeps mothers and wives ignorant of methods of contraception was prompted by love of the people . . . I also believe that for breaking the law, I should have been arrested . . . I gave them the opportunity . . . I wanted the fact that this law was vicious driven home to the people through its enforcement . . . and I considered such a result worth going to prison for. . . . You are right as regards the advocacy of sexual restraint, but I am glad you have doubts as to the efficiency . . . I wish you could read the seven or eight hundred letters I have piled up before me now, they would convince you that it is not enough. . . .

I'd like this to be a round robin to the family, as I wish them to understand.[65]

Anson answered immediately: "Thank you very much for your letter of May 29 which makes your position clear and helps me to understand the reasons which led you to adopt conscientiously illegal and sensational methods for accomplishing what you believe to be important. Of course, I think the methods unwise. . . . However, we must each work in the way we believe right."[66] A few days later Rose concluded the exchange:

Although it is true that Jesus spent most of His time making a few men understand his message, it is also true that He raised his lash one time and drove the money changers out of the Temple. . . . Quiet and simple in His manner, His strongest appeal was yet an emotional appeal: Lovest thou Me? . . . Always that question, when He asked obedience and following . . . an appeal to the emotions first. So that we find Him adopting the methods of sensationalism and emotionalism even though His main method of propaganda was of the "orderly constructive" type. . . .

In a word, dear Anson, it seems to me that history supports both methods: the orderly constructive as well as the emotional and illegal, and each is wise and justified as it aids in accomplishing worthy socially-progressive ends.

Please consider this a postscript to the discussion and pay no further attention to the matter.[67]

The high level of public exposure resulting from the uproar at Carnegie Hall brought hundreds of letters to Rose from troubled women and men from all parts of the country: from thirty-year-old Mrs. Tear in Providence (who had four children and did not want any more so that she could bring these up a little better); from Jessie Bloom in Fairbanks, Alaska; from Mrs. R. Stevens in Swampscot, Massachusetts (who had seven children and could not afford more); from nineteen-year-old Ida Weiser, who had a seven-month-old baby (asking for a pamphlet); from Mr. J. Sweeny in New York (who wanted her to enlighten his wife and help them to live because with five children they could barely exist). Mrs. Sweeny was two months pregnant, and Rose answered her husband's plea by special delivery: "I know nothing about abortion."[68]

Not everyone agreed with Rose, of course. Percival Meigs, Jr. of Ridgewood, New Jersey, returned her pamphlets fearing that conditions would "exist when sex-intercourse is looked upon as a social pleasure only and irresponsible people in violation of laws of both God and man lose entirely the sense of difference between right and wrong."[69]

The publicity also generated numerous requests for Rose to speak to various women's organizations on birth control. And Margaret Laing, secretary of the Associated Charities of Columbia, South Carolina, asked for the "contraception formulas . . . I have so wanted to know what to tell a few people from time to time."[70]

Rose, characteristically, had thrown herself deeply into this movement, as is demonstrated in her own words spoken at an interview with a reporter of the *Baltimore News* at the ISS Sherwood Forest Conference in Maryland. The reporter wrote:

> I met her in the forest of Sherwood, against the green and leafy background of which the copper glints of her wonderful hair took on an added luster. If it had not been for her ultra-modern garb of tailored linen shirt-waist and white skirt, Rose Pastor Stokes at that moment with the sun streaming down on her bare head and her youthful figure, graceful, lithe and supple swinging toward me . . . might have passed for one of those happy, carefree goddesses with whom Corot loved to people his woodland groves. . . . And when, later in the afternoon, she appeared on the little pier jutting out from the edge of the forest and plunged right into the cool September tide, without the usual preliminaries of wetting first her toes, then her feet, then her ankles, one realized again the complete harmony between herself and her surroundings. . . .
>
> I broached the subject of birth control. Was it true that she had been associated with Miss Goldman in advocating it?
>
> She gave me a searching look then explained . . . she and Miss Goldman had not actually been working together, Miss Goldman being an Anarchist and Mrs. Stokes a Socialist. On the one question of improving the race by means of birth control they were agreed. "And I was enraged," she added with a touch of vehemence, "at the discrimination which the arrest of Miss Goldman represented. . . .
>
> "Yes, the class discrimination. The middle and upper classes know all about birth control and practice it. In suppressing Miss Goldman and Mrs. Sanger they are discriminating against the people, and they are the very ones who need [their] doctrines most."
>
> Her voice rang with deep conviction as she added that for the present, "as a woman it is the most important duty confronting me. It means so much to me that I am willing to go to prison for it."[71]

Rose, who was a writer as well as an agitator, directed her efforts to the problems of the day, becoming a literary propagandist. Her major theme was feminism. During her activity for birth control she wrote, with Alice Blaché, the screenplay *Shall the Parents Decide?* and other feminist plays.

Though Rose's interest in birth control never waned, her involvement declined during 1917 as she became absorbed in her health, World War I, and other political interests. But she was still thought of as a birth control agitator.

The activity of Rose Pastor Stokes and other socialist women on birth control and other feminist issues provoked a woman socialist to address a question to the *Call*'s women's page editor. She wanted to know whether "it is a good thing for Socialist Party women to take an active part in affairs that are not really Socialist propaganda." The writer of the letter refers to "birth control," to "the case of Margaret Sanger," to "helping Elizabeth Gurley Flynn," and to support of "the Anti-enlistment League." She cites Rose Pastor Stokes as a prime example of the type of activist she has in mind.[72]

A few days later the *Call* carried Rose's reply:

> I try to avoid doing any work, taking any position, joining any organization that will compromise my principles or the pledge I signed when I joined the Socialist Party.
>
> I labored for Elizabeth Flynn's freedom on principle as I would labor for any earnest, radical thinker and worker who had served the workers as she had served them and who had, as she, been persecuted and hounded for it.
>
> I am helping to focus public attention on the Sanger case because I believe the free discussion and thorough understanding of the subject of birth control is one of the workers' most immediate needs.
>
> In these two instances, as in others I might quote, I feel that as a Socialist I have, incidentally, helped many people to approach the question of Socialism with a more open mind and sympathetic spirit.
>
> You urge me to explain my position, Dear Comrade, but there is not much to explain. There are almost as many ways to work for socialism as there are roads to heaven. Some ways are open to some of us, and other ways to others. We need be careful always but of one thing: to know our ground and never to compromise our principle. . . .
>
> I write for Socialism sometimes, and speak for it a good deal and sometimes I work for it in ways whose effectiveness may not always be apparent to some of my earnest comrades but which, I am satisfied in my own mind, are real and helpful to the cause.[73]

Rose Harriet Pastor (back row, third from left) with workers at Gleichman's Cigar Factory in Cleveland, spring 1896

Rose Pastor and James Graham Phelps Stokes on their wedding day at Brick
House, Noroton Point, Connecticut, July 1905

Rose Pastor Stokes at her desk in the Stokeses' apartment on Grand and
Norfolk streets, Lower East Side, New York, in 1906. (Yale University Library)

Rose and Graham Stokes in their library on Caritas Island, 1909. (Photograph by Clarence H. White)

Maxim Gorky (standing) at the Stokeses' housewarming on Caritas Island, July 4, 1906. Seated, left to right: Alexander Irvine, Miriam and Leroy Scott, and Bernard Pastor, Rose's brother

Rose Pastor Stokes with glass globe on the lawn at Caritas Island, 1909. (Photograph by Clarence H. White)

Above: The Stokeses' house
on Caritas Island, designed
by Isaac Newton Phelps
Stokes, Graham's brother

Left: Anna L. Pastor,
mother of Rose, at Leroy
Scott house on Caritas
Island, summer 1909

Rose with Lillian P. Fletcher, her sister, at Leroy Scott house
on Caritas Island

James Graham Phelps Stokes (standing between Frederick Brockhausen on the left and Victor Berger) and Rose Pastor Stokes (seated at left) with delegates to the Socialist party convention in Milwaukee, 1907. (Lena Morrow Collection at Tamiment)

Rose Pastor Stokes (right) with John and Prestonia Martin at the Martins' camp in the Adirondacks

The Stokes family reunion at Anson P. Stokes's camp at St. Regis in the
Adirondacks. Rose is seated on the floor, second from right; Graham is standing,
second from right.

Rose with roses presented to her at the second big meeting of the beginning of the hotel workers strike, 1912

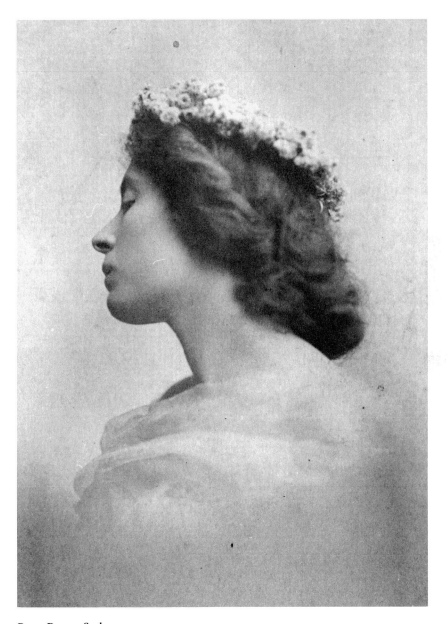

Rose Pastor Stokes

Rose Pastor Stokes from the *New York World*, December 12, 1909

Delegates arriving at Petrograd railroad station for Fourth Comintern Congress, November 19, 1922. Zinoviev (head of Comintern) and Lunacharsky (Soviet cultural commissar) frame Rose Pastor Stokes (in black fur hat). She stands in front of Max Eastman (partly hidden).

Sketch of Rose Pastor Stokes from *New Masses,* June 1933

Feminist groups working for women's liberation were no more unified in Rose's time than today. The one sustained note then as now was the goal—women's liberation. The primary organization in the early twentieth century was the suffrage movement. Once the vote was achieved, the feminist movement became even more fragmented and diffuse, but then as now, there was the striving for "consciousness"—to make all women aware of the need to seek independence in a male society.

Today, though "consciousness raising" has attained a more formal level there is still division and diversity among women's groups. In her analysis of the varied feminist groups, Barbara Deckard claims that there is a "great need for experimentation, both in organizational forms and in tactics. . . . Women . . . are not yet all sisters. . . . Class and race divide us."[74] This critique is just as applicable to the first quarter of this century as to the last. The term *feminism* has never been subject to a precise definition. The dictionary definition, "organized activity on behalf of women's rights and interests," is serviceable enough. But active feminists have rarely identified themselves with the full agenda that may be associated with women's rights and interests: not every militant suffragist was also a dauntless advocate of birth control.

Mari Jo Buhle in her generally fine history *Women and American Socialism, 1870–1920,* denies Rose Pastor Stokes the honor of the title *feminist.*[75] That Rose herself did not claim the title is beside the point. She was active in every women's struggle of her day—suffrage, birth control, peace, and equal rights for women and men. After she joined the Communist party, which in its early days had a narrow view of the scope of feminism, she aimed her appeals almost exclusively to working-class women. If this denies Rose membership in the feminist circle, the worthy pioneers of women's rights of the nineteenth century and the first fifth of the twentieth must also be denied it, for they largely excluded the lowly woman worker from their appeals.

In her letter to Maxim Lieber, quoted at the beginning of this chapter, Rose separates in her thinking the ideologies of socialism and feminism. She reveals her political view clearly and defends herself as a woman—but feminism "as such" remains undefined. If this presented her with conflict, it did not remove her from activity in both areas. Rose was for womanhood, and therein lies the significance of her activities. Nor did her ideologies condition her response to the cultural and historical concept involved in realizing female emancipation. Her life revealed her understanding instinctively and experientially of sex discrimination and women's position in society. She never hesitated to align herself with any group that sought to achieve freedom for women, but she was convinced that her political philosophy was correct and was the essential means to this achievement.

IX

The Pen as Weapon

When Rose Pastor Stokes wrote to "Dear Comrade Sinclair" in 1911, she told him: "I am still reading your book. I should say: 'I am still reading your heart.' Your other books may possibly be your soul, or your genius, or your mind or your spirit; but *this* book is your heart and nerve fibre and marrow."

By this time Rose had found her calling as a platform speaker. Her fame was based on her highest skill—an earnest, sincere, persuasive gift as a speaker. And she knew it. She told Upton Sinclair: "I covet your joy of being able to crowd so much work into the days, and so undisturbedly— *these* days, I suppose. If I could work so—but then the platform work would suffer much. Your 'Jungle' may reach the readers, but I have the joy of reaching the earnest men and women who have never so much as *heard* of your book—who may yet read much some day, because I have reached them with *my* message." In the same long letter, she recalled a talk they had had "some years ago—(four?—or five?)": "You talked, talked, talked to me. About . . . love and marriage and the world and hypocrisy, and you spoke of many other things. Well, dear comrade mine, from that time . . . I have been looking for this book that is your heart. . . I want you to know that I know your heart—that I knew it that day on the hill, and that all my heart goes to you in a keen but inexpressible sympathy—as you might guess from the things I am putting in my play."[1]

Rose had gone from cigar roller to journalist, from political propagandist to agitator for women's rights, from lecturer to author, from teenage verse writer to minor poet, from pencil sketches to artist. She had written her way out of the ghetto and into the heart of James Graham Phelps Stokes. She did not follow her literary and artistic bent in a disciplined and relentless manner. The development of these talents was hampered by the time and energy she devoted to using the spoken word to change the social system. Charles Leinenweber says: "Socialism was also a movement of culture derived from ethnic and class tradition and . . . experiences. . . . The shop floor singing of Rose Pastor refuted the bourgeois distinction between high and popular culture."[2]

In 1927 her early friend Sonya Levien, whom Rose had counseled at the settlement house, was a prominent Hollywood script writer. She and Rose had drifted apart. Sonya wrote to their mutual friend Philip Russ: "If you want to be a friend, write me a long letter about Rose Stokes. I have always loved Rose and it hurts me to think that we have just lost track of each other. How is she getting on? What is she doing? Where does she live? My, if that woman had stuck to her writing she would have been best of them all now." Russ sent Levien's letter to Rose, adding his own endorsement: "May I add Amen to Sonya's last two sentences. I feel quite elated over the fact that so eminent an authority as Sonya Levien voices my own opinion of your tremendous potentialities as a writer. Why not try your hand at it again? It may yet be the very making (artistically and creatively) of you."[3]

Rose began writing verses, jingles, and prose while still a cigarmaker. For the rest of her life she toiled over her poetry. She wanted to be a poet; she felt she was a poet. She sought criticism and help to improve her skill. In 1909 Rose sent some of her verses to Lincoln Steffens and received a letter from him which she said "was like an inspiration." She acknowledged that the demands of the movement curbed her ability to listen and—in the poetic sense—sing: "Propaganda absorbs me almost utterly." A year later she sent Steffens another batch of verses and urged him "to criticize most frankly and freely and relentlessly."[4] The poems were not great, but many of her contemporaries regarded them highly. Their subject matter was often agitational; they were relevant to the problems of her day. Readers and listeners responded to them.

Daniel Kiefer, an old friend of Rose, the lecture agent and manager for Lincoln Steffens, arranged for Rose to read her verses at Henry's Studio in Philadelphia on January 23, 1921. The hall was crowded; people were turned away. Kiefer commented that there had never been "an evening like it in all my connection with things of a radical nature." He made this statement in a letter to the publisher Benjamin Huebsch in which he told him of Stokes's reading of yet unpublished poems. Kiefer suggested publication. He believed such a book "would be a big seller."[5] But Huebsch told him there was no market for poetry. After her Philadelphia reading, Kiefer told her, "I hope I said enough before you left us to let you be under no misapprehension as to our regard for you, and that your brief visit with us, including the reading, will ever be a great memory to us."[6]

Another reading of Rose's poetry was arranged by Symon Gould of the American Service Library, who described the event:

> I had arranged a reading of her poetry in order to circumvent the governmental objections to her public appearance. . . . During World War I, I had the distinction and honor of presenting Rose Pastor Stokes in a literary evening, even though she was under government onus . . . at the Labor Temple, located at 14th Street and 2nd Avenue but I did not reckon with the authorities that govern the renting of the auditorium. . . . They seemingly were approached by some officials and they cancelled the contract. . . . However, I did not permit this obstacle to hinder me from running down to 4th Street, renting a small hall and then we had the spectacle of about 150 men and women marching down Second Avenue from 14th Street and paying admission and listening to Rose Pastor Stokes very enthusiastically.[7]

In 1913, when Rose was deeply involved in Socialist party work, her need for more artistic expression was on her mind. She complained in her diary: "The days here [Caritas Island] are spent quietly reading, writing, housekeeping. I get terribly, unbearably restless. We are in a transition period—all in turmoil in Society. There is work to do right among the people and my desire is to spend at least half my year in the work for the people *direct*. My writing bears upon the same theme, arises from the same motive, but it is not enough, I must be in and of the struggle."[8] But it was only after her life was threatened by poor health that she decreased her platform appearances and turned to sedentary occupations such as writing poetry and plays.

Rose's writings, like her speeches, spoke of the people and to the people. Her agitational themes were absorbed by them, not as "mere propaganda" but as truths. Rose was a forerunner of the proletarian writing that did not find its fullest expression in the United States until the 1930s. It is not known what inspiration directed her to express herself in poetry in her youth. She was not really a reader and had little acquaintance with poetry. She was, however, passionately inspired by the "Man with the Hoe" by

Edwin Markham, and she was introduced to Shelley by a fellow worker in Cleveland. In her adult years she was absorbed by the radical themes of Walt Whitman and by the romanticism of Dante Gabriel Rossetti. These examples indicate that her taste in poetry was pointed to the common man and to the woes, struggles, and triumphs of life.

Basic themes from these first influences made their appearance in her own work—themes ranging from personal experiences and her responses to toil, nature, personal unhappiness, and frustrations, to love, and to God in the early adult period of her life. Finally she turned to political and social themes. The early poems were expressions of the toil that filled her deprived childhood.

An example is the poem "The Song of the Cigar," one of her earliest. Seven stanzas, six lines each, rhythmically direct the performance of her hands, making her cigars. Each line proclaims a step her fingers use to complete the process:

> Cut, cut cut!
> The sumatra as brown as a nut.
> Cut finely the selvage to-day
> The Foreman is looking my way
> And I may be docked from my pay.
> Cut, cut, cut!

The verses go through "Roll, roll, roll!" "Paste, paste, paste!" "Clip, clip, clip!" Then the finale:

> Count, count, count!
> To what does this day's work amount?
> One dollar and twenty-five cents
> And I must keep eight souls alive!
> Oh! how can man's faith in God thrive!
> Count, count, count![9]

The *Jewish Review and Observer* of Cleveland on page 1 of its issue of July 5, 1901, published Rose Harriet Pastor's "Sub Silentio," an ode to God. Rose was almost twenty-two years old when it appeared. These early poems reflect solemnity, loneliness, frustration, and an identification with nature.

At the time of the announcement of her engagement to Graham in 1905, Rose was briefly "discovered" as a poet. The *Evening Journal* led the way with a satiric poem written as a list of "don't's"; two days later the *Evening Telegram* published "Love and Fame" and two days after that the *Telegram* picked up "Feeding the Sparrows" from the *World,* complete with a musical setting by F. Fanculli.

Several of Rose's poems were published in the *Call* from 1908 to 1913. They appeared mostly in the women's pages, and their themes were children, labor, and the struggles of working people. Among them were "Come Little Daughter" about a little girl who had to leave the fields and flowers to enter the factory, "Golgotha" on the death of a soldier, "On the Day," "Adult Labor," and "It's Every Day."

In February 1915 Rose was the opening speaker in a course called "The Poetry of Today" given by the literary department of the Commonwealth Club of Upper Montclair, New Jersey. A newspaper story described her participation:

> Mrs. Stokes talked . . . of the group of writers who had interpreted the life of the "spinners and toilers. . . ."
>
> Mrs. Stokes . . . who has portrayed the situations of the workers' world in her own poems, was well fitted to glean the gems from the many heart and soul stories that have been woven into verses. Rather would she call them poems of protest than of revolt. . . . She quoted from many . . . writers . . . that made the audience feel in touch with each writer. Mrs. Stokes was requested to read from her own work. . . . She read "An Honest Man and His Skeleton," a protest poem against keeping a skeleton in the closet. When the skeleton takes a walk among the "proper folks," the citizens . . . hurry home to lock their own skeleton more securely in.
>
> "In England," which Mrs. Stokes also read, was an exquisite poem showing the beauties of the hedge and the thorn and the harmonies of the song bird . . . but turning the singer sees a man with a burden on his back and England seems less lovely.[10]

In Rose's later years, she made an effort to support herself by selling her poetry and prints. She had little success. Her work was not broadly accepted. The *Forum* did publish her "Woolworth Girl" and a print, and she won the Tyng Prize in 1926 for a "little poem" sent to the *British Poetry Review.* These publications and the prize brought small amounts of money.

Rose also published poems in the *Liberator,* successor to the *Masses.* One, "We Who Stay," was reprinted and reviewed unfavorably by the

Literary Digest. These verses exalt the Russian proletariat. Daniel Aaron, in *Writers on the Left*, considers this poem an example of the "rhapsody" into which some intellectuals were led by their passionate response to the Russian Revolution. It did not always produce the best art, but it was deeply felt.[11]

Rose's translation from the Yiddish, in collaboration with Helena Frank, of Morris Rosenfeld's *The Song of Labor* was highly regarded. The translators were acclaimed not only for bringing the stirring poetry of Rosenfeld to the English-speaking public but for maintaining the quality and tone of the originals. Reviews in England and the United States were complimentary. Rose had read Rosenfeld's poetry in the Yiddish. His poems told of the lives of immigrant workers and were highly regarded by Jewish intellectuals of the period.

In August 1914 Upton Sinclair wrote to Rose that he had read her poem on Paterson and was reading the Rosenfeld book, which he found to be "very remarkable stuff." He was to review it for the *Intercollegiate Socialist Society Review*. "I like your translations very much indeed," he said, "though I am not the best judge of them as I do not know the originals."[12]

Rose was always fond of Rosenfeld's verses. In 1908 the *Independent* carried her poem "Whither," "from the Yiddish of Morris Rosenfeld":

> Say, whither, whither, pretty one?
> The world is still a present!
> O list how quiet 'tis around!
> Ere dawn—the streets hold not a sound.
> Oh, whither, whither do you run?
> Sleep at this hour is pleasant.
> The flowers are dreaming dewy-wet;
> The birds'—nests—they are silent yet.
> Where to, before the rising sun
> The world her light is giving?
>   "To earn a living."
>
> Oh whither, whither, pretty child,
> So late at night a-strolling?
> Alone—with darkness round you curled—
> All rests—and sleeping is the world.
> Where drives you now the wind so wild?
> The midnight bells are tolling!

Day hath not warmed you with her light.
What aid canst hope then from the night?
Night's deaf and blind!—Oh, whither, child
Light minded fancies weaving?
　"To earn a living."[13]

Rose wrote poetry nearly to the end of her life. Her themes became more revolutionary, passing from expressions of protest to expressions of revolt. They became didactic and too freighted with ideology to be sustained by her poetic quality. Pablo Neruda, Nazim Hikmet, and Mayakovsky could find the fitting poetic language and imagery for such material. Rose could not.

Ten days after Rose Pastor Stokes wrote Upton Sinclair the letter quoted at the beginning of this chapter, she wrote to "My dear Upton" again. She was working on the play she had mentioned to him. He had apparently made some critical suggestions, but she did not like them. Her tone is confident:

> I've fallen back to my original plan for it; for I find the *fourth* act changes the entire motive of the play—shifts it to something else.
>
> I am also resolved that you shall find my *curtain* not weak and insipid. I firmly believe I will make the final scene (with *all* its teacups, etc.) a most powerful, dramatic "curtain." You'll see. . . .
>
> The Spring is singing in my heart and pounding through my arteries. So—it's hard work. I've had to fight to get started again.[14]

From 1911 on, and particularly from 1913, Rose was usually working on a play. She evidently liked to use dramatic characters to project struggle and protest. Her plays are concerned with social issues, mostly with workers trying to survive in a society they do not control, and they stress the special problems women workers face in relation to work, love, marriage, motherhood, and birth control.

On the publication of her play *The Woman Who Wouldn't* in 1916, Rose was asked how she happened to write a play. She responded: "How did I happen to write a play? I didn't happen to. I had to. The thing took possession of me . . . about five years ago and for months . . . the play was crystallizing in my mind, but there was other work to do that absorbed me completely." Then because of fatigue as a result of activity in a strike she was ordered to bed for two weeks. "That gave me the necessary freedom and quiet . . . I started my play. . . . When I was a little girl, I used to think in dialogue. . . . There would be sometimes two, three, or four imaginary people and they'd thresh out questions, or things dramatic, tragic, comic that would happen to them."[15]

Her first play, *Mary*, was never published or produced. It was the subject of a conflict involving plagiarism. Dr. Frederick Robinson, president of the Sociological Fund of the *Medical Review of Reviews*, had asked Rose to be on the production committee of another play, *The Guilty Man*. After reading the play she charged "unconscious plagiarism," claiming that the "doctor's scene" in her play *Mary* was now part of this play. She had read two acts of *Mary* to Dr. Robinson on his visit to Caritas Island several months before *The Guilty Man* was prepared for production. When Rose's sister Lillian saw *The Guilty Man* on October 1, 1913, she told the *American* that one scene had been taken from Rose's play.[16] Letters flew back and forth between Robinson, Ruth Helen Davis, who had translated and dramatized *The Guilty Man* from a novel by François Coppe, and Rose Pastor Stokes. After some bruising exchanges, Rose withdrew haughtily from the battle.

Mary was offered through an agent to the producer Winthrop Ames. Though he praised the play, he called it "in essence, propaganda; and the public can only be made to swallow a 'propaganda' play by disguising it with an excess of dramatic action. To Mrs. Stokes and perhaps to me, this action and progress is supplied by the sincerity of the author's belief and first hand observation. . . . A selected audience could see it and sympathize."[17] Ames's criticism points out a frequent flaw in Rose's writing. She had ability, but her heavy-handed emphasis on social significance detracted from the dramatic quality of her work.

A few years after the quarrel with Dr. Robinson, Rose used the basic ideas of *Mary* in the *The Woman Who Wouldn't*. It was published in 1916 just about the time *The Guilty Man* was to reopen. An unrelenting Rose wrote to the *Times* that she hoped that those who saw *The Guilty Man* and later read her play "will not believe that I was the 'pilfering tailor'."[18]

The first of her plays to be staged was the one-act *The Saving of Martin Greer*, which was shown with three others at the Berkeley Theatre in New York under the auspices of the Socialist Press Club. The hero, Martin Greer, has reached the age of diminishing returns. A younger worker, accepting a lower wage, can better increase the boss's profit. Two months in arrears on rent and facing eviction, Greer attempts suicide. A sympathetic nurse, daughter of the landlady, finds him gasping from inhaling gas. "Saved," he cries, as he looks at the world again, and the curtain drops.

The *Call* review reported that "Mrs. Stokes makes her first appearance as a playwright. Martin Greer is said to be another name for a well known person, and people are wondering why he or they need to be saved and how Mrs. Stokes has managed to save him or them."[19] The review in the *Sun* commented on the line "saved . . . which ends Mrs. Stokes's playlet with everything which should be right quite as wrong as in the beginning."[20]

Another one-act drama, *In April*, met a better reception. It was opened by the Washington Square Players at the Band Box Playhouse on a program with three other plays under the direction of Holland Hudson. Most reviews were favorable, and it was subsequently performed in little theaters in many cities throughout the United States and in England. Its story of tenement life could be partly autobiographical. The main character is a young working woman who sacrifices love and marriage (not autobiographical) to remain with and give support to her mother, who is living in poverty with a wretched, alcoholic man.

Of the four plays presented, the *Tribune* considered *In April* "the most successful both of intention and achievement." The *Telegram* said, "Mrs. Rose Pastor Stokes's study in the misery and fatality of tenement life and sacrifices of the young to the poverty and weakness of the old had reality and truth." *Drama News* called the play "an effective story of a poor working girl who gives up hope and happiness." The *New York Press* and the *Brooklyn Daily Eagle* reviewers wrote in the same vein.[21] Olive Dargan had called the play "perfect" and said there was "not a flaw in it" when she read the script late in 1913.[22]

Rose was by now deeply into "proletarian literature." She may have gotten her inspiration from Emma Goldman's *The Social Significance of Modern Drama*.

Rose's play *The Woman Who Wouldn't* was published by Putnam's in October 1916 but was never staged. It is a heavy drama devoted to the development of young Mary's character from adolescence to an independent, socially conscious womanhood. The plot is based on Mary's abandonment by her lover and fiancé because of his love for another woman, leaving Mary pregnant and fearful. She has kept her pregnancy a secret from him. When he learns of it through her father, he agrees to marry her. He accepts his responsibility and is willing to protect her honor. She rejects his offer. Responsibility for her child leads Mary to the realization of her potential. Befriended by only one person, the leader of the mill union, under his direction Mary develops into a mature woman, secure and efficient. She devotes her life to the cause of labor.

Rose here portrayed an independent woman who understands her position as a worker, mother, and union member and who can face life with the strength of her convictions. The dramatic development is clumsy, but the characters are plausible. But Rose overburdens the play with too many social and political issues, which detract from those that are vital to the independent woman. Reviews of the published play ranged from fair to good. Most said the characters were well drawn and the scenes realistic. They also remarked on the "nature of propaganda."

A Mrs. Mumford gave *The Woman Who Wouldn't* a negative review, which Rose accepted with uncharacteristic forbearance, telling her friends that Mrs. Mumford was a "good critic" and a "brilliant woman" and that "intelligent reviewing is rare."[23] Nevertheless, Rose must have been much happier with a letter from John Spargo saying, "Your Mary is a glorious creature. . . . I do not know of another character of equal beauty and inspiration in the whole range of our literature."[24] A reviewer for the *Philadelphia Press* struck a fair note in the opening paragraph of his careful review:

> It is always difficult for an ardent reformer to achieve complete artistic success. Even so great a playwright as Ibsen found his theories of social betterment a distinct hindrance in the working out of many of his dramas. Consequently it is not surprising that Rose Pastor Stokes in her zeal for the cause of industrial justice, should have fallen somewhat short of the highest esthetic possibilities of her play. However, she has given a strong picture of the grim war between capital and labor, which is, after all, the dominating feature in American life at the present time.[25]

Rose wrote three or four more plays. Her play *On the Day* was given at the People's Playhouse, which sponsored and encouraged Socialist playwrights in an attempt to further proletarian literature. The *Call* announced that Rose was taking an important role in the theater, not only in writing plays but in selecting actors and directing. The *Call* considered *On the Day* "thrilling drama. . . . Depicts the mental process of a philosophical anarchist." Two other plays written by Rose are *Chat about People* and *Squaring the Triangle*.²⁶

During the period when Rose was trying the hardest to be part of the American cultural scene, she lived in Greenwich Village. The Stokes home at 88 Grove Street and Helen Stokes's next door at number 90 were located on Sheridan Square, the very heart of the Village, the capital of Bohemia.

In the 1910s, the years of the magazine *Masses,* edited by Max Eastman, the Village was in its zestful prime—a radical mix of anarchism and socialism, flamboyantly expressed by serious writers (Walter Lippmann, Van Wyck Brooks), poets (Edna St. Vincent Millay, Alfred Kreymborg), feminists (Susan Glaspell, Henrietta Rodman), journalists (Lincoln Steffens, Hutchins Hapgood), artists (John Sloan, Art Young), radicals (Emma Goldman, Carlo Tresca), and many more.

Curiously, although she had a political or social relationship with many of these people, Rose Pastor Stokes was not herself a Villager. She rarely attended the soirées of Mabel Dodge. She and Graham lived sedately, aloof from the liquor, sex, and eccentric dress that were part of the "typical" Village scene. Rose at 88 Grove was untypical. John Reed at 42 Washington Square reveled in it all. By 1919 both were among the founders of the new Communist party.²⁷

Late in 1918, after the war had ended, left-wing socialists were founding the People's Playhouse, and of course Rose participated, as did Samuel Ornitz—who thirty years later would be one of the "Hollywood Ten" who were jailed for refusing to answer questions of the House Un-American Activities Committee. Ornitz lived in Brooklyn, and Rose sent four of her one-act plays to him for criticism. He was straightforward: *Squaring the Triangle:* "brilliantly novel. But you do not do the splendid satire justice with the dialogue"; *In April:* "There is no lagging drama; forceful, pregnant with purpose and meaning; unforgettable"; *The Saving of Martin Greer:* "Done with the sympathy of the world woman . . . and mother that you are. . . . You rage with revolutionary anger at . . . any suffering"; *On the Day:* "A big theme but I am not satisfied with the way it is developed . . . I'd like to talk to you about this play." Ornitz concluded, "I'm very keen about the People's Playhouse and I dream of big achievements.

It means work and I'm ready for it." Ornitz's evaluations reveal the force in Rose's character that drove her—sometimes without restraint—and was responsible for both her successes and her failures.[28]

By 1915 the infant silent screen had reached the age of discretion and had produced on United States soil *The Birth of a Nation,* which despite its racism and ideological infamy represented a high level in the technology of movie making.

Carl Beck, director of the Labor Forum, wrote to Rose Pastor Stokes in December 1915 to express his pleasure that she had agreed to serve actively on the forum's Labor Drama Committee. He also told her that at a meeting of the Unemployment Committee there was discussion on a "proposition of requesting you to write a scenario for *Martin Greer.*"[29] Labor films—mostly antilabor films—and films with related subject matter had already appeared frequently in the modest movie theaters that proliferated in the early years of moviemaking.

Rose was offered what seemed at first to be a more important enterprise than the one broached by Carl Beck when she was approached in 1916 by Madame Alice Blaché, one of the earliest of the small number of women film directors and, judging by her screen credits, one of the more serious. In 1912 she did *Fran Diavolo,* based on Daniel François Esprit Auber's opera of that name. In 1913 she made *Dick Whittington's Cat.* In 1914 she did *Dream Woman,* adapted from a novel by Wilkie Collins. The leading film trade journal of the day carried her article "Woman's Place in Photoplay Production."[30] She came to Rose because she wanted to do a film on birth control. The first title proposed for this film was *Sacred Motherhood;* it was later changed to *Shall the Parents Decide?*

The script was tried out in Rose's home at 88 Grove Street with Alice Blaché, Rose, and Helen Stokes reading aloud. Each scene and its characters portrayed one reason for the need for birth control. The overall theme as stated by Stokes was: "A woman should not have children more frequently than her health and strength and the proper birthright of her children dictate. . . . The science of contraception comes as a great measure of safety for the future of the race."[31] This propagandistic statement was dramatic and pointedly presented even if a bit obvious. The preparatory work proceeded well, and the ultimate failure to produce the film was not for lack of goodwill on the part of the coauthors. Rose did balk when she became aware that her membership in the Authors League of America precluded her acceptance of payment on a "net receipts basis," but she told Madame, "You are quite welcome to take material I have placed at your disposal." This hurdle must have been cleared for in October Madame wrote to Rose: "I am working now and hope to be able to see you next week with my version and hope the financials will decide to help us for I am very interested in this myself."[32]

Madame Blaché did not own a distributing company, and that hurdle caused the project to founder. In December Bert Adler, an executive with Solax, the film company Madame was president of, wrote to Rose: "I have discouraging news again. A craven spirit seems to dominate the producers; they will take a 'sex play' if it is sufficiently sugar-coated, but not if it is red-blooded and points a real lesson. Universal accepted and produced 'Where Are My Children?' with its half-lesson but return 'Shall the Mother [sic] Decide?' with its whole lesson. So there we are. However, I am again casting around for a market." But in 1916 there was no market. Bert Adler approached the Selznick company, which had released a similar film. Adler reported to Rose that "it is my own belief that [Selznick] was simply afraid to produce this subject."[33]

Rose's many talents were evident in her production of plays, playlets, and poems. In the later years of her life she proved herself gifted in the graphic arts. A friend from this period and a surviving relative treasure Rose's drawings in their possession. Of course, it was as a platform speaker that she excelled, using her fine speaking voice.[34] Her untrained singing voice had been praised in the uncritical stogie factories when she was a teenager. In 1915 for a while she took singing lessons from Laura P. Elliot, who wrote: "Your voice is fine and comprehensive. I so want to develop the noble and legitimate quality in it, so that no matter how little you sing it will be free and simple and expressive of what you are." In another letter Elliot asked Rose "to bring with you tomorrow Schuman's Album Vol. III for the low voice . . . later you will sing the high, but at first so as not to bring any strain upon the voice teachers use the low."[35]

Rose did not long continue voice lessons, but her interest in music remained. She became involved in furthering the career of a young singer, an immigrant from Russia, who had been blind since the age of four. He was poor, he needed help, and he had a fine voice. He came to Rose's attention through a society woman who had sponsored him at a home recital. More such recitals at the homes of wealthy persons were arranged. Rose Stokes soon took over the main responsibility for advancing his career. Not all his singing was for society; one night at the Socialist Consumers League, his folk songs had the old folks dancing in the aisles. His name was Vladimir Resnikoff, and his singing voice needed further training. Mince Parker of the City Club warned Rose that he was abusing his voice by not using it correctly: "He is courting . . . disaster if he pursues his present course." She felt that in his last concert he did not show "beautiful bigness and fullness of tone . . . in his voice."[36]

When Rose was on her speaking tour in November 1916, Graham assumed responsibility for finding Resnikoff housing where he could practice his singing. A series of letters between Rose and Graham deal with this hunt. The temperamental Resnikoff was very fussy but finally settled in Chelsea not far from the Village. Resnikoff was interviewed at the Stokes home, 88 Grove Street, early in March 1917. He told a reporter:

> I always sang . . . all my people sang . . . the peasants sang as they worked and the children learned the songs. . . . The Russian peasant's music comes from the heart. . . . It is all about the sky, the birds, the flowers. Very often it is not even written but passed from one generation to another. . . .
>
> They were all very good to me . . . they sang me their songs and told me their fairy tales and legends.

He knew nothing about music and had never been to a concert. The only music he had heard besides the songs of the peasants was the soldiers' when they went through the town. His older brothers and sisters went to America and then sent for him and his parents and another sibling. They were initially refused admission at Ellis Island because of his blindness, and the family was detained there for two weeks. Assurances from his brothers and sisters that he would not become a public charge made it possible for them to enter. On arrival he immediately was placed in the Institution for the Blind at 34th Street and Ninth Avenue:

> I was taken sick with the loneliness of it and was in bed for a long time . . . but when I was better I was ready to go back to the Institution . . . I used to sing the Russian peasant songs to them and they found I had a voice, and they did every thing they could to cultivate it. . . .
>
> But they discouraged me. They told me that with my handicap I

could not be successful. But I kept on working. I studied all the time. I knew I must succeed.[37]

Rose took Resnikoff to visit the great Enrico Caruso, and she wrote to a friend: "I must tell you of the wonderful, interesting hour I spent when I took my blind boy to sing for Caruso. 'Bravo' and 'respect' were some of his exclamations." On this visit Rose "did not tell him for whom he would sing. 'You must sing your best,' she said in the elevator as they were going to Caruso's studio. He sang for Caruso and Caruso sang for him. He recognized Caruso's voice. He had heard him once four years before this visit at the Metropolitan where he was taken by friends to attend an opera."[38]

Rose arranged many concerts for Resnikoff, some with the help of other women who sponsored him. He sang in many cities and was well received. Reviews were enthusiastic and complimentary. He sang at a meeting at Carnegie Hall on March 20, 1917, sponsored by the Society of Friends of Russian Freedom celebrating the revolution that had just dethroned the czar.

Reporting on a November 28, 1918, concert in Chicago, the *Chicago Tribune* headlined its review "Blind Russian Boy's Voice and Smile Wins Society Plaudits." (The "boy" was then twenty-five years old.) Rose was sensitive and sensible about the reviews Vladimir Resnikoff was receiving. She welcomed praise for her protégé, but she was leery of reviews that praised the quality of his performances excessively. On November 11, 1917, after reading reviews on a Chicago concert, Rose wrote to a Mrs. Leight:

> Could you help to correct the impression among the Chicago critics particularly—that my young singer is credited with having a *phenomenal voice?* This is unfortunately an error. He has a most *unusual* quality of voice, he is dramatic to an altogether exceptional degree and is a creative singer. But letting the impression go out that he had a *phenomenal voice* may lead people to expect a voice that will make the welkin ring! And that wouldn't do. Would it? . . . I do not wish *too* great expectations raised, as people are apt to expect a voice like Caruso, and this of course he is not![39]

Vladimir Resnikoff's death in 1920 put an end to Rose's attempts to further his career.

X

The Great War

Rose Pastor Stokes was heavily involved in the years 1913 to 1917 with the nagging case of Patrick Quinlan. It was one of those pathetic civil liberties violations that has mired the pages of labor history repeatedly from its earliest days. The Quinlan case was a product of the silk workers' struggle in Paterson, New Jersey, that began in mid-January 1913, when the weavers of the Doherty Mills struck because they balked at being required to operate four looms rather than two. Doubling their load resulted in the layoff of half their number.

Carlo Tresca, Elizabeth Gurley Flynn, and Patrick Quinlan were invited to address a meeting on February 24 at which five thousand weavers unanimously endorsed a call for a general strike. Quinlan had arrived late that afternoon and had been present when Joe Margini, chairman of the Doherty Shop Committee, shouted from his seat in the hall, "Let's all go to picket the Doherty Mill." Quinlan, and not Margini, was later charged with having interrupted the meeting to move that the audience go to the Doherty Mill and "club, beat and drive the workers out."

The police chief arrived at the hall after the crowd dispersed and ordered Tresca, Quinlan, and Flynn to leave town within twenty-four hours. They refused to do so, and all three were arrested. They were charged with unlawful assembly and inciting to riot. In April the three were indicted by a "silk jury," so called because of its intimate connections with the owners of the industry, which was still crippled by the strike. Quinlan was the first to be tried in April in the midst of the strike. The jury disagreed. He was then tried again by a more carefully selected jury composed of small business men. After twenty minutes of deliberation they brought in a verdict of guilty, laughing and applauding as they did so.

Quinlan was sentenced to serve two to seven years. Two higher courts reaffirmed the verdict, and in March 1915, long after the strike was settled, Quinlan was imprisoned at Trenton. It would be hard to disagree with Rose's statement: "It is indeed tragic that of the fifteen hundred people arrested in Paterson the man who is the victim and must pay the extreme penalty is Patrick Quinlan, who was 'framed up' by police perjury. The recent vindication of Miss Flynn and the affidavit submitted by Margini—to the effect that he spoke at the time Quinlan is alleged to have interrupted—give the lie to the Paterson police."[1] For the next two years Rose Pastor Stokes, working with Dolly Sloan, wife of John Sloan, the famous "ashcan" artist, led the vain struggle for his freedom. He served the full two years of his minimum sentence.

Elizabeth Gurley Flynn's case was still pending when Quinlan started his term, and while Rose continued the fight for Quinlan's freedom she organized a defense committee for Flynn as well. Charles Edward Russell, a journalist, author, socialist, and reformer, wrote to Rose that he knew "nothing about the case. But if you are interested in it I feel sure it is all right and will be a member of the Defense Committee as you request."[2] Several notables joined the committee, and Flynn was cleared in 1916.

Other civil liberties cases proliferated in the period leading up to the war which was "to make the world safe for democracy." Betty Edelson was on a hunger strike in prison in 1914. On August 10, a mass meeting to protest the forcible feeding of Edelson, an obscure anarchist, brought three hundred women and a few men to Murray Hill Lyceum, where Rose Pastor Stokes presided. Elizabeth Gurley Flynn and Anna Strunsky Walling denounced the persecution of Edelson. "A captive revolutionist," Matilda Robbins called her, "giving her life in protest against denial of her rights."[3]

Scott Nearing was dismissed from a professorship at the University of Pennsylvania in June 1915 for opposing child labor, and Rose became instantly involved in the futile campaign for his reinstatement. On October 24, 1915, prompted by Gurley Flynn, Rose sent a wire to President Wilson reading: "I beg the kindliest, most humane President since Lincoln for the life of Joe Hillstrom." Hillstrom was better known as Joe Hill. Falsely accused of murder, this sturdy IWW songwriter was executed by a firing squad at a Utah prison on October 19, 1915. In 1916 the capital cases of Tom Mooney and Warren K. Billings made demands on all civil libertarians.

Some fifteen years later, Rose looked back on these years of war in Europe and the preparation for United States entry into it. She recalled:

> For years I have gone about the country stirring interest in Socialism. I had thrown myself into strikes with the fury of a true soldier in the ranks of my class. Nothing was too difficult; all-night picketing, all-day activity, at times no sleep, no food; it did not matter. Often I kept going until I broke, and had to be dragged away from the scene of battle. There came no call of any kind to aid in the struggle to which I did not respond with joy. Another blow at the enemy, another and another![4]

In the background, from 1914 to 1917, there was the war. It started as a European war and became World War I. The combatant nations fought under glorious banners and eloquent slogans. President Woodrow Wilson enunciated the classic slogan of the war when he said in his War Message to Congress, April 2, 1917, "The world must be made safe for democracy. Its peace must be planted upon the tested foundation of political liberty." When the war was safely over he acknowledged: "This war was a commercial and industrial war. It was not a political war."[5]

World capitalism reached its imperialist stage around 1900. Great Britain then held in subjection more foreign territory than her rivals—Germany, France, Italy, Russia, and the United States—combined. But she had lost her industrial leadership, and her competitors sought to divide Britain's spoils, her colonies and spheres of influence. Germany had her eyes on Britain's holdings and those of France as well. Germany also aimed at seizing the Ukraine, Poland, and the Baltic countries from Russia. The czar wanted to dismember Turkey and take the Dardanelles; Britain wanted Mesopotamia and Palestine and a weakened Germany; France wanted Alsace, Lorraine, and the Saar from Germany. The United States wanted to protect its huge loans to Britain and to achieve world domination.

As early as 1892 Friedrich Engels saw a war coming and predicted that at its end crowns would be rolling on the sidewalks of Europe and there would be nobody to pick them up. The Second (Socialist) International repeatedly discussed the war danger in its congresses. At the Congress of Stuttgart in 1907 an antiwar resolution was passed, which contained an amendment proposed by V. I. Lenin, Rosa Luxemburg, and L. Martov: "In case a war should nevertheless break out, the Socialists shall take measures to bring about its early termination and strive with all their power to use the economic and political crisis created by the war to arouse the masses politically and hasten the overthrow of capitalist class rule." The same resolution was adopted at the Congress of Copenhagen in 1910 and, unanimously, at the Congress of Basel in 1912.[6]

But when war came in the summer of 1914, the German Social Democratic party voted for war credits with only Karl Liebknecht and a few others dissenting. The Socialists of the western European countries followed the German party's lead, supporting their respective governments' declaration on both sides. The big and, as it proved, important exception was the Russian Bolshevik party, which opposed the war in its own country and attempted to organize the antiwar forces in all countries.

In America there was no immediate pressure on the socialists to choose sides. Neutrality was the order of the day. The Socialist party of America denounced the "senseless conflict." It resolved that it was against all wars "waged upon any pretext whatsoever." Its pacifist program was implemented by agitation against war in general and against the entry of the United States into the European conflict in particular. In September 1914 the SP National Executive Committee mildly declared, "We do not presume to pass judgment upon the conduct of our brother parties in Europe. . . . They did the best they could under the circumstances."[7]

The long-expected war took everyone by surprise. Rose Stokes's friend the writer Joanna F. Cooke, left Providence on July 21, 1914, intending to spend the rest of a peaceful summer in northern Italy and Switzerland. But when her steamer arrived at Marseilles "the American and English Consuls most urgently advised the Americans of our party to go to Paris and thence, if possible, to the coast or to England. Already, we learned, tourists were scrambling to get out of Switzerland." Cooke wrote Rose ("My Dear Comrade") on August 13, from Paris:

> But now that I am here, I feel like staying for a while, at least. I lack entirely the impulse to run to cover. I know Paris, sufficiently well for my needs—I spent several months here in bygone years—if only I had some Comrades! . . .
>
> Paris is wonderfully calm, and the streets are quiet even for August. It looks like a feminist city now. Women wearing their men's old straw hats, sweep and wash the streets, and in the caps of the employees of

yesterday, they are acting as streetcar conductors, ticket sellers and punchers, etc. I hear they are rapidly being organized for other lines of work. The press is rigorously censored. So far nothing has been published unfavorable to the French and Belgian side. But tales of German "brutalities" fill every column. Nothing was said of the treatment of the poor Germans in Paris. What madness! . . . Sometimes I fancy it is all a huge conspiracy to block the progress of the Revolution.

I wish I knew what the socialist press at home is saying . . . I am alone and cut off from the divine light of the torch of the Revolution. . . . Dear Comrade, if by chance you should have the address of some French socialists, I am sure you will send it to me. I feel woefully cut off from the news sources in which I can put faith.[8]

Joanna might have seen similar scenes in New York less than three years later. In the meantime Rose and Graham did their socialist best to agitate for an end to the war. Early in 1915 Agnes D. Warbasse, a Brooklyn socialist, wrote to say that "Helen Keller will give another anti-war speech at Carnegie—January 5th . . . for the Cause. Can you give us the benefit of your advice?"[9] And at the end of the year, when Helen Keller spoke at the peace rally in New York's Washington Irving High School, she spoke against the Ford peace ship.

The peace ship project was a matter Rose Pastor Stokes knew something about. She and Graham had each received identical telegrams from Henry Ford which read:

Will you come as my guest aboard the Oscar II of the Scandinavian American Line sailing from New York December 4th for Christiania Stockholm and Copenhagen, I am cabling leading men and women of the European nations to join us en route and at some central point to be determined later establish an international conference dedicated to negotiations leading to a just settlement of the war a hundred representative Americans are being invited full letter follows with twenty thousand men killed every twenty four hours tens of thousands maimed homes ruined, another winter begun, the time has come for a few men and women with courage and energy irrespective of the cost in personal inconvenience, money sacrifices, and criticism to free the good will of Europe that it may assert itself for peace and justice with the strong probability that international disarmament can be accomplished.[10]

In conformity with Socialist party doctrine, both Rose and Graham sent their replies within twenty-four hours of receiving Ford's telegram. Rose's reply said:

I think I have a sufficiently modern outlook to discard the purely "moral" attitude toward a problem and cling to the scientific which, to eliminate a given condition seeks out the cause.

It was in this spirit of research that I have become deeply convinced that the system of production for private profit is the basic cause of the great European war.

If I thought you saw eye to eye with me in this matter, I would be glad to join you in a propaganda among the belligerents for the establishment of permanent peace; but I feel on the contrary, that you stand for and foster the very conditions that have caused this war—conditions which, if fostered further, will make for future wars, plunging even the United States into a violent conflict.

Concerning the prospects of immediate peace, I am firmly convinced that not the question of the humanities but the question of markets will end (as it began) the war and that nothing but a complete test of arms will be allowed to settle this question: Because powerful capitalist groups, not the people, are in control of the governments involved.

Doctors widely disagreeing on the diagnosis and, consequently on the form of treatment, should not together attend the patient upon whose case they disagree. It is confusing to the doctors and bad for the patients. I believe that you and I are two such social "doctors." I regard your diagnosis as wrong and your proposed treatment as futile as you, no doubt, regard mine. Therefore, much as I desire "peace by Christmas" and the establishment of permanent peace for the future, I fear we cannot work together and I must (regretfully and with deep thanks) decline your exceedingly kind invitation.[11]

Shortly after spurning Henry Ford's invitation, Rose was invited by the Twilight Club to address one of its series of "What is Wrong" forums. Speakers were free to choose their own topics—"What Is Wrong with Advertising?" "with Legislation?" "with Education?" Rose spoke to the

Twilight Club on December 21. Her subject was "What Is Wrong with Our Defense?"

There is evidence in January 1916 of the beginning of a separation between the Stokes couple and the orthodox SP position. This rift is shown, for example, in a letter from Graham to "Dear Uncle Will" (William Earl Dodge Stokes), who had been so infuriated by Rose's activity in the waiters' strike. Graham refused to join in issuing a public statement Uncle Will had proposed on the matter of preparedness. But he told his uncle, "I feel that the Socialist Party, officially, is entirely wrong as regards this preparedness matter." Two months later he told a Socialist comrade: "I am not in accord with the present extreme to which anti-preparedness sentiment has gone in the Socialist Party. . . . The United States should be much better equipped than it is to face the risks of war with unfriendly powers."[12]

In March Rose was still in good standing as an honorary vice-chairperson of the Women's Peace party of New York City, and late in May Emma Goldman invited her to a meeting of those in the city who might sign an antimilitary manifesto. But at the end of 1916, Rose and Graham were not willing to participate in the New Year's Eve peace demonstration to be held in Washington Square, a few blocks from their Grove Street home.

Professor M. MacNeille Dixon at the University of Glasgow wrote in February 1917 telling Graham that his name had been given to her as one who was sympathetic to the cause of the Allies and the principles for which they were fighting. Dixon may have been premature in approaching Stokes, but it would not be long before he would publicly announce his hostility to the neutralist position. If a rumor of his change in attitude had reached Glasgow, there must already have been some talk.[13]

On March 17 Rose ended any speculation that might have existed about her position. She sent her letter of resignation from the Women's Peace party to her "Dear Friends" in the party. She must have sent it to the papers even sooner, for it was in the next morning's press:

> Through long and earnest seeking of light I have come to the attitude which was not my attitude at the outbreak of the war . . . I love peace but I am not a pacifist. I would serve my country but I am not a patriot. My love of peace does not blind me to the lessons of history, nor could it—though I have not the spirit we call patriotism—turn my back on a people in the throes of a conflict and refuse to help

during a state of general suffering. I seek for this country as for the world the highest good and consider it essential to support peace or conflict as means best for the world's progress toward unity.

If the United States enters the war I would regard it as the perfectly natural result of causes being inherent and deep-rooted in the world-wide competitive system. This system no man or nation is responsible for. In the long, slow plan of human society we have moved from less to more desirable systems. We have not yet come to the best. If through our common misfortune of not being born after the arrival of the "best" we find ourselves still impaled in violent struggle it seems to me as futile and unscientific to inveigh against it as it would be to scold an earthquake.

I would fight or serve if called upon and would recognize myself to be fighting or serving not for national glory or for those petty spheres of influence which our loudest voiced patriots would perhaps be definitely seeking through the war, but as an infinitessimal part of a great instrument in use since the beginning of history for the perfecting of human unity and human freedom.[14]

Her letter of resignation, written to the Women's Peace party about three weeks before the United States joined the Allies in the war, was no doubt the expression of a strongly felt belief. It may also have been the product of exposure to the discussions of the "millionaire socialists" in her own living room, which resulted in the Kruesi-Stokes manifesto.

This manifesto was drafted by Graham Stokes and Walter E. Kruesi, with some help from William English Walling, and was issued privately on March 10. It was published as "A Socialist Protest" in the *New York Call* on March 24, with the signatures, in addition to those of the three drafters, of Charlotte Perkins Gilman, Charles Edward Russell, Charlotte Kimball Kruesi, Leroy Scott, and Robert Bruere. The address 88 Grove Street headed the letter.

The manifesto criticized the SP's antiwar position. After ten ringing paragraphs, it concluded: "To refuse to resist international crime is to be unworthy of the name Socialist. It is our present duty to the cause of internationalism to support our government in international law and order which are essential alike to Socialism and to civilization."

It was one of many high-minded statements that proliferated among the earnest prowar socialists of this period. Unlike Rose's statement, it made no reference to the "loudest voiced patriots," "national glory," or "spheres of influence." The signers of the "Socialist Protest" were doing their duty "to the cause of Internationalism."

A student of those wealthy intellectuals counted sixteen millionaire socialists (who were called by some irreverent contemporaries the "rebel rich"). Only two of this unstructured group eventually turned against the war and found a place for themselves in leftist politics. They were Rose Pastor Stokes and William Bross Lloyd.[15]

Whatever the subjective motivations of the affluent socialists in support of the Allies, the hard fact was that the United States entered the war to protect Wall Street's major investment in the Anglo-French-Russian cause. It feared a powerful German empire and was confident it could handle a weakened British one. On April 6, 1917, three weeks after the revolution in Russia—and seven months before the next one—the United States declared war against Germany.

The Socialists in March had set an emergency convention to meet in St. Louis on April 7. This proved to be the day after a majority of the U.S. Congress voted for the war. There were 193 delegates. A War and Militarism Committee of fifteen, with Kate Richards O'Hare its elected chairperson, spent five days holding hearings and preparing reports. It was soon apparent that the great majority of the delegates were strongly opposed to the war for a variety of reasons: "Many delegates held that the party should oppose every war; others held that the party should oppose every imperialist war. . . . Still others held that the party should oppose the war as one of aggression but that it should support it should the United States be involved."[16]

The resolutions committee finally defined three basic positions. One of these, drafted by Spargo, declared that now that the war had come, the Socialists were duty-bound to help the United States and its allies win as speedily as possible. This position received 5 votes. A second resolution, presented by Louis Boudin, condemned the war but omitted any program for fighting against it. This limp document received 31 votes. The majority resolution, which received 140 votes, was drafted by the centrist Hillquit and the left-winger Charles Ruthenberg. It called on the workers of all countries to oppose their governments in the war and stated that the war was not being fought to destroy militarism or to preserve democracy. A seven-point program of action was proposed in opposition to the war.

The convention was required to submit the resolutions to a referendum of the party membership. Boudin's resolution was considered too like the majority one and was not submitted. In the referendum the majority resolution received 21,000 votes. Spargo's got 350. The Socialist party thus committed itself to "continuous, active and public opposition to the war, through demonstrations, mass petitions, and all other means within our power."[17]

The results of the referendum on the antiwar proclamation were not published until the beginning of July. Rose and Graham Stokes were then members of the Stamford local of the Socialist party. On July 9 they addressed a letter to their "Comrades":

> A majority of the votes cast in the referendum on the reports on military affairs and preparedness, having favored the so-called Majority Report which has thus been adopted as an authoritative expression of the position of the Socialist Party, and many declarations in that report being, in our judgment, unwise, undemocratic and intolerable, we hereby regretfully tender our resignations from the Socialist Party.
>
> We withdraw not because we have ceased to be Socialists, but because we have lost faith in the Socialist Party as an effective instrument for advancing the Socialist cause. We retain our faith in Socialism unimpaired, but we believe that under present conditions we can render more effective service in the movement, outside the Socialist Party than in it. . . .
>
> We believe that sincere advocates of a just and lasting peace should now press every nerve to overcome the Prussian war machine, which supports autocracy and reaction everywhere, and devastates insofar as it is able, all that it cannot control.
>
> Socialists talk much of their belief in "world-citizenship." Let them now rally as world-citizens in defense of the threatened democracies of the world. To withhold their aid in such a crisis, is in our opinion to betray the interest of the working class whose cause can triumph only in proportion as democracy is made secure.
>
> Sincerely hoping that many friendships that we have formed in the Socialist Party will endure even though party bonds are now severed.[18]

The pious hope that friendships made in the party would survive their severance from it was not fated to be realized. Fierce hostility often characterized relations between those who left the party and the great majority who stayed in. One after another the Stokeses' circle of Socialist friends left the party—Walling, Spargo, A. M. Simons, Upton Sinclair, Gustavus Myers, Charlotte Perkins Gilman—and almost all used fierce language against their former comrades. An exception was Upton Sinclair, who defended the rights of those who stayed in to oppose the war.

Leroy Scott soon told Graham, "For a long time I have been sick of the Socialist Party." Charles E. Russell wrote, "I am not willing to be connected with an organization that labels itself Socialist."[19]

Eugene Victor Debs, however, remained a staunch antiwar Socialist. On July 22, 1916, Rose had written to him from Caritas:

> Dear, dear Comrade Gene! It was especially kind and sweet in you to send me greetings on the eighteenth [her birthday and wedding anniversary] and I thank you warmly for remembering or noticing the accident.
>
> One forgets birthdays, these terrible times—remembering days of world-wide death and the moaning of the women, who have lost. But sometimes, perhaps, it is well to remember, remembering the struggle to which we are born—and dedicated vow anew our allegiance to the cause of the People. Great leader of that cause, loving greetings to you, from Rose Pastor Stokes.[20]

"Knowing Rose Pastor Stokes's sincerity," wrote a biographer of Debs, "and her unflagging devotion to the workers' welfare, he realized that her support of the war sprang from her belief that it was, in all truth, a war for democracy."[21]

Though Rose and Graham waited until July to resign formally from the SP, they did hide their disagreement with the party in the months following the St. Louis convention. On May 13 they sent a cable to the European Socialists demanding the overthrow of the kaiser as essential to peace. In May Graham threatened to resign from the party if it refused to stop its opposition to the draft. Both he and Rose volunteered to assist the New York State Military Census in June. The Woman's Section of the Navy League thanked Rose for her $10 donation.

During the summer of 1917 the Stokeses, together with Spargo, Walling, Russell, and Hunter, planned a new "Socialist" organization, the Social Democratic League of America. Graham announced on July 12 that a new socialist organization would be formed, "probably in September in response to a nationwide demand for a Socialist Party which at the same time puts America first." The "nationwide demand" was never registered. During its short life span the league devoted itself principally to prowar propaganda.[22]

The league joined with remnants of the Progressive party, the Prohibition party, and some woman suffrage supporters and, in October, met in conference in Chicago to form the National party. With the support of Charles A. Beard, A. M. Simons, and Frederick Howe, it adopted a progressive but nonsocialist platform. This party died almost aborning, and the Social Democratic League never attracted followers to its group of leaders. In a desperate outreach on April 5, 1919, Graham Stokes appealed to John D. Rockefeller, Jr., for help.

Though the Socialist party suffered the defection of most of its affluent intellectual stratum, it did not lose more than 750 members following adoption of the St. Louis Proclamation. In 1917 its membership held steady and its vote-pulling power increased. Morris Hillquit got almost 150,000 votes in New York running for mayor, four times the 1912 score for the party. In 1918 the party increased its membership slightly, but its effectiveness was curbed by the ruthless repression of the government, the suppression of its press by postal authorities, the vigilante actions of civilian groups, and the weakness shown by some Socialists who had been elected to public office.

Some of the upper-class former Socialists were vicious to their former comrades and to others whose commitment to the war was less than total. A. M. Simons accused Victor Berger of accepting subsidies from German agents to slant his *Milwaukee Leader* in favor of Germany. Walling was so savage in charging pro-Germanism to the Socialists in the conservative newspaper at Greenwich, Connecticut, his hometown, that the editor of the little journal labeled the charges as "exaggerated." Spargo was writing pamphlets accusing the Socialists of pro-Germanism.[23]

Graham Stokes, soon to be fitted handsomely into a National Guard uniform as a member of a Coast Artillery unit, wrote hysterically to Vice-President Thomas Marshall and House Speaker Champ Clark urging investigation of possibly treacherous activities by Senator Robert M. La Follette and two other senators and three congressmen. He suspected them of treason; he demanded immediate trial; and "if any are guilty let the guilty be shot at once without an hour's delay."[24] Graham's brother-in-law, Rose's youngest brother, Bernard, was, like Graham, in uniform by

November 11, 1917. On that day he arrived at the U.S. Naval Training Station in Newport, Rhode Island. A month later he was assigned to the battleship *Utah.*

Graham's intransigent position on the war led him into a vindictive spirit, a harsh, brutal attitude toward those who did not agree with him. Rose's tenure as a patriot, however, turned out to be brief.

In November 1917 she published "A Confession" in the *Century* magazine, acknowledging that, for the first time in her twenty-seven years in America, she was indeed "an American." But by the time this claim appeared in print she had already begun to change her mind about the war, which she now criticized, and about the Socialist party, to which she was ready to return.

Her husband never experienced such a reversal. Rather, his history, once he had rebuffed Henry Ford in 1915, was one of a steady movement to the Right. On November 23, 1917, Graham sent his letter of resignation, as both president and member, to the Intercollegiate Socialist Society, which he had helped to found in 1905. His reasons were principally that the ISS did not take a stand against the SP antiwar position and that it had invited Morris Hillquit to address its convention.

Harry W. Laidler replied to Graham Stokes five days later in a seven-page, single-spaced letter deploring Graham's resignation and taking issue with the reasons he had given:

> I think that from the standpoint of democracy and freedom, it is dangerous for an educational organization like ours to begin to boycott thoughtful speakers because they do not represent the point of view of the President of the United States. . . .
>
> Personally I cannot but feel that it is not at all inconsistent with one who wishes to back the President in this war crisis to give Mr. Hillquit an opportunity to be heard at the convention. It seems to me that such a course is thoroughly in accord with the spirit exemplified by President Wilson in his most democratic utterances.[25]

Rose's article in the *Century* sounded as if she had passed a point beyond which there was no return:

> America as I now conceive her, stands among the free nations of the world, eager to follow where Liberty beckons, eager to fight for a

newer, better world, burning to strike a blow at Injustice and Oppression wherever these may rear their heads, whether they appear in the guise of German autocracy abroad or special privilege at home. . . .

No narrow nationalism could have moved me one inch from my old position. It was only when our President, and the American people behind, stood where the Socialist Party of this country should have stood that I became an American.[26]

Even as the November *Century* appeared Rose began to turn away from the patriotism expressed in the article. She was thereby moving slowly into a confrontational position with Graham. The marriage would last, legally, for almost eight more years, but as their political views continued to diverge, the marriage became increasingly unstable. Patrick Renshaw, writing on the marriage, says of Rose Stokes: "Never without fervent admirers, she almost certainly began embarking on minor love affairs, which probably continued for the rest of her marriage to Graham." We find this speculation too conditional—"almost certainly," "probably continued," "minor love affairs"—and unsubstantiated. As documentation Renshaw invites us to "see, for example, the letter from an unknown man, October 31, 1913 . . . proposing an assignation in New York. Rose cut off the signature . . . but the letter was on City Club notepaper, indicating that the man was probably an artist or writer with socialist leanings."[27]

This is the only example cited by Renshaw because there is no other evidence available. And as evidence this letter fails entirely. The salutation is: "My dear Rose of the World." The signature, which, indeed, is not cut off, is "Rose." It is not a letter "from an unknown man" but one from her old friend Rose Strunsky, who often addressed Rose Stokes in this way. It was an affectionate letter full of gossip and bright chatter from a friend eager to see Rose, trying to arrange such a visit between caring for her daughter, attending meetings, being interviewed by editors, and being very busy on a run into the city from her residence in suburban Cedarhurst.[28]

Renshaw makes better use of an entry in Rose's diary dated March 27, 1915 (which he erroneously dates 1914):

Today marked a deep change in me—mentally—spiritually—in my attitude toward G. He *accused me of loafing*. Blurted it out quite innocently—because I stayed in bed late in the morning. I returned on the

22nd after a week's speaking tour in Penn. and Ohio, with a bad bronchitis and a stay-in-bed temperature. I didn't give up the rest of the
tour (tho I had to speak one night with a temperature of 102°) until I
completely lost my voice. On top of my bronchitis attack the chronic
infection in my jaw became active again and I have to have it lanced.
The two have all week kept me too below par to be very active and I
have merely been trying to get stronger and reduce my temperature
to normal. "Loafing"! I didn't reply. What's the good? But it put the
iron into my soul, and this time I feel it's there to stay.

The terrible loneliness of one's soul in such moments! Only those
who suffer it can understand.[29]

It may have been a minor incident. The marriage wore on for ten more
years, but after 1918 it would slowly get worse despite Graham's earnest but
clumsy attempts to control it.

More than ten years later, Joanna Cooke recalled to Rose a 1915 (1916?)
episode when she had stayed the night at the Stokes home on her return
from Europe. As Cooke recalled, it was the time of the strike of the transit
workers—one of the greatest battles in New York's labor history:

Graham was furious against the men—I saw it was no use to speak;
you said very little; he was peremptory and dogmatic. I was at his
table and I could not begin a quarrel. I felt savage—I wanted to lick
my knife or turn down my plate or pour my coffee into the saucer. I
never even glanced at you and I know you did not dream of my real
feelings. From that time I divined him very well and although you did
not seem to be unhappy, I felt a dreadful fear that unhappiness was on
the way.[30]

Joanna Cooke must certainly have remembered well the day she returned in 1915 from western Europe in wartime. But the transit strike she
recalls actually took place in the summer of 1916. She evidently telescoped
two incidents. Graham's mood as she describes it is perfectly plausible—
his arrogance and dogmatism had been evident on previous occasions.
And by the summer of 1916 he was becoming seriously alienated by Socialist party doctrine. In the transit strike the party gave total support to
the harshly driven workers of the transit monopoly. Only the *Call* among
the numerous daily papers in the city fully endorsed the strike. It even

issued a special evening edition each day to facilitate coverage of this great struggle.

In the long run, the Pastor-Stokes marriage was not destroyed by "minor love affairs." It was eroded by political differences that became acute after 1918.

XI

"Espionage"

The year 1918 was a climactic one in the life of Rose Pastor Stokes. She found new fame and notoriety. Her politics moved increasingly to the Left, and her marriage began to erode beyond the possibility of remedy. She was confronted with a ten-year prison sentence following conviction on a felony charge. It was also to be her last full year on the enchanting Caritas Island.

In January Rose announced that her attitude toward the war and the Socialist party, to which she sought readmission, had changed. These changes stirred the malice of her husband's Uncle Will and doomed Rose to years of persecution by a vengeful government. William Earl Dodge Stokes had shown his antagonism to Rose's political activity in 1912, at the time of the waiters' strike, when he threatened to devise a lifetime trusteeship over Graham's fortune if Rose's strike activity was not curbed. In 1917 he had published his racist eugenic tract *The Right to Be Well Born*, subtitled *Horse Breeding in Its Relation to Eugenics*. It includes the following observations:

> It is well known that the Jews are a thrifty people. They are known for their ability to accumulate money. A thoroughbred horse has no greater tendency to run than has a Jew to succeed in the business of accumulating money. (p. 175)

> [On the foreign-born:] We cannot forever absorb this influx of the scum of the earth, this off-scouring diseased, imported blood with its evil customs. (p. 74)

> Why do we not breed human beings to endure hard work and do it with ease without straining, just as we breed the dray horse. . . ? This

will do away with the crying need of labor unions, for walking delegates, business agents and bomb throwers to protect the weaklings of their number.[1]

William Stokes became a volunteer informant to government investigative agencies and caused a surveillance of Rose's activities that culminated in her trial under the so-called Espionage Act.

The act was passed by Congress on June 15, 1917. It bore the title "An Act to punish acts of interference with the foreign relations, the neutrality, and the foreign commerce of the United States, to punish espionage and better to enforce the criminal laws of the United States and for other purposes." Its scope was so broad that it is curious that it was given the short title "Espionage Act." To be charged under this act—no matter how petty the alleged offense—was to be placed instantly under a cloud, which, in wartime, was almost as sinister as being charged with treason.

The government lost little time in testing the strength of the Espionage Act. The indomitable Kate Richards O'Hare, an editor of the lively socialist organ the *National Ripsaw*, based in St. Louis, was on a barnstorming tour of the rural West delivering—scores of times—her speech "Socialism and the War." She was arrested following a speech at Bowman, North Dakota, on July 17, 1917, about a month after passage of the act. O'Hare received a five-year sentence, which she began serving after the war was over, on April 15, 1919. She served her time in Missouri State Prison. On May 29, 1920, President Wilson grudgingly commuted her sentence to time served. (Calvin Coolidge later granted her a pardon.) When O'Hare was released, Rose Pastor Stokes was out on bail, still threatened with ten years in Missouri State Prison, while she waited for due process.[2]

"Justice" was more temperately meted out to four socialist defendants found guilty by a federal jury at Albany, New York, on November 17, 1917. They had distributed an antiwar tract, *The Price We Pay*, by Irwin St. John Tucker, issued by the Socialist party national office. The offending four received sentences ranging from four months in jail and $50 fine to one year and $600. Dennis Lucey, the prosecutor, reported to the attorney general: "I expressly and publicly requested the court to make the sentences imposed merely impressive enough to make it undesirable to be a martyr, but at the same time light enough so that no one would feel that there was any element of vengeance in the prosecution."[3]

No such consideration had been shown to Kate O'Hare. And when

Rose Pastor Stokes's turn came, the "element of vengeance" was clearly present. When Rose wrote her "Confession," for the November 1917 issue of the *Century,* she had gone as far to the Right as she would ever go. She still regarded herself as a socialist, but she was passionately devoted to Wilson and his war "to make the world safe for democracy": "I wanted peace but came blindly to stand for war. It was a war for markets, but I began to see it wrongly as a 'war for democracy.' It was a war of European and American capitalism for control of oil in the East. I came to see it distortedly as something beside—as a war of liberation—a war that would precipitate the Social Revolution."[4]

By January 1918 she had changed her mind. She no longer had faith in the country's war aims; she no longer considered the Socialist party an impediment to the struggle for world democracy. Although she did not consider the party's position on the war entirely correct, she did believe that the best hope of bringing the war to a conclusion with a democratic peace lay in the party. At any rate, she saw no future for socialism in James Graham Phelps Stokes's stillborn National party, and she had come to the conviction that the Socialist party of America was indeed the vehicle through which to work for her democratic, socialist, and anti-imperialist ideals. At the same time, she revived her membership in the ISS.

We can only surmise how Rose went through the process of turning from an ardent patriot to a stern critic of the Wilson administration's war policy. One safe guess is the obvious one: that an event that took place far from Greenwich Village, the Bolshevik Revolution, on November 7, 1917, caused her to rethink her orientation. The majority of those who had remained in the Socialist party after the April 1917 convention hailed the revolution, at least at first.

Rose Pastor Stokes's return to the party was not part of a great movement of former members back to the ranks. The return of Rose Pastor Stokes was announced in the *New York Call.* Among the less radical, ranging from Woodrow Wilson to James Graham Phelps Stokes, the new Soviet Russian government was as unwelcome as the plague. But those who had long hoped for a socialist breakthrough somewhere—anywhere—in the world greeted the earth-shaking event in Russia as a new dawn. Eugene Debs, of the party's left wing, proclaimed himself a Bolshevik from the crown of his head to the soles of his feet, and Victor Berger, the right-wing leader, saw in it a political and industrial democracy.

One bit of evidence shows that Rose Pastor Stokes's change of mind antedated the Bolshevik Revolution. Before the ink was dry on the issue of the *Century* that carried her "Confession," she announced in the press her last-minute support of Morris Hillquit, the Socialist party candidate for mayor of New York. Hillquit, generally considered a centrist in the party, was campaigning on an antiwar platform.[5]

Graham informed Rose that Samuel Gompers, the opportunist president of the AFL, was moving closer to socialism. She was surrounded by "reactionary AFL officers, bourgeois reformers, birth control advocates who offered birth control . . . as a panacea for all the evils of wage slavery, liberal dinner clubbers, petty-bourgeois anarchists, government officials." She was used in prowar publicity. Madame Alice Blaché based a scenario, "The Best Loved Rich Woman in the World," on her. A film company made a test reel, declared her a Sarah Bernhardt, and offered her a role in "Sacred Motherhood." Wealthy townswomen drew her into their homes because of her interest in music. Margaret Wilson, the president's daughter, invited her to dine with her and her father at the White House. She was surrounded by Stokeses waving the flag—even the Union Jack of Great Britain. The Baroness Halkett, Graham's sister, professed love for the Labour party. The sudden friendliness of the baroness seemed to push Rose over the line, convincing her that she had joined her class enemies.[6] Rose's unfinished autobiography indicates that she finally realized her working-class instincts were in collision with the political atmosphere within which she lived.

Even before the Bolshevik Revolution, the Bureau of Investigation (BI) put socialists under surveillance. A BI agent covered a speech by Socialist party candidate Morris Hillquit on October 31, 1917, and reported the next day to the attorney general that "a stenographer was engaged and instructed to attend the meeting. . . . It was determined that the only practicable scheme was to have him occupy a seat with the newspapermen. . . . In order to accomplish this it was essential to take into our confidence several newspaper reporters who were well known to this office." This instance of enlisting the working press in intelligence activity may not have been the first of its kind. It certainly was not the last.[7]

W. E. D. Stokes is described in a marginal note as "informant" (a soft synonym for *informer*) in a communication to A. Bruce Bielaski, chief of the Bureau of Investigation, sent from the State Department early in February 1918. It acknowledges receipt of information in January from Stokes "with reference to Rose Pastor regarding Bolsheviki activities in this country and possible German interest therein."[8]

Rose Pastor Stokes, who at this stage was either unaware of or indifferent to the fact that she was the subject of Department of Justice inquiry, continued with her public speaking. This was always her principal activity in the socialist movement and sometimes a source of income. She was aware that some of those who had booked her before the public declaration of her return to the Socialist fold might not still want her as a speaker. She wrote to these groups to give them a chance to cancel. Annette Moore, who chaired the Program Committee of the Kansas City Woman's Dining Club, waived the opportunity Rose offered to cancel, as did the Philadelphia Club of Advertising Women, which she was to address on Lincoln's Birthday. The club president, Anna M. Kelly, reassured her on February 1: "We women . . . know you and know your work, and on that basis, alone, you will honor us, by being our guest of honor . . . and we will be very glad indeed if your splendid husband has the time to come with you; if not, please say to him that we will take good care of you."[9]

In January public perception of Rose's attitude toward the war was still so ambiguous that L. Ames Brown, director of the Division of Publicity of the Committee on Public Information, had hopes of engaging her in his division's propaganda activities. The Committee on Public Information was also known as the Creel Committee for its chairman, George Creel. Creel had made a reputation as a crusading liberal before the war and was named by Woodrow Wilson to the propaganda (and censorship) agency. The Creel Committee's zeal for propaganda often exceeded its zeal for the truth.

On January 7, 1918, Rose wrote to Brown stating her reasons for declining his invitation to "prepare some rallying patriotic piece" for him. They had to do with her "convictions regarding imperialism and freedom of speech." Nevertheless, on January 10 Brown wrote again, saying that he was "most emphatically unwilling to give up a hope of getting a contribution to our war propaganda from you." On the same day, the Eighteenth and Twentieth Assembly District organization of the Socialist party invited Rose to speak at one of its meetings. Rose told her old comrades, "I want to come back because I see no hope of functioning 100 percent for the common people except through the Socialist Party. . . . The crisis created by the [April] St. Louis [antiwar] resolution is past, and the present immediate danger is imperialist peace which, I believe, only a unified and strengthened international Socialist movement can prevent." At about the same time she resumed her support of the ISS and Laidler told her, "We are delighted to have you again with us."[10]

Early in February, speaking to the Brownsville Labor Lyceum in Brooklyn, Rose said that she finally had lost her faith in the policy of the government because, after first supporting Russian democracy, it turned its back on the Bolsheviks, who, she thought, were most likely to bring permanent peace.

On February 17, 1918, Rose addressed a meeting in Baltimore. According to an agent's report to the Justice Department, she said "that President Wilson was a tool in the hands of capital, she did not believe in conscription, that the United States did not have the right to draft men into service and send them overseas to fight against their wishes, that there is very little difference in the United States and Germany as to reasons for engaging in world war and that the United States was wrong in entering the war."[11] In this report she does not call for unilateral withdrawal of the United States from the conflict. Rather, it was her belief that, now that battle had been joined, Germany must be defeated. She hoped that the resulting order would be democratic and prolabor and that the socialists, as in Russia, could have some influence. When Rose was arrested a month later it was for language far milder than that reported above.

Meanwhile, Uncle Will was tightening the noose around his despised niece, whose foreign and Jewish origin he could not forgive and whose socialism he could not tolerate. On March 4, 1918, from the grand Hotel Ansonia, assuming the role of adviser on domestic peril, counselor on foreign policy, and, not least, fingerman against the hapless Rose, he wrote to Charles Warren, assistant attorney general, in Washington:

> You will find that the suggestions and warnings, which I have made, will sooner or later begin to develop, and that I have written in the true interest of our country, and the Administration. . . . Mr. Warren this government needs practical, intelligent men, and it needs the standing up of German spies against the wall and shooting them. We will never lick the Huns with kind words, candy and ice cream.
>
> Now, my nephew, J. Graham Stokes, the ex-Socialist leader, married Rose Pastor. He is as fine a young man as ever lived, but he is married to a woman who was born under a cloud with a grievance, and she is dangerous. You will find him so, and I have tried to break

him away from the influence of this misalliance, and I think to a certain extent I have succeeded. He tells me he knows nothing about what is going on in the so-called Orthodox Socialist party which, as you know, is today a party of Anarchists, Bolshevikis and I.W.W.'s. That President Wilson, Frank Polk and others of authority have not been shot is a miracle. We have let into this country a dangerous, rotten lot, by our free methods of emigration. . . .

In the Village of Greenwich, New York City, there took place a meeting yesterday afternoon, and while I do not know what it was for, I have serious reasons to believe that it forbade no good to this country or to our Allies. I know that the Bolsheviki and Hun elements in this city are trying to arrange for a peace conference. . . . Do not fall into the trap.

The movement of the country to allow Japan and China to intervene in Siberia is a good move. . . . It will give China the chance to get back her property which Russia took away, and it will give Japan a chance to expand where she wants to expand, but all this time, realize that the Grand Duke Nicholas, who is the only man in Russia that holds control over the soldiers and the best element in Russia, is sitting still and sawing wood . . . I know him personally and I know he is a grand man and wants the freedom of Russia, and he would make a great Dictator for Russia, and I believe that he is the only man in Russia who could save the day.[12]

Uncle Will evidently saw no contradiction in recommending his friend the Grand Duke as a dictator to bring freedom to Russia, nor was he squeamish about plotting the entrapment of a favorite nephew's wife.

The site of that entrapment was the State Dinner of the Woman's Dining Club of Kansas City, Missouri. A woman named Reinike was president of the club. Presidents held office for one year. As Annette Moore later told Rose, Reinike "was anxious for her year as president . . . to rank first." Reinike had been an ardent admirer of Rose Pastor Stokes for years. When she learned from the press that Rose had left the Socialist party she decided that if she could have Rose speak at the State Dinner, the culminating event of her tenure, her success was assured. "And it would have been too, had it not been for some jealous old 'cats' that were just watching for a chance to pounce upon her administration," Annette Moore told Rose after the indictment. According to Moore, the jealous, anti-Reinike group "deliberately misconstrued" Rose's speech "and imagined a lot of things beside."[13]

In January Rose had notified Reinike that she had rejoined the Socialist party and offered her the option to cancel the engagement. Reinike no doubt hoped that the charismatic Stokes would give a presentation that would make her administration outstanding and memorable. Indeed it did.

Rose spoke at the Kansas City dinner on March 17. The next day the *New York Times,* which would not ordinarily cover such an event, reported:

> Rose Pastor Stokes, in a talk which astonished members and guests of the Woman's Dining Club at the Hotel Baltimore . . . completely reversed her unqualified support of America's entrance into the world war by asserting she had returned to the principles of "pure socialism."
>
> She called our present system "industrial serfdom."
>
> She said: "Some of you may be disappointed by what you hear from me tonight. . . I have turned to the views I formerly held.
>
> "Surely there is not a capitalist or a well-informed person in the world today who believes that this war is being fought to make the world safe for democracy. It is being fought to make the world safe for capitalism." She was hissed by some and some of the audience walked out.[14]

The *Kansas City Star* gave a somewhat fuller account of the dinner. Rose felt some lines reversed the meaning of what she had said. Before leaving Kansas City to fill other speaking engagements, she wrote a letter of correction to the *Star*: "I am quoted as having said: 'I believe the government of the United States should have the unqualified support of every citizen in its war administration.' I made no such statement. I believe no such thing. No government which is for the profiteers can be also for the people, and I am for the people, while the government is for the profiteers."[15]

Rose proceeded with her tour, speaking at Neosha, Missouri, on March 20 and going on to Springfield, where she found the theater she had been booked to speak in locked against her. When she attempted to make a speech to the large crowd that had gathered in front of the theater, she was prevented by the chief of police.

"We want no poison spreaders in this city," he told her.

"I will not speak about the war," Rose assured him. "I will discuss economics—about bread and butter problems: quietly and sanely. And I want you to stay right here and arrest me." "No, you have no permit. But I would like to be chivalrous to a lady." "Never mind that!" said Rose. "You can leave that out. We are men and women here. You can just give me my rights and never mind your courtesy."[16] He arrested her. The case was dismissed the next day when she left Springfield forfeiting $100 bail.

On March 22 Rose spoke at the Opera House in Willow Springs, and the next day she was arrested there by federal officers in the lobby of the Horton Hotel, charged under the Espionage Act for her letter to the *Kansas City Star*. On the twenty-fourth she was brought to Kansas City and held in the matron's quarters at police headquarters. She complained to the press that this was "a pleasant sitting room with barred doors and windows" and told the U.S. marshal that she "wanted to be held in the worst part of the jail."[17]

Graham Stokes learned of her arrest at Willow Springs through the newspaper accounts, and he wired his wife: "Dreadfully troubled. Don't arouse people against cause of social democracy. Awful reports in papers here. Graham." This shrill communication drew an acerbic reply from Rose: "Your message misdirected dear; send it to jingo capitalist press. Am under arrest; leave this afternoon for Kansas City. Break news gently to Anna [the housekeeper], Boy [Vladimir Resnikoff], Lily [a sister], Mother. Rose." This time Graham replied with a more sympathetic grasp of the situation: "Dreadfully, dreadfully sorry. Telegraph % Western Union at Union Station, Chicago. Advise where I can find you. Much love, Graham." The answer came back: "At the United States Marshal's office, Federal Building, Kansas City, Monday. Rose."

A BI agent promptly obtained copies of these telegrams from the Western Union operator at Willow Springs, disregarding the existing privacy statutes.[18]

The U.S. marshal, Purcell, said that while she was a prisoner Rose Pastor Stokes said, among other things, that she did not believe newspaper reports about the Russian Revolution. She thought there were no more casualties there than in some American strikes. When Purcell asked, "Is it your point to cause a revolution in this country?" she said, "Yes, that's my point." And when the shocked marshal exclaimed: "Then you want people to kill each other off like they are doing in Russia," she said, "they are not doing that to each other in Russia despite what is reported in the papers."[19]

But the rhetoric and the repartee were not relevant to the issue that was to come before the court. In fact, the question of whether Rose had violated the Espionage Act in Kansas City had little to do with anything she said while there or anything she said in the following few days of speaking in public and fencing in private with local and federal police. The entire case against her depended ultimately on the meaning placed by the government on her letter to the *Kansas City Star,* and not on the entire letter but on the brief statement: "No government which is for the profiteers can also be for the people, and I am for the people, while the government is for the profiteers." When the case came to trial, the government reduced the question to little more than a semantic quibble over the meaning of the offending sentence—with a ten-year sentence for the loser of the argument.

Meanwhile Rose was out on $10,000 bail arranged for by Graham, who had engaged a local law firm to handle the preliminary phase of legal defense. Graham told the *Star* in an interview that his views on the war and those of his wife did not entirely agree. "I am profoundly convinced that the interest of world democracy and of American liberty require the prosecution of this war with the utmost vigor by the American people," Stokes told the interviewer. He had not heard his wife express disapproval of American participation in the war, but he added, "She has been fearful that the profiteers have gained so great influence over the government as to thwart its purposes." Nevertheless, according to the *Star* reporter, he made it plain that "he would stand behind his wife." Before leaving New York Graham had prepared a statement of about three hundred words on the difference between his own and his wife's viewpoints: "Mrs. Stokes had emphasized the danger to the democratic movement of the times that lies in governmental interference with the free expression of their views by honest and high-minded radicals. I share Mrs. Stokes's recognition of that danger, and yet I recognize the no-less-great danger to the democratic movement that lies at times in the utterances of honest, earnest and high-minded radicals."[20]

Rose said she was sorry her husband had taken "all the trouble to come to Kansas City." When asked, "Have you received many telegrams of sympathy?" she replied with typical spirit: "No, but I have received telegrams of congratulations."[21]

Congratulations were also received in another form when federal snoopers interviewed a young Mr. Lipscomb in Willow Springs. Lipscomb had been deputed by his father, Caleb, a businessman and socialist of Springfield, to accompany Rose on her train journey to Willow Springs. Young Lipscomb was enchanted by her. The agent reported to Washington that the young man thought "Mrs. Stokes was a wonderful woman and that he had learned more from Mrs. Stokes on the way from Springfield than he ever knew." An attorney, W. B. Wilkerson of Springfield, also thought she was "a wonderful woman." He told the BI man "that she was a very persuasive speaker, that he became very amused at the Chief of Police of Springfield in his little encounter with Mrs. Stokes and she showed the complete control of mind over matter; that the Chief was no match for Mrs. Stokes." In the speech she delivered at Willow Springs, Rose said: "I have never tried to get anyone to evade the draft law. . . . What I wanted and what every Socialist is trying to do is explain what may come of it, what may not." Her experience with the *Star* reinforced her conviction that as long as people believed "that the common press tells them the truth, just as long they will not learn the truth." Chief of Police Rathbone's statement to the federal agent showed moderation. Rose told him she "did not come to Springfield to arouse opposition to the war. . . . But I do say I am opposed to war on general principles. I believe we are all opposed to war; even the President and his advisors are opposed to war; the Chief of Police here I venture to say is opposed to war, so are Rockefeller and Morgan; I am opposed to everything that will mean profit for the wealthy few and suffering for the working many. I believe that this war has been dictated by the capitalist system."[22]

Meanwhile, back at the Ansonia Hotel, William Earl Dodge Stokes continued his campaign against Rose. On March 24, with his nephew and Rose off in Kansas City coping with the formalities of bail and arraignment, Uncle Will put in a call to 88 Grove Street. He then informed Charles Warren:

> From my conversation with Anna [Webb] the maid it was apparent that she had warned Rose Pastor Stokes that she was going to get in trouble with her IWW, Bolsheviki and socialist views and her ideas of doing away with the constitutional government of the United States and the introduction of her ideas of taking from everyone everything they had and dividing it among the laborers of the country. But she

and her friends are worried that she will get herself into trouble by her remarks in regard to the government and that Anna is prepared to tell everything and that she [Rose] has in her possession in her apartment important information in connection with Bolsheviki, IWW, socialistic and anarchistic subjects and that they are afraid that your department [Justice] will order a search and examination of her apartment.[23]

It was not long before such a search was carried out.

Exacerbating the hysteria, the *Kansas City Post,* journalistic rival of the *Star,* urged the attorney general to prosecute the *Star* for printing Rose's letter. The *Post* also sharply attacked the U.S. district attorney for not moving against the *Star.* And in June, when Vice-President Thomas Riley Marshall launched a drive for a third term for Woodrow Wilson, he referred to the *Star* as the paper that had "published the Rose Pastor Stokes letter and other seditious documents."[24]

Some ten days before the grand jury brought in a three-count indictment, W. E. D. Stokes came up with an idea which on April 13 he submitted to the assistant attorney general in Washington. Uncle Will reported that he

> had a talk this morning with my nephew, J. Graham Stokes, who is the husband of Rose Pastor, as a result of a conversation I had with Rose Pastor yesterday. She seems to be conscientious in her views of upsetting the government of this country, in fact the government of the whole world with her Bolsheviki and socialistic theories and ideas.
>
> She states that she is crazy to get a passport to leave this country. Her husband says of course he could not consent to such a thing as that. He thinks she has gotten a good scare, and the U.S. Grand Jury will not indict her for her remarks in Kansas City. She, on the other hand seems to covet jail or anything else for the good of her cause and theories.
>
> Now, in case the Grand Jury at Kansas City indict her, do you suppose an alternative could be given, that she could be given a passport to go to Russia, the country from which she came, and let the matter end there?[25]

This letter suggests that Rose could only have been baiting her uncle-in-law. The idea of running away was alien to her, and she would no more have discussed her "Bolsheviki and socialistic" ideas seriously with Uncle Will than she would with her sister-in-law the Baroness Halkett.

The case of *United States* v. *Rose Pastor Stokes* on a charge of violating the Espionage Act began on May 20 and proceeded without surprises. Judge A. S. Van Valkenburgh made it clear that it was not necessary for the government prosecutor to prove any physical act of obstruction. Simply expressing opposition to policies of the government made one subject to prosecution.

Character witnesses such as Florence Kelley counted for nothing against such a simplistic reading of the Espionage Act. And the defendant's claim that she had merely criticized the administration could not prevail against the prosecution's argument that she had subverted the abstract concept of the government, as provided for in the Constitution.

Rose took the stand in her own defense and delivered essentially the same speech she had made at the Woman's Dining Club two months before. She also gave an account of her early life in Russia, London, Cleveland, and, in 1903 to 1905, New York. She said her husband never was a millionaire, although his family was wealthy. When she was asked to explain how she became a socialist her reply was in the grand tradition of revolutionary self-defense. She said: "For twelve years I was a cigarmaker in Cleveland. I was ill-nourished and poorly clad. I worked night as well as day to help piece out my family's existence. I never had anything I wanted. But the moment I left the working class and got into the leisure class . . . I had all the money, all the clothes, in a word, everything I wanted. I realized then conditions were unjust and not above criticism."[26]

It was a fine statement, and it has been widely quoted. But like Nathan Hale's statement that his only regret was that he had but one life to lose for his country, it had no effect on the outcome of her trial. Neither did other bits of testimony, as when she mentioned that her chief concern was that the war might not accomplish the democratic purposes for which America claimed to have entered it or that her husband was a member of the Ninth Coast Artillery of the New York National Guard. (The judge told Graham he was unfit to wear the uniform.)

"Do you believe in patriotism?" asked the prosecutor.

"I love all countries," said Rose.

And so, on the third day, she was convicted on all three counts of the indictment: attempting to cause insubordination, obstructing recruiting, and making false statements to impede the success of U.S. forces and to promote the success of its enemies. The next day, May 25, the *New York Times* in its leading editorial—more than a column of austere self-right-eousness—gloated and rejoiced at western states' intolerance of what it called "anti-Americanism." "Mrs. Rose Pastor Stokes had the misfortune to be tried by a Western jury. . . . It is probable that her unhappy experi-ence will teach our Bolsheviki and pro-Germans the advisability of confin-ing their anti-American utterances to New York, where juries are more amiable."[27]

In a letter to the *Times* a few days later, James Graham Stokes declared: "I stand and always have stood absolutely and unqualifiedly back of Presi-dent Wilson and this Government in the prosecution of this war. Mrs. Stokes also stands back of President Wilson in this way, notwithstanding widely publicized misrepresentations to the contrary, and she desires as I do, that the war be pushed with all possible vigor until the foundations of democracy are effectually secured."[28]

This was a fair, if imprecise, statement of the areas of agreement be-tween the Stokeses. But the unmentioned differences between them were to grow and become more undeniable and decisive than Graham's bland statement suggested. She opposed U.S. intervention in Russia; she wel-comed the beginning of people's power in Russia; she looked toward an anti-imperialist, democratic end to the war, with Socialist parties of the world helping to write the peace treaties. Graham wanted none of these things. The list of differences would grow until they became "friendly enemies" (Rose's phrase), until they lived separately under a single roof, until they lived separately. This process covered about seven years.

Senator William E. Borah got a letter from his friend Earl Wayland Brown of the magazine *Golden Trail*, asking him to have a talk with Rose Pastor Stokes: "I have always believed and believe now that she is true to the highest ideals of fundamental patriotism—even though she has been con-victed by a jury and sentenced by a judge for a technical violation of the espionage act. . . . Have a heart to heart talk with her. Am sure that if you do it will result in establishing between you a mutual understanding and esteem that will be lasting."[29]

No such meeting took place. Nevertheless, on May 31, 1918, William E. Borah, Republican from Idaho, in a speech to the Senate, said that Rose's conviction "was due partly to the fact that she stated that no government that is for the profiteers can also be for the people." He continued: "Nothing is truer than that statement. If the government of the United States possesses the facts as to the existence of these profiteers, and fails to prosecute, fails to deal with them, the Government itself is derelict and subject to the criticism of everybody who is for the people. And I am for the people where the Government is for the profiteers."[30]

But on June 1, the day after Borah's speech, an unblushing Judge Van Valkenburgh sentenced Rose to ten years' imprisonment in the Missouri State Penitentiary. She was continued on $10,000 bail pending appeal to the Circuit Court.

The conviction and the harsh sentence were not isolated events at the time but part of a pattern of abridgments of the Bill of Rights. On April 1, 1918, trial had started in Chicago of 101 IWW members charged with a conspiracy to obstruct the war. For five months the defendants were tried in a courtroom presided over with the most casual decorum by Judge Kennesaw Mountain Landis. (John Reed, covering the proceedings for the *Masses,* said Landis looked like "Andrew Jackson three years dead.")[31]

In three days on the stand Bill Haywood became the principal witness for the defense. In words curiously anticipating the famous speech of Martin Luther King, Jr., Haywood said he had a dream of a society in which there would no longer be a conflict between capitalists and wage workers and every man would have access to the land and its resources. But these were only a few of the million words presented to the jury in the five-month trial, and who was listening? An hour after the jury got the case, the verdict was brought in: the 101 Wobblies were guilty; 15 received sentences of twenty years; 33 got ten years; 35 got five years; and fines totaling more than $2.5 million were levied. Most of the convicted Wobblies spent many years in prison.

On the front of freedom of the press, as distinct from freedom of speech, the Department of Justice did suffer a defeat in its two 1918 attempts—the first in April, the second in September—to convict the editors of the *Masses.* Both prosecutions ended with hung juries. But this was exceptional; the government won almost all of its cases.

In Bisbee, Arizona, for daring to strike against the Phelps-Dodge copper interests, twelve hundred strikers and sympathizers in July 1917 were forced by vigilantes onto a cattle train and deported to New Mexico, kept in the desert for thirty-six hours without food or water, beaten, and held for three months in a federal stockade, then released without charges. It was all part of "a war to make the world safe for democracy."

The ten-year sentence of Rose Pastor Stokes drew mixed reactions. The *New York World* said the sentence would remind "other persons of Mrs. Stokes's opinion . . . that this is not the right season to spread disloyalty." The *Brooklyn Eagle* declared pacifists of the socialist school to be "public nuisances." The *Portland Oregonian* said the sentence showed the government was waging war against "treason and sedition." The *New York Tribune* carried the opinion of John Spargo, a former friend and comrade of the Stokeses, that the national interest was not served by ferocious prison sentences "while millionaire newspaper owners can in safety carry on an insidious attack upon our morale." And William English Walling declared that unless "a certain newspaper publisher" could be legally convicted, "all lesser offenders ought to go free." Most readers would have understood William Randolph Hearst to be the "certain newspaper publisher."[32]

Rose Pastor Stokes meanwhile bravely bore the burden of heavy bail and a sentence of ten years. Moral support came from friends, including some who did not agree with her political stance. In a dozen years of social and political agitation, Rose had won the loyalty of people from a wide band of the political spectrum. She especially appreciated the confidence expressed by her old friend and former employer Abraham Sarasohn, who wrote on behalf of himself and his wife, Belle: "Just a word of goodwill, a line expressive of confidence in you, in these trying days, from Belle and me. We who have known you for so many years, who appreciate your high ideals and lofty motives, your unselfish and self-sacrificing work for humanity, cannot conceive of your doing anything that is seditious or blameworthy."[33]

Rose replied immediately: "I am strong in the knowledge that all who know me, know that I have been mistried. . . . The one thing more than any other which drove me back into the SP was my fear of an early imperialist peace . . . I do not agree with some of the most quoted clauses in the St. Louis resolutions. . . . We do not need to agree on anything but principle to be members."[34]

To those who wrote to assure her of their continued friendship and love Rose offered explanations and assurances: "I have not for a moment attempted to interfere with the war, and the one thing more than any other which drove me back into the Socialist Party was my fear of an early imperialistic peace, that I am convinced was then in the air—the secret air of diplomacy." "Ten years is a long time, at my time of life, I shall come out an old woman. But if I find a young social-democracy, I know it will make me young again. Last week I heard from some one very close to the highest circles in the administration who said she was coming to tell me 'good' news but when I intimated that, whether in prison or out, I would have to, so far as I was able, give expression to the truth as I conceive it, she failed to show up. I could not of course accept 'personal favors' from Washington and be 'duly grateful.' I will not buy my liberty and pay the price of silence."[35]

Rose made her first speech following imposition of her ten-year sentence on July 9 at Webster Hall in Manhattan. She insisted that she intended to criticize the war aims of the government "if I have to go to jail for the rest of my life." The Department of Justice agent covering this event thought it important to inform his boss that "the audience last night was composed mostly of Jews."[36]

Ten days later she told a small audience in Brooklyn at the Brownsville Labor Lyceum that "the IWW [then in the fourth month of its five-month trial] were the most misunderstood class of workers in the country." She said: "I believed in this war because it was inevitable, but those great things the war stood for—freedom of speech and freedom of thought— have been removed, and hence the war is no longer worth fighting." Rose was becoming less restrained in her public statements despite her pending appeal.[37]

Olive Dargan had the fanciful idea of using influence to rescue Rose. She went to see an uncle of her late husband, Pegram. The uncle, a federal judge, was a friend of the attorney general. She returned, however, "touching no goal." She then thought of going to "her best friend" to tell him "how staunchly pro-war you had been from the first. But perhaps I would only muddle things." Her prediction fulfilled itself. A distraught Olive Tilford Dargan wrote to Rose once or twice a week during the month of June. One night she cried out:

> Darling—Rose—sister—it has come over me like a thunderclap— just now at midnight—that you may be shut out from the world of sun and green things—and I cannot bear it. I had no fear till now. My heart is cold as death and almost as still. Write me that it is a black dream—a demon lie. . . .
>
> I got out of bed to write you. The house is asleep. I hear nothing

but the river and I think of you . . . I shall not be able to bear it and I won't believe it. I am so weary of this wicked star. If we could fly to another.

During the summer of 1918 Rose corresponded frequently with Olive, who was devastated by the fate confronting Rose. Rose tried vigorously to fortify her friend. "People must pay for liberty," she wrote. "Not one particle of freedom has been won without sacrifice. . . . Never think of me as suffering for myself. . . . This is certain—they will only make more Socialists—wake the worker up—we can only take joy—they will never bend us!"[38] Rose told Flora Raugh that "Caritas Island has been sold . . . a couple of weeks ago to a Mr. Bartram, a very rich man who made his money on sugar during the war period. We have had great joy of the dear island and it is well that others enjoy it now. Graham and I are planning to build a little house in a sweet woods that we have back on the mainland . . . just as if I were really going to live in it . . . Graham will not believe that I will ever go to prison."[39]

Eugene Victor Debs had been uncharacteristically passive during the first fourteen months of U.S. participation in the war. The journals for which he wrote were being hobbled by government prosecution and arbitrary denial of second-class mailing rights. A combination of reasons may have kept him from the speaking platforms. Poor health, his wife's urging, his brother Theodore's cautionary words are among reasons that have been suggested.

But as he saw growing numbers of his comrades being put in jail or at liberty on bail, and as rumors, mistaken to be sure, spread that he had repudiated the Socialist party resolution against the war, his energy revived and he made a speaking tour of Ohio. The harsh sentence of Kate O'Hare led Debs to tell her, "I shall feel guilty to be at large." The even harsher sentence of Rose Pastor Stokes propelled him into the antiwar campaign. In his autobiography Clarence Darrow wrote: "During the war Mr. Debs said very little on the subject. I have always felt that he would have gone through the period without accident except that Rose Pastor Stokes was indicted for opposing the war. The case was ridiculous and flimsy, but the judge and jury were deeply prejudiced, as all of them were during that period, and Mrs. Stokes was convicted. Mr. Debs immediately protested in the strong and vigorous language that he knew how to use."[40]

Debs was in Canton, Ohio, where a state convention of the SP was taking place on June 16, 1918. He visited the Canton county jail and spoke with the three socialist leaders imprisoned there, Charles Baker, Charles Ruthenberg, and Alfred Wagenknecht. Then he crossed the street to Minisilla Park, where a supportive crowd of twelve hundred was waiting, and gave the speech that headed him toward a ten-year penitentiary sentence. In the course of a fiery two-hour speech he referred to "Rose Pastor Stokes, another inspiring comrade. She had her millions of dollars. Her devotion to the cause is without all consideration of a financial or economic view. She went out to render service to the cause and they sent her to the penitentiary for ten years. What has she said? Nothing more than I have said here this afternoon. I want to say that if Rose Pastor Stokes is guilty, so am I. If she should be sent to the penitentiary for ten years, so ought I."[41]

An industrious Department of Justice stenographer took down Debs's words. The authorities took him into custody on June 30, just as he was about to address a crowd in Cleveland. An agent of the Bureau of Investigation was on the scene August 11, 1918, when a Socialist meeting took place on the Boston Common to protest U.S. intervention in Russia and the arrest of Debs. Louis D. Fraina, Ella Reeve Bloor, and Rose Pastor Stokes were among the speakers. The agent reported that when Rose was asked by someone whether she was for or against the war she said "I am for the war until the democracy of the Socialists triumphs."[42]

In September Rose was in Chicago to attend the trial of Debs for violating the catch-all Espionage Act. She, Margaret Prevey, and five others were brought before the judge for applauding the eloquence of Seymour Stedman, the defense attorney, who had also conducted Rose's defense. A reporter noted that Mrs. Stokes was "plainly dressed as usual" and stood before the judge with bent head as if to say "in trouble again." She said quietly, "Yes I applauded." The seven miscreants were duly fined.[43] On September 12, when the jury brought in the expected verdict of guilty, Rose was holding the defendant's hand. She told the press, "The verdict will greatly help the movement and makes us hopeful and joyous."[44] Speaking at Beethoven Hall at a meeting supporting Debs after his conviction, Rose said of the jurors at his trial, "They looked to me as though most of them had gone to sleep before the Civil War."[45] They knew only of chattel slaves and had no understanding of a wage slave.

Debs expressed his respect and affection for Rose late in 1918 when he wrote from Sandusky, Ohio:

My dear Comrade Rose: A thousand thanks for the beautiful letter from your hands which came to me here. Each word from you has cheer and strength and inspiration and how deeply I am touched and [how I] have greatly appreciated your continued kindness and devotion I shall not attempt to tell you.

I have heard of your wonderful meeting with your inspiring picture of the trial including your precious personal tribute. . . .

I am just leaving for Cleveland. There is no chance to write. You well understand. They still follow us and report my speeches to the Department of Justice! Let them. We have nothing to fear. The comrades everywhere ask about you—they all love you and well they may.[46]

On the day of Debs's conviction, James Graham Phelps Stokes denounced the Socialist party as disloyal to the American people's idea of democracy. He praised the wisdom and ability of Woodrow Wilson and his administration. "The working people of America never had any group in government or outside of it working more earnestly or intelligently to promote justice for all," he told the *Times,* "than the group which now administrates the affairs of the nation in Washington." The "hopeful and joyous" comment of Stokes's passionate and emotional wife appeared in the same issue of the *Times* as Graham's dour denunciation of the Socialists.[47] This curious juxtaposition provokes the question, How was it possible for two politically aware people to function under one roof when their differences of opinion were so enormous? It seems doubtful that the "compulsive ardor" was responsible for the seeming amity, which lasted for years while Rose moved inexorably to the Left and Graham resolutely to the Right. It may have had much to do with the will and wishes of Graham, a "Puritan" and a businessman, who regarded the marriage contract as unbreakable, as well as the residual affection that remained of the large store he had felt for Rose.

Rose was aided by the self-control with which she was able to moderate her emotions when necessary and by the "inner sweetness" on which she prided herself. She told a friend in June: "Please believe that I am not bitter, and I am glad you trust me not to be. It is not in me to feel bitterness. I have often said that I could not live with myself if I did not feel sweet inside."[48]

The well of emotion that Rose possessed was tapped to a surprising degree by a simple expression of friendship that reached her from Charles Drake, a Chicago socialist. She replied:

> Beloved Comrade Drake: How can I ever compensate you enough for the beautiful gift, the sacred gift of your loyal comradeship! Do you know your letter almost choked me with emotion? I have been used so long to standing alone, and waiting for the years to bring understanding, that now I am almost bewildered by the love my comrades shower on me. . . .
>
> You blind my eyes with tears when you expressed the wish that I had permitted the Party to take over my defense. I am so grateful for the wish, even though it is too late for the deed. . . . It was a bitter thing for me to take the money from Mr. Stokes's people, but the comrades generally never could have understood, and it was best. I felt like a Christ nailed to a Cross when I was told how much I was costing—how much they had to pay for my "folly" . . . I have a letter from Gene [Debs]. When I think of him, my heart weeps and sings; and I want to be a great mother with arms to enfold him.[49]

Of course, the comrades would not have understood why the wife of a millionaire socialist should turn to the party to pay for her defense. Of course, Rose, kept on a short financial leash by Graham, could not meet the heavy costs of a legal defense and appeal. And, of course, the convocation of Dodges, Phelpses, and Stokeses who were involved in the expense of keeping her out of prison would let Rose know the cash price of her "foolishness."

In 1917 Gene Debs had introduced Rose Pastor Stokes to Mabel D. Curry through a letter. Later, when Debs faced prison, he felt that Rose and Curry should know each other better. He wanted her to be a confidant of Mabel's and a support for her after he had been imprisoned. Curry and Gene Debs had become lovers some time before his speech at Canton. This created a painful situation because both had been long and loyally married to others. Gene apprised Rose of his love for Mabel, whom he had placed on a pedestal. Mabel anxiously awaited the time when the two women might meet. "*His* 'lovers' are all mine," she wrote Stokes, "and I want to put my arm about you as I know he does." Especially after Debs had entered prison, Mabel often wrote to Rose out of the warmth of her affection and to engage her in activities on behalf of their mutual friend.[50]

A bit of farce followed the high drama of Rose's prosecution under the Espionage Act. Although the Nineteenth Amendment did not become effective until August 26, 1920, the state of New York had given women the right to vote in the election of 1918. Rose, who had worked for suffrage, was not going to pass up her opportunity to cast a ballot. She registered to vote in the November elections. The local police responded by raiding the 88 Grove Street house in the early morning on November 5 and placing her under arrest. The charge was that, as a person convicted of a felony, she had lost her franchise, thereby making her registration a criminal act. She was transported to Jefferson Market Courthouse a few blocks from her home. The magistrate took a dim view of the nighttime raid and released the prisoner on low bail. The case was dismissed on November 9, when the district attorney agreed that the element of criminal intent was lacking.

On November 17 Rose was in Harlem on the familiar platform of the New Star Casino. She opened her remarks by saying, "A little while ago, it was suggested to me that this may be a good time for me to leave the country. The suggestion was made seriously. I replied that it was the best time for me to stay here . . . I am in no fear. I will stay in this country, though it promises to be the country of the greatest reaction in the world, and fight it out with my fellow-workers." She told her audience that after she was sentenced on June 1, "there came word to me from a certain gentleman in New York that if I desired to leave the country and go to Russia, I could get my passport and safe conduct. This offer was made twice. It was made by a gentlemen too, who had a great deal to do with my arrest in Kansas City." Toward the close of her speech, Rose said: "Comrades, this may be the last time I address you. Next month my appeal comes up. I may go to prison."[51]

But, in fact, it was May 12, 1919, before the Rose Pastor Stokes case came before the U.S. Circuit Court of Appeals and March 9, 1920, before the circuit court reversed the lower court and ordered a new trial. Finally, in 1921, the government abandoned prosecution of the 1918 indictment.

In responding to a letter from Anna Strunsky Walling, Rose told her, "I was glad to hear from none so much as from you . . . who embody for me all the things for which I am contending. Yes, the sentence is a terrible one, and will serve only to make the conflict between the forces of light and the forces of darkness more bitter." In the course of this long letter Rose wrote:

> In glancing through a "shelved" manuscript yesterday, while putting things to rights here [88 Grove Street] before closing for the summer, I came upon a *dream* that I had years ago, which I had incorporated in this story, and it struck me with a new, strange significance. I must copy it here for you:
>
> "I had a strange dream last night. I dreamed God turned me into stone and set me far out, into a wild sea. A high cliff I was, against which the waves beat with a fierce, lashing fury. As each wave struck my sides I tried to move, to fight back, to strike the waves as they struck me, but I could not stir. And because I could not, I was in agony. 'Oh God!' the heart in me cried, 'if I could but lash them as they lash me—if I could but hurl my weight against them as they hurl their weight against me—if I could only fight back, Oh God! if I could only fight back. . . . Then strangely through my agony there stole a sense of power and of glory: But I was a *cliff*—an immovable cliff against which the sea hurled itself in vain. Oh God! make me to be that high cliff!"
>
> That dream strikes me with new force today, as almost something prophetic of these days. Much like the sensation I felt in that strange dream was present in me all through the trial, and during the morning upon which sentence was pronounced. I did not shed one tear for myself, or have an extra heart beat. I felt all the immovable power of the organized proletariat of the world in me. These courts and these governments of the master-class were hurling their power against me but I was a cliff—an immovable cliff. God *had* made me to be that cliff![52]

XII

"A Dangerous Woman"

The war was over on November 11, 1918, and the principal reminder that it had ever taken place was the new configuration of the map of Europe. The chief element of such a map was a Russia somewhat shrunken in size by the Brest-Litovsk treaty, a Russia no longer ruled by a czar or even by a bourgeois-democratic entity but by a strange socialist movement and a Soviet government—whatever that might mean. Whatever it was, the U.S. government and her wartime allies did not like it. After the Bolshevik regime had been forced to sign a separate, costly peace with Germany, troops of the Allied powers, including those of the U.S. government, were on her soil giving aid and comfort to the counterrevolutionary forces waging a civil war.

Theoretically it could be argued that the revolution should not have happened in Russia, the most backward and undeveloped of the principal capitalist states. American socialist theoreticians had expected that the socialist revolution would occur first in one of the technologically advanced countries, one with a large industrial proletariat such as the United States or England.

But Marx and Engels in their day had believed the revolution they worked for might start first in Russia; and Lenin did too. He analyzed capitalism in its imperialist stage and saw the imperialist countries as a chain that would break at its weakest link, which could be and, in the event, was czarist Russia, "the prisonhouse of nations."

Inevitably the commercial press in 1918—and afterward—was hostile to the new regime in Russia. With the same inevitability, public opinion in general was hostile to the Bolsheviks, and the U.S. government certainly was. But at the same time there were many people who welcomed the socialist revolution in Russia and many more who at least accepted it. Radicals, socialists, anarchists, and syndicalists hailed the Russian Revolution. The Socialist party was overwhelmingly supportive. Even the more fainthearted of the Socialists were moved by this triumph of the Russian workers, peasants, and soldiers. That they had lived to see the day when a Marxist revolution should triumph touched a deep chord inside of them.

American radicals had been roughly treated during the war, and those who voiced their sympathy with the Soviets—or were believed to have such sympathy—were handled even more roughly when the war was over. Some saw the wisdom of being quiet. Some fearfully saw the wisdom of changing their minds. Some were dismayed by real or reported or fancied aberrations in the conduct of the revolution and its aftermath. But initially most Socialists, left, center, and right—one might say Debs, Hillquit, and Berger—welcomed the events in Russia. These events were being reported in the *Call* by John Reed.

The disagreements in the Socialist party of America had to do principally with the practical lessons that the revolution had for Americans. Should the American party apply these lessons to the United States? Should it become a truly revolutionary party? The Center and the Right—Hillquit and Berger, for instance—would say maybe or no. The left—Fraina, Ruthenberg, Reed, and Stokes, for example—gave a hearty yes.

Even on the Left there were distinctions, as Philip Foner has pointed out: "Some left-wingers saw revolution in the United States as the order of the day and put forward as the immediate aim for the Socialist party the slogan of Soviet power. . . . Other left-wingers, however, felt that the slogan of Soviet power in the United States would find no echo among the American workers and the American people and would be used as a club by reaction to destroy the party. The lessons of the Bolshevik revolution should be applied to revitalize the party without calling for immediate revolution."[1]

Rose Pastor Stokes was, of course, on the Left. On May 5, 1918, she attended a three-day conference of laborites and Socialists that had been called to protest any move for United States intervention in Siberia. Rose presented the resolution of protest, which was passed unanimously. That was a few weeks before her trial and conviction. A few weeks after her conviction she spoke at a conference of the Liberty Defense Union. Again the subject was intervention. In mid-August U.S. troops were landing in Siberia.[2]

Olive Dargan, who always made a loyal effort to follow Rose politically, wrote that "never in the history of man has there been such a piece of colossal fiendishness as our present attempt to stymie Soviet Russia." (The same letter contained Olive's obituary for Peter, the Stokeses' pet dog, whose full name was Peter Pan. She could never look at Peter's pictures "without smiling, although he was a comrade for the spirit if ever doggie was.")[3]

The left-wing forces within the Socialist party were the principal and the most ardent supporters of the new Soviet state. The powerful leadership of V. I. Lenin in that country began to attract the attention of American radicals. In December 1917 the left-wing journal *Class Struggle* published a portion of his *State and Revolution*. The socialist educational institution, the Rand School, published a pamphlet in 1918 titled *The Soviets at Work*. This was a translation of Lenin's article "The Immediate Tasks of the Soviet Government." The Rand School pamphlet became an instant best-seller.

The American Socialists were generally moving to the Left as, for awhile, political parties of the working class elsewhere did. In Germany and Hungary revolutions were attempted, only to be aborted. In the United States by the end of 1918 the left wing of the Socialist party was an organized force in Boston and Chicago. New York was still to be organized. In the spring of 1918 John Reed returned to the United States after six months as a journalist in Russia. He wrote and lectured on Russia and produced his famous book, *Ten Days That Shook the World*. In the summer of 1918 he joined the Socialist party and became part of its amorphous left wing.

In January 1919 the left wing of the New York Socialists organized a city committee of fourteen that met for the first time on February 2 at the James Connolly Socialist Club at 43 West 29th Street in Manhattan, a club led by the charismatic James Larkin. Larkin was absent from the meeting, but he, Nicholas Hourwich, John Reed, and Rose Pastor Stokes were elected to the International Bureau. Reed and Bertram Wolfe were designated to draft a manifesto. Rose became treasurer of the Left Wing Section of the greater New York locals of the Socialist party, a party within the party with monthly membership dues of ten cents. Rose was now launched on the rough seas of organized left-wing politics leading to the founding of the Communist party.[4]

It could have been about this time that a letter came to Rose from Graham's sister Helen: "I send you my love—and though we seem to differ often as to the best way to help to make this world a happy world full of justice and peace for those who live in it, I know that we both want to help to bring in that kind of world."[5] Helen Stokes kept a steady course. She did not leave the Socialist party with Graham, support the war, or leave the ISS. Nor did she follow Rose out of the Socialist party and into the Communist party. But she remained a steady friend of Rose until the end.

While Rose was busy forming the new Left Wing Section, Graham was busy writing a long letter—over two thousand words—to the *New York Times* exposing "Bolshevist Propaganda," as he saw it, through the words of John Reed and Rose's friend the Reverend Albert Rhys Williams. It must have been a very cold February at the breakfast table at 88 Grove.[6]

But from the hinterlands Rose received warmth: she got a letter from Henry W. Youmans of Sedalia, Missouri, which told her, "You and Kate [O'Hare] are the sweethearts of the revolution in America." And it was good to hear from Mabel Curry, no doubt echoing Debs, "that the left was 'absolutely right.'" In a fervent sentence Curry expressed the emotional power of the Russian experience on American leftists: "The revolution in Russia has been a university course for all radicals who wish to know the way."

Mabel Curry was in the Senate chamber when the Suffrage Bill passed. "It is pitiful," she wrote, "to think what women have paid for such a little bit of justice." "I ache to see you, Rose," said a letter in May, "I've admired and loved you so long you seem my very own . . . Gene loves you so very dearly. It has been a loving ambition of his to put us in each other's arms! Let us hope he may yet do it."[7] It is not clear that Rose and Mabel ever met.

The late winter and spring of 1919 were weeks and months of skirmishing between the new left wing and the ruling center of the Socialist party. The party was slipping away from its leadership. A referendum election for the National Executive Committee (NEC) and for international delegates went overwhelmingly against the incumbent NEC. But these entrenched, die-hard bureaucrats were not to be dislodged by a mere vote. In retaliation they took a drastic step. With only two of the old members of the NEC supporting the newly elected committee, the repudiated body declared the election illegal and fraudulent, and to guarantee their own victory they expelled and suspended the majority of the party members. At its May 24–30 meeting the NEC expelled the six thousand members of the Michigan organization and "suspended" more than forty thousand members of various language federations. In the following weeks Massachusetts and Ohio were severed as were Chicago and branches in New York and elsewhere. Fifty-five thousand members were thus disfranchised, and the property of the party was transferred to a corporation of seven members of the old National Executive Committee.

The left wing had not been idle. On May 5 it sent out a call to a national conference to be held in New York on June 21.

It was a period of intense political struggle for all supporters of socialism. There were few among them on any side—certainly more than two sides could be discerned—who did not affirm, at least in words, their support for the newly formed government of Soviet Russia.

Rose took little ostensible notice of the May 12 hearing in St. Paul, Minnesota, that was the appeal—almost a year after the event—of her conviction for violation of the Espionage Act. The three-judge court took the matter under consideration. It was ten months before a decision was made.

Rose had hardened herself not to expect justice from the courts. She was convinced that ultimately she would have to serve her time. (Debs had been incarcerated in April.) She was so convinced that she did not take kindly to being argued with or reassured by concerned friends who tried to convince her otherwise. Rose had Debs's assurance that she was walking the right path: "Twenty centuries ago there was One appeared upon earth we know as the Prince of Peace. He issued a command in which I believe. He said, 'Love one another.' He espoused the cause of the suffering poor—just as Rose Pastor Stokes did, just as Kate Richards O'Hare did."[8]

From within the family walls on Grove Street the two ardently political Stokeses carried on their diametrically opposed campaigns. In May Graham Stokes still took his Social Democratic League (SDL) seriously despite its failure to attract members. He wrote to Upton Sinclair in support of an SDL resolution endorsing the proposed League of Nations and the peace treaty that had been presented to the Germans. "I am indeed glad," he told

Sinclair, "to note that you are not consciously advocating Bolshevism . . . Bolshevism to my way of thinking is a very hideous tragedy."[9] (But he and a "Bolshevik" found shelter under the same roof.)

Rose did steal time from the factional activity that had split the Socialist party to satisfy her creative urge. On April 18 Rose Pastor Stokes (as director of players) and Felix Sper (as president of the People's Playhouse) addressed a circular letter to the secretaries of all the New York Socialist party branches announcing, "The Proletarian Drama is here." A program of three playlets, one of them by Rose, was announced for May 7. It was suggested that branches "might arrange benefit performances on a 50-50 basis." Tickets were fifty cents each.[10]

Thirteen years later Samuel Ornitz, by then a successful screenwriter and novelist, remembered 1919 and the People's Playhouse and the strange relationship between Rose and Graham Stokes. Ornitz wrote to Rose from Hollywood:

> It is Sunday today, and I recall a bright wintry Sunday afternoon, dining in your Grove Street house, my wife and my little son with me; how, before dinner, a dentist (who later ran from fire) and another comrade (who went to prison for it) and you read the American Communist Manifesto—was it '19 or '20? [It was 1919.] (We were then organizing the People's Playhouse.) In any event, I remember asking that the Manifesto be translated into the American idiom. . . . Then dinner . . . Graham came down: lean, long, cadaverous, spectre of Capitalism, lugubrious, laconic (a dead man is the perfect example of bourgeois good taste), but he came to life in defense of his property, his skeleton bones clattering, his cry like a death rattle because my little boy, Arthur, lost his balance on his spindly New England chair, and his hearty young legs (he was a little over two then), lifted the table from its foundation threatening the delicate china and silver which the spectre rescued with his last strength. . . . We talked after dinner, Graham leaving us. . . . Then my wife Sadie and you sat and talked while I took Arthur for a walk. . . . We walked north and when we were near 14th Street my child was attracted by the music of a brass band, playing military music and we went toward the music. Behold there was a parade on Sunday when parades are forbidden, but this parade was permitted because it was a parade of National Guardsmen, and they were filing out of the Armory on Fourteenth

near Sixth Avenue, I think, and we watched and there I saw Graham, in the uniform of a petty officer, drilling the guardsmen, now that the war was over, to fight the revolution of the masses: while his wife was at home refining the appeal to revolution!!! Do you remember?[11]

A month later, in May 1919, Norman Springer sent Rose a copy of his play *Rough Stuff,* which had been performed successfully by the People's Institute in San Francisco: "I wanted the story to say that class loyalty was the first workingclass virtue. . . . The dialog is vulgar, but it is natural, and it does not sound obscene out in front. The People's Institute Players presented your sketch *In April* again. . . . We had a large hall, a good stage, and a packed house. The sketch was well done, and very well received."[12]

Rose wrote to Debs not long after he arrived at Moundsville Penitentiary in Virginia:

> And among other things, what do you think I am doing now? Launching a dramatic movement—the People's Playhouse is giving a first performance of three proletarian plays for the first time on the stage, and the players, young workers all of them, are also to be "for the first time on any stage." I am the dramatic director and the author of one of the plays. The other two are also written by comrades. . . .
>
> So you see, dear Comrade, life is made up of a number of things. If we stand in the shadow of the bastille, we still serve the people and art, joyously—aye, even *gaily.* . . .
>
> Yours with the dear love of Comrades.[13]

The letter was delivered on May Day and was one of scores that arrived for Debs on that special day. He could not physically handle a response to all that mail and he asked his brother Theodore to respond to Rose. Theodore wrote her a letter in the very spirit of Eugene. He closed by saying: "Gene wished me to send you his greetings, his love, and his thanks for all you have done and are doing to bring light and peace and happiness to a struggling world."[14]

Debs was placed under strict correspondence regulations after he was transferred from Moundsville to Atlanta penitentiary. There he succeeded in having Mabel Curry be his secretary with special privileges for visitation and correspondence. Mabel then became his surrogate in the communication between him and Rose Pastor Stokes. When Mabel's daughter got married, Mabel told Rose: "If I believed that marriage today could promise fulfillment my heart would not feel so empty. But it is built too conventionally and fed too artificially to serve my high ideals of love and mating. The mother in me is mourning."[15]

The skirmishing between Left and Right continued through the spring, much of it through such organs of the Left as the *New York Communist* and the *Revolutionary Age*. But it was an article in the *Call* by Morris Hillquit that bluntly stated the facts: it would be better to have two small Socialist parties, each one unified, than a larger one torn by internal dissension. The Left gladly accepted the challenge, but not in a unified way.

In the left wing there was determination to form a Communist party. When the ninety-four delegates to the national conference of the Left Wing assembled at the Manhattan Lyceum in New York on June 21, 1919, they were divided as to when the new party should be formed. The Socialist party had scheduled an emergency convention for August 30 in Chicago and, as Hillquit's article in the *Call* showed, it was quite prepared to live without its troublesome left wing. At the June conference it was soon apparent that the foreign-language federations and the Michigan party were determined to form a new party as quickly as possible. They proposed that it be done right then and there at the conference. But a majority of about two-thirds, mostly the English-speaking delegates, balked and voted it down. Thereupon, the foreign-language delegates and those from Michigan departed the conference.

The remaining delegates elected a national council of nine members, designated the *Revolutionary Age* its official journal, and directed Louis Fraina of Boston to draft its manifesto. The manifesto included the important statement, "The upsurge of revolutionary Socialism in the American Socialist Party, expressed in the Left Wing, is not a product simply of European conditions. It is in a fundamental sense, the product of the experience of the American movement—the Left Wing tendency in the Party, having been invigorated by the experience of the proletarian revolution in Europe."[16] It was also decided that the left wing would try to win control of the SP at the emergency convention and, failing that, it would meet in its own convention to found the Communist party. Those who had walked out of the left-wing conference decided not to attend the SP convention but to meet in a founding convention in Chicago and set up their own Communist party on the first of September.

While Rose Pastor Stokes and her comrades were making these decisions at the Lyceum on Fourth Street, the agents of the infamous Lusk Committee were raiding and ransacking the left-wing headquarters on 29th Street. The Lusk Committee was officially known as the Joint Legislative Committee Investigating Seditious Activities; its short name came from its chairman, state senator Clayton R. Lusk. It was dedicated to the prosecution of all shades of "radicals" and caused much mischief in its day. Now it is gratefully, if ironically, remembered by labor historians for its four-volume, forty-four-hundred-page report, *Revolutionary Radicalism,* which contains documents, names, and historical records that might otherwise be very hard to obtain.

Rose had much to do in the period of the left wing's establishment and development. At about the time the court ordered a new trial for her she received a curious form letter from Laura Steffens Suggett, librarian of the Sutro branch of the California State Library in San Francisco. It contained the branch's offer "to act as the custodian of two copies of each article or book written by an author, one copy in the form in which it went to the editor or publisher and the other the final form in which it appeared in print."[17]

On the back of the letter Rose wrote a note to Upton Sinclair: "Is this a scheme?—a sort of literary espionage bureau for reaction? We get to suspecting everything these days." Her note to Sinclair was the beginning of a correspondence with him relating to his work in progress at the time, which materialized as *The Brass Check,* a study of the venality of the contemporary commercial press. Rose had many stories, she said, of her victimization by the press and she promised to write them when she had a chance. In July she was getting ready to go to Stamford for the summer and there, she was sure, she would "get time to look up the mass of material I must have, laid away somewhere, on the subject of press misrepresentation in my own case."[18]

A couple of weeks later Rose sent Sinclair the longer, more detailed account she had promised. She sent four single-spaced pages from Stamford, written on the letterhead of the People's Playhouse ("The Drama of the Masses") of Brooklyn. Rose was the treasurer of the playhouse. She described a number of her charges against the press, beginning with a tirade against "This man Kitchin [a reporter for the *World*] . . . a three hundred pound infantile specimen that would make you marvel at even such a paper as the 'World' employing it for reportorial work. Honestly, Upton, the most unintelligent, unintellectual type of male that I had ever set eyes on." She went on to tell of various sins committed against her by the *Kansas City Star,* her Missouri nemesis. She told also of an interview with a *Tribune* reporter in New York who turned out to be a card-carrying Socialist. He was assigned to get her life story to be run parallel with another reporter's similar story on her husband. But the story was written too sympathetically, the interviewer later told her, and was therefore turned down by the editors. She told of a recent mass meeting at Madison Square Garden at which she had denounced the violence then being rampantly used against workers. Two of the city papers quoted her as advocating violence. She told Sinclair: "The press works hand in glove with the capitalist class and today not only expresses its point of view, but takes first-rank part in its conspiracies against labor—on a national and international scale. How then can we look for any justice or fairness from the press? Have not the Associated Press and Associated Powers fought from the selfsame trench against the world's proletariat throughout these recent years of the clarified international class struggle?"[19]

In 1920, by the time Sinclair's *Brass Check* appeared using her letters, Rose had hardened her political line. Sinclair limited his use to her accounts of dealings with the *Kansas City Star.* Rose complimented him on the mobilization of facts in his book, which she thought could be very useful. But, she said,

> Your method of *appeal* . . . spoils your book for me. I find you constantly appealing to the "public." There is no "public." There are only *we* and *they;* the working class, and the capitalist class. Throughout your book, you seem to be identifying yourself with, and expressing your faith in, the "public". Who do you conceive to be the "public"? the soft-worded liberal ladies and gentlemen who are wise enough in their own class interest to treat the burning questions of the day with a genial "kindness" and handle all radical situations with kid-gloves— until, their policy failing, they turn and rend the workers to save their miserable little "income"? *Who* are the "public" in your view, if not these? You do not identify yourself with workers. You speak *of* them—not *to* them, not *with* them. You appeal to the "public's" sense of "fairness". You expect them to come to the "rescue" of the workers. That the workers might come to their own rescue, you merely hold

up as a threat to the "public" if "it" should fail of finding a solution. . . . But you are asleep, doped by some "liberal" soporific. You'll
wake up, I believe, for you are destined to an early awakening. . . .
The *burning* sincerity of Upton Sinclair, born comfortable, but now
a white-collar slave with a collarless reaction to the struggle, will sting
you into wakefulness. . . .

Perhaps, my hope of you is as foolish as your hope of the "public".
Perhaps, I am warning you against a blindness which I myself share.
Still, I feel that you properly belong with the workers. And I can't
give up the hope that you are, under your deep sleep, the Upton
Sinclair I used to know.

All power to the workers![20]

Thus ended the correspondence relative to *The Brass Check*. Despite
these strong chidings, their long-standing friendly relations continued.
Poor Sinclair was not far enough to the left for Rose. For Graham he was
too far to the left.

Sinclair wrote to Graham in June 1919, telling him that "without realizing it, you are allying yourself with universal Reaction. Mark my words—
if Kolchak [a leader of the counterrevolution] ever gets into Russia he will
kill twenty people for everyone the Bolsheviki have killed, and he will
settle complete reaction on Russia for a generation." Graham replied icily:
"It appears wholly preposterous to one who has as much personal contact
with the American Bolsheviki as I have, for you and others like you to
attribute to the Bolsheviki an admiration for any of the principles and
methods of democracy."[21]

Sinclair sought to clarify his stand when he replied to Graham: "You
are mistaken if you think that I do not see the matter sent out by the
Russian Information Bureau . . . I try to understand both sides—neither
side is what I would prefer. . . . I am not advocating Bolshevism in America . . . I am merely saying that the American people should let the Bolsheviks alone in Russia."[22]

For some reason the managing editor of *Hearst's Magazine* asked Rose
to contribute a definition, in not more than one hundred words, of the
term *freedom of speech*. Rose saw this as "a trap to catch unwary radicals."
She spurned the invitation.

Democracy and *dictatorship* were prominent words in the vocabularies of
all parties to the debate forced on Americans by the continuing survival of

Soviet Russia. Rose's friend Nathalie Ells, for instance, recognized the darker side of formal democracy. She wrote from Baltimore in June that she had "got up a big meeting for Mrs. Mooney [Tom Mooney's mother]—she stayed with us from Friday till Tuesday—a perfectly dear little woman." Ells also informed Rose that she had seen "a number of Mr. Stokes's articles in *The Federationist* [AFL journal] and elsewhere—against the Soviet Gov-[ernment] and I think of you. —Read what Lenin says about Social Demo-crats et al. in the last part of *Soviets-at-Work*."[23]

What Lenin said had to do with the difference between a dictatorship by the many against the few and one of a few against the many. He stressed the necessity of stern discipline by the workers and ruthless repression of the enemies of proletarian democracy. It was not Jeffersonian democracy; he would call it revolutionary necessity. Perhaps Graham *had* read *Soviets-at-Work*.

The young Soviet government made some bizarre diplomatic gestures. One of these was to designate John Reed, returning from Petrograd to New York, as its consul for that area. This designation was soon dropped. Somewhat more permanent was the establishment of an information bu-reau and trade agency in extensive offices occupying two floors at 110 West 40th Street in New York. Ludwig Christian Alexander Karl Martens, a Russian citizen resident in the United States, was appointed representa-tive of the People's Commissariat for Foreign Affairs. Martens organized his bureau into five departments, each headed by a member of the So-cialist party. The Lusk Committee stated later that "as might have been expected, his staff was recruited largely from the most violent revolution-ary elements to be found in this vicinity." "Violent revolutionary" cer-tainly did not describe Martens's head of his legal department, who was Morris Hillquit, and probably did not fit the other four either. The Lusk Committee did acknowledge that the principal duty of L. C. A. K. Mar-tens was to reestablish trade relations between Russia and the United States.[24] Nevertheless, on June 12 the Lusk Committee, armed with a search warrant, raided the bureau's premises, seized its files, and subjected Martens to examination on his life and his intentions.

The left-wing section of the SP promptly rented Madison Square Gar-den for a protest rally. On June 19 Rose got a letter telling her she was to speak there, along with Ludwig Martens and several others. "Prepare yourself and come early," said the letter.

Alexander Spokletsky, of the *Novy Mir* (New World), spoke in Russian, and a police captain asserted that everyone understood him though only half of those present understood English, the language in which Rose Pastor Stokes told the audience: "The capitalist class has started a campaign of terrorism against the working class of America but they will fail to terrify . . . I see by the afternoon papers that Mr. Charles Evans Hughes warns against the Reds in America. We warn Mr. Hughes that we will go on, that we know the work before us and can no longer be confused by the slogans of race, or of religion, of creed or color or nationality. . . . We shall refuse to fight our comrades in Russia."[25]

The *New York Times* did not like such talk. It editorialized against the "Red Night at the Garden" and called for the Reds' punishment. It cited Governor Alfred E. Smith of New York, who said with some confusion: "These people have their choice of either education or nightsticks. But how many have had the nightsticks . . . or believe it will be applied to them? Besides who is to apply nightsticks when these people are so crafty as to keep within the law?"[26]

Olive Dargan was ill again in mid-June 1919 and Rose urged her to come north. She could stay at the Stamford cottage, and Anna, the housekeeper, would feed her and give her whatever the doctors prescribed. She could keep her whereabouts secret if she wished. And she would have privacy—Rose was away four days out of seven and Graham came home only two or three times a week. His schedule was "bath—then supper; then an isolated corner of the house with a book or paper, then bed."[27]

By the time the offer arrived, Olive was in a hospital. She was hemorrhaging, her blood count was unsatisfactory, gallstones were suspected, and surgery might be necessary. But a few weeks later she was much better and surgery was postponed. She got "a wonderful message" from Gene Debs about her poems in July 1919, which may have had a therapeutic effect.

Toward the end of August 1919 came the climax of all the inner Socialist party skirmishes that had been taking place since early in the year. Chicago was the site for the action.

The official SP convention, called by the Socialists-in-possession, was the opening bout. It began on August 30 at Machinists Hall on the second floor. The left wing, determined to capture the party at the convention, rented the ground floor and met there in caucus on August 29. The first convention of the Communist party of America (CPA) was slated for September 1 in the hall of the Chicago Russian federation. This hall was now being called Smolny Institute after the headquarters of the authentic Bolsheviks in Petrograd.

At the left-wing meeting on August 29, Benjamin Gitlow, L. E. Katterfeld, and John Reed were elected as a steering committee to lead the Left at the SP convention. At this convention the left-wing found itself hopelessly outnumbered and so, on Sunday, the thirty-first, eighty-seven of them decided to withdraw to their caucus room and form the Communist Labor party (CLP). After much debate, it was decided to send a committee to the Smolny the following morning to consult with the new Communist party opening its convention there. A small left-wing group remained in the Socialist party, unwilling, for the present, to break away.

At the Smolny on the morning of September 1, a delegation was present from the Communist Labor party to invite the Communist party to merge with it. Proceedings were delayed briefly when the police raided the premises, destroying decorations and placards and arresting Dennis E. Batt, who was about to declare the convention opened. Rose Pastor Stokes, according to David A. Shannon, cried out: "They are arresting our comrades—three cheers for the revolution." "Shut up," a police sergeant shouted. "It's always a woman that starts the trouble." The police raid was soon over and the delegates settled down to the business at hand. When the Communist party rejected the Reed group's overtures for unity, the Communist Labor party moved its convention to the IWW hall on Throop Street and proceeded independently. Within a few months, the newly founded parties, and other portions of the American Left, were to suffer blows sufficiently severe to drive them into a semilegal, even underground, existence. On the Left, there was a three-way split resulting in two Communist parties plus a faction remaining within the Socialist party.[28] A year later the bulk of the Communist party and Communist Labor party merged to form the United Communist party. Some members of the Communist party refused to participate in the merged party and continued for a while to call themselves the Communist party.

Some opposition was expressed to permitting Rose Pastor Stokes to join the United Communist party. She was challenged as a "bourgeois element" because her husband derived income from rent. Rose claimed, however, that she depended on income from royalties and was exploited by publishers, an argument that prevailed and permitted her to become a founding member.[29]

Rose got a taste of the early anticommunism, a carryover of anti-socialism, when she spoke at Union Hall in Yonkers on November 9. She also got an instance of tendentious reporting (which she gave to Upton Sinclair for his *Brass Check*). Her meeting at Union Hall was invaded by the Reverend Dr. Francis Theodore Brown of Saint Andrews Memorial Church, accompanied by a sizable cluster of his parishioners. They heckled the speaker, sang the "Star Spangled Banner" (according to the *Times*) or "America" (according to the reverend doctor). As a result, Mrs. Stokes bowed out (*Times*) or continued beyond the scheduled time for conclusion (Rose).

Brown received some letters criticizing him for "infringing upon the rights of free assemblage and free speech." In a letter to the *Times* he pleaded that he had merely poured some Americanism into the meeting. Besides, he said, he did not start the fuss—this was done by Commissioner of Public Safety O'Keefe and Captain Collins of the Home Guard. Nevertheless, he pointed out, Pastor was free on bail and he questioned whether she had a right to speak.[30]

Rose was back in the news a few days later when an investigation of "anarchism and revolution" was held up because of her refusal to answer a subpoena. The district attorney said she would be brought "by means of a body attachment" if she did not come voluntarily. Rose, it appears, refused to permit the process server to enter the house and vowed she would have him arrested if he tried to "push the maid" aside. This episode occurred, of course, before Rose had time to talk to her lawyer, who later that day told the district attorney that his client would appear.

The Red-hunters were now proliferating. Rose's subpoena was for a Bronx grand jury conducting hearings on communist activity. Benjamin Harrow, a teacher at DeWitt Clinton High School, was being dismissed for teaching "political theories" and assigning a book on Bolshevism. The Lusk Committee was abroad in New York state, and Attorney General A. Mitchell Palmer's raids had started, supervised by young J. Edgar Hoover. Eighty persons had been removed to Ellis Island pending deportation. The *Times* headline was "Red Plot to Kill Officials Bared."

Rose was not named as a plotter in that particular fantasy. Rather, she was supposed to have contributed $11,000 to various radical publications. This, if true, would have been her legal right. But it was not true—she did not command such wealth, and her lawyer properly dismissed the "charge" as ridiculous.[31]

Rose was not silenced by the attention being paid to her by various authorities. She would not have known, in any case, that a speech—not one of her best—at a Communist party public meeting at the Manhattan Lyceum on December 11, 1919, was of interest to J. Edgar Hoover. But a raid on the offices of *Novy Mir* in New York produced a transcript of Rose's talk, and it was duly sent to Hoover.[32]

A couple of weeks after the Manhattan Lyceum meeting, and still months before the equal suffrage amendment went into effect, Rose was nominated for Congress on the CP ticket in the Fourteenth Congressional District. (This was a nice gesture when it is considered that neither of the new Communist parties had placed a woman in their top leadership. Rose was, however, elected to the CP executive committee.)

The Fourteenth District incumbent was Fiorello H. LaGuardia, a Republican populist with whom Rose later became friendly. Victor Berger, in Milwaukee, also sought (and won but was denied) a congressional seat. He, too, was under indictment for violation of the Espionage Act. Berger was, and remained, a Socialist.[33]

A sweep by hundreds of police and special agents on November 8, acting for the Lusk Committee, had resulted in the apprehension of a thousand persons in New York City and the confiscation of tons of publications and records. Most of those arrested were soon released, but some 75 were indicted on various charges. Many of them were aliens who were added to a federal roundup of "Russians" and were among 249 deportees aboard the former troop transport *Buford,* which became known as the Soviet Ark, and were carried off to Soviet Russia, without "due process," sailing on December 21, 1919. Emma Goldman and Alexander Berkman were among these deportees. Ultimately three thousand more faced deportation.

But the most devastating blow to the new parties was the notorious Palmer Raids, which took their name from the attorney general of the United States, A. Mitchell Palmer. These raids took place across the country on January 1 and 2, 1920, and resulted in more than five thousand arrests. Many were indicted, and some three hundred were convicted and sentenced under whatever pretext was handy. Though relatively few actually served their full time, the drastic roundup and the tension and cost of numerous defense cases were devastating acts of intimidation and enforced a two-year-period of "illegality" on the Communist parties. During this time the most ostensible activity was the continued publication of a number of journals. And the dedicated cadres of the movement remained when the preponderance of the membership fell away. Rose was one of those who stood fast during this "illegal" period.

She was again wanted under subpoena in January 1920, this time as a witness in the case of Benjamin Gitlow. Gitlow was one of five assembly-men-elect who were denied their seats in the legislature. He and James Larkin were arrested in the November Lusk raids. Both were defended by Clarence Darrow and Charles Recht.

Two detectives were posted in front of 88 Grove Street, where they were to wait all night with warrants for Rose's arrest. Anna Webb, the housekeeper, told them that Mrs. Stokes was not at home but had informed her by telephone that she would "be in court tomorrow." Webb told a reporter that she herself had been in court that day. "No, I wasn't frightened," she told him, "I was just afraid I would say something that would hurt Mrs. Stokes."[34] Rose did appear in court but was not called as a witness. Larkin, Gitlow, and the others were sentenced to five to ten years and served about two years.

Even as the trial of Larkin, Gitlow, and the others was proceeding in New York, scores of communists were being indicted in Chicago charged with conspiracy "to overthrow the government by force." Rose Pastor Stokes was one of them. (The total number of "conspirators" was eighty-five. It is not clear whether this figure included Harrison E. Ellis, who was arrested in Beacon, New York, by police who thought they had grabbed John Reed. Reed was in Moscow at the time, but neither the Beacon nor the Chicago police was aware of that.) Each defendant was required to post a bond of from $5,000 to $10,000. Graham posted $5,000 for Rose.[35]

An extradition order was signed by Governor Alfred E. Smith on February 12, 1920, to bring Rose from New York to Chicago. It was requested on February 3, but Rose was suffering from the flu and said she would go to Chicago only after her physician pronounced her well. She left for Chicago on February 16 in custody of a female detective. Earlier that day, accompanied by Graham, she had appeared in the Tombs Court, where the extradition papers were processed. Interviewed in Chicago, she wanted to speak only of her race for Congress in New York, maintaining that "there is a great likelihood that I can win. There is a great constituency of my people there."[36]

Graham's involvement in partisan politics was growing more tenuous as Rose's became more sturdy. He confessed to a friend, "I am no longer actively interested in party politics of any kind, but do try to help along, in various ways, the general movement towards a larger and finer type of democracy." Graham's love for Rose had to transcend her devotion to "a dictatorship of the proletariat," a concept he abominated. The friend to whom he wrote was Major Hector Munro-Ferguson, whom Rose and Graham had visited in Scotland on their wedding trip in 1905. Graham told him he could make no definite plans for the summer because "so much depends on how my wife's very unfortunate affairs turn out," but he hoped that they would have the pleasure of a visit from Munro-Ferguson while he was in the United States. He explained, "Of course we live exceedingly simply here," but the major would be welcome "if you think you could be comfortable in a very small room in a little house with only one servant."[37]

It was a period of much strain for Rose. To illness and government harassment there had been added the sadness of the death of Vladimir Resnikoff, her blind protégé. At the age of thirty, when his career was stabilizing at a self-sustaining level, he died in the Presbyterian Hospital of pneumonia on February 5, 1920. His last public appearance was at a concert sponsored by the Workers Music League at the Manhattan Opera House on January 18. He shared the program with Eddie Brown, a violinist, and the composer Sergei Prokofiev, a pianist.

In a letter more than a year after Resnikoff's death, Rose brought the news to the attention of A. Lunacharsky, then in charge of cultural affairs in Soviet Russia. Lunacharsky sent the letter to the chief of the musical department of the School for the Blind in Moscow remarking on the "enthusiasm and faithfulness on the part of the deceased artist to Soviet Russia and to the Great Russian Revolution . . . I have heard comments on his singing on several occasions. He was an unusual artist." Rose's letter was published with Lunacharsky's in *Izvestia*, the government newspaper.[38]

There was a bit of pleasant news in the offing, and it came from the legal side, which had been generating so much bad news for Rose. The U.S.

Circuit Court at St. Louis, on March 9, ruled on her appeal from the conviction and ten-year sentence that had been passed on her in June 1918. The appeals court declared that, though there was substantial evidence at the trial to support a verdict against the defendant, Judge A. S. Van Valkenburgh in his instructions to the jury failed to set forth Mrs. Stokes's explanation of the crucial passage in her letter to the *Kansas City Star*. The "partisan zeal of the court below . . . led it to place too heavy a burden on the defendant in her endeavor to meet the evidence." A new trial was ordered. Rose took this victory with what may be considered excessive calm. She told the *Times:* "I am neither pleased nor displeased. I don't care. Had the news been the other way it would not have made any difference to me."[39]

She expressed the same indifference in a different tone and more politically when she wrote to Theodore Debs:

> Many warm thanks for the thoughtfulness expressed in the sending of the press clipping from your local paper in re the reversal in my case. Of course the matter has little significance. They have framed much more repressive and reactionary laws and have infinitely better cases against the real radicals now. I am satisfied to be tried anew—on real issues—and to go to prison for big principles will be truly a privilege. In the class conflict we must expect that more rather than decreased repression will be the outlook. We should not be deceived or fall back into a state of passivity in our propaganda because such camouflaged decisions as in my case look like a straw in a "liberal" wind.[40]

The tone of this letter suggests that Rose's consistent protestation of indifference to her own fate insofar as the "espionage" case was concerned was not an avowal of defeatism or passivity but rather a mode of fighting back.

Later in the year Attorney General A. Mitchell Palmer, who was feeling a backlash as a result of his unscrupulous raids, asked President Wilson for advice on proceeding against Rose. The president replied on October 4:

> I have your letter of October first about the case of Rose Pastor Stokes and hasten to reply. I believe that Mrs. Stokes is one of the dangerous influences of the country and I hesitate to advise that the suit against her be dropped, but I feel the embarrassment of pressing the suit now which began under the authority of the Espionage Act, because I think the country feels that the time for that is past. I hope,

therefore, that you will not make an exception of Mrs. Stokes' case, but rather put it on the same footing that you are putting all others that have arisen in the same way. I think this is the fair and wise thing to do.[41]

There is no doubt that Rose was being discussed in the intelligence community. On January 10, 1921, Major W. W. Hicks, chief of the Army's M.I. 4, sent a memo to J. Edgar Hoover asking for "any information" he might have regarding Rose's activities "from January 1920 to the present date." Apparently he wanted an annual update.

XIII

Troubles

The years immediately after World War I, while Wilson was still president, were years of mean-spirited attack on the Left. The left wing of the SP, the Socialist party itself, the anarchists, syndicalists, Wobblies, and—as soon as they were organized—the new Communist parties became targets for government agents, free-lance vigilantes, employers' associations, and religious groups. By 1920 the National Historical Society published *The Red Conspiracy* by Joseph J. Mereto—four hundred pages denouncing the targeted entities. The book contains many citations of furious rhetoric but none of violent acts.

The lynch atmosphere that led to the castration and hanging of Wesley Everett in Centralia, Washington, the legal parody that kept Nicola Sacco and Bartolomeo Vanzetti imprisoned for eight years and then executed the innocent pair, the jailings, and the deportations all coincided with the great open-shop drive, which was called by its corporate sponsors the American Plan. It lasted for most of the next fifteen years.

The American Federation of Labor, which had 4 million members in 1920, was beaten down to 3 million in 1923.

Health problems and health remedies became central in the correspondence of Olive Dargan and Rose Pastor Stokes in mid-1920—first Olive's "lung trouble," then an illness of Rose that caused a suspension of her activities. Olive began to worry about an illness in March. Later x-rays revealed her lung problem. A determination was made that she must go to Saranac Lake in the Adirondacks to the Trudeau Sanitarium. Olive wrote to Graham: "Dr. Brown returned and came forthright to see me. The magic of your name seems to be opening the door for me. I shall know definitely tomorrow if I am to be admitted to Trudeau. I feel very, very grateful."[1] Actually, she stayed on at Saranac Lake as an outpatient until late July. Immediately after that Rose got a letter in Olive's high-key style:

> Yes, darling sister, come! Just any day, any hour that you feel like starting, and can, just come. I don't want mother to know, and think we can keep it from her. She is so *scared.* You will be Mrs. Rachel Phelps. That is true enough. I will write you a postal card thus addressed for our postmaster's eye, before you come. And, dear Heart, I want Graham's approval. You know I took you away once without his full consent. But I feel sure he will have no reservations this time. There will be no Anna—no bathtub, no corner grocery—but my warm heart and the free hills, and the throb of the world that is coming.
>
> I shall let you do everything for yourself—just as I do. For you understand how willingly I *would* do if I could. But I am not strong enough to take a single added care. I am dropping everything that I can possibly let go. This old machine—my body—won't stand much more patching, and when it runs at all, I want it to grind for the gods. Oh, the years and years I've wasted! Always saying next year it will be different—next year I will begin. . . .
>
> My precious, it will be so sweet, so wonderful to have you here. May it be soon! Sister[2]

Olive's cautionary words to Rose about the need for a pseudonym for her stay in Almond reflected a wisdom born of intimate knowledge of the social and political climate of the North Carolina hills. The same knowledge told her that Anna Webb could not be happy there after the relative freedom at 88 Grove Street.

No letters have been located from Rose to Olive save those of which Rose kept copies or which Olive may have returned to her. There are several depositories of Olive Dargan material in various institutional libraries, but none contains a letter from Rose Stokes. Many may have been destroyed in a fire in 1918 and another in the 1920s in Olive's home. But fear may have led her to burn the others.

In the 1930s Olive showed more boldness after the success of her novel *Call Home the Heart* and under the transparent cover of the name Fielding Burke. In the 1940s, perhaps in memory of Rose, and under the influence of the wartime "legality" of the Communist party (and the U.S.-USSR alliance) she helped the North Carolina communists by lending her home for occasional meetings. But after 1950 Olive—then in her eighties—must have been very frightened by the anti-Red atmosphere of the McCarthy era. When she published her poem "Rose Pastor" in a 1958 volume, she changed the title to an impersonal one. She was then ninety years old— and much younger people had their own well-grounded fears at that time.

The nature of Rose's illness is not known, and it may have been simply a need to get away, including away from Graham. There is pitifully little affection for him displayed in the letters they exchanged during her stay with Olive, which lasted from August to November 1920, and Graham's writing is only slightly more ardent.

A letter dated August 10 tells Rose that he had called her lawyer, Joseph Brodsky—"I did not want to write to him"—who said he had "no word from Darrow or anyone connected with your case in Chicago." On August 13 he sent $40 to Olive to cover Rose's board for two weeks. He would "send more later if you decide to stay." A week later he wrote that he had gone to Stamford to see their house, which was still being readied. On September 28 he had been away on business and was sorry not to find Rose at home when he got back but realized "the South is good for you." She stayed for another two months.[3]

On October 19 Rose sent him a "Dear Grey" letter, written in her vigorous hand with a stub pen. Like most of her letters, the four pages deal mainly with chores she wanted him to perform. She was going wild-grape-gathering and, on Sunday, mountain climbing—four miles each way—only half of which would be on the fine mules "Bill" and "Bob." Her canvas shoes would be finished by this excursion. Would he "be so kind as to take my old brown tennis shoes with the high tops and low brown walking shoes to the cobbler, then send them to me parcel post." Another half page describes the deplorable condition of her canvas shoes, apparently the only footwear she had left. She made another request: when Anna goes to Wanamaker's "please get several packages of the bronzed crinkled wire hairpins that I use, and send them—or I'll have to return with hair bobbed to look respectable." Animadversions on the necessity for the hairpins consume another page. Most of the final page predicts a deterioration of the weather. In a day or two she would no longer be able to sleep out-of-doors on the porch but would have to move to the attic. A marginal note says: "If you should see Mother, or Helen, or Emma please give them my love." The signature is "R."[4]

From Anna Webb in the servant's quarters at 88 Grove came a letter: "That woman came over that you told me to give some meals to and she seems very nice. But I want to know—how do all these nuttie people find you? They all seem to find this house when they get down and out. Well, I suppose we must help each other in this life."[5]

Daniel Kiefer wrote to Rose frequently during her stay with Olive. His writings were like a newsletter exchanging the views of Francis Garrison, Frank Girard, Bob Minor, Lincoln Steffens, and others of that intellectual circuit. In one he quotes a few paragraphs in which Steffens tries to strengthen Rose's estimate of Lenin (an exercise we might have supposed was superfluous):

> The letter from Mrs. Stokes is beautiful, and she is right about Debs, about his generalizations. I mean that I agree there. But I think she misses Lenin. She doesn't know how much he feels; burns; suffers. Gorky knows that inside. And Gorky understands and says that Lenin thinks he has to keep his head. Surrounded by hard-heads and impossibles for so many details of "the revolution" he feels as the captain of a ship feels: that he must keep open house in his head; hear, consider and gently decide. So he saves a lot of splitting. He lets one side try out its way, even against his own conviction, and waits. When the wrong way fails, he returns to the right way. But his plan is complete. It is not the way I'd take, but it goes clear through to my end and Mrs. Stokes' and his own. I would warn her always to think maybe Lenin is right and that she and I may be wrong. We are only thinking; he is a doing and thinking too.[6]

While Rose was in her retreat in North Carolina John Reed died of typhus in a Moscow hospital and was buried with state honors in the Kremlin wall. His death at age thirty-three, at the height of his usefulness to the young communist movement, was a shock to the radicals of the United States and Europe. Tributes to him were written by many of the comrades who had known him during his half-dozen years as a progressive, a socialist, and a communist. Rose wrote one, and so did Steffens, and Kiefer promised to send it to her in her isolation. He often sent her a bundle of radical papers, her main contact with the world she was obliged largely to forgo.

She did take the trouble while on Olive's mountainside to end her membership in the ISS, which was now being called the League for Industrial Democracy. Harry Laidler received her resignation with regret: "Sorry to hear that you feel you cannot longer be a member of the Society. . . . It is broad enough to include all interested in Industrial Democracy and . . . there is no inconsistency in your remaining a member." He said also that the society appreciated all she had done in the past and he hoped her "cooperation will not cease with her resignation."[7] But cease it did.

Finally, in November, Rose was able to tell Graham she would soon be back home. This was good news to Graham, and some real warmth breaks through in his reply: "I am ever so blessed to think you will be back soon. I shall expect you for supper on Monday the 22nd." A few weeks later there was a letter to Rose from Olive: "I have been making my will this week . . . I decided to give you the lower farm, for I think you like that best."[8] It was not old age—Olive was only fifty-one—but rather the frightening series of illnesses she had experienced that put Olive in mind of her mortality. Her fears were premature. She had forty-nine more years of life, and some of her best work, ahead of her. She died near the end of her one hundredth year in 1964.

Two curious letters reached Rose around Christmas 1920, both in the same hand, without salutation or signature, and apparently part of a more extensive correspondence. The two letters indicate a feeling of affection and admiration that appears to have extended over a long period of time. We do not have Rose's part of this correspondence with the unidentified person who writes:

> I did not feel that I could reply at once to your letter for I did not want to write until I could do so quietly and in full realization of all that you had said. What you read between the lines, you read correctly. Indeed, you could hardly have read anything else. That which I meant to tell you then, and which I hoped would not surprise you, I ought perhaps to have told you long ago, for the thing itself goes back to the first time I saw you. Yet I was not free to speak out, nor am I free now, and you too are bound. And we met so rarely and could talk so little that much, too much, had to be taken for granted. Now that you know what has always been in my heart . . . I am glad

even if that which I had been silently offering could not in any way have your response.

And the second letter goes on:

> "I do not know whether I am to go away for a time or stay here. . . . You will understand . . . why your letters are an additional joy to me . . . bringing a new stimulating atmosphere . . . I must not speak until we can speak together . . . would like to drop by for lunch . . . will wire you."[9]

In sketchy notes made while working on her autobiography ten years later, Rose may have been alluding to this correspondence and the aftermath: "The reply was, friendship I want. Love I reject. The result, Silence! Well, another friend lost—because it seems so absolutely impossible for a man to be a woman's friend without seeking to be more than friend."[10]

A kindly estimate of one of Rose's ventures into what may be called Off East Broadway theater appeared in the *World* and generated a bit of controversy:

> Rose Pastor Stokes yesterday stepped across the dividing line of platform and stage. In lieu of the agitator, she became the actress. She has now established a Proletarian Theatre, a movement she began two years ago but was obliged to abandon.
>
> Mrs. Stokes apologized for her first playlet as "a miserable little cross-section of bourgeois life." She produced it for the garment workers as a complimentary performance in a little east side theatre at number 66 East 4th Street. But there was slight suggestion of the Red in the speech she made to introduce it and no implication of the amateur in the character she portrayed.
>
> If she is resting from the labors as propagandist of Bolshevik principles, her followers may be assured she will put the same instinct for drama into her new expression with an unleashing of womanly graces her sterner mission tended to obscure. . . . Mrs. Stokes spoke of the one-act plays she has written that are ready for production, one of them to be translated into Yiddish and brought out at the Yiddish theatre. Her dramatic organization has been formed within the Civic Club, which she described as "made up of people of all beliefs, with some radicals and a few Communists."

"King Arthur's Socks," the one act play by Floyd Dell was the vehicle. Mrs. Stokes showed herself sufficient mistress of a somewhat mawkish situation to elevate the episode to the class of sex drama. . . . Small as the sketch was, Mrs. Stokes invested it with power. To ease and charm she added the fire and spirit of a varied personality.[11]

The writer's report that she "has now established a Proletarian Theatre" and his reference to "her dramatic organization" brought a letter of protest to the *World* from Cornell Ridderhof, an active member of the Civic Club. He protested particularly what he said was her allegation that several members of the dramatic club were communists. Rose wrote to Ridderhof that she did not tell the reporter that the Drama Club was "her organization" and that the reference to communists was to the Civic Club and not to its much smaller drama department.[12]

During this time, Rose was carrying on a heavy correspondence with Daniel Kiefer, who often signed himself Dank. He was an ecumenical radical who functioned as lecture agent for Lincoln Steffens, who had a long reputation as a liberal and muckraker. He had received notoriety as a result of his travel in and reporting from Soviet Russia, which was somewhat more extensive than his celebrated remark that he had "Seen the Future—and it works."

Kiefer does not appear to have corresponded with Rose regularly until about 1920. In March of that year the Kiefers rented an unfurnished apartment in Philadelphia, "in the Jewish quarter," he wrote, "the approach to which [is] as slummy as getting to 88 Grove Street."[13] But 88 Grove—and number 90 next door, where Helen Stokes lived with Mary Sanford—was by no means a slum. A noisy crosstown streetcar passed near the door, and there was a livery stable around the corner, and there were parts of the Village that had not yet been annexed to Bohemia. This ambience may have been what Kiefer had in mind.

Kiefer, basically a Henry George single-taxer, was in touch with many prominent radicals and progressives of the early Communist party period. In his communication with Rose he sometimes acted as self-appointed intermediary between her and other people. He respected her views highly but admitted that he had no taste for her poetry, or anyone else's, although his wife did. The day after Rose's appearance in *King Arthur's Socks* she was in Philadelphia to give the public reading of her verses at Henry's Studio. Kiefer, with his professional know-how, had managed the affair.

Kiefer wrote to the left-leaning publisher Benjamin W. Huebsch in New York (Huebsch had recently published *The Great Steel Strike* by William Z. Foster): "When I spoke to Mrs. Stokes this morning about putting her poems into a bound volume, she said she had not thought about it. I suggested her seeing you, believing that you would find publishing them a good business proposition. Feeling some diffidence herself about approaching you on this, I said I would write you. It goes without saying that if you do undertake it, that I will give you what help I can towards effecting a sale of the book." Huebsch replied: "I have always admired Mrs. Stokes' courageous stand, and I hope that if her *poems* are expressive of the spirit she had displayed, they may see the light of day. With the publishing business as it is and the poetry business as it has always been, it seems impractical for me to take up the project."[14]

The young socialist Jessica Smith was now executive secretary of the Intercollegiate Socialist Society (which in October 1921 became the League for Industrial Democracy). Smith was just beginning a lifetime career of radical activism that would run for more than sixty years. She had asked Kiefer to arrange lectures for Lincoln Steffens at various branches of the ISS across the country. Kiefer confided to Rose: "I haven't yet taken the matter seriously with them as for some reason I did not know how worthwhile it might be. Their letterhead contains a great mixture of names. Some of them are good ones, notably, Roger Baldwin, H. W. L. Dana, and Alexander Trachtenberg, and Norman Thomas. So also the name of Helen Phelps Stokes. It may be that I can allot them some of Steffens' time on his way back from the coast, or from Mexico. Let me know what you think of the worthwhileness of so doing."[15] In this letter, as in most of them, Kiefer asked to be remembered to Anna, the housekeeper. He never mentioned Graham.

Early in March Rose sent Dan Kiefer a long letter reporting on a political discussion she had had with her good friend and comrade Agnes Ingles. Agnes came to see Rose just when Rose was trying to thrash out some tactical questions with another old friend, a brother of Anna Strunsky Walling. Agnes, Rose felt, had come to New York hoping to "get away from all the endless discussions and differences that . . . she suffers so much from at home." Most of the discussion dealt with the stern measures the Soviet government was taking against some who proved to be hostile to the revolution—the anarchists, for example, who were becoming an opposition if only because of their traditional hostility to the state—any state. Rose took great pains to explain her own position to Kiefer, possibly because she thought he too could use some bolstering. In any case, Kiefer immediately sent a copy of Rose's letter to Agnes Ingles, on which he scribbled, "I am going to send a copy of this to Steffens." Here are some excerpts from Rose's letter to Kiefer:

> I felt really helpless. She resents the Russian policy of putting some anarchists in jail. I insist that if it is necessary to save the revolution, it must be done. I myself would want to be put in jail under such circumstances. If ever I become a Babushka, gentle, sympathetic with the people generally, but a meddlesome person in a time of revolution when the workers are fighting for their lives in the ways they must, not in the way I would like them to, then I trust I shall get safely tucked away in some nice double-locked cell until the danger from my muddled, obstinate self is over . . . I trust the Bolsheviki in Russia with this job because they have held the whole pack of imperialist, counter-revolutionary and millennium-fools at bay and conserved the revolution for the workers. . . .
>
> Some of our anarchist friends would like to see us enter the heaven of a perfect Communal state, without the necessity of the proletarian dictatorship. Bureaucracy? surely! nobody loves one, but if there is no other way to keep your machinery going while you beat off all the vicious packs of exploiters.

A week later Rose called off the discussion. "The creative impulse is upon me," she explained, "and I want to work. Besides I am a little heartsick for the moment and want to get away from some of my indulgences."[16]

She received such an opportunity when she was invited to speak at the Round Table Conference for Work among Colored People in Greater New York. The invitation came from the conference president, Adam Clayton Powell, pastor of the Abyssinian Baptist Church. It is not clear whether he invited her because or in spite of her Communist party membership. During this period, however, Rose received a constant flow of letters asking her to address various groups.[17]

Among these invitations was one from Cyril Briggs, leader of the militant African Blood Brotherhood. Briggs, who soon after began a long career as a Communist party activist, sought to bring about an alliance between the brotherhood and Marcus Garvey's Universal Negro Improvement Association. He tried to bring the proposal before the Convention of the Negro Peoples of the World in 1921 and "arranged for Rose Pastor Stokes . . . to speak to the convention on the significance of the Bolshevik Revolution." A resolution from the floor calling for endorsement of the "international Communist movement" was tabled because of the bitter opposition of the Garveyites, who also refused affiliation with the Blood Brotherhood.[18]

There was a new president in the White House, not Woodrow Wilson, who thought she was dangerous, but a member of the "Ohio Gang," the very model of a presidential figure, Warren Gamaliel Harding. Toward the end of April Rose's fate was being slowly but favorably resolved in the newly staffed Justice Department.

George H. English, an assistant U.S. attorney, wrote to R. P. Stewart, assistant attorney general, that "in consideration of the improbability of a conviction, the bad effect which an acquittal would have on the public mind and the expense of preparation for such a trial . . . I feel constrained to recommend . . . dismissal of the case."[19] But there was no rush. The wheels of justice persisted in their slow grind. Rose declared herself resolutely indifferent to the ultimate outcome of her case. But there was a disadvantage besides the holding of the bail money for over three years in being under indictment and out on bond. Some thought this justified curbing her civil liberty, though her conviction had already been nullified.

On September 12, in her suburban hometown of Stamford, an American Legion protest led to police action against her. She was supposed to talk on aid to Russia, but threatening groups of legionnaires surrounded the hall, and police forcibly removed Rose and took her to headquarters on order of Mayor John J. Treat. She demanded that formal charges be lodged against her. This was refused and she was dismissed. The meeting, under the auspices of a committee of local socialists and workers' organizations, had heard other speakers, including Jeanette Pearl, and raised $300. But the legion intervened when Rose was announced as the next speaker.[20]

Rose was determined to have her say. She announced that she would address a group at her home on Willowbrook Lane on Sunday, the thirtieth. Justus J. Fernel, a local patriot, promptly reported to the Department of Justice and suggested that an agent cover the meeting, to jail her if she made "seditious" remarks.[21]

In New York she was not so bothered by officials of the law. More than one thousand people at the Lexington Avenue Theatre heard Rose attack Herbert Hoover's Russian relief plan. She charged the scheme with trying to turn people in the famine-afflicted areas against the Soviet government: "If the government of the proletariat had not been established she would have been supplied with railroad equipment and locomotives and every capitalist government would have rushed to her relief long ago," Rose told the audience. This meeting was conducted by the Jewish Division of the American Labor Alliance (a "legal" form of the CP). After marrying Graham, Rose did not emphasize her Jewish ethnicity though she did not try to hide it. This was one of the few times it was a factor in her selection as a speaker. She proposed a resolution that "we favor the stand taken by the Soviet Union in accepting relief from capitalist causes to be administered solely by the Russian workers and peasants."[22] She must have been mindful of a Soviet leader's remark that "food too is a weapon."

Rose Pastor Stokes had become active in 1921 as national secretary of the Women's Division of the Friends of Soviet Russia (FSR). One of her principal efforts was the organization of the Famine Scouts, a fund-raising group of children aged eight to sixteen. In three months their efforts generated $1,500 for the FSR.

In October Rose was told by her doctor that an x-ray of her lungs showed she was in danger of developing tuberculosis. This meant she would be unable to campaign for the office of Manhattan borough president, for which post she had been nominated by the Workers party, another "legal" face of the Communist party. Her work for the FSR would also have to be suspended.

Rose and Olive exchanged letters arranging for Rose to stay at Olive's home in the South. ("Don't go to Saranac—you could not endure it"; "Don't bring Anna—she would be miserable here.")[23]

In mid-November Rose learned that the government was abandoning further prosecution in her Kansas City case. The U.S. attorney in Missouri was convinced that no conviction could be attained. The *New York Times* said Rose was prepared to show, in defense, that her husband and siblings served in the war and that she had shown by contributions to Liberty Bond campaigns, knitting for "our boys," and other activities that she had no intention of obstructing the war effort. The conjectures about the line of defense she might have made were flatly contradicted by Rose in a letter to the *Times* two days later. She said: "In the event that the case was tried again my plans were to offer no defense whatsoever."[24]

By the end of November she was resting at Olive's home in Almond, North Carolina, where she remained till the end of February 1922.

The intramural warfare that had been slowly poisoning the relationship between Rose and Graham Stokes for several years flared up sharply in 1921. At the beginning of the year Graham told Rose that he wanted her necessary consent to sell their lot on Avery Street in Stamford to a buyer who was willing to pay $800 for it. Graham told Rose testily: "I am asking you to let me do it—to apply to your legal expenses which have amounted to $5633.85." That was it to the very nickel as of that moment. And as the year drew to a close, Graham expressed his fierce resentment at having their home—"my" home, he called it—frequented by Rose's communist associates in a letter Rose received just before Christmas:

> I am sorry to discover that notwithstanding your knowledge of [my] feelings in the matter you have again arranged for Jean Pearl to come to my home. Your disregard of my feelings in this matter is so outrageous, Roselie, that I will not stand it any longer. I have notified Anna that unless she can succeed in keeping that woman out she will have to leave my employ. If Anna goes I shall get someone to tend the door who has more regard for my feelings than my wife has shown. It has been a great imposition, Roselie, your continuing to bring or send that woman to my home and I will not stand it any longer.[25]

Graham was on the wrack. At about the time this cry of imperious pain arrived at Almond, a batch of cheery Christmas mail from Rose arrived in New York. The letter Graham received from her on Christmas Eve brought him "the first happy Christmas I have had in a good many years." But he did not savor this moment of happiness, for he replied:

> I'm sure you don't realize Roselie, how very, very mean you've been to me during the last several years or more. I've seen a lot of meanness during the forty years or more that I have been observing people's conduct toward one another. But I've often thought that never throughout that period have I known any human being to be so consistently mean to any other human being as you have been to me

during the latter years. You who when I first knew you were so wonderfully kind! You've let wretched people like Jean Pearl flatter and cajole you and for the time being mold you like clay, and the result has been distressing, and some day you will be very, very sorry. . . .

Anna was so happy over your letter to her and Mother was much blessed with your letter to her . . . I sent you some fleece-lined shoes. . . .

With love, dear, dear Roselie[26]

Rose immediately answered this painful and uncomprehending letter, writing with some attempt at tact and forbearance. The man she wrote to was certainly a domestic autocrat, though a loving one. She began with thanks for the portrait of the Harold Stokes family he had enclosed with his letter. "The baby is a Stokes baby to his little fingers even." She thanked him for sending the shoes, which would keep her feet warm. Then she turned to the substance:

One word more with regard to J. P. She is my Comrade. But you can have no conception of the influences that guide me if you think that she or any other personality in the movement affects my point of view, or my conduct. If you cannot see that great, world-shaking events have clarified my thinking for me, as they have for you, there is little use, dear, in discussing the matter. I don't know what my letter contained, aside from assurance that J. P. will not come to "88" any longer since from now on there is no real need. When I was in town and had no other suitable place to see her or any of my friends except in my home, it was necessary, from time to time. Now I'm away and since, when I return, I shall have a studio room where I can see her or them without annoying anyone, they will need never again to set foot on the doorstep of "88."

In our *thinking*, dear Grey, we must agree to disagree. I shall remain a Communist always—events can modify my tactics, make them more aggressive or less, perhaps, but my principles are what they [are]. I stand by them unalterably. As to what you call my "meanness" dear—there are two sides to every story.[27]

That same day Rose sent a cheery New Year's note to "the dearly-loved MacInneses," which spoke of her "banishment for six months to get strong again. . . . This is a log cabin . . . very primitive. But O, the joy of being with [Olive] and the simple mountain folk here." Actually, Rose's banishment lasted about four months: late in February she was back in New York.[28] In January she had received a long letter from Graham, heavy with business, written from his office at 100 William Street. He urged Rose to sell a piece of property she had acquired in the early years of their marriage. Mary Sanford wanted to buy it, and Graham thought Rose would be wise to accept her offer. He also enclosed a paper which he asked Rose to sign before a notary. It was for an exchange of a bit of swampland in Rhode Island in which Rose had dower rights for another equally worthless piece of swampland so that the two swappers could make better use of their adjacent properties. The letter also referred to a request Rose had made for $200. "I would gladly send you the $200, dear Girlie," he said, "but I must send it to Harry Forbes in payment of his bill. Recent doctor's bills have been in the aggregate so high that I can scarcely pay them from my income alone."[29]

This was one of a number of times Graham claimed to be broke, apparently suffering from a cash-flow problem. He evidently was guided by an upper-class policy that one must not touch principal but live strictly on the yield, though he did on occasion borrow from his mother. One does get the feeling, however, that Graham was parsimonious in his management of his affairs and Rose's.

Soon after this Graham was pleased to be able to tell Rose that "Anna is doing well at 88. She is just as kind as can be and the troublesome people have been staying away. . . . Come back and we'll find a safer place for you near home and maybe at home soon."[30]

Letters came to Rose in Almond from a number of friends and comrades. She had sent an article written early in the year to Jean Pearl, who promptly submitted it to the *Voice of Labor* in Chicago, which "was very glad to get it." The *Voice* was a midwestern radical weekly of which William Z. Foster was a sometime editor. Rose also asked Jean to pass on another article to the *Toiler*. Jean did so but told her that "you must hardly expect the present cocks to use it. There is going to be a change in personnel of that paper . . . I wish you would rather write on the women's question . . . you should assist in those lines that need assistance most."[31] By the end of January, the *Toiler* had merged with *Workers' Council* to become the weekly *Worker* (and, in 1924, the *Daily Worker*).

Elmer Allison, the director of the Workers Party Lyceum-Literature Department, wrote that he appreciated "your suggestions and the comments you make upon the Women's committee and its work."[32] When Rose returned to activity in New York it was again as national secretary of the Women's Division of the Friends of Soviet Russia.

Daniel Kiefer, as usual, wrote many letters to Rose in her mountain retreat. Eugene Victor Debs's name often appeared in them, as in his quotes from Lincoln Steffens when Debs had been out of prison only a month:

> Rose Pastor judges Debs, as Debs judged Russia. I made Debs remorseful for his sin, and he said he would do penance. . . . If a man as pure and sweet and loyal as Gene Debs cannot be forgiven his errors; if we are not willing patiently to speak to his willing ear and heart, then I say we are not up to our job as propagandists. . . . Woodrow Wilson said one thing that is fiercely true. He said that Russia was the "acid test." He himself could not survive that test. I think that very, very few can. We have dreamed of heaven, and we find that we must go through hell to get to it.[33]

Rose replied to Kiefer at length, taking issue with Steffens's tolerant, patient attitude to the veteran Socialist Debs. Debs's ambiguities about Soviet Russia and the Communist party annoyed communists, and in early 1922 Rose had scant patience with him, though the old man deserved better. Rose, apparently willing to try his ear and heart, paid a visit to Debs around June 1922 in Terre Haute, and the consequence was a distorted, and generally anticommunist, press release which Debs did not take the trouble to repudiate.

When in July 1922 Debs publicized a cable he had sent to Lenin demanding clemency for twenty-two social revolutionaries who had been accused of counterrevolutionary activities, he brought a shower of criticism down on his head, including a letter of protest from Steffens, a patient man.

But Debs remained a contributor to the *Liberator,* which was communist-influenced, and in August he came to the defense of the communist leader William Z. Foster and told him, "I shall be with you shoulder to shoulder in your stand for the working class and industrial freedom." And in October he said of the members of the Workers party, "They are actuated by the best of motives and that they are as honest as we [the Socialist party] in their efforts to build up a party to serve the working class in the revolutionary struggle."[34]

In general, both socialists and communists were able and eager to claim

Debs as their own though intermittently one side or both would take sharp issue with him. He was an extraordinary personality, a charismatic speaker and polemicist. He paid little attention to theory, and this made him unsteady when theories became the subject of battle. He was a revolutionary, and, despite his vaunted pacifism, in 1905, when "Big Bill" Haywood and others were threatened with execution, he said that if that was attempted "a million revolutionists at least will meet them with guns." Soon after, he warned the authorities: "Beware the wrath of an outraged and avenging people." William Z. Foster considered Debs's main weakness to be a belief in "bourgeois democracy" (although he was often enough victimized by it). "St. Eugene Victor" a newspaperman called him: "With his head he never understood Marx, but with his heart he instinctively felt the answers that the great Karl pondered."[35]

XIV

The Red, Red Rose

In 1922 Rose attended two important political events. The first was the underground convention of the Communist party of America, from August 17 to 25. Elaborate plans for keeping the location a secret were frustrated by the presence of Francis A. Morrow as a delegate to the convention—he was also an agent of the Bureau of Investigation. He had been given a delegate's rail ticket to St. Joseph, Michigan, and sent a letter to his superiors with that information. After arrival at St. Joseph he was taken to the convention site, a summer resort at Bridgman, Michigan, some fifteen miles away, where tight security was being maintained. But by August 19 two experienced Red-hunters from the BI had arrived in St. Joseph and had little trouble deducing where a gathering of some eighty people might be held.

A prying agent in the vicinity of the convention spotted a delegate—William Z. Foster. The agent was in turn recognized by Foster. While the agent went off to organize a posse for a raid, the convention succeeded in spiriting away most of its more vulnerable delegates and burying material that could not be immediately carried off. By the time the federal agents and their local support force struck on the morning of August 22 there were only seventeen left on the grounds. They included Charles E. Ruthenberg, party secretary, and Francis Morrow, also known as Special Agent K-97.

K-97 tipped off his "captors" to the location of the buried items, which included the registration forms of the delegates. It is of at least passing interest to us that to the question on the form, "Are you married or single?" Rose answered: "Self-supporting," thus foreclosing the 1919 issue of Graham's wealth.

One of the questions the hastily aborted convention meant to discuss was the propriety of ending the existence of the underground Communist party in favor of the legal Workers party, founded in December 1921. The Communist party merged into the Workers party at a convention on April 7, 1923. (The party resumed the name Communist in 1929.)

The second important event for Rose in 1922 was her designation as a delegate to the Fourth Congress of the Communist International.

That body (also known as the Comintern or CI or Third International) was founded at a congress in Moscow in March 1919. It was conceived to fill a void created by the collapse of the Second (Socialist) International, the members of which had been involved in the separate sides of World War I.

Selection of Rose as a delegate to the CI Congress in Moscow was an honor and an expression of confidence. The delegation of a dozen or more people included representatives of the factions that were institutionalized in the formative years of the Communist party of the United States. The party did not purge itself of these factions until 1929.

Rose was a member of the so-called Goose Caucus, which claimed a small majority of the party. The principal rival faction was the Liquidators. The Geese were for preserving a dominant underground party; the others were for liquidating it and merging with the open Workers party. The issue was decided during the Fourth Congress. The Liquidators won. In the next few years many of the leaders of the Goose Caucus left the party. Rose did not.

The congress lasted from November 7 to December 3, 1922, and touched on many relevant issues. A booklet, *Resolutions and Theses,* that resulted from the congress fills 124 pages. In the "Resolution on Communist Work amongst Women" Rose could be gratified that the American party already conformed reasonably to the resolution's mandate that all parties should take "necessary measures for the organization of women Communists within the party" and establish "contact with the masses of working women." Rose's political activities reflected this policy.

At the congress Rose served on the Negro Commission. Its main report was signed by Otto Huiswood, a leading black communist, and by Claude McKay, a highly regarded black poet. Huiswood's presence at the congress reflected his importance in the sparse black ranks of the American party. But McKay's presence was a fluke of his own making. He had been an editor of the *Liberator,* a successor to the *Masses,* assisting Max Eastman.

He left when Michael Gold replaced Eastman. Gold was too abrasive for McKay's taste. McKay then made his way to Moscow, where he had the good fortune to meet an old friend, Sen Katayama. Katayama, a Japanese, had been a member of the Socialist party in America and had attended Fisk University, a southern black school. Now he had sufficient influence to get his friend McKay designated a "special" delegate to the congress.

McKay was erratic politically and later wrote contemptuously of most of the radicals he had once associated with in the "*Liberator* Crowd." But in his 1937 autobiography he remarks on the enthusiasm with which he was greeted in the Russian streets in 1922 by "all the people": "Never before had I experienced such an instinctive sentiment of affectionate feeling compelling me to the bosom of any people, white or colored. And I am certain I never will again. My response was as sincere as the mass feeling was spontaneous. That miraculous experience was so extraordinary that I have never been able to understand it."[1]

The report of the Commission on the Negro Question was made to the congress by Otto Huiswood, the first black delegate ever elected from the United States to a CI Congress, and Claude McKay, probably the only nonelected delegate in the entire history of the CI. The thesis adopted by the congress marked the beginning of the truly serious concern with Afro-American liberation that was later to be an important aspect of the Communist party's activity.

There was also a minority report on the Negro question, submitted by "Sasha," the *nom de guerre* of Rose Pastor Stokes. It was not a dissent from—or a substitute for—the main resolution. Rather, it was Rose's appendix to that document. It dealt mainly with intercomradely relationships between black and white communists. "It is necessary," she said, "that the white Communists meet the colored Communists in a spirit of complete emancipation from color dogma. We must guard against the slightest misunderstanding on our part which might tend to prevent the fullest confidence and cooperation on the part of the enlightened representatives of the most oppressed portion of the world's proletariat."[2]

After Rose was back in the United States a bit of nastiness arose deriving from her presence on the Negro Commission. A malicious story appeared in the *New York World* declaring that Rose claimed to be qualified as an expert on the Afro-American question because she employed a black maid. Of course, Rose wrote to the editor asking for a correction of the story, which she declared was untrue.

Some weeks later Rose got a letter from Samuel Spewack, who was at the *World*'s Berlin bureau. He reported that his wife, Bella, had told him, "I have been guilty of a grave offense in crediting you with a statement which you never made. In justification, I think it is fair to divulge that my authority was Max Eastman who (I presume) had no interest in being inaccurate. His source of information was McKay."[3] The Spewacks, a popular husband and wife writing team, had long been friends of Rose and remained so. Claude McKay, however, was always antagonistic to Rose. He described her arriving in Moscow "still pretty and purring and sly as a puss."[4]

Soon after Rose returned from Moscow, the League for Industrial Democracy showed that it was not ready to write her off. A letter from one of its activists, Solon DeLeon, urged her to attend a meeting at Helen Stokes's studio next door at 90 Grove. DeLeon told her, "We very much want to have some representative people with strong opinions of their own." But Rose told him that if she did come she would not be on the program and would participate only if the spirit moved her in discussion from the floor. A year later Harry Laidler asked Rose again to present the communist position, but Rose refused the invitation.[5]

Rose did not spend all her time at 88 Grove, for she had taken a furnished room, which she regarded as her studio, where she felt she could work more freely. Though proof is scarce, Graham must have been outraged by Rose's attendance at the Bridgman convention and then her sojourn in Moscow. Life under the family roof must have been trying. In early March 1923 Rose told Olive the room she had taken was too expensive. She wanted to move but couldn't because the woman with whom she was living needed the rent money. But in the spring she returned to the townhouse at 88 Grove.

The Stokes clan was in Europe at this time. Helen was with Mary Sanford in London; Mother Stokes and sons Anson and Isaac Newton and their wives were jaunting around the Continent, sometimes together, sometimes not. But word of the tension between Rose and Graham reached them. At the end of a chatty letter Helen told Rose: "I have been thinking of you and Graham wondering where you were and how you were faring—and how he was faring there at 88. For you see I love you both. Do let me hear from you."[6]

Helen may have heard from Rose immediately that she was back at 88. In any case, Mother Stokes, now in London, heard this good news, and hastened to tell Rose how "very glad and thankful" she was "that you have come home to Graham and that you *no longer hold the extreme views* that have made him so unhappy." It was an unfortunate opening sentence. Rose underscored the words we have emphasized and scrawled in her heavy black editorial pencil "*Who* said so!?" Mother's letter went blithely on: "In all the world you could not find a husband as loving and faithful, and patient, and forgiving, and forbearing as he, because *he loves you,* and he had had no doubt but that you would in time realize that you had been misled. I hope you will appreciate his love more and more and that there may be many years of true happiness for you both together." Using her fat black pencil, Rose scribbled a note at the bottom of the letter: "I don't know where Mother got her notion that my views are *modified.* On the contrary, they are more left than ever in my life before—and will not go *right* again because based now in Marxian clarity. R."[7] Probably Rose left this letter with its addendum where Graham would find it, on a living room table or dresser top, rather than seek a face-to-face confrontation. They lived together as under the terms of a truce. This marital reconciliation was unstable and temporary.

In addition to the strains staying married to Graham Stokes entailed, Rose underwent other painful incidents. On May 7, 1923, her twenty-three-year-old sister Florence was killed by an automobile near the house where she lived with their mother in the Bronx. Anna Webb wrote to Daniel Kiefer to break the news to him. Kiefer was in the hospital with an illness at the time. His last letter to Rose was dated August 1. He died on August 18. His death deprived her of a staunch friend. It also made the connection with Lincoln Steffens more tenuous. For several years Kiefer had been a clearinghouse for almost all that Steffens and Rose had to say to or about each other.

Rose's fragile health interfered with her party work. In September Rose wrote to Olive: "I feel myself overwhelmed by distressing symptoms when on the platform . . . I am in my 45th year, Dear Heart, and I am not succeeding in cheating nature."[8]

When bad things happened, she applied herself with devotion and seriousness to her art, sketching and wash drawing. For advice and criticism she sought out Kahlil Gibran, the writer and artist. Years before, in December 1918, Gibran had responded warmly to a letter from Rose: "How gracious and generous you are to write me so wonderfully about my little book. And though your letter reveals a world of truth and beauty far beyond my reach yet I cannot but be moved and strengthened by it. . . . And how well you have expressed the unattainable by likening my little book to Olive Shreiner's 'Dreams'—and how much you have comforted me."[9]

Gibran was a Lebanese by birth and a Maronite Christian. He had been a pupil of Rodin in Paris, and it was in Gibran's nature, his freewheeling spirit, to improvise praise by Rodin of Gibran's work, including a wholly fictitious comparison with the art of William Blake. In the same nonchalant way, Gibran was ambiguous about details of his biography. His spiritual, mystic, and inspirational writings are still in print. Some were of the kind that are published in small format, on gilt-edged paper, in leather bindings, to be carried easily in the pocket for instant spiritual help.

Gibran "was also praised by social reformers," say his biographers: "One in particular was Rose Pastor Stokes, the nonconforming activist whose devotion to material revolution was as intense as his was to spiritual evolution. Although she believed in violent change while he held out for the exercise of sincere, intelligent love, they established a rapport and he began to understand and lean toward the Socialist position as a method 'for more justice in the condition of life—for a better distribution of opportunity.'" He once wrote a parable, "The Capitalist." When he read it publicly for the first time only one person in the audience applauded. It was Rose Pastor Stokes. He told the audience he was waiting for their applause—and then they shouted.[10]

Rose went to Gibran now as to a guru. One such visit was in September 1923. She was working in the election campaign of her party, but she found it impossible to do soapbox speaking so she returned to her drawing board. Gibran's advice pleased her. He told her not to go to art school: "Just draw—draw—draw—and get criticism . . . no one can teach you." She was thrilled with this suggestion. She told Olive, "I drank of it and carried it away in my soul . . . I spent an hour with a truly great man." There were other good hours with Kahlil Gibran. Once she brought him a sketch drawn with a carbon pencil. He said he was "astounded" and urged her to give all her time, for three months, to self-study. All she needed, he told her, was to get fully acquainted with that tool—the pencil. Another time she attempted a pastel. She told Olive: "I did not know the first thing about the way, yet when I finished the head (the girl with the copper colored hair I used to have when I was twenty) it appeared so real and alive that I could hardly sleep . . . over the success of the experiment. I venture to say that no artist ever used a scrap of kneaded rubber to apply the color. Necessity made me discover this means. And I find it good."[11]

She told Olive of her charcoal sketch of Graham in Anna Webb's words: "It looks just like when he found the toast burned. That's Mr. Stokes to the life!" Rose told Graham when he refused to smile "that he has one look for the mirror, one for his friends and quite another for me! . . . Most of the time when he is looking at me he is saying 'bad, bad Girlie, bad Girlie.'" Her sketch, she affirmed, was indeed Graham " 'to the life' looking fearfully injured and bearing it with the stoic New England gentlemanliness. . . . He is greatly pleased with my work generally, recently. One of Anna in a few strokes—is so perfectly herself, Graham breaks into loud praise, then cautions me against being too proud. I assure his Puritan conscience that I am only very glad and not at all proud and he is pleased to see that I am not going wholly to the bow-wows and we both laugh almost as in the old days." So there *were* a few good moments to be enjoyed, but they were too few and too late to cure the failing marriage. In the same letter that reported her upbeat moments with Gibran and Graham, she acknowledged to Olive: "But of all the many people I touch in the city, and I know there are many who are good and true friends, I feel always utterly alone here. You alone ARE, Heart of Me, others are shadows to me. And when my personal spirit flags in this city, it soars to your hilltop and you where the holy bread and wine your heart has always offered revives it again."[12]

In that September she hoped to get to Olive's hilltop in November. But it did not happen. In October Olive told her Gibran was right, and she was glad Rose had "found a heart of authority to which you will listen. The picture of Graham is wonderful—the nostrils tremble." At Christmas Olive urged her to come to Almond in the spring and to bring phonograph needles and records—dance records—one-step, two-step—toddle and waltz. Rose said she would and that she "would dance her head off." But it did not happen that spring either.[13]

Rose would put aside drawing and sketching and would never take three months off from party work to study. Drawing was then for rest and relaxation, for those frequent occasions when fatigue kept her from anything more physical. Otherwise she lived the life of a political activist pulled in various directions by constantly changing demands. Her visit to Soviet Russia generated an ardent article on the women of Petrograd.

Based on her experience at the Fourth Congress, she also wrote an urgent plea to advance the organization of women's committees in the United States.

She felt obliged to correct the *Times* (in a long letter) when it said that the Soviet Political Bureau had ordered the Third International to spend its funds in ways other than it was doing. The story had emanated from the rumor mill in Riga, Latvia, and Rose pointed out that the truth was that the Soviet government and party had no power to do what was alleged.[14] She wrote a series of "Proletarian Mother Goose Jingles," and both Charles E. Ruthenberg and Max Schachtman told her that they might be suitable for a projected children's magazine. But she felt they were too adult for that and would better fit the *Young Worker,* the organ of the Young Workers League. She got into a hassle over an unintentional affront to a Comrade Bail in Philadelphia and had to write a lengthy and apologetic letter of explanation to Ruthenberg when she reached her next stop in Rochester, New York.

Rose was nominated for the Board of Aldermen from the good old Lower East Side. Despite the paucity of farmers on that bleak landscape, nomination was by the Federated Farmer-Labor party, with which the Workers party was in coalition. But a few weeks before election day she was notified by the Board of Elections that she had insufficient signatures on her petition. She was disqualified.

Early in the summer, party work brought her to Cleveland, where she used the occasion to make contact with a number of the women who had worked with her in the stogie factory a quarter of a century before. Rebecca, a friend and comrade, shared the occasion and wrote her:

> I certainly did enjoy that day with your friends. It was a study to me. It was good to see the bond of friendship which had been made between you and the girls, years ago, survive, and bring them flying from all corners of the city and at all hours to see you and talk to you. And I was glad to see that at least one of them, yourself, had remained true to the working class, and its cause, although you were placed under circumstances which might have put you in the same class in which the rest of your working girl friends had fallen.[15]

In November Rose spoke to a crowd of seven hundred socialists at the Engineers Hall in Buffalo, New York, at a celebration of the sixth anniversary of the Russian Revolution. To her dismay—and the dismay of the entire crowd—her fur coat was stolen from the cloakroom as she spoke. The theft of the coat put the story on page 1 and grabbed the headline. Rose sorely missed that warm coat, which she had acquired a year before in Moscow.[16] A few days later she was the speaker at another celebration in New York. A few weeks before she chaired a meeting at which Foster, Moissaye Olgin, and Omario Ruotola were the speakers. It was part of the drive to launch the *Daily Worker*. It was part of the grind of being a communist leader.

The Workers party was trying to organize the paper's staff, raise the requisite $100,000, and transform the weekly *Worker* into the *Daily Worker*. Also needed were statements from prominent individuals welcoming the forthcoming paper. Rose was briefly on vacation at Old Forge in the Adirondacks when she got a letter from John Ballam, manager of the campaign committee, asking her "to shake Sinclair up a little . . . to push him into line for the *Daily Worker*."[17] Nothing could have been simpler, and ten days later Rose had the required statement from Upton Sinclair, who told her he was fearful "the weatherman will bust up the show." The "show" was an outdoor rally that he was working on for Eugene Debs in Los Angeles the following night.

In October Albert Rhys Williams, who as a young, radical, maverick minister had been inspired by Rose Pastor Stokes's "fire and grace" to dedicate himself to the cause of socialism, was preparing to issue a Russian edition of one of his books on the Russian Revolution. Rhys Williams had spent the first ten months that shook the world looking, almost literally, over the shoulder of Lenin.

As a preface Williams asked Sinclair for one of the latter's writings about Russia. Sinclair chose a piece about four years old which was based on a discussion he then had with Graham Stokes. It was published first in the *Appeal to Reason* and became the basis for Sinclair's prosecution in Los Angeles for "criminal syndicalism." Sinclair spent two days defending it on the witness stand. Now he had adapted it for Williams's book and did not know whether he should say that "Graham *is*, or *was* your husband." He asked Rose to write to Williams and tell him which word to use. It was just a legalism, of course, but the word was still "is."

Samuel Ornitz had been out of contact with Rose for several years. In mid-December Rose got a letter from him. He and his wife, Sadie, and their son Arthur were living in the Bronx. Arthur had caused Graham some nervous moments when they visited 88 Grove Street in 1919. Now

Ornitz was finishing his second book. He had "buried himself" to do "a lot of writing" that he had long been thinking of. Now "more than anything I want to know again and enjoy my friends." He wanted to see Rose. His first book had already been published. It was *Haunch, Paunch and Jowl,* and it portrayed Lower East Side life. It purported to be the auto-biography of a jurist, now deceased. Ornitz asked Rose not to reveal the secret of his authorship until the publisher saw fit to disclose it. Rose must have found the book interesting, if only because in it the central character loves both Esther and Gretel. He marries Gretel and then is devastated when the beautiful Esther marries a non-Jew, a *goy*, a settlement house worker, a millionaire. A postscript reveals that Rose had by this time given thought to writing her own autobiography, for Ornitz writes: "I am particularly interested in your biography that you and Fawcett [the pub-lishing house?] were working on . . . I hope you haven't dropped it. I think within the next year or so it will be apt and timely. American thought is slowly coming out of the war mad anesthesia. Your fight for free speech should be the big note of your book. Do you mind the suggestion? You see I have been thinking about it."[18]

Several years later, Ornitz and Rose did begin an ill-starred collabora-tion on Rose's autobiography.

Lenin died on January 21, 1924, and Charles E. Ruthenberg asked Rose to speak at a memorial meeting to take place on February 10 in Wilkes-Barre, Pennsylvania. But the meeting was banned. That action was typical of the harassment Communists were subjected to at that time. Three hundred people were turned away from the Bloom Garage, where the meeting was scheduled to be held. The American Legion helped the police bar people from the garage. But Rose and Herbert Benjamin persisted, and, in the open air, quietly, during the afternoon they did hold a meeting attended by some thirty-five people at Sugar Notch, five miles from Wilkes-Barre. Rose's speech was titled "Race War between Capital and Labor."

Alvin Olmsted, of Philadelphia, was one of those who participated in the secret meeting at Sugar Notch. He was also a member of the Ameri-can Legion, and that evening he attended a legion meeting at which he berated his colleagues, insisted on free speech for the Workers party, and told them of the memorial meeting that had been held at Sugar Notch. His fellow legionnaires threatened to tear him apart. Some peacemakers escorted him to the railroad station and put him on a train to Philadelphia.[19]

The entire episode was so commonplace that it would hardly bear mention were it not that a year or so later it would become a part of a fierce argument between Graham and Rose in which her recollection of the Wilkes-Barre date was deemed to be crucial.

Rose's planned spring visit to Olive's farm in Almond, North Carolina, did not take place. In fact, many months passed before there was such a visit. Both women were very busy, and both were plagued with symptoms of poor health. Olive, as often happened, was trying to solve the health problems, as well as the financial and general circumstantial problems, of various close relatives, usually several at a time. Rose decided to give her some advice, although usually Olive was the giver of advice and Rose the recipient. Rose told her she was taking too much responsibility for family affairs. She

> must cut loose from all the entanglements. . . . Often we do not alone smother ourselves but suffocate their own initiatives by solving and . . . assuming burdens of our kin folks. . . . The early years of my girlhood in my own mother's and stepfather's family, taught me that it is the part of wisdom to knock the crutches (myself) from under the crippled wills of my kin folks. They grew stronger by exercise. But it was not until after my own willingness to assume every burden had hopelessly demoralized my stepfather that I learned the lesson, which I strictly applied to the children.[20]

In early June advice came from Olive to Rose. Rose was planning to go to St. Paul, Minnesota, to attend the founding convention of the Farmer-Labor party. The Federated Farmer-Labor party of 1923 had foundered when it lost the support of John Fitzpatrick and the Chicago Federation of Labor, its principal noncommunist backer. Now in June 1924 the communists wanted to try again. They gathered their own forces and a slender coalition in St. Paul to launch a new national Farmer-Labor party.

But while the communists were isolating themselves in the narrowly framed organization, the broad masses of dissidents in the United States were rallying to the banner of the Progressive ticket headed by Robert La Follette. Everyone to the left of Calvin Coolidge and the Democratic lawyer John W. Davis was moving toward La Follette, including the Socialist party, the NAACP, and the American Federation of Labor.

Olive Dargan told Rose, "Dear and ever dear: I don't want you to go to St. Paul for two reasons. First, the convention will be nothing unless it unites the masses so that they can be better guided later on; and the more famous of the Communists should keep in the background. Your turn will come, at a time when you will be sorely needed." Olive was showing sound political sense. Her second point was that "I want you to take your well earned rest. Loaf and fill up with enthusiasm for your work. . . . Give the summer to your art, darling, and through that to men." Rose took none of this advice.[21]

Olive had a busy June ahead. She went to Chapel Hill to receive an honorary degree from the University of North Carolina, then on to Raleigh on business, then to Asheville on legal matters. July and August she dedicated to finishing her book of mountain sketches, which Scribner's published as *Highland Annals* in 1925. Her soft heart was guided by a hard head.

Rose was at the St. Paul convention, which ended on June 18 and founded a party that included as affiliates the Minnesota Farmer-Labor party and the Workers party and garnered 542 delegates, mostly farmers. When Rose was called to the platform, the convention gave her a standing ovation as she ascended the steps. She delivered a short, punchy speech on behalf of the abolition of "this whole system of exploitation." It was a message the conventioneers were fully familiar with. The *New York Times* reported that "Mrs. Stokes was wildly cheered as she left the platform." Rose could still captivate an audience.[22]

But the Farmer-Labor party almost instantly found that it could not carry on a national campaign. It nominated Duncan McDonald, a coal miners' leader, for president, and William Bouck, a farmers' representative, for vice-president. A few weeks later, on July 3, Robert La Follette was nominated by the Progressive movement and even the stalwarts of the Farmer-Labor party seemed to fly to him. The Farmer-Labor party candidates were withdrawn, and the Workers party nominated William Z. Foster and Benjamin Gitlow to head its ticket and go it alone.

Rose plunged into the campaign, but she dropped out before November. In September a newspaper reported that Rose Pastor Stokes, the "famous radical," had spoken with presidential candidate William Z. Foster in Elizabeth, New Jersey. A few weeks later, she got a letter from Olive that said, "I was not disappointed when I heard that you had to retreat from the campaign, for I knew you didn't have the strength for such a battle." She had to assure Rose, "No, oh no, precious, most precious! You are not even temporarily old. Not even jokingly old!" Rose was forty-five; Olive was fifty-five. She told Rose: "I am younger than I have ever been, notwithstanding this old stomach with its silent glands and falling perversity. This is my one ailment left, and I am going to Mayo's or Battle Creek and get rid of it. I shall submit to no imperfection." She had not finished her book of mountain tales. There were still two or three more to be written: "I have just finished one about an old man who was buried a few miles from here last summer, by the Masons. He was married six times and had affairs on the side, but he was a 'good brother, in fine standing.' I am boarding with a close relative of his, so got the inside story, which 'furriners' don't hear."[23]

Rose's poor health record, her energetic forays followed by almost inevitable collapse, could hardly have been the product purely of physical frailty. The impossible home situation with the constant emotional drain involved in enduring the living arrangements at 88 Grove may also have been a factor. Upton Sinclair declined an invitation to dinner because he could not face the tension in that household: "I should have felt so unhappy about meeting Graham under the circumstances existing. I am very fond of Graham personally, and I should like to sit down and have a heart to heart talk with him, but to meet him and not refer to the subject of politics—I just wouldn't know how to do that."[24]

Seven years was a long time for two committed people who were politically alienated to live under the same roof. A reluctance to make public the failure of such a "perfect marriage" may have contributed to prolonging it. Habits of life, slowly changed, were gradually adjusted to. A modus vivendi was developed. Tentative breaks adjusted situations and prevented a permanent break. Residual affection exerted its pull after sex had been retired. The wear and tear on the emotions must have been considerable. Ending her relationship with Graham also meant ending relationships with other members of the Stokes family for whom she had developed affectionate regard—Mother Stokes principally among them. Only Helen Stokes could be expected to retain an active friendship.

Rose had dropped out of the election campaign activity. She was scheduled to speak at Binghamton, New York, on November 5, but fatigue prevented and Sadie Van Veen Amter was sent as a substitute. Graham was away on a business trip. Rose stayed home and found it restful, as she innocently mentioned in a letter to him. He picked up the message as a stick to beat her with:

> I am indeed glad that you find the house so quiet and restful and "healing" but am so sorry that you have had to live so excitedly and so needlessly exhaustedly during so many years that no one can accomplish the most of which he or she is capable for any cause—good or bad—when attempting to function under such conditions and in such an atmosphere of [illegible] excitement and futile haste as you have chosen to indulge in during recent years. The "slowing down" that you now complain of is but the sane and kindly way of doing for you what you would not do for yourself. I have seen your day dreams of "revolution" and "triumph" blow up and vanish one after the other because the excited judgments on which they are based have no true relation to any wide realities. Some day you will feel, I feel sure, that this slowing down which seems so hard to bear has been just a very real blessing to you and, second, a means of enabling you to prepare for a far realer service to humanity than any you have been able to render, and through realer service you yourself will [illegible] as you never did before.[25]

Some may be impressed by the "common sense" shown by Graham in this well-intended lecture. But it could only have antagonized a revolutionary like Rose. What Graham called "day dreams" were to her the "wide realities."

Like all communists at that time who had made the transition from the Socialist party, Rose did need to adjust her dreams to changing realities. Everyone misjudged the tempo of the revolution. The success in Russia led initially to an expectation by its leaders of similar revolutions in Germany, Austria, and Hungary. The leaders of the bourgeoisie, on the other hand, predicted that the revolution would fail in Russia and took measures to see that it did. The Russians were wrong in that the European revolutions did not succeed beyond the czar's former empire. The international capitalist class was also wrong—the new Soviets survived.

In December 1919 Rose Pastor Stokes had told a public meeting called by the Communist party that "in the end . . . ninety percent of the people" would stand behind the party in the United States, "and it won't be long, I repeat—it won't be long."[26]

These words showed no inclination to heed the message, a year before, from V. I. Lenin: "We know that help from you, comrades American workers, will probably not come soon." She was more inclined to interpret freely his fiat: "We are invincible, because the world proletarian revolution is invincible."[27] Rose, like all the more durable communists, adjusted to that open-ended promise. But sometimes she became overwrought from the tension between her home and the wide, wide world.

How else could one explain her charge to Comrade Bail? And how could one explain her charge in the fall of 1924 that her close friend Jeanette Pearl was an enemy agent? Pearl reacted with appropriate outrage. She wrote to the Central Executive Committee of the Workers party:

> I hereby prefer charges against Rose Pastor Stokes in that she is publicly declaring that I am a spy. . . . Such a charge lends confirmation to the contention of our enemies that the WP harbors spies and that it is publicly so admitted by one of its active spokeswomen. . . .
>
> I want you comrades to consider the source from which this charge emanates, a highly neurotic woman openly living with a white guard, a member of the millionaire class. . . . When she was indicted in Chicago, he refused to go bail for her . . . I secured [her] bail.
>
> I had urged Rose to leave him on the ground that a Communist who is the Party's standard bearer has no right to be living with a counter-revolutionist while preaching solidarity to the workers. This evidently came to his attention and he forbade her to associate with me . . . I have no doubt that her charge against me is based on a subconscious desire on her part to escape the humiliation of being compelled to accept such a tyrannical ruling as to her associates.[28]

Secretary Charles E. Ruthenberg asked Rose for a statement on Pearl's charges, and Rose answered coolly, repeating her "profound suspicions that Comrade Pearl is not square with the party . . . nothing has happened to weaken or uproot that suspicion." Then she added: "Comrade Pearl . . . knows (what I cannot be expected to make clear to every comrade in the party) that I live *at* my home, but not *with* Mr. Stokes, nor have been for many years. Mr. Stokes's principles and mine, as well as our conduct in the class struggle, are diametrically opposed, as the world knows. I am responsible to the party and to the working class only for my own, not for his conduct."[29]

Rose's suspicions regarding Jeanette Pearl were baseless. She had thought she noticed that Pearl was withdrawing from party work. The reason, as she was soon to learn, was that Pearl had undertaken an assignment at the party's request. Rose acknowledged her error. The two friends were reunited and even shared an apartment for a while.

Life at 88 Grove Street in the three months that followed Graham's letter of admonishment—the well-meaning but hopelessly cruel and divisive letter of November 6, 1924—is impossible to reconstruct. There must have been more of the strained attempt to continue life as usual. But a fuse was sizzling and would burn to an explosion.

Perhaps it was during this three-month period that Rose became friendly with Irving Grossman and members of his family. The Grossmans operated a summer resort at Sharon Springs in the countryside some fifty miles west of Albany and a winter resort at Lakewood, New Jersey. Mrs. Grossman, presumably Irving's mother, and a female friend of hers were guests at dinner at the Stokes home on Saturday evening, February 7, 1925. On Sunday morning a hapless, perhaps innocent Graham asked Rose the name of Mrs. Grossman's friend. Rose did not identify her further to Graham, and there is no indication as to who she was. The marriage ended at that moment. Rose was infuriated by the question. She said it implied that the woman was not just Mrs. Grossman's friend. In a devastating fury, Rose declared that the question showed disbelief in Rose's statement. Graham said he had no such disbelief—he just wanted to know who the woman was, her name. In her anger, Rose's language went out of control. She showered him with "perfectly outrageous abuse—abuse so outrageous that [he] could not stand it. . . . And when in a cyclone of abuse you said you would leave the house 'tomorrow,' I replied that *if that was the way you felt*, I should put no obstacles in your way. . . . I have knocked around the world a good deal, Girlie, but I have never heard from human lips such wicked abuse as time and time again you have hurled at me."[30]

These words were written in reply to a letter from Rose, sent on Wednesday, February 11. She had left the house on Monday. "Dear Grey," she wrote: "I have still a few things to do at '88' before I am quite out of the house. My going would have been much harder—perhaps I had not gone at all, who knows? If you had not said 'it suits me!' This revealed to me that by leaving home I would relieve you of a burden—give you personal satisfaction. The fact that you agree so readily and cheerfully to my going, makes the going quite simple."[31]

From this exchange—the accuser Rose saying that Graham said, "It suits me" and Graham replying that he merely said, "I shall put no obstacle in your way"—in which the rebuttal is tantamount to the accusation, we might conclude that Rose's departure was but an angry response to an angry phrase. "I might not have gone at all," says Rose. "Come back, Girlie. You owe it to yourself as well as to me to undo *the hideously brutal thing that you have done,*" replies Graham.

But the two principals in this painful drama could only momentarily delude themselves that the ultimate quarrel was over a semantic misunderstanding. Seven years of political differences had preceded the denouement. Finally, Rose, not without some hesitation, had slammed the door.

XV

Divorce:
Riches to Rags

Rose left 88 Grove Street on Monday. On Tuesday she was back to remove her bags and folios. Irving Grossman, as she wrote to "Grey," helped her move. She found a room at 436 West 24th Street in the Chelsea section. "I shall not starve," she told Graham, "and work will be sweet once I am free from the suffocating atmosphere of the house . . . where love is not, nor understanding possible."[1]

The next day Rose sent a copy of this letter to Olive Dargan and assured her that, unlike in 1923, this time "there will be no returning. No matter how hazardous and hard life may be in the future . . . it was the better choice." She wanted to draw, "with a pencil and sketchbook lingering where I will to play at this new game which fills me with an ecstasy that I have never known before." And most important, "there will be no solemn faced, puritanical person to tell me that this is 'a most unlady-like, hazardous thing' to do and that I am 'utterly crazy.'"[2]

Rose waited almost a week before replying to Graham's plea—or was it a command?—"Girlie, come back." She had achieved an impressive degree of calmness, and her lengthy letter seems a perfect statement of her case—of what had finally driven her out of "88":

> You ask me to return—at the end of a long letter in which you accuse me of treating you brutally by the act of leaving "88". Not a word of the refined cruelty I suffered from your attitude toward me in relation to my work and my *interest* in my comrades. While I recognize that your attitude comes from the fundamental antagonisms inherent in our opposite points of view, to our adherence to principles mutually exclusive, you, on the other hand, seem to see nothing of this; appear

to have the notion that I am just a naughty child who, from some strange contrariness in her nature (or some evil influence exerted on her by her friends) refuses to be "good."

You scold me a lot; tell me that in all your experience no one had ever done a more brutal thing than I to you by leaving home. And you say, "Come back, Girlie." Apparently, you think there is no problem. Certainly, not an insoluble one. Perhaps, in a measure the manner in which I have tried (particularly in the past two years) to meet in a conciliatory spirit the crises you threatened by your attitude to precipitate may have led you to believe that with each "punishment" for my active support of Communism I was becoming more "amenable to reason." Last year, for example, after you had in silence permitted me to get the cottage in shape for the summer (even to draw John [the handyman] into the work altho you knew all the while that he knew the cottage was rented) I learned from you long after the event that you had rented the cottage as punishment for my having spoken in Wilkes where the American Legion attacked me. My humiliation was so profound, my protest so deep, I could have broken a storm over your head neither of us would have soon forgotten. Instead I was silent. I wanted to leave but said to myself, I promised to make life at "88" possible. Perhaps I haven't tried hard enough.

Again, when you could bear to see me start on a thirty-two-hundred mile trip by foot offering me a ten-dollar bill and the stern reproof of a righteous person to a wicked soul, I wanted to throw the bill in your face and return no more. Yet I said to myself, he hates my Bolshevism and will not aid it thru me. This is the reason for his attitude.

When you denied the house over and over to my comrades I said to myself "This must end." Several times I was on the point of leaving. That I went ultimately is due not to a fit of temper or of mean disregard for your feelings as you would infer, but from the most profound conviction that even the kind of armed truce that existed between us at the house was impossible to maintain, because of the deep-going fundamental difference in our aims, our ideals, our principles and convictions.

I returned two years ago because you held out the hope that we might maintain, even tho formally, some sort of peaceful existence while each did the work he believed in. I have come to realize that the hope was vain. A week ago Sunday when, once again, after repeated catechisms you took me to task about a visitor you suspected of being a bolshevik, the break that was threatening came.

You said it suited you that I go. I went. It is the first time in almost two years that I have breathed a free breath. I should stifle if I returned. I am willing to undergo any struggle rather than come back. This confession should give you at least some idea of the extent to which, under a restrained exterior, I suffered. I don't place the blame on you. It is the old story. We two look two ways. Add to this the fact that you had no idea of what I thought and felt, it was inevitable that I should suffer intensely.

When you taught Bunny to sit up and look docile and pretty for her dog-cracker, remarking to me with not a little of significance that the gesture pleased you as a "nice" way of asking, I determined to steal my bread if I must, but never to sit up and beg like "Bunny" to please a self-complaisant master.

No dear, I cannot return. We'll be better friends, respecting ourselves and each other if each goes his own way. It is not your fault, it is not mine. If invited to dinner by you, I shall be pleased to accept. But I MUST GO ON MY OWN. I feel sure that we shall find more peace—I, here in a hall room (from which, for example, I went Sunday to speak in Philadelphia and returned at three A.M. with none to question or be disturbed by me) you, at 88, where you have the comfort of a good servant, good food and no "bad, wayward child" to harass you.[3]

Graham's reply to Rose's letter is a point-by-point rebuttal, in some respects not unlike a legal brief. About half of three pages deal with the disagreeable matter of the lease of the Stamford cottage to Mr. Moos. Although he attaches documents to prove that she is amiss in claiming he did not inform her of this until "long after the event," he concedes that he rented the cottage without first discussing it with her and while she was absent at Wilkes-Barre "on an errand of which I deeply disapproved." He says defensively, "I could under no circumstances permit the place to be used again as a rendezvous, a place of recreation for ingrate enemies of America such as you had had there before." As for his refusal in 1924 to finance Rose's hitchhike to the Middle West to attend the Farmer-Labor party convention, Graham said: "I told you I disapproved so strongly that

I could not honorably contribute to the expenses of the trip. But I realized something of the dangers you were incurring, and so told you that while I could not give you a dollar for the *expenses* of the trip, I would give you $10 to hold in event of some emergency arising that would make it necessary for you to communicate immediately with friends." This stern epistle contained no invitation to dinner. Rather, Graham assumed the stance of a benevolent but despotic "puritan" when he said: "Notwithstanding all that has occurred you will be welcome at home whenever you choose to come, but I would prefer not to be there when you come unless you can feel regret for what you have done."[4]

Rose replied on March 6, enclosing with her letter a refund check for $63.81 payable to her from the Fifth Avenue store of Lord and Taylor. She had endorsed the check to Graham. "I shall soon be at work I hope and earning my own living. In the meantime I manage to subsist." She made no attempt to refute Graham's documentation of her "wrongdoing." Instead she stressed the extent to which their political differences had separated them. She told him:

> It appeared to me for a time, that I might succeed in doing my work from "88" without molestation. I was mistaken. Neither of us [was] able for one moment to forget that the other was a soldier in a hostile camp. . . .
>
> The bitterness with which you make reference in your last letter to my principles and convictions would convince me, were I not already convinced, that life for us under the same roof is impossible. . . .
>
> We are active soldiers in opposing armies, you and I. We cannot set up for ourselves a peaceful tent in No-Man's Land.
>
> Still, and forever, without bitterness,
>
> > Roselie[5]

If one might suppose that leaving home and ending a relationship after twenty years was an instantaneous process, for Rose and Graham it was not. Driven by some need for justification, Rose returned to the fray on March 16. She had found a memo book which, in her view, documented the validity of her complaint that for weeks he had concealed from her that he had leased the Stamford cottage to a Mr. Moos—and revealed it only when he learned she had invited her sister Lil to spend some time there in the summer. "I see in all this," she writes, "not any meanness on your part because I see that even in this our sharp political differences [remembering

Wilkes-Barre] play a most important part." And then, in a first reference to a divorce, she goes on: "Free me, dear Graham, and free yourself."[16]

Graham replied promptly with a quibbling defense and denial that he had long concealed the offending lease. With more relevance he added:

> You should realize, Roselie, that after ten years of faithlessness as you have shown to me I had no heart to call you up each moment and tell you what I was doing—what you were forcing me by your faithlessness to do. . . .
>
> "Political differences" have little if anything to do with our trouble, Girlie. There are lots of people whose political differences are even greater, who have no quarrel at all. Our troubles are due, or at least 99% of them are due, to your selfish determination to disregard my feelings in our home and to do exactly as you like at all times wholly regardless of anybody's feelings but your own. With deep regret, Graham.[7]

The accusation of "faithlessness" cannot be regarded as an accusation of sexual infidelity. Graham would not have tolerated that for ten years—or ten minutes. It is equivalent to his charge of disregarding "my feelings in our home." It is interesting that ten years would mean a period dating well before the split over World War I and the Bolshevik Revolution. That time span—ten years—coincides almost to the day with the entry Rose made in her diary on March 27, 1915, when Graham "innocently" accused her of "loafing." "It put the iron into my soul," she wrote. (Had Graham taken a peek into that volume?) Could Graham really believe that their political differences were so irrelevant? Were there really "lots of people" with such differences (theirs was more than a difference of Republican versus Democrat) "who have no quarrel at all"?

During this period when they were firing missives at each other, Rose had the pleasant distraction of having some of her black and white drawings and pastels shown at the sixth annual exhibit of the Society of Independent Artists on the Waldorf Astoria roof. The *Times* called it her debut, but she had shown her art works at the Independent Artists show two years before. The paper said there were "weird works" at the show. A headline proclaimed that one of the artists showed Adam and Eve as Ethiopians. Futurists and cubists displayed their work, and it all sounded very avant-garde to the *Times*.[8]

Major J. G. Phelps Stokes was at this time involved in a more conservative endeavor, preparing for publication his "A Brief Sketch of the History of the 244th Coast Artillery (previously known as the 9th Regiment, N.Y.)." Stokes traced the outfit and its antecedents back to 1673, when its British commander surrendered to the Dutch. It was this regiment that Samuel Ornitz and his son Arthur had seen being led by Graham Stokes in a Sunday parade in 1919.

Rose Stokes's financial situation was not critical at this time. Starting at the end of May she would be fully, and more than fully, employed at the Pavilion Hotel in Sharon Springs, the resort operated by the family of Irving Grossman. By Memorial Day Rose was at Sharon Springs doing publicity and public relations for the Grossmans' hotel.

But sometime before that, according to testimony at the divorce hearing in October given by the janitor of the building, Irving and Rose had become lovers at the 24th Street address. And sometime before Memorial Day Graham had acquired this information and had taken the first steps toward divorcing his wife on a charge of adultery, the only grounds then available in a New York state divorce proceeding. It was a ground used most often in collusive action in which the husband—being a male and thus safe from scandal—did not contest the charge.

On May 23 Rose had an appointment in the afternoon with George Houghton Gilman, a Connecticut attorney who for many years had been well known to both Graham and Rose. Gilman was to represent Graham in the upcoming divorce. It was her naive, and slowly surrendered, hope "that we can find a way without scandal for either of us and that you will find it possible to consent." In the morning of that day she wrote to Graham expressing that hope. She also told him: "I came in for my mail and Anna again mentioned (as she has done repeatedly) that she suggested to you a *money settlement* on me. I want you to know that I told her (today and on every occasion) that she is under no circumstances to suggest such a thing, as I desire *nothing* from you but my freedom."[9]

Graham informed her that Anna had never mentioned such a matter to him. Helen Stokes called Rose's problem with Graham a "tragic subject" and told her that their mother "refused absolutely to believe that your action was final." Helen believed it, however, and felt bad about it.[10]

Graham Stokes was pressing for an early divorce, but Rose balked: suit before autumn "might completely risk the livelihood of the family who have started the business here [i.e., at the Pavilion Hotel]." On July 8, Gilman had assured her that there would be no publicity until he had filed notice with the clerk in Rockland County late in September. That would take care of "any unfavorable effect on Mr. Grossman. Of course, Mr. Stokes and you will have to take your chances when the time comes."[11]

By this time Rose must have been resigned to taking her chances. She had investigated other possibilities: Graham owned much land in Rhode Island, a state that had reasonable divorce laws. Rose thought he could establish residence there and have the divorce proceedings under its liberal provisions. Graham would not consider it. Rose found that Yucatan offered ready conditions to partners seeking divorce, and she would be willing to spend the two or three weeks there that would be necessary to achieve a decree valid in New York.

Rose appealed to Helen to intercede for her to persuade Graham to adopt one of the more painless roads to divorce. Helen, however, told Rose that Graham never mentioned his marital problems to her and she regretfully could not bring the matter up. A few weeks later Rose told Helen:

> I am simply appalled at Graham's insistence upon his legal pound of flesh and cried out to you because I am straining to so affect his attitude as to be able to avoid being driven into some manner of desperate action to protect my future against the threatened attack. . . . But I can see that you can do nothing. Please forget, if you can, that I appealed to you.
>
> I am working as I haven't worked in many years, but it is, of course very good for me.[12]

Her hard work kept her busy, but she entered the political world in such small ways as were available. She had to deny to the *Pittsburgh Chronicle Telegraph* that she had "forsaken" her political position; she wrote to C. E. Ruthenberg that though she was not very active at the moment her "position is unshaken and unshakeable." Her present struggle was twofold,

> to earn a living after twenty years of absence from that field (with only the brief interval at the FSR [Friends of Soviet Russia] and to re-order my personal life. I am expecting to get my freedom and to re-marry in the fall. . . . We are forming a group from among the waiters etc who will study this season . . . then later we think, will join the Party. . . .
>
> Please be assured that . . . I may grow physically weary at times

and as at present be hampered in several external directions from full party activity but these things are temporary. I look forward to the day when I can get into the fight as usual.[13]

Rose was unable to attend the fifth Workers party convention on August 25 at which the name was changed to Workers (Communist) party. But she made two very brief trips—via the Albany night boat—to the city to vote for delegates, and she submitted a lengthy statement urging the importance and necessity for women party members to join nonparty women's organizations, especially those of a proletarian character, to influence them along lines of struggle. This was a tactic not unlike that which the Workers party and its close adherent the Trade Union Educational League advocated in relation to trade unions.[14]

Rose was disappointed that her country labors kept her from meeting with Mr. and Mrs. Julius Hammer. The Hammers had just returned, early in August, from more than two years in Moscow and were to return there in four weeks, a schedule that kept Rose from accepting their invitation and kept them from visiting Rose at the Pavilion, where, she assured them, they need not fear the food: "We won't feed you pickles for green vegetables." Julius Hammer and his sons were friendly entrepreneurs who founded a mammoth fortune on dealings with the Soviet state over several generations.[15]

Once the summer had rolled away happily enough, the brief ordeal of the divorce trial had to be faced. It was also an ordeal for Helen Louisa Stokes, Graham's mother, who feared the breath of scandal. Graham reassured her in a phone conversation four days before the event and then felt the need to put it in writing:

> Dear Mother, . . . I assure you I shall do everything in my power to protect your feelings and those of all our family in the very sad situation that has ensued. Everything possible will be done (on my side) to avoid publicity, and there will probably be none at the time of the trial anyway, unless Rose causes it. The judge has promised to hear the case "in chambers" (that is to say privately) and will undoubtedly do so unless Rose through misunderstanding or folly compels him to try it in open court.
>
> Rose has made some big mistakes in the past two weeks in her relations with witnesses. . . . Now it is in chambers as a default action—undefended. Rose has sufficiently admitted to the essential

facts and has specifically refused to deny them and there are plenty of witnesses who *know* what has occurred and when. So controversy, I think, would be very foolish. . . .

I hope she will feel that controversy at this time with all its attendant publicity and scandal would be much better omitted. It would injure her much more than it would injure me.[16]

Rose's lawyer was Charles Recht, who had counseled her as attorney for the strike committee at the time of the hotel strike in 1912 and had remained her friend. Recht had offered his services free of charge. She did not greatly impose on his time—they had their first consultation four or five days before the case was heard. Recht's advice was to put in a defense based, first, on the ground that the arrangements were collusive and, second, that the matter for other reasons should be returned to the status quo ante. Rose was against any opposition, fearing that this would defeat the purpose of a hearing in chambers—secrecy.

There was some effort to defer trial of the case. Rose even asked her mother to call Stokes to request a deferral. But Graham sent a letter to Rose giving his argument against any delay. Recht wrote to Gilman asking him to defer the trial. Gilman replied with a notice of trial. Recht wrote to Gilman and the judge that, because time was not fixed in the notice, and because the trial was to be in Nyack, in chambers, and on Saturday morning, he (Recht) presumed it would be sometime about noon.

Charles Recht arrived at court at about 10:50 and waited until all other business was finished—about noon. He was then told that the Stokes case was one of the first to be called and the judge had granted the interlocutory decree. The judge asked if he wanted an order to reopen, but Recht said no—he had no instructions from his client. Recht was amazed when, on Sunday, all the papers carried full accounts of what had happened.

The lawyer did not think Rose should waste too many of the ninety days nominally available for rehearing. He told her:

> As you know, I have constantly, and now do, advise you not to permit this default (interlocutory decree) to stand against you, but to open it. You stated that you had three months within which to take any action. I think, however, that if you will let the matter stand for the statutory time that it will make a very unfavorable impression, and that later, if you make an application to open, you will have to explain

to the Court why you waited all of three months, and the question of what we call "laches" might come in.

My motives in advising you to do this are the following: In the first place, you have explained to me, the whole arrangement was collusive. In the second place, no provision was made for the support of yourself and your mother. I understand from you that neither you nor your mother has any substantial means at your command, while Mr. Stokes seems to have plenty of money. An agreement to contribute for you and your mother's support would not hurt him in the least. I am the first person to condemn a woman who having lived a short time with a man then desires to be pensioned for that for the rest of her life. I have seen too many cases where men have been driven into desperate situations and poverty by revengeful ex-wives and wives, who insist on their alimony when there is no moral consideration for such support. In your case, however, we have no such conditions. The small amount of money that you would require from Mr. Stokes for your support and maintenance would hardly be burdensome to him, and the chances are that if he did not give it to you, that it would go to some such bodies or individuals whose aims are diametrically opposed to ours. Thirdly, you and Mr. Stokes have lived together for twenty years. Disregarding the last few years of disagreement and estrangement, there has been in the past so much in common between you which allowed your relationship to carry itself, despite of all the divergencies, for almost a life time. It seems to me that that alone, in a case of this sort, entitles you to some sort of an arrangement which at least would shelter you from abject poverty and need during a period of life when the glamour of youth can no longer gloss over the barrenness and sadness of one's existence.[17]

The principal witnesses against Rose were the janitor at 436 West 24th Street and a housekeeper at the Pavilion Hotel who testified to seeing her enter Grossman's room at the hotel. The janitor had seen Grossman, wearing a bathrobe, leave Rose's room at 24th Street. Attorney Gilman said he had known Mr. and Mrs. Stokes for eighteen years. Three weeks ago he had spoken to Mrs. Stokes at 24th Street, and she told him she would marry Grossman when she was free.

James Graham Phelps Stokes testified that he and his wife had been separated for more than the required year—which was not true—and that they had not both agreed to the divorce—which was also not true. It was of such trifles that Charles Recht wanted to ask for a rehearing, for the proceedings were technically collusive.

This quiet divorce was reported in all the New York City evening papers that night and all the morning press the next day and papers throughout the country. It was mentioned on page 1, column 6, of the *New York Times* on the eighteenth and page 1, column 5, on the nineteenth. A reporter had interviewed her mother, Anna Pastor, at the apartment at 1178 Clay Avenue in the Bronx, where Rose was then living with her. Mrs. Pastor was "surprised" at the divorce and could give no information about it.

Rose Pastor was not at home. Typically, she was down on Grand Street on the Lower East Side addressing a rally of the Workers party. The *Times* man reported that before her marriage she had been a cigarmaker on the East Side, but the fact is that she was a Jewish journalist on the East Side. He also said that Woodrow Wilson had commuted her sentence under the Espionage Act. That was not true either.

The *Times* reporter waited for Rose to come home, and he was rewarded with a statement. Rose handed him a portable typewriter and dictated about 375 words. Some of it covered territory we have already surveyed. In addition, she remarked:

> The mantel of shame seems to fall on the defendant in our case. It should be placed upon the shoulders of the State of New York where it properly belongs. There is due no small measure of disgrace to any state whose laws will not permit one to get a divorce unless one is willing to be made a subject for scandal. . . .
>
> The prevailing social system degrades lovers and sanctifies the most unwholesome, degrading and destructive relationships . . . the real scandal—the wife who gives herself to the husband without love and the husband who gives himself to the wife without love—the real breach is given a veneer of sanctity by the church and covered with a cloak of decency by the law.[18]

She would not be drawn into further colloquy by the reporter.

The wide publication of Rose's statement brought instant fan mail. A letter came from a stranger, Minnie F. Corder of Poughkeepsie, who hoped that the generations to come would benefit "by such true and beautiful ideals on love and life expressed in your statement. You are and always will be the one only great woman in the U.S.A. of the present period. Your name and your spirit will never die."[19]

Eugene Victor Debs sent her a note immediately: "I drop you this line of loving greeting to you this morning. You may know I remember gratefully your loyal [support] in the days that were dark and trying and that I hold you, as all do who have the privilege of knowing you, a strong and courageous and able woman in the service of humanity. Believe me I am dear comrade always, Yours faithfully."[20]

Rose answered him saying she was not "nearly so strong or courageous as I must appear," and she expressed the wistful hope "that we may yet fight from one platform." Debs replied promptly in his ardent style:

> We are perhaps none of us as strong and courageous as we sometimes appear but when the trying and testing experience comes, as they will do, we at least have each other to comfort and sustain us in our crucial hours and to keep alive the faith that after all life is well worth living. . . . What now seems cruel adversity will but strengthen you for greater service to the cause that is your life and add fresh lustre to your radiant soul.
>
> It does not matter how widely our viewpoints may be at variance. In these days of readjustment and realignment the time will come when we will again stand beneath the same banner as we have in the past and meanwhile, whatever betides, I beg you to believe me always
>
> Faithfully your friend and comrade.[21]

It was a warm, sincere, and generous statement such as only Debs could have written. It justified the faith that Lincoln Steffens had in him and renewed Rose Pastor Stokes's flagging love and respect for him.

For all her strength and courage, Rose, some ten days after the hearing at Nyack, was to feel pangs of bitter grief over the crash of her marriage, which had begun twenty years before at such a celestial level. She passed Graham on the street. He did not see her, but she caught a look in his face, his eyes, and she had wept herself blind over it.

She had sought to make it possible to part "without dragging our beautiful years in the mire. But he was unyielding," she told Anna Walling. "His puritanism (which was the original cause of our estrangement) made what came inevitable. He demanded his legal pound of flesh." When she passed him on the street, it seemed to her as if "it was *his* life, even more than *mine*," that must bleed for that extortion. But those who read the letters of this period by Rose and Graham must doubt that this was so. Graham reached a point of vindictive bitterness toward Rose even before the formality of the interlocutory decree. There was more hardness in Graham than she had ever realized and more softness in herself, and more tears. As for Irving Grossman, there were problems. While Irving and Rose spent a long summer of work and love, his wife gave birth to his child. Rose and Irving agreed that the mother and child needed his presence, and he returned to her. A divorce would come in due course. In the meantime he and Rose would wait and see.[22]

Rose continued to live with her mother, and Olive urged her to continue there "for a little while" at least—she was sure the rent would be paid. She even thought—though she was very wrong—that Graham would help her "after the first hurt is over and some day they would be friends again." Rose and Olive had lost their haven in the Great Smokies. Their farm was gone, and Olive did not think Rose should live in a place "totally without artistic stimulus and where your party activities might arouse tragic opposition." Her triumph, Olive told her, "lies through that one way—your art—and that means hard work and concentration—as well as the white inspired moments."[23]

Rose spent sleepless nights and tearful days. She was torn between love for Irving and grief for his wife. She sent him away "forever," but he came back pledging devotion. She had found that tearing all three of them to shreds was no solution. She could not work without peace, and Irving's love gave her peace. He was planning to make good provision for his wife and child and then leave them, though the family business would require him to spend a day or so each week in Lakewood, New Jersey, where they were living.

Her economic stringency was relieved by a $400 check from *Collier's* weekly for her article "There Are No Bad Divorces," essentially an elaboration, with some literary flourishes, of the principal theme of her *Times* statement: a denunciation of the cruel divorce laws, a belief in love, and an endorsement of "free marriage" unrestricted by laws.[24] She hoped to retain such freedom for herself. She also received a few dollars for a poem from *Theatre Arts* magazine.

"If there is to be marriage," she told Olive, "it will be free marriage." Olive certainly approved: "Your way of triumph is through yourself, not another. Irving is dear and fine, but mere mated love will never bring you content. It may help, but it is not your goal."[25]

Financial problems again weighed heavily on Rose when she wrote in painful distress to Graham on March 2, 1926. He had declared his intention to reduce, and then eliminate, the $100 per month subsidy to Anna Pastor which he had paid since 1905. Frantically Rose described case by case the hard times being endured by her siblings to whom Graham said her mother must now turn. The most prosperous of the lot, her sister and brother-in-law Lillian and William Fletcher, would find it hard to contribute $5 a month. Mother and Rose were ill. She had paid for her mother's expensive but essential dental work and the medical expenses from the proceeds of her writing. Then she went on:

> There should be no need to speak of these things but, you are so far removed from poverty and want. I can only account for your attitude on the ground that you lack imagination. I am hoping to make you realize something of the irony of your offer of "thirty-five dollars a month provided her children do their share"! From the whole of your letter I realize something of the bitterness you feel. . . .
>
> I had always hoped that our ultimate parting would leave you without bitterness. My hope was not realized. This is doubtless partly my fault but also, no doubt, partly your own. You can help yourself, dear Graham, and I shall be glad to learn that you have.
>
> As for myself and my old mother—somehow, I trust, we shall manage to spend "the last of life, for which the first was made," beautifully.
>
> With memory only of the fine things.[26]

It was important to Rose that she should treasure their good years together, which she accounted, somehow, all but the last two. And her words were hopeless against Graham's smug conviction that he was, and had been for ten years, the injured party. She did not mail the letter of March 2 immediately. But neither did she tear it up as she had several earlier versions.

Graham's indifference to any need to "help himself" became suddenly, and shockingly, evident to Rose when she read in the *New York Times* ten days later, on March 12, on page 1, the headline:

STOKES TO BE MARRIED TO
LETTICE LEE SANDS
HE DIVORCED ROSE PASTOR
LAST OCTOBER

On that day Rose sent Graham a letter: "The enclosed letter—stamped and addressed—lay on my bookshelf for a long time. I have not been able to bring myself to post it. But on reading the announcement of your marriage tomorrow I have decided to send it on. . . . I wish you happiness. . . . I'm posting the other letter instead of enclosing it."[27]

Graham Stokes and Lettice Sands made their vows at a small wedding performed in the home of his sister, Mildred (Mrs. Ransom) Hooker, at 173 East 71st Street. Officiating was the Reverend Charles Hampton, pastor of the St. Michael's Liberal Catholic Church, 144 West 64th Street. The word *obey* was omitted. Lettice came from the same social stratum as Graham. Her sister had married a Rhinelander from a family as prestigious as the Stokeses. (Lettice was still charming and attractive when we interviewed her more than fifty-seven years later.)

Toward the end of March, misguided again by Anna Webb, Rose made an effort to obtain some of her old possessions and some discardable odds and ends from the garage at the Stamford cottage. John the handyman had changed the locks and would not release anything without specific instructions from Graham. She wrote to Graham that Anna had led her to believe there would be no impediment. Graham wrote back that John had behaved properly. If she would give Graham a list of what she wanted, he would arrange to let Anna go up some day and help get the items out. "There are quite a few things in the garage that I should be glad to let you have," wrote Graham. "Certainly nothing should be taken without authority from me."[28]

"You must know," Rose replied, "your offer of Anna's 'help' is an offer to add insult to injury. You must know that I cannot accept." Thus ended another episode.[29]

There was yet another a few days later. At Graham's direction, his secretary, E. P. Behringer, sent Anna Pastor a $35 check "in response to a request made of him by the former Mrs. Rose Stokes. This will continue monthly until next autumn. . . . He hopes that your children will have found it practicable to make adequate provisions for your comfort."[30]

On behalf of her mother, Rose returned the check on the day it was received "as both the cheque and his expressed intentions in no way represent a response to the request I made of him."[31] Thus ended the twenty years of Graham's support of Rose's mother. This had been part of the marriage contract, so to speak, because by marrying Graham she was foregoing the means of contributing to the support of her mother and the younger children. Graham undertook to do it and gave her $100 per month until March 1926, two months after the final decree.

With money saved and money borrowed and a mortgage from somewhere Rose took possession, probably in April 1926, of a small plot and small cottage in Westport, Connecticut, and for a while it became the focus and fulfillment of her dreams. For $300 she gathered from various sources antiques to fill four small rooms. Her prize was a hand-carved, solid mahogany bed with a fine box spring and a heavy two-piece hair mattress. It must once have been "the possession of some super-Graham" she thought. Irving Grossman had also bought a "darling bit of woodland" not five minutes' walk from her cottage. There on the bank of the Aspetuck River he planned to build a studio-cabin with a little garage. Irving was painting and sketching. Rose was sure he would do fine work someday "because he has something finely human to say," she wrote Olive early in May. His wife, Sarah, and the baby were still with him but would not be when his cabin was built. Sarah was becoming interested in other men. This time he hoped their separation would come about "quite naturally." Rose's mother shared her fireside. Her mother was white-haired and past sixty-five, but she had helped Rose break sod for a cabbage patch that morning. Irving would let Mother Anna be his mother, too, when he had settled by the Aspetuck. And when Olive had *her* cabin in this sweet bit of woodland, Anna would be *her* mother too. The little dirt road on which the properties abutted was peacefully quiet. On Sundays a few cars might come through and perhaps a couple of riders on horseback, but that was the only traffic. Rose had obtained a 1924 Chevrolet with which she could travel to New York when she had need to. She and Olive could make the run into town that way in an hour and a half and save rail fares and avoid the smokey cars. Rose delighted in the thought of being south with Olive in the winter and having Olive in Westport for the summer. Irving would be in Sharon Springs all summer, working like a beaver to earn enough to give them all a simple living in their little communal colony. "It is all going to come true," Rose wrote to Olive.[32]

Rose was feeling cheerful because, if for no other reason, she had received a small flurry of checks. *Cosmopolitan* was running an article in June. Her agents had placed some verses and sketches that would appear in *Forum* in June and October. And a small verse she had submitted to the *British Poetry Review* had won the Tyng Prize and brought her the equivalent of about $50 that would be used to fix the gutters, screen the porch, and bring her some prestige. She had sufficient prestige—or notoriety—so that her arrival in Westport was noted in the local newspapers, which emphasized her art rather than her politics.

She wrote to Joanna Cooke that same day and told her the good financial news. Joanna lived not far away, in Stamford. Rose would drive there some fine sunny day and bring Joanna to Westport. If her health endured and she continued to produce, she was sure she would manage. Of course, the wolf was always at the door. "But let him howl as he will; so long as I am surrounded by the love of friends, he is powerless."[33]

Busy at Sharon Springs as host and boss, Irving Grossman was negligent about writing to Rose, and she must have prodded him with a lover's anxiety. On July 1 there came a hasty note:

> Dearest—you will forgive me—I know—when I explain—someday later, verbally—why I could not—or did not write sooner.
>
> Don't doubt my everlasting love and—devotion—I will be there thru it all and at the finish—no matter what the hardship—
>
> Count on my love—if it fails, slay me, for I would then deserve no more of life—

Irving's words sounded positive, and a trusting Rose was willing to be reassured. But her plans of two months previous were falling apart. On July 8 she had to tell Irving that Olive would not, after all, be part of their threesome at Westport. Because of her history of respiratory problems, Olive had decided she could not leave her North Carolina mountains for the Connecticut shore. "I *could* be very sad to think that her cabin will never snuggle in this sweet bit of woodland. But I won't permit myself. I have her love—yours. These are all that matter."[34]

Irving did protest too much. During the next weeks of the summer, both Sarah, the wife, and Rose, the lover, were to lose this undeserving charmer to a third party. In early September Rose had to tell Olive: "Irving remains dear and kind—to mother and me. But a slender young hand has plucked the sun out of my skies. . . . I try to hold the thought that our year and a half of love-life was worth the plodding lives of countless 'comfortably married' pairs. But I bleed at every cell of brain and body."[35]

Rose was mature enough to handle this relatively minor disaster within a reasonable time. From some friendly souls among the women who were attracted to Irving, including the woman who married him after his divorce from Sarah, she received plenty of evidence that she had trusted a man who could not be trusted.[36]

The cottage in Westport was not fully winterized, and as fall came Rose's mother returned to the Bronx and Rose was delighted to find an apartment at 133 West 15th Street between Sixth Avenue and Seventh where the Village becomes Chelsea. It was "a miracle in low rent," she believed. The steam-heated flat was $40 a month, which she split with her roommate, Jeanette Pearl. The two were once again the best of friends. Rose had been "insanely mistaken" about her.[37] Rose was working hard on her freelance writing and sketching. She hoped to own her cottage debt-free.

A new friendship she had formed with a young intellectual in the communist movement, Jerome Isaac Romain, was proceeding exceptionally well. Jeanette had to leave New York in December. Establishing a stimulating friendship with Romain had saved Rose from the painful loneliness which her absence would have brought on. Jerry Romain was managing to see her every evening. He, too, may have been lonely. He had been married to a writer, Frances Vinciguerra, who later wrote several successful biographies as Frances Winwar (English for Vinciguerra). They had a son who was about six years old and were now divorced.

One evening Rose and Romain had read manuscripts together until the wee hours; the following evening he invited her to the union headquarters where he had his office. The local was on strike. "They are men who go to one's heart," she told Jean. "They make you laugh and they make you cry." The following day he invited her to the meeting called by the General Strike Committee at the Manhattan Lyceum. The naive, good-natured local president hustled her to the front and maneuvered her into a seat. The party comrades on the platform were a bit uneasy, but she recalled old times as she sat in on that meeting. The next day Romain took her to see Sergei Eisenstein's film *Potemkin,* which Rose thought was greater even than *The Cabinet of Dr. Caligari.* At New Year's she had supper at the home of Romain's parents. "I'm afraid I'm getting deep in love," she told Jean Pearl. "I find him so rare and fine a spirit that it would take more than human will to resist his appeal." (A contemporary remembered him as a studious, idealistic, likable young man, a description that might apply to his later years as well.)[38]

He was taking college courses and must study for exams. "I'm interfering with his studies and I'm afraid he's interfering with my peace of mind." She wrote happily to Jean: "It was so good not to be in love! I'm mighty near being at that extent that I shall lose all sane judgment. Don't fall in love, Jean. It's an enslaver of life."[39]

Evidently she was being vigorously courted. Though it remained concealed from the press and idly curious for two years, Rose and Jerome were married early in 1927, probably in February. There was no political divergence to disturb this romance.

Rose performed her party work in 1926 mainly with the pen. In April the *New York Times* reported that an article by the "former wife of J. G. Phelps Stokes" had appeared in the March 8 issue of the Moscow *Pravda,* the special woman's day issue. Her article was her contribution to a symposium by noted women communists from many countries.[40]

In August, Alex Bittelman, editor of the magazine section of the *Daily Worker,* began an effort to enlist Rose as a regular contributor to the magazine. He wanted a weekly or bimonthly flow of thousand-word pieces dealing with particular incidents in the lives of working-class and farm women, plus small drawings to illustrate them. "The style should be kind of direct . . . from writer to reader in an intimate fashion." The proposal appealed to Rose. She was willing to send in a story and drawings each week, but she must be paid. She was "now a pen-proletarian, living from hand (frequently empty) to mouth. I mention this, Comrade . . . merely to impress you with the fact" of her changed circumstances.[41]

Her first story and drawings were received at the paper's Chicago office by September 16 and were used in the September 18 issue. Bittelman told her, "We will place you on our payroll, and as conditions permit, would pay you five dollars a week, or twenty dollars a month. . . . In order to keep up this arrangement we must have your second article and drawing within a few days." But conditions apparently did not permit the fulfillment of this modest reward. Back in New York from Westport in October Rose told Bittelman that she would not be able to contribute regularly to the magazine because "she must look for work." She would contribute "on occasion" and asked to be paid by the piece. Rose had submitted another little story and a drawing by October 23. On that day, in a letter that did not mention remuneration, Bittelman "insists" that Rose "contribute as regularly as is physically possible for you. We absolutely must have your contributions." But Rose's contributions arrived erratically.[42]

Rose told Bittelman she had ideas for the women's page. When she was economically able, she would accede to his request. The time, however, was in the "lap of the bourgeois gods." She said: "I laugh with those gods that this should have come to be true in this case. Had I a fighting spirit where I personally am involved, I'd fight for a place in the party. But I am not built that way. However, this must not prevent my expressing appreciation of your interest. I am grateful that you at least, one of the old crowd . . . appreciate my potential usefulness to the movement, even though the platform has, after twenty years, ceased to be my medium."[43] (Bittelman, "one of the old crowd," was then about thirty-two years old.)

Requests continued to come for speaking engagements, but Rose did not feel able to accept them; the platform was no longer her medium. Intolerable health symptoms generally affected her these days when facing an audience. She worked instead in the women's peace movement, in the United Council of Workingclass Women in a campaign for better housing, and in conducting an outing for women and children of the women's United Council. A letter came from J. P. Cannon, assistant executive secretary of the Workers party, congratulating her on her work with women and children and telling her that he wanted to speak to her and other comrades "active in women's work" when he came to New York.

Rose Pastor Stokes's new husband, Jerome Isaac Romain, was twenty-nine. She was forty-seven. Like Rose, he had been born in a Russian-Polish *shtetl*, in Lodz, and begun his education in London. In the succeeding years he became a leading intellectual in the Communist party, a functionary in its educational department, an editor of its ideological journals, and a writer of pamphlets and books. In the McCarthyite period of the 1950s he was indicted during the second wave of Smith Act prosecutions, convicted, and imprisoned. After completing his sentence, he returned to the work for which he had been jailed. From about 1930 on, he adopted the name V. J. Jerome and was known to his comrades as Jerry.

The union of Rose and Jerry was not, at least initially, accompanied by an improvement in their financial situation. Rose even considered—and rejected—a suit against Graham for a sum estimated at between $6,000 and $10,000, the value of stocks she held at the time of her trial under the

Espionage Act. Graham took them over to meet the expenses of making bail and conducting the trial and for his personal expenses in this connection, even including the nickels he spent for carfare. He had kept the accounts and, a few years before the divorce, showed her that her stocks had just covered the expenses he had undertaken to pay. At the time, under a common roof, it did not seem to matter. Now it was too late to pursue.

During much of 1927 neither Rose nor Jerry was able to get other than temporary jobs at minimal pay. She clung to her Westport retreat, and they shared low-rent flats at locations on the Lower East Side, initially at 107 East 10th Street. Jerome had custody of his son, Germinal—usually called Jerry or Little Jerry—and Rose made Germinal her charge and nurtured a good relationship with him. He spent much time at Westport with her. After 1930, when Rose became ill, Germinal returned to the care of his natural mother.

In January 1927 the Communists moved their party headquarters from Chicago to New York and the *Daily Worker* moved with them. Rose busied herself with the event, which was marked by a conference and dinner at Yorkville Casino on January 14. Scott Nearing sent a message of support and greeting. She tried to get one from Fiorello La Guardia, a maverick Republican congressman from a New York district since 1916. She invited him to have dinner with her, but he had a speaking engagement. He told her: "I am sure a good talk in a restful place as you suggest would have done me a great deal of good. . . . At any rate there is always a standing invitation for you for a spaghetti dinner at my home, 1852 University Avenue."[44]

She may have hoped to obtain help from La Guardia in finding a job. Mike Gold's brother George Granich tried to help her get a job at the Pleasantville High School, but she would have had to use a false name and lie about her formal education—or lack of it. Gertrude Haessler sent her a veritable catalog of comrades to contact, but there was no result. Her time was filled with looking for work, drawing her sketches, writing articles and stories, and doing party tasks. She and Romain were barely managing. J. Louis Engdahl, editor of the *Daily Worker*, wanted her to help with the paper's women's department. Bittelman told her in March: "It is too bad you are so financially pressed, but this does not in the least satisfy me that you cannot be of service to the magazine at present." He, too, wanted her work for the women's section: "Your stories and drawings are just the thing necessary." It seemed hard for some of her comrades to accept the image of a poverty-stricken Rose Pastor Stokes.

During the years 1927 through 1929 Rose wrote intermittently for the *Daily Worker* and for the *New Masses,* which had started monthly publication in May 1926. Her sketches and light verse were accepted by the *Forum,* and she sent her story "The Door" to every serious monthly in the country, all of which rejected it. She agreed to work on the publications committee for a projected "Anthology of Revolutionary Poetry," an enterprise greeted with enthusiasm by such as Edwin Markham and Percy Mackay. Her poems "The Alarm Clock" and "Paterson" were to be included in the volume.

In November 1928 the Civic Club invited her to attend a dinner and reception honoring Upton Sinclair. She sent her regrets, probably because she could not afford it. Two weeks later, when the Society of Arts and Sciences invited her to an O. Henry Memorial, she again sent regrets.

The Jewish Biographical Bureau pressed Rose in February 1928 to furnish biographical notes for inclusion in the second edition of *Who's Who in American Jewry,* though Rose's ethnic and religious identities were fairly obscure by this time. In April Globus Press wanted her "memoirs which we have been asking you to do. . . . Let's get together for the purpose of arriving at an agreement. . . . I am confident you have an absorbing tale to tell."[45]

Joanna Cooke had heard of Rose's financial problems. She was furious with Graham and reminded Rose of Graham's anger at the transit workers' strike. She said: "It seems to me that he has never been truly generous with you—never was—and that his soul is not a giving soul . . . I would speak things to him he would not forget." Joanna proposed that they work together on the story of Rose's life. She did not want her life "to go out like a flame. . . . There is fire and passion and love and sincerity to make it immortal." What she had in mind was a novel covering a short period, abridged to achieve dramatic momentum and to end with the inevitable separation. It was "to be a picture of two natures with a superficial affinity, but in their deepest layers antagonistic." But Rose was already thinking about writing an autobiography and discouraged Joanna's plan for a novel. Joanna told her: "After seeing you last spring I have left off thinking of you as the writer of the book I *wanted* you to write because—it seems to me—you love and forgive and understand too profoundly to resent. In other words you are not a good hater."[46]

It was one of the most difficult periods of Rose's life. Since spring she had been living with her mother at Westport together with Romain's son and another child who was being boarded with her—an effort to augment the family's failing income, which was sometimes frustrated by the parents' failure to pay for the child's board.

Jerome Romain, in New York, was trying to sell insurance, or advertising space, or printing—trying, but generally failing, to sell. "Unless something materializes I shall lose hope," he wrote her. "Something will have to materialize or I shall go under." In a curious ordering of priorities he told her that "the first few dollars I get will go for a *Freiheit* sub." By July 10 Rose was desperate. The boy she was caring for was a problem, and she could no longer tolerate the situation. She begged Jerry, "Darling, get work—any kind—."[47]

The next day the unthinkable happened: her mother left. Rose's letter to Bernard, her youngest brother, tells the story:

> Mother is returning to New York. We cannot live all summer together without making life intolerable for each other. Today she announced that she is leaving. The other day I was ready to do any desperate thing to myself to escape the close relationship. She is full of complaint against me, and I against her. She'll tell you her side of the story and you'll curse me. I haven't heart or time to go into my side. I can only hope for your sake that, when you go into a home of your own that mother does not come to live with you. You will not be in the house long enough to feel it. But your wife, who must bear the companionship every hour of the day, will be made miserable. It isn't just our mother. It is true of every mother who has grown old, and so "touchy" that you are in constant dread of treading on a toe!
>
> I offered to give her the cabin, and thus pay my obligation to her for the several hundred dollars she lent me on it. She refused it. I am putting it on the market. As soon as I have sold it, I will pay her back with interest.
>
> I hope none of the children will condemn me in this situation without hearing my side of the case. At any rate, I wish they'd first take mother to live with them for a season, before they judge. I challenge Lil or any of the boys to invite mother to stay with them in their own homes before they make up their minds that I am to blame in this.

Old parents should live in their own homes and be visited by the children. It is hell on earth for both.

Don't you ever do it, Babe!

And if you haven't read this to mother—DON'T. It will only add another hurt. It's tough all around. Never again will I suffer it, if I have to beg my bread. At least, I shall eat it in peace—hurt nobody and be hurt by none.[48]

It was October before the strain between mother and daughter eased.

The situation in Westport touched bottom on October 17. Rose had only thirty-six cents and no credit except with the milkman. She told Romain:

My pantry will be empty tomorrow. My tires are so bad I don't dare risk running on them. . . . You know the situation, why haven't I heard from you? You are silent. . . . Ask S[teinberg, father of the child Rose was boarding] to send me remittance at once. I cannot wait another day. I can pull the belt in but the children must eat. . . . I can't understand the lack of cooperation, dear. I know how much you care. But you seem to lack imagination. I have a roof over my head, but have nothing else . . . my 36 cents will buy a few eggs for the children and I can hold out till Friday—then I don't know what.[49]

That same day she explained to the League of Mutual Aid, which was asking for payment on a loan, the details of her situation and promised to send money "the first breathing spell I get." She had joined the league before her break with Graham, never expecting that she would be one of its clients—and a delinquent one.

On July 18 Rose had written a quietly agonized note to Romain. "Love to you on my 49th birthday . . . you have my best years. And if life under the present order did not so oppress us, I could make you realize it every moment of time."[50]

By December Rose had found a steady job as assistant secretary of the Workers International Relief (WIR) at its headquarters in Room 604 at One Union Square. The WIR was a service agency helping victims of class warfare, strikers and their families mainly, who needed financial, moral, and other assistance. She held the job through 1929. Jerry Romain also had steady employment. He was making a niche for himself in the ideological sector of left-wing politics. He and Rose lived in an apartment at 329 West 17th Street in an unfashionable part of New York's Chelsea area. Their wages were low, but they sustained a simple life.

On Monday, February 18, 1929, Rose Pastor Stokes was arrested with 229 other pickets in the garment manufacturing district of New York City. She was accompanied by nine-year-old Germinal Romain. The mass picket line, as well as the mass arrests, was routine in this strike called by the left-led Needle Trades Workers Industrial Union. It is possible that her WIR duties took Rose to that picket line. More likely, she was there because Monday had been designated Left Wing Artists' Day, one of a series of "days" for supporting the strike. Adolph Wolf, a sculptor, was also arrested that day. Twenty-eight pickets, including Stokes and Wolf, were dismissed, and the others were given suspended sentences. During the proceedings, young Jerry was taken in charge by the Children's Society.

The prisoners sang and joked with their captors as they were carried off to Jefferson Market court and jail. They filled the prison yard and sang "communist" songs until their attorney pleaded for silence on the ground that court procedures were being hampered. His appeal had only a temporary effect. Singing was heard in the court. Sympathizers brought coffee and sandwiches to the throng of prisoners.

They were all freed, but Rose was directed to return to court to face a charge of violation of the education code. She had described herself as Jerry's mother "in all but birth" and claimed, unwisely as it turned out, that the boy was being taught by tutors at home, "and we plan to send him to a good school this spring." (Application for a scholarship had been made to Walden.) The matter was cleared up on March 7, when the simple truth was told that Jerry Romain regularly attended PS 23 on 20th Street and had been absent only on the day of the picket line.

One result of this episode is that for the first time the press and public were made aware that the former Mrs. James Graham Phelps Stokes was now the wife of Jerome Isaac Romain and had been for two years.

The life of Olive Dargan slowly began a new turn in the spring of 1929. Her friendship with Rose had made her a fellow traveler of the Communist party, a sympathy not expressed in action but in understanding and words of encouragement to Rose. She recognized that rural Almond, North Carolina, and even urban Asheville, could be a fatal setting for a lone radical sympathizer flaunting her views. Her humanitarian instincts drove her to help any family member or neighbor who needed help. She felt the need to apologize to Rose for trying to help people one at a time rather than being part of a mass movement to bring a better future for all. Early in 1929 she was painting the home of a woman neighbor to make it more attractive for transient boarders who might drop in for the summer mountain air or while driving north from Florida.

But on April 2, 1929, a strike was called at the Loray textile mills in Gastonia, North Carolina. In February a small group of communists had started building a local of the National Textile Workers Union (NTWU) in the Loray mill of Manville-Jencks. An attempt by the United Textile Workers Union of the AFL to organize in North Carolina in 1920 and 1921 had found a warm response among the desperately poor workers in the mills. But the forces of "law and order" had driven off the union organizers and caused the union to abandon the struggle and leave the workers to their fate. The NTWU succeeded in overcoming the workers' resulting distrust. It built a small local. When several of the union members were discharged, a strike was called. Twenty-five hundred workers stopped work and joined the NTWU. The next day the governor of North Carolina sent in five companies of militia.

On April 4 the *Gastonia Gazette* carried an ad which said the strike was being led under "the blood red flag of Bolshevism . . . the flag of the country that does not believe in religion, which does not believe in the sanctity of marriage. . . . It was started simply for the purpose of overthrowing this government and destroying property and to kill, kill, kill." The organization for which Rose Pastor Stokes worked was in Gastonia by April 15. The Workers International Relief brought in food, erected tents for evicted workers, and established a relief store.[51]

The strikers were facing terrorist tactics from Chamber of Commerce members, the Loray Mill Committee of 100, the military commanders, and the civil authorities. Within about a week, Olive Dargan, now in her sixtieth year and living in Asheville, was for the first time lending a hand in a class struggle. She traveled the one hundred miles that separated Asheville and Gastonia and fraternized with the strikers.

In the last week of April Olive asked Rose to write to the Gastonia headquarters of the textile union and tell them that Olive "can be absolutely depended on . . . I have met many of the strikers and it is not necessary for me to go in and out of the Union Headquarters, but I'd like to—

and they have to be so careful. I'm stamped 'middle class' all over you know and they *must* guard against treachery. But the strikers like me and make me feel blood-kin—bless their weary bones! If you write, dear, sign as R.P.S.—the name they know."[52]

The strike was full of drama, including folk drama of the kind Olive Dargan was very sensitive to. On June 7 it climaxed when the strikers repulsed an armed assault on their headquarters in the course of which the police chief was killed. Sixteen workers faced death sentences and prison terms and were held without bail.

From her experience with the Gastonia textile strike Olive Dargan, a well-published poet and a chronicler of southern folkways, who had remained relatively obscure, wrote a novel, *Call Home the Heart,* published by Longmans, Green, which became a best-selling "proletarian novel" and made an impressive reputation for Fielding Burke, the pseudonym under which it was published. It did little for Olive Dargan, its faceless author.

XVI

Last Years

The political and temperamental differences between James Graham Phelps Stokes and Rose Pastor Stokes made it almost inevitable that they would go separate ways. While Rose was taking every struggle of the working class for her own, Graham was indulging his philosophical interest in comparative religions.

In the summer of 1929 he was in Holland and went to hear the Hindu Krishnaji. He wrote to his mother: "None of us [ever] heard as wonderful a discourse as he gave us last Friday, and perhaps we never shall again. . . . Someone called it his 'Sermon on the Mount'. . . . In me there is no doubt that the same Divine Being who spoke 2000 years ago spoke again last Friday . . . Krishnaji's message is very different from the message spoken by the Christ through Jesus—the whole emphasis now is on uncovering the Inner Light." In a small chamber on the top floor of 88 Grove Street, after it had been physically merged with 90 Grove, he established a meditation room from which daylight was excluded. He filled it with objects of Hindu and Christian worship and kept it as a place to which he could retreat and contemplate a narrow world. It was a long time since he had tried, in the words of Karl Marx, to change that world.[1]

In December 1929, though Graham would be unlikely to have known it, the *Daily Worker* was carrying frequent reports on the revolt of the Haitian people in a "struggle against foreign oppression," by which it meant control of the country by the National City Bank and the California Packing Corporation. The Communist party called for a mass demonstration of protest in front of the Federal Building on Park Row near Broadway on Saturday, December 14, at 1:15 P.M., to demand withdrawal of United States forces from Haiti.

Two thousand people showed up. As soon as the demonstration began, the police rushed in and began to club the demonstrators, pursuing them for blocks. The main body marched to nearby City Hall.[2] Rose Pastor Stokes was in the demonstration and felt the blow of a policeman's club. It was conjectured that this blow caused the cancer of the breast that plagued Rose's few remaining years.

The stock market crash on October 29, 1929, was soon followed by an accentuation of the Great Depression, which was already evident to the 3 million unemployed. As the economic crisis grew more acute, the unemployment figure would rise to 15 million. The Communist party, to which Rose Pastor Stokes was completely dedicated, now entered upon its heyday, which would last for the next ten years. But Rose was not fated to have any part in the successes and defeats of that period.

On March 6, 1930, the Communist party launched a national campaign for unemployment insurance, other forms of relief, and jobs. Demonstrations were held in major cities across the country. The leaders claimed that a total of 1,250,000 persons came out that day. In New York City they claimed 110,000. But Rose was too sick to be part of the excitement. On March 8 she was admitted to Memorial Hospital for breast surgery; she had a malignant tumor.

Olive Dargan, living in Asheville, learned of Rose's illness on February 26. Rose hoped for two more years of life to complete her autobiography. Olive assured her she would have "ten times two." She herself needed three months "to finish a novel and a book of poems. But I go for weeks without securing a day." She wrote to Rose: "Precious, you know that one lives years with that trouble in the breast. You will have time. Would it be possible for an old mountain doctor to get at it with that secret, inherited formula of his? He has cured many. . . . Yours may be not too deep seated for him. O, I don't want you to go to the knife."[3]

But Rose did go to the knife, and on March 8 Olive Dargan sent a special delivery letter to Memorial Hospital full of the passionate hyperbole of which she was so capable:

> My dearest in all the Worlds—I've just come in from four days out in the mountains. . . . My darling. I did pray with you on Friday because there is no minute of the day that I do not hold you wrapped in love and prayer and confidence. You *shall* be well, Precious. You don't

believe in healing through spirit, but I do—so strongly that your own doubts are powerless before my faith. You have so much to do yet. We have so much to do *together*. This book I am on—it is something you will like—the story of a mountain girl struggling with crude stinging poverty of the hills—her flight to the lowlands and the harder struggle out of which knowledge comes. She is caught in the Gastonia strike—and there are two chapters unfinished, that you must censor or approve. I can't send the book out until you have said yea. . . .

[This summer] you must be with me, darling. I am going to make it possible—and you are not to have a care from May to November . . . I shall have enough for us both to live in some sweet, simple way. Yes, my heart, our very ashes will know each other. I am not afraid of losing you in eternity—but we are to have a great joy here and now . . . in our present being. . . . Since you wrote, March 6th has passed. O, my beloved, from what hidden waters do we drink to be able to endure? And yet how great it all is![4]

Rose's name had not been mentioned in the press since her arrest in February 1929 while picketing for the Needle Trades Workers Industrial Union, when she was charged with failing to enroll young Jerry in school. The arrests were routine and unresisted and not accompanied by violence.

Nevertheless, when news of Rose's operation and her poverty hit the press, as it did on March 20, 1930, the *New York Post* reported that "Mrs. Romain's friends say, she has been in ill health ever since, during a scuffle between garment strikers and police last year, she was struck on the breast by a patrolman's club." The *Journal* said the tumor was "caused by a blow from a club during a Communist riot." This beating was often alluded to as the cause of her illness, especially after her death. The "Communist riot" was the Hands-Off-Haiti demonstration that had been dispersed by the police in December, when Rose did receive a blow, which did not seem to require treatment. In later years Rose's husband discouraged the idea that this blow was a causal factor in her affliction. And in a 1932 interview Rose told Marguerite Young she had suspected a problem since 1924.[5]

The publicity advertised the gravity of her illness and the marginal economic position to which she had been reduced. She was living with Romain in a tiny top-floor tenement at 215 Second Avenue near Thirteenth.

The news of her circumstances reached many people who had known and loved her and been separated from her for years. Lillian Wald sent her a check asking: "Will you please me by using the enclosed for any little needs that may arise? I have been reminded how many unexpected calls are made upon one's exchequer when things go wrong."[6] She got well-wishing letters from William MacDonald of the *Nation*, from Peggy Tucker, and from Solon De Leon. Many friends wrote asking her to rest.

She was doing that; how much more could she do? She went first from the hospital to sister Lil and brother-in-law Bill and, on April 30, was admitted to the Loeb Convalescent Home in Westchester. The arrangements were made by Cecilia Razovsky Davidson, a medical social worker, who advised Rose that at the home she would "be a guest . . . [and] receive attention needed for your recovery. . . . Mrs. Israel is in charge . . . knows of you and your work and assures me you will have all the privacy you request."[7]

The Communist party, through Herbert Benjamin, its New York organizational secretary, told her it would "be glad to do anything that is possible for us to assist you." Elizabeth Gurley Flynn wrote to Mary Heaton Vorse from Oregon that "Rose Stokes is very ill at the Betty Loeb Convalescent Home. I hope you can see her while you are there."[8]

On May 1, the day after Rose entered the Loeb Home, the day Rose would have called the "Workers' Holiday," her mother died. The tension between Rose and Anna had long been resolved. Rose promptly notified Olive, who replied:

> I wish I could have seen the darling mother once more. She had been precious to me since that night twenty-six years ago when she read—translating—the Rosenfeld poems and broke down, with tears on her cheeks, because of the heart in the Yiddish words. . . . Beautiful and great! And she must have her red ribbon—O, beloved! Brave soul and brave day. It belonged to her—that brave day. . . . We mustn't think that we have lost her, darling. Though the sweet face can't smile on us anymore. I shall wear two red ribbons every May Day. One will be for her.[9]

After her surgery Rose devoted herself to intensive study of the history, causes, and therapy of cancer. She found many references in medical journals and news articles to modes of treatment, including some bizarre notions. She even tried some of the less menacing prescriptions such as diets of uncooked vegetables, exercises, and living and sleeping in the open.

Advice poured in on her from friends and strangers. Flora Raugh tried to convert Rose to Christian Science because "there are many authentic cases of permanent healing of cancer on record." She asked Rose to send the practitioner's bill to her. Rose received the urging in a friendly manner, but it was one of the therapies she never accepted.[10]

Her first awareness of a more scientific course of treatment came while she was at Loeb. Mrs. Rachel Kaplan, who was a fellow sufferer from cancer, told her of the work of Dr. Hans Holfelder, head of the roent-genological clinic in a hospital in Frankfurt am Main. He was experimenting with an x-ray technique and was confident of favorable results. Mrs. Kaplan was planning to make the journey to Frankfurt. Rose cabled Holfelder: "Can you treat successfully radio resistant cells?" Holfelder replied that if the tumor was not too big he could be of help. He advised her to come without delay.

Rose's friends and relations opposed her decision to go to Germany. Dr. Levine, a cancer specialist, agreed to care for her without "regard to financial payment." But Rose was beguiled by the seriousness of Dr. Holfelder and the supposed efficacy of his treatment. Rose had planned to travel with Mrs. Kaplan, but Solon De Leon, a Communist party representative, obtained a reduced-fare ticket for her on the *Europa*. On June 17 she was on her way.

A telegram came to the ship from Olive and another from Cecilia Davidson. Oswald Garrison Villard, editor and publisher of the *Nation,* sent a letter carrying the assurance that his cousin had Rose's ailment twenty-five years before and was now fine. "I cannot let you go on this voyage," he said, "without a word of greeting—I always . . . had a deep regard and admiration for you."[11]

Mrs. Kaplan was the mother of Anne Kaplan Williams (later Anne Feinberg), who became acquainted with Rose when Rose and Anne's mother were receiving treatment in Frankfurt in 1930. Rose and the young woman became close friends. When Rose was an outpatient she and Anne traveled briefly in Germany together and took a trip on the Rhine. Rose told Anne at that time that "Hitler was the most dangerous man in the world!" Anne Feinberg believes that Rose went to Communist party meetings in Germany but, fearing for Anne's safety, would not take her. Rose, however, told Adelaide Schulkind Frank, "I long to go to meetings here but this, of course, I cannot do."[12]

Anne Williams agreed to work with Rose on her autobiography when they returned to the United States. During the next two years she often worked with Rose on this project and sometimes stayed with her at West-port while working. The living arrangements were primitive. There was no heating system, and winter days were frequently too cold for work. The autobiography remained unfinished at Rose's death, and Anne Williams did not feel capable of completing it.

Olive Dargan had been fearful when Rose underwent surgery. She was no less apprehensive of radiation therapy. But Rose's messages from Frankfurt were positive, and Olive wrote to Dr. Holfelder: "The word has reached me that you will be able to cure Rose Pastor Romain. This is great news for humanity. . . . How wonderful it is to hold the keys of life! I congratu-late you and the world."[13]

Rose returned to the United States late in July, and soon after she was with Olive in West Asheville. She was for a while under the care of Dr. G. E. Pfahler. Pfahler wrote to Dr. Holfelder in October reporting on the result of x-rays he had made. Early in November Rose was convinced that she needed to make another visit to Hans Holfelder.

In need of financial aid, she turned to the Mutual Aid Society, then under the guidance of Lucille Milner, Grace Hutchins, and Solon De Leon. Hutchins was a bit stern. The Mutual Aid was a loan society and was not able to give anyone more than $100 a month for four months. The Communist party had just moved its headquarters from Union Square to a loft building on East 12th Street. Its resources were drained, its staff accumulating unpaid weeks. Hutchins explained, "All our friends who have had the same trouble as yours—all seem to find that specialists here can do everything that the German doctor can do, without the heavy ex-pense of a trip abroad. Even those who can afford *the very best* of medical care go to Dr. [Frederick] Bancroft. . . . Dr. Pfahler in Philadelphia is of course also very fine and knows the method Dr. Holfelder uses." Five long pages of careful reasoning in careful handwriting explained the situa-tion.[14]

Rose assured Grace Hutchins that she was well aware of the party's dire financial condition. She was asking the party for nothing. She said: "In fact the party is doing for me *by merely being,* more than I can ever hope to do for the party. The existence of the party (and the intensification of the proletarian world struggle) gives me zest for living . . . save for these I'd find no sense in the personal struggle to survive." The $400 Mutual Aid provided plus $200 or $300 from a few friends would be all she needed.

She would travel third class; she would not stay in the expensive clinic but privately at rock-bottom expense. Rose informed Hutchins that "it would be no less an economy to live (and get treatment) in Frankfurt than in Philadelphia or New York." Besides, "In the Roentgen Institute in Frankfurt a radio-resistant type of cancer-cell is *non-existent*. In America we have yet to find an expert so far advanced in the practice as to feel justified in making such a declaration." Unfortunately, only the second sentence of this affirmation was true.[15]

On December 19, 1930, Rose left on a second trip to Frankfurt. This time she stayed until the end of July 1931. She was treated as an outpatient, residing in a small apartment with kitchen arrangements on Weisenhutten Platz, Frankfurt. She was able to prepare her own meals. Rose wrote all details of her condition to Olive. She was optimistic about the treatment and possible cure. Olive answered with an equally high-spirited and newsy letter: "But O, Precious, how I am rejoicing at your letter. I wish I were there . . . yes we'll get to Florida next year. . . . How I love Holfelder!"[16]

Rose was undergoing intensive radiation therapy. She complained to her friend Adelaide Schulkind Frank of her inability to apply herself to her tasks and work on her manuscript. She was unable to use her arms and fingers. The intensive radiation had incapacitated her, but Dr. Holfelder assured her that there was "nothing wrong," that she was receiving "precautionary radiation," and, she says, "I must accept his word." She was convinced that Dr. Holfelder was a "lap ahead of the rest of the Roentgenological world . . . and I am doing the best I can for myself by being here." She wrote:

> I prepare all my food; board and lodging does not amount to more than $15 weekly. . . .
>
> Yes, there are books and good things to eat here. The shops are crammed with edibles of every delicious and appetizing kind, but the poor workers here, as elsewhere in the world, stand outside the shop windows, looking in with hunger in their eyes, and emptiness in their pockets and stomachs. The well-fed German burgher is such a shocking contrast to the lean, pale, almost cadaverous-looking workers one sees on the streets . . . I'm learning the tongue after a fashion—simply by the inner necessity to waken some of these workers.[17]

Adelaide was handling her manuscript and art work, trying to sell her prints, and also having the autobiography typed.

In spite of her critical, painful, and demoralizing illness, she kept in touch with the world. Despite painful fingers, she wrote to friends, tried to work on her autobiography, read, and kept up with current affairs, thinking only of the day when she would be part of it again.

In January she received a letter from Germinal, who had not been in her charge for some time. He told her he was "getting better in school" (he was getting B's), and "the principal said he had a good chance of being promoted." Rose commented on this information in a letter to Germinal's father: "Our son's letter to 'Mother', as you see, was written in a spirit of levity. . . . Perhaps in his young mind he thought this was the way to cheer me up. Well! send him my love . . . I enclose a few scraps of things for his interest and amusement."[18]

In response to a note from Lillian Wald, Rose wrote her a full report of her condition and treatment: "I still take the X-rays daily . . . and have no idea how much longer I must stay. But today the Prof. announces that he will cure me—*absolutely!* He does not say these things to cheer his patients. I have heard him say gravely to inquiring patients, Well, you can't expect—So I am naturally most hopeful. . . . He has effected many cures that appeared hopeless . . . and I have great confidence." She told Wald that Dr. Pfahler of the University of Pennsylvania was in Germany. He said, "It is not fair to judge America by [Dr. Holfelder] any more than it is fair to judge Germany by Holfelder. Holfelder is Germany; in fact there is only one Holfelder in the world!" Rose's letter to Lillian Wald continued: "I'm trying to get ahead with my 'Life'—20,000 words is all I have done—and now must wait till my right arm is freer. I am promised that it will be, by-and-by. World conditions are such today that one longs for youth and vitality to join in the struggle. It is hard to be wholly inactive—merely an onlooker!"[19]

Anne Williams was one of Rose's few visitors during this stay in Frankfurt. When Anne reached Paris, she wrote to Jerome and told him his wife's courage was great and that she looked fine. "But," she admitted, "I don't know what that means."[20]

Rose kept up a continual flow of letters to Jerome, and he answered them dutifully and carried out her many requests. In April she wrote frantically requesting information on the "Red Indian." "I'm offered an opportunity of earning a little money." She needed historical information on the subject and asked Jerome to research it for her: "You know how to dig for facts." Then, typically, Rose told him how to dig: "The Public Library," "the periodical room," "maybe Bob Dunn will put you in touch with data . . . two statistical pages including the children." She too was doing some research on the subject when she was "feeling good." There were days when she was "feeling very good and they happen frequently now—though I have my 'downs' too—frequently." A postscript to this letter asks Jerome to write a review in his paper on a children's book written by a friend of Rose and recently published. She knows Jerome can handle it—especially since she proceeds to write the review for him, minus only a few commas.[21]

Several letters passed between Adelaide and Rose during the months she remained in Frankfurt. In February Rose told Adelaide she had enough money for her own subsistence but needed $180 to pay Dr. Holfelder. In March Adelaide told Rose that the Mutual Aid had approved a loan for that amount.

Adelaide had other bits of good news for her: she had sold three engravings and sent the money to Romain; Mrs. Dreier, the art critic who taught at the New School, had arranged for an exhibit of Rose's works; the art critic Horace Kallen and his sister, who was connected with the Boston Museum of Art, were "greatly" impressed; the manuscript was being typed.

Rose was eager to go home in June. She had come to use Adelaide as her channel of communication with her comrades. At the end of May she informed Adelaide:

> I should be free to sail third week in June. . . . Much depends on what [Holfelder] finds when again X-rays are made of the arms and the mediastinum. The swellings around the neck and supraclavicular spaces are down quite noticeably, *this* week. But there have been such queer "ups" and "downs" that I can't be sure yet that this is regression [remission?] come to stay! . . .
>
> I'm hoping, *hoping* I can be through early—and that my sacro-iliac joint which had been so troublesome and is now subsiding, aching and again subsiding will really prove to be nothing specific of [cancer].[22]

Rose wished to get back to New York—sick or well—to stand trial in the long-pending Bridgman, Michigan, case with other comrades. She rejected the assurance of the International Labor Defense that her participation could be severed. But then the indictments were dismissed and she was relieved of that particular pressure.

On the first of May she went to the Frankfurt May Day observance. There she had brief contact with members of the German Communist party, which at the time was a legal movement and near the peak of its strength.

But getting well was her main concern. Her doctor told her he could do just so much—"the patient does the other half." She believed that she was "making as determined, intelligent and cheerful a fight as can be made. . . . But, remember, I am fighting the deadliest of all known maladies. A hydra-headed disease." Mrs. Kaplan was going home. Holfelder had "absolutely cleared up her tumor."[23] Mrs. Kaplan died less than two years later.

In July Rose wrote to Anne Williams: "Sailing from Bremen on the 'Europa' on the 28th—this month—and flying from here to Bremen. I find it is *cheaper* than going by train—and sleeping car. I'm thrilled at the thought of attaining to the experience at last. I've always longed to fly!"[24]

Rose returned to the United States at the beginning of August and soon reestablished herself at Westport, where she applied herself to work on her autobiography. She had some correspondence with Villard at the *Nation* regarding an article written by Holfelder which Rose translated for publication in the *Nation*. Villard rejected the article because it was too technical, but he told Rose that he would accept an article on cancer treatment that might "appeal to the general reader."

Rose thought her book would bring her money for another stay in Frankfurt or perhaps in Liverpool, where a "new medicine" was being talked about. Maxim Lieber had become her agent and was confident they would find a publisher. The *Frankfurter Zeitung* wanted to publish the book after first serializing it. Lieber would negotiate with them. Coward-McCann was interested. But the manuscript remained incomplete.

The thought that she might go to Liverpool for the new medicine was fanciful. The "medicine" was a concoction controlled by a family that operated a women's clothing store. They were unwilling to let it out of their closet but would sell the rights to it for $20,000. The father, Mr. Swerdlow, had found the formula for the medication in the diary of a Dr. Levitas. It might as well have been found in the cabinet of Doctor Caligari. It is a measure of Rose's desperation that she could be beguiled by it.

More realistically, she was attracted by the news that William Donner, a retired steel manufacturer, had donated $2 million to found a cancer research center. She thought he should know of the work of Dr. Holfelder and wrote to him of her experiences—"my lungs have remained free to this day of recurrence." She spoke also of Julia Turitz, a Bronx resident, whom Dr. Holfelder had cured of stomach cancer.[25] She was also in touch with Dr. Willy Meyer in relation to his theory of curing cancer by rendering the bloodstream resistant.

She was following a rigorous regimen. It was summer and she lived in the unfurnished cabin in the woods back of the cottage. She slept on the open porch and ate mostly uncooked foods. When she cooked vegetables she used a Kampkook, a marvelous two-burner gasoline stove. At the beginning of August her book was one-third done. In October she reported to Dr. Holfelder that her condition was good and that her book was almost completed.

Holfelder replied in English: "I was very much enjoyed with the good news I had from your state of health, but—of course—I didn't expect otherwise. The last tracks of the disease of which you are still complaining are only due to the scar-formation, but nothing else. I hope to get still better news from you in the future. . . . Conditions over here are rather hard and the misery is just as great as all over the world."[26]

From the summer of 1931 until late in 1932 Rose spent most of her time in Westport. Her extensive correspondence with friends continued, but she did not have the company of the vast number of friends she had known intimately before she became a communist and when she was Mrs. Rose Pastor Stokes, wife of the socialist millionaire. Of course, her illness hindered her ability to get about town and socialize. She had friends and acquaintances who loved her for herself and were not troubled by her politics or poverty, and their letters during these trying years reveal their admiration and respect for her, often despite political differences. Her old and good friend, Leonard Abbott, after a cordial visit in Westport, referred to their "battle" that day and stated, "The day I spent with you lives vividly in my memory." He admitted that he had been neglectful for not contacting her and added: "Our long friendship means much to me, in spite of the fact that I can not share your one hundred per cent communist convictions."[27]

Romain had been assigned to bring Abbott to visit her. Knowing Romain's notorious absent-mindedness and neglegence in matters calling for precision, Rose had admonished him sternly: "Look here, Jerome! get in touch—or write him *at once*—to meet you on that 9-something to South

Norwalk on Sunday morning, or at the S.N. station *And Don't Fail Him!*"[28]

Rose was very deprived financially at this time. Her attempt to live frugally on simple food in bare surroundings owed as much to destitution as to her quest for health. She had no heat indoors, and the cold weather became unbearable. She probably moved from the cabin to the cottage with its fireplace when winter set in. Romain gently urged her to move back to the city: "Perhaps it would be best if you came to town for the rest of the winter . . . really, darling, think it over. You could work at your book in warmth and quiet all day long." But Rose was fighting for health and stayed in the fresh air and simplicity of Westport.[29]

Clara Renner of Brooklyn must have heard from a friend of Rose Pastor of her need for blankets. Renner sent her two soft, light, warm ones with a note that said: "I hope dear Comrade, some day to have the pleasure of meeting you, as I must confess you have a great place in my thoughts. Trust you are feeling better and if I can be of service (I am a nurse) nothing would be too much." Rose responded to Renner: "How can I tell you how your gift and thought of me have moved me. I have slept two nights under the soft, light blankets. I have awakened less tired . . . I will do more work because of this. This is what we make sacrifices [for] to further the work and bring closer the day of working class emancipation. My love and thanks for your brave offer of personal service which I shall always remember."[30]

From Culver City, California, on a Metro-Goldwyn-Mayer letterhead, came a warm note from Bella Spewack and a copy of the latest play she and her husband, Sam, had written. They were going to see Lincoln Steffens. She asked Rose to "pocket her pride" and accept the $100 enclosed for her blessed cure. "I think of you often," wrote Bella, "and wish I had the courage of your convictions."[31]

In January Rose heard from her brother-in-law William Fletcher a story that shocked her profoundly and provoked her to reflect upon her finished life with Graham. She hastened to pass it on to Olive Dargan:

> Billy was in the neighborhood of 88 Grove street, and on an impulse stopped in to see Graham. Graham was apparently very glad to see him and they talked. Billy naturally got on the subject of the collapse and what this has done to the workers; the unemployment, the star-

vation wages, the stagger plan, the vast misery of millions of men, women and children. *And what do you think Graham said to all this?* Graham said he thought "the public health" was better today than it ever was because *people weren't eating so much!* . . . Can you believe it? . . . Can you? . . .

To think that once I had such faith in his loyalty to the people— that I had implicit confidence in his genuine devotion to the cause! But how can it be possible that any time in such a man's life was a time of true devotion to the principles which for more than ten years he professed! It is utterly *impossible,* IMPOSSIBLE![32]

Through 1931 and 1932 Rose continued to work on her book, but her poor health hindered her ability to concentrate on completing it.

For the past two years Hermynia Zur Muhlen, a German communist writer living in Frankfurt, had carried on a correspondence with Rose about health and literature. Hermynia wished to translate Rose's short stories and get them published. She may also have thought of translating and publishing her autobiography. But these ideas never materialized. As Hitler came closer to power, the chances of German publication for Rose's writings became more remote.

In the United States her agent and friend Maxim Lieber made every effort to obtain a publisher for her. There were a number of setbacks. George Putnam, who had published Rose's play fifteen years before, heard about her autobiography from Anzia Yezierska one evening at his dinner table. He wanted to buy the book and sell serialization rights to *Liberty* magazine. But *Liberty* did not want it, and Rose told Lieber she did not want to appear in that magazine. Putnam's interest cooled.

Samuel Middleboro, of E. P. Dutton, told Rose that Dutton "cannot fit your book into their list," adding "such a forthright and telling document will find its way to the public." A friend of his wanted to read the manuscript. He permitted her to do so and "returned to find her in tears." Benjamin DeCasseres told Rose that "Arthur Leonard Ross . . . and Ben Sonnenberg [the father of the present editor of *Grand Street*] would like to handle her book . . . [Ross] is the friend of all radicals . . . he has great admiration for you." Coward-McCann was now "interested." Rose scribbled a letter to Lieber: "I doubt if any publisher other than International will take my book."[33] She was wrong. It was accepted by Covici-Friede with the help of Sam Ornitz, who obtained an advance of $500 to be paid to Rose in a lump sum of $250 and then $25 a month.

Olive Dargan was also having difficulties with publication of her *Call Home the Heart,* but they were of a different magnitude from those of Rose Pastor Stokes. In March 1932 Olive told Rose that the book was being published. But she complained bitterly that her "best Communist Party chapter was cut out bodily." (Olive never joined the Communist party, but she wished it well, cheered Rose on, made Rose's friends her friends, and seven years after Rose's death, helped the Communist party in practical ways in the North Carolina hills.)[34]

Dargan had chosen the pseudonym of Fielding Burke for her first novel to cover her real identity in what she perceived as the hostile territory of the South. But *Call Home the Heart* was well received by the mainstream critics, one of whom promptly revealed her identity. She wrote two more novels by Fielding Burke, neither of which enjoyed the success of her first. After *Call Home the Heart* appeared, she used her nom de plume in her infrequent left-wing activities, such as the First American Writers Congress in 1935.

In the early spring of 1932 Rose was receiving treatment from Dr. Willy Meyer without fee. When he died suddenly, his son, Dr. Herbert Willy Meyer, arranged for x-rays for her when she was unable to pay Lenox Hill Hospital for them. The films were sent promptly to Dr. Holfelder in Frankfurt.

At about the same time, she arranged to enter Lenox Hill to receive a five-week course of treatment from Dr. Linder, basically a series of injections of the mistletoe extract. She had heard that Mrs. Kaplan had taken the "brew" in Liverpool. Her blood had been normalized from the alkaline side to the acid. A cure was certain, Rose believed. She was ready to try anything. She told Romain when she entered the hospital to tell friends not to send flowers but rather to send vegetables and fruits because she did not expect to get these at the hospital.

Soon after she was released, Dr. Linder informed her that "the Amerlabs Corporation will send you a bottle of Birch Elixir. Take it three times daily, one teaspoonful in a third glass of water before main meals." He also prescribed "an abundance of fruits and vegetables, with exception of tomatoes . . . and only a little of potato and corn."[35]

Meanwhile, from Heidelberg, Paula Jacobi wrote joyously to Rose, "We [Jacobi and Anna Van Vechten] have been to see your wonderful Dr. Holfelder with his extraordinary 'cannons.' He has treated my friend . . . and we have been dismissed for six months! This means a new lease on life." A month later another letter said that Paula's friend was again unwell and taking parathyroid tablets under Holfelder's prescription. But no amount of bad news could undermine Rose's confidence in the Frankfurt physician. Shortly before Rose died, and unknown to Rose, Anna Van Vechten committed suicide.[36]

From what seemed like the wrong side of the barricades, June Burr, a member of the Guggenheim family, made a sardonic query: "Why should my father, poor perverted human being, be permitted 86 years here when you and I must live under this cloud of haste lest we be snatched before we even half-finish what we want to do."[37]

Rose believed that correcting her blood's pH was the key to a cure. Late in August 1932 she was still sure Dr. Linder had achieved this. Her friend Jeanette Pearl was traveling through Europe seeking help and rest for a nervous disorder. She wrote to Rose from Berlin that there is a "serum they use here for cancer that is said to be very good called 'mistel'." Rose replied promptly:

> Mistel—is Mistletoe. . . . How thrilling, no longer in the experimental state in Germany and Switzerland. . . . It literally unnerved me to read your letter on this score. I am talking my head off to doctors and laymen ever since I have had my report on the pH of my blood. The mistletoe *corrected it completely.* Of course I must get the news to our friends at once. With your letter to add to what I already know and believe, I can possibly impress them more deeply with the fact that this is not "just another will-o-wisp" . . . but the answer to the mysterious malady.[38]

But Olive had been worried by Rose's enthusiasm for the magic potion. She questioned whether Rose should take both Holfelder's radiological treatment and Linder's remedy at the same time. "You must not make a mistake," she cried out. "To have you well and eagerly working is the thought that thrills me."[39]

In September Rose parted for the last time from her dearly loved stepson, Germinal Romain, who was returning to his mother, Frances Vinciguerra. To the painful parting Rose added a painful letter:

> Perhaps you felt that I turned away and did not say a word to you in what I felt was our parting, because I could not trust myself to speak at all. It was doubly difficult because there was an outsider present. This is just to tell you that my heart ached in that moment. You looked so pale, so really ill, and in need of care, I could have cried. In the restaurant I saw you eat unwisely—*mustard* on your bread and similar harmful stuff. Yet I felt it was no longer my part to caution you.
>
> Be earnest for the movement, Dear Boy. And if, in love, things don't always go well believe that there is something more wonderful ahead that cannot yet be seen. I wish I could save you suffering—despite everything.
>
> Your Mother. (Still!)[40]

By October Rose knew that her health was declining. In November she told Dr. Holfelder that "friends are trying to get a new fund for me to stay at your clinic for treatment. If the fund materializes I shall take the next boat out." On December 28, 1932, she wrote to Holfelder: "Can you give me any hope that under your treatment I will recover my health again for a desirable period of time? At best I could hope to check the disease for a year or more. Could you help me if I come soon? I shall anxiously await your answer."[41]

But the next day Rose, who was staying with her friend Dr. Grace Bates at the doctor's apartment at 2 Gramercy Park West, became extremely ill and was taken by ambulance to Flower Hospital. The diagnosis was pneumonia. In the hospital she started a diary of sorts in an appointment book marked off in weekly pages. She sketchily noted her progress and plans until March 20:

January 8–14:	Still improving—temperature 99.2 Learned that Helen Stokes took care of the hospital fee. My heart goes out to her
January 16—	Holfelder cabled—Come immediately—so there is still cause for hope
January 17—	Ornitz 9 A.M.
January 18—	Sam Ornitz 2 o'clock

January 22—	Lil and Bill take me to their home
January 26–27	Ornitz comes. Works with me
February 8—	Sail on *Hamburg* to Frankfurt
February 17—	Land at Bremen. Land journey [to Frankfurt] near killed me
February 20–25	Can I survive such terrible food and conditions
March 5–12	Am sinking daily, cannot bear the suffering
March 12—	Letters at last
March 12–15	Difference in my condition, but food still a problem. Stale vegetables, meats, sour sauces
March 19—	Chicken at dinner was literally decayed
March 20—	Holfelder sends me back to Haus Baden[42]

She was unable to work on her book. She had arranged with Samuel Ornitz for him to do the unfinished portion as a biography. Olive was pleased with this news: "An unfinished book can weigh so heavily on vitality. You will get well faster when getting well is your only business."[43]

Rose turned to the willing, able, and reliable Anne Williams for many small favors: "Covici-Friede has not begun to remit. Can you stir Max Lieber to action? No *Worker*—no *Times* yet. Scold Jerome for me."[44]

Outside the hospital walls Hitler was settling into power. He had become chancellor on January 28. On February 23 Rose, in spidery block print letters, wrote to Romain: "Hitler speaks around the corner tonight. The hall is in a rich respectable neighborhood. If I were not so ill they'd probably throw me out of the country. I agitate everybody!"[45]

Holfelder was making a long stay possible on limited means. ("Holfelder never charged a penny for X-ray treatment.") She told Max Cohen that "nights are torture—coarse leaden bed covers torment the sore tissues." She begged friends to send her a pair of soft, very lightweight, white woolen blankets. When a month had passed and not a letter had been received, she begged Anne Williams to send her the news. "Conditions here are more depressing than I can describe . . . I'll die fighting . . . I am nearly dead."[46] That was in mid-March. She had three months left.

She worried about money. She told Joseph Brodsky that she had to pay the hospital two weeks in advance; she had to pay $29 for a bed pad, blanket, and down quilt; $25 went to the hospital doctor. "I find," she wrote, "here one must pay nurses not to suffer neglect and some days to bring extra food when what they offer will not go down." She could manage with $25 weekly. That was the amount due from Covici-Friede. "Can I hope that you will prevail upon these friendly pirates to begin these weekly remittances at once?"[47]

Back in the United States, Dr. Maximilian Cohen, a dentist and Communist party leader, was laboring mightily as chairman of a large Rose Pastor Stokes Testimonial Committee to raise funds for Rose. Sixty-three distinguished political and cultural figures placed their names as sponsors on the committee's letterhead. They ranged from the prisoner Tom Mooney to the actress Alla Nazimova; from Sherwood Anderson to Genevieve Taggard; from Professor George S. Counts to Oswald Garrison Villard.

The centerpiece of the committee's efforts was to be a mass meeting in honor of Rose. It took place at Webster Hall on April 14 and was attended, according to the *New York Times*, "by about 500 Communist and labor representatives . . . primarily to raise funds for medical treatment for the divorced wife of James Graham Phelps Stokes." Her present husband refused to say where she was staying in Germany because "he feared the Nazis would persecute her, because she was a Communist and a Jew."

It was two weeks before Rose got the *Times* issue with its story on the testimonial. Interestingly, what disturbed her in the account was Romain's reluctance to disclose her precise whereabouts. On April 29 she sent a letter to the *Times* stating that she was "under treatment by Professor Hans Holfelder of the University of Frankfurt, director of the Roentgen Institute in the Medical Centre of the city."[48] When Rose wrote this she was confined in the Stadtisches Krankenhaus in Frankfurt to which she was transferred from Holfelder's Haus Baden on April 15. At the Krankenhaus she was under the immediate care of Professor Vito Schmieden.

On April 19, 1933, she inscribed a simple will and had it notarized at the hospital: "I leave all that is mine to J. I. Romain, Philip W. Russ, Dr. Maximilian Cohen, Max Bedacht, and Joseph E. Brodsky, Atty. They know my wishes." It was signed Rose Pastor Stokes. In a letter she asked Brodsky to keep her "old wordy will." She had torn up a "high falutin' legal document" because it made her "sound like a Morgan partner."[49]

There was never enough mail. "If my friends write only when I do, I shall die of loneliness" is a message she repeated often. She longed for company and wanted Anne Williams to visit her. But Williams's husband would not permit it. He was fearful for her safety in Nazi Germany.[50]

Olive Dargan wrote often, trying to sustain a mood of hope: "Maybe I'll turn something over here and join you. . . . What if at last we may go on to Russia!" But Olive broke down at last. She asked the question all of Rose's friends must have been asking each other: "If you are not getting well why can't you come back to us . . . I don't understand, they must be helping you or you wouldn't stay."[51] Rose's only visitor in Frankfurt in her last months was Clara Renner, the nurse. Renner was on a trip to Moscow, but an essential part of her travel plan was to visit Rose. Her letter to Romain on April 17, 1933, reported that Rose's condition was dismal. She told him that "Rose was upset—looked weak—lost most of her hair be-cause of X-ray—general condition poor." Renner reported that Dr. Hol-felder told Rose daily there was a "chance." That is Rose's only hope. He told Renner, however, that there was no hope. "Her blood count is low and tommorow she is to have a certain treatment she is looking forward to . . . please write if you ever received a letter with some verses from Rose. She wants to know . . . write soon . . . no one there can conceive how much a letter means mentally and physically. Rose feels you do not write often enough. Knowing your habits she believes you wait for a letter to send an answer. She urges you again to write often without expectation of reply in each case."[52]

Clara Renner spent a week visiting Rose. She became friendly with Miss Patti, Rose's nurse, who took her around Frankfurt. On one occasion the three of them had dinner together in Rose's room. When Miss Patti left, Clara spent the night by Rose's bed. But Rose had mixed feelings about Clara. She was pleased to have a visitor from America, but Clara overwhelmed her. Clara was in the full bloom of health and energy. She radiated good cheer—and it was too much for Rose. Clara was not an old and trusted friend. Rose really wanted Anne Williams, who had gone through her mother's cancer experience. She understood Rose's needs and wishes and was competent at handling everything.

Clara went on to Moscow, then stopped to see Rose on the way home. She found it depressing and did not linger. She undertook to deliver Rose's typewriter to Romain. Rose appreciated her good intentions but was not sorry to see her go. Rose wrote to Joseph Brodsky soon after: "Thanks, Old Joe. The urn with my ashes will go to your office long before the summer's end. I am slowly dying of starvation—a characteristic of the course of the disease."[53] She was losing the function of the organs of digestion.

She viewed her imminent death calmly and made what feeble use she could of her remaining days. Sometimes she wrote, sometimes she dictated letters and cables; she read hungrily the English-language papers and periodicals that arrived in bundles; she worried about the integrity of her small estate in Westport and the royalties that would be her legacy to the movement she loved.

Long before, she had stated part of her credo about death. In 1916 she had reviewed a book by her friend Anna Strunsky Walling. It was a tale of the Paris Commune, *Violette of Pere Lachaise*. Rose wrote: "The end, however, leaves the reader unsatisfied. At least it did this reader. Violette seems to me to be resigned to death, and I don't like resignation—even to death."[54]

On Wednesday, June 21, 1933, Olive Tilford Dargan received a cable from Frankfurt dispatched that same day. Through someone's negligence, it had been delayed. It read: "Olive dearest write me wire going out of my mind."[55] But Rose had died the day before. She felt she was dying and asked the head nurse to play something lyrical by Franz Schubert on the piano. Afterward she wrote brief letters to a few friends. She lapsed into a coma for twelve hours and quietly died.

In May, when she was failing, her physicians asked the American press not to publish information about her condition because she was a constant reader of American newspapers. Her death was prominently proclaimed in the evening press on June 20 and in the morning press the next day. For one more time the papers retold the story of her life, from Poland on, adding only the circumstances of her death. The reports were generally sympathetic, none more so than in the *World Telegram* where a four-column, two-line head stated: "Stokes' Dream of a Soviet U.S. Remains Vision, but Her Ringing Cry for Economic Justice Lives On."[56]

A report in the *New York Times* that Rose had died after an operation performed by Dr. Schmieden troubled both Jerome Romain and Dr. Grace Bates, and they wrote to Dr. Holfelder for clarification. Holfelder answered in detailed clinical terms, denying the report, adding only: "I assure you that I myself admired Mrs. Rose Pastor Stokes." (He assumed that Dr. Bates was a male.) Jerome Romain had thanked Dr. Holfelder for his efforts and expressed his regret at not being there at the end. He had planned to go in July. He had not known, he said, "that death was so imminent. If only I might have been informed!" Dr. Holfelder replied in laymen's language:

With many thanks I received your letter of June 27 simultaneously with the request of Dr. Bates. I wrote him today and gave him the report the physician wanted and the friend desired. I trust you will learn by my letter that your wife, Mrs. Rose Pastor Stokes, had not to suffer greatly in her last weeks. The anemia increased and, therefore, she was very weak, but you may be assured we all did our best to soothe her illness and to give her any help and relief we could and to make everything as comfortable to her as possible. As I wrote already to Dr. Bates, an operation has not been made. I do not know from where the press got this information.

She had a quiet and calm end, without pains and suffering and passed away quite silently.

I beg to assure you of my sincerest sympathy.[57]

Rose had made a bold request of Romain just before she sailed on her last trip. While aboard the vessel she penned a note to him in which she recalled their good-byes. She told him she "had not forgotten that in the most important request you failed me utterly but at the parting it was senseless to go over the earlier struggle with you." After her death he wrote down his thoughts in a letter or essay without date or salutation:

The most important request—to provide her with a dose of kindness when the pain became unbearable. My mind realized the justness of this request—but my heart kept me from complying. One reason was uppermost in my thoughts even at the moment when she pleaded with me, her nearest: I could not—though I know it was cruel—let her exit be that of a suicide, even though I knew the world would not deem it weakness or surrender on her part—she had struggled as far as human being could struggle, to live and take again her place in the workers' battles toward freedom.[58]

The two persons most affected by Rose's death were her loving friend for twenty-nine years, Olive Tilford Dargan, and her husband for six years, Jerome Romain. "Dear, Dear Jerome," wrote Olive:

Your telegram! Is she gone? How can I bear it? My very best and dearest for so many years! I thought for her sake I was better pre-pared, but life chokes me.

You dear, I know how your deep, tender heart is torn. But is it true that the end has come? Must I believe it? In some strange unaccountable way I have kept hoping that she would come back to us for the end. O, why didn't they bring her back when they learned she must go from earth? . . . I couldn't believe she was going so soon—that I wasn't ever to see her. . . . My love, my blessing to her dear Jerome![59]

In his reply Jerome shared their love and their loss: "It has happened. She is gone. Can it be? Every ell of space is in motion with her step. Her laugh, her unforgettable voice, her eyes—are in the day about me, fill life for me." Jerome enclosed a photograph of the young Rose Pastor: "Look with me at the beautiful ethereal form. Features keen for purposeful living, hair luxuriant. . . . See the outlines of nobleness in her face. See the eyes gazing with pained eagerness, as it were, far out toward that world for the achievement of which she was to dedicate her life. . . . Only to you dare I speak so, dear Olive. . . . But my heart must weep, even though I know I should steel it. What, my dear, what shall I do! . . . The failing must be in me that I cannot choke my private grief."[60]

After their first meeting, in Canada in 1904, Olive Tilford Dargan was moved to celebrate in verse her response to her new friend Rose Pastor. With a letter dated May 27, 1933, certainly one of her last to Rose, she enclosed a new poem:

TO ROSE PASTOR

Voracious Earth must constant feed
On priceless seed;
Beloved heart and bone
To her are sown;
Dear treasure of the brain,
Effort and triumph, turn to ash
With briefest flesh,
For her unsurfeited;
That life may lift again, again
A bruised and yearning head.

But where you fall she will receive
Ashes of gaiety.
For you are sad that joy may be;
And tears are yours that none may grieve;

And if, a fleet earthwhile,
You anger's armor bear,
It is that love may live
And the cradled future wear
Your smile.[61]

Afterword

The death of Rose Pastor Stokes, at the age of fifty-four, created a sense of deep loss among her friends and comrades. Her protracted sickness and self-exile to the ill-chosen health facilities of Frankfurt am Main had removed her from the publicity that kept her fresh in the minds of many. Nevertheless, she was a vivid figure, widely admired, extensively known, and sadly missed.

A memorial meeting was held for her on July 24, 1933, at the New Star Casino. Also honored on this occasion were Clara Zetkin, the prominent German revolutionary who died in Moscow on the day Rose died in Frankfurt, and Sergei Guasev, a founder of the Communist International. Among the speakers at the memorial were Robert Minor, Samuel Ornitz, Rose Wortis, and Joseph Brodsky.

Rose's ashes, together with her meager possessions, were returned to the United States by the consulate in Frankfurt and arrived in time for the memorial. Her ashes were borne to the platform by a young woman with an honor guard and placed on a table covered with a red cloth. The further disposition of the ashes is an unresolved question. After the ceremonies, they were placed in a safe at Brodsky's law office. They remained there until after Brodsky's death late in the 1930s. We were told in 1985 by attorney David Freedman, who succeeded to Brodsky's practice, that, probably before World War II, "a young Jewish poet" came for the ashes and carried them away. This must surely have been V. J. Jerome, who died in 1964. What finally was done with the ashes of Rose Pastor Stokes is not likely to be known.

Ten days before the memorial meeting, the five executors designated by Rose in her notarized will met to carry out the wishes she had communicated to Joseph Brodsky. The estate was reported as valued at less than $2,000. The main business of the executors was their decision to implement Rose's wish to create a refuge for sick and needy radicals at her cottage and property in Westport. With no cash for development of these small premises, the wish was a forlorn dream. The executors decided to create a Rose Pastor Stokes Foundation to further her purpose. Alexander Trachtenberg, the communist publisher, and Roger Baldwin of the American Civil Liberties Union were invited to join in the organization of the foundation.

Jeanette Pearl became the prime mover of the foundation. Rose's equity in the Westport property was sold in the hope that the money could be used to purchase property in Croton-on-Hudson, New York, that would be more suitable as a rest home. Rose's wish to provide a facility for her aged and ill comrades was not backed by any realistic financial means. She had probably fantasized that the royalties from her autobiography would provide the necessary funds. Jeanette Pearl worked for years to get the funds for a Rose Pastor Stokes rest home. Six acres and a fifteen-room house, well equipped, in Croton were contracted for. Sponsors were sought by a committee to raise funds, with playwright Clifford Odets as chairperson. Almost four dozen prominent people agreed to join the effort. Ten persons or so declined. Some of these names were impressive too—Freda Kirchwey, Corliss Lamont, Mary Van Kleeck, Elmer Rice, and Oswald Garrison Villard were among them. But in the end, which was the middle of the Great Depression, the money was not to be had, and the project fell through.

A similar fate befell the autobiography. Apart from V. J. Jerome, no one was more committed to the publication of Rose Stokes's autobiography than the publishing firm of Covici-Friede. Year after year, at least into 1937, the firm believed someone would be found who would do the job that her illness and death had barred Rose from doing.

Sam Ornitz, indeed, had promised Rose that he would complete her book as a biography. Covici-Friede was agreeable to having so prominent and successful an author undertake it. But there were problems. Ornitz had told Rose he was working on a play about Kentucky coal miners, which the Theatre Union, a politically advanced off-Broadway company, was pressing him to complete. Rose agreed that he must finish the play before undertaking the book. He told Joseph Margolies at Covici-Friede on December 30, 1933, that in two weeks his play would be finished and he would proceed to New York to "bury myself in the public library" researching the book on Rose. He wrote: "Principally I'd like to have the three to six months that I shall need to tell Rose's share in organizing the Communist Party and its thrilling history—with plenty of terror and bloodshed—rising to the historical climax of Rose's death in Germany as Hitler took power."[1] Ornitz pleaded guilty to dilatoriness but pointed out that finding time to work on Rose's biography depended on his selling a couple of screenplays to finance himself during the period of work. The screenplays were soon sold.

But five months later Jerome wrote to Ornitz that he had just learned from Maxim Lieber "that the publication date of Rose's book has been further postponed." He urged Ornitz to let him know "by return post when you think the work will be completed."[2]

Jerome spoke of the matter to Earl Browder, general secretary of the Communist party, and at the end of July Browder wrote to Ornitz: "I feel that I need hardly impress upon you that the life of Rose Pastor Stokes, autobiographically couched and rendered complete by you who would bring to bear both intimacy with the milieu and warm sympathy for what she did politically, would mean a definite service to the Party." Ornitz replied in a long letter explaining that his Kentucky play had taken a year longer than expected and that he had been blacklisted for a year and had just reestablished himself financially in Hollywood. By September 15 he would be in New York for rehearsals of the play and to begin work on the Stokes book.[3]

Six months later he was still busy, making a living and revising his Kentucky play—and promising Jerome that after one more month of screenwriting he would be ready to start research on Rose's biography.[4]

By December 1935 Ornitz must have given up the biography project. Joe Margolies wrote to Jerome in appreciation of his efforts to get a suitable writer to finish Rose's autobiography. "We [Covici-Friede] are becoming a bit impatient with the constant delays." He asked Jerome to "return to us the manuscript which is now in your possession in order to enable us to turn it over to someone we may select to finish the book."[5]

Margolies wrote to Jerome again in May 1936. By this time, Jerome was committed to Covici-Friede for a book of his own and was receiving a weekly check in advance. Margolies pressed him for a quick reply as to whether Fielding Burke would undertake Rose's book. In February 1937 Fielding Burke—Olive Dargan—had not yet agreed. Covici was also trying to get Grace Lumpkin to do it. Burke was working on a novel. She told Jerome: "Now that the biography has been postponed so long, I think it will be all the better if it is delayed longer. The immediate interest connected with her death is already lost. The book must rest on its permanent significance. It must interest people who never heard of Rose Pastor, and make them hear of her with wonder and admiration. This can be done as easily two years from now as at the present time."[6]

Pascal Covici would agree only if Fielding Burke would sign a contract to write the book as soon as she finished her novel. "Nothing could please me more than to sign her up, not only for the novel she is doing but for all her future work . . . I hope you will agree with me that we are the logical publishers for her."[7]

But no one could find the time to write Rose's life. V. J. Jerome always retained his interest in Rose Pastor Stokes's story and a fading hope that it would be published. Cedric Belfrage told us in 1984 that sometime around 1940 Jerome asked him to undertake it. Belfrage was interested, and Jerome gave him about thirty letters, mostly between Rose and Olive, as samples of the available material. But World War II plunged Belfrage into activities that prevented his attention to Rose's book. In 1984 he turned over to us the letters in his possession.

John Whitcomb began a correspondence with V. J. Jerome in November 1955 regarding biographical materials relating to Rose Pastor Stokes. Whitcomb was an industrious collector of such items and made possible their acquisition by Yale University after Jerome and his wife Alice had died. In 1958 Jerome told Whitcomb he was still trying to find someone to write Rose's biography. The correspondence between Whitcomb and Jerome ended with the latter's death and was continued by his widow.[8]

In the period immediately following her death, Rose Pastor Stokes was not permitted to fade from memory: the efforts to sustain her foundation, the naming for her of branches of the International Labor Defense, scholarships to the Workers' School established in her name, a pamphlet in Yiddish by Reisel Beilis, a memorial meeting on the second anniversary of her death at which A. B. Magil and Fielding Burke were among the speakers. A novel in Yiddish, *Reizel of the East Side,* by Chaver Paver was serialized in the *Morning Freiheit* from January to March 1942 with Rose as the prototype of its heroine. A generation of radicals from 1933 to 1953 was kept aware of Rose Pastor Stokes's story by commemorative articles, mostly by her friends Jeanette Pearl and Elizabeth Gurley Flynn, in the pages of the *Daily Worker*. Little mention of her appeared after that until the fiftieth anniversary of her death approached, when articles appeared in the magazine *Jewish Currents* and (by Arthur Zipser) in the *Daily World*.

"Eloquent and beautiful," Elizabeth Gurley Flynn called her, "this radiant flame-like woman. . . . She was an agitator, of whom we have too few in a period which demands tremendous agitation of the people. She fought for equal rights for women. . . . She would have been a great leader of the people. . . . Women of yesterday like Rose Pastor Stokes . . . are a great inspiration to the rest of us, to fight on in their spirit."[9]

And what was Rose fighting for? Her own answer was "A world in which there will be no unemployment, hunger, insecurity or war."

Notes

I. The Cub Reporter

1 Ira Kipnis, *The American Socialist Movement, 1897–1912* (New York: Monthly Review Press, 1972), p. 152.
2 Jacob Rader Marcus, ed., *The American Jewish Woman: A Documentary History* (New York: American Jewish Archives, 1981), pp. 112, 209, 210, 485–88.
3 *JDN,* August 13, October 25, December 7, 1903.
4 Quoted in Stanley Feldstein, *The Land That I Show You* (Garden City, N.Y.: Doubleday, 1979), pp. 175–76.
5 *JDN,* July 12, August 4, 1903.
6 *JDN,* July 26, 1903.
7 *JDN,* July 10, September 7, August 4, October 3, 1903.
8 Emily Dunning Barringer, *Bowery to Bellevue* (New York: Norton, 1950), pp. 158–61.
9 Jane Addams, *Twenty Years at Hull House* (New York: Macmillan, 1945), pp. 43–113.
10 Katherine Kish Sklar, "Hull House in the 1890s: A Community of Women," *Signs* 10 (Summer 1985): 660.
11 Beatrice Shustko, *The Edgies* (New York: Educational Alliance, n.d.), pp. 3–26.
12 *JDN,* July 7, 1903.
13 Jeffrey Scheuer, *Legacy of Light* (New York: University Settlement, n.d.).
14 *JDN,* July 19, 1903.

II. The Immigrants

1 "My Childhood Days in London," *New York World,* April 12, 1905.
2 Ibid.; AB, pp. 1–30.
3 Lloyd P. Gartner, *History of the Jews of Cleveland* (Cleveland: Western Reserve Historical Society and Jewish Theological Seminary of America, 1978), pp. 101, 123; maps of Cleveland, 1896–98, NYPL.
4 Gartner, *History of the Jews of Cleveland,* pp. 125, 127, 129.
5 *Cleveland City Directories,* 1895–1902.
6 AB, p. 41.
7 AB, pp. 52–53.
8 AB, p. 53.
9 AB, p. 62.
10 AB, pp. 68–78.
11 Rose Pastor Stokes, "From Poverty to Protest: Excerpts from her Autobiography," *Jewish Currents,* June 1983, pp. 23–28.
12 AB, pp. 62, 64, 67, 68.
13 Letter to the authors from Lester Zwick, whose mother worked with RPS, June 1, 1983.
14 AB, pp. 70–79.
15 AB, p. 79.
16 AB, pp. 91–97.
17 AB, pp. 84–89.
18 AB, pp. 79, 95–101.

19 Miriam Shomer Zunser, "The Jewish Literary Scene in New York at the Beginning of the Century," *YIVO Annual of Jewish Social Science* 8 (1952): 290–93.

20 AB, pp. 101–2.

21 AB, p. 101.

22 AB, pp. 102–9; Death certificate of RPS's half-brother, Samuel Wieslander, Yale.

III. The Engagement

1 The early pages of this chapter are based principally on material in Genealogy Division, NYPL, relating to Dodge, Phelps, and Stokes families; and Stokes Papers in CU.

2 *DAB*, 18:69–70.

3 *NAW*, pp. 384–86.

4 Ibid.; *DAB*, 18:65–70.

5 P. S. Hunter (nephew of JGPS) to JMW, July 6, 1967, JMW; *Who Was Who*, 8:2792; JGPS, CU.

6 *DAB*, 18:66.

7 "Isaac Newton Phelps Stokes (1867–1944)," *Columbia Encyclopedia*, 3d ed. (New York: Columbia University Press, 1968), p. 2047.

8 *Trow's City Directory of Manhattan and the Bronx.*

9 AB, pp. 112–13.

10 AB, p. 112.

11 Philip S. Foner, *History of the Labor Movement in the United States*, 8 vols. (New York: International Publishers, 1947–88), 2:213.

12 AB, p. 114.

13 Virginia Terrell Lathrop, "Olive Tilford Dargan," pp. 1–13, manuscript at Pack Memorial Library, Asheville, N.C.

14 AB, p. 115.

15 *New York Sun*, April 6, 1905.

16 JGPS to Mother, March 1905; Mother to JGPS (cable), March 1905, CU.

17 *New York Sun*, April 6, 1905.

18 Ibid.; Solon De Leon, ed.; *The American Labor Who's Who* (New York: Hanford Press, 1925), p. 221.

19 *New York Tribune*, June 5, 1905.

20 *New York Sun*, April 7, 1905; *Philadelphia Press*, April 8, 1905.

21 *New York Times*, April 6, 1905.

22 JGPS to Mother, April 12, 1905, CU.

23 *New York Evening Journal*, April 7, 1905.

24 *Philadelphia Evening Telegram*, n.d., 1905, clipping in Box 75, CU.

25 *New York Evening Telegram*, April 11, 1905.

26 Hearst Syndicate, April 1905.

27 *New York Evening Journal*, April 10, 1905.

28 *New York Evening World*, April 11, 1905.

29 *Chicago American*, April 28, 1905.

30 *New York Sun*, September 6, 1905.

31 *New York World,* April 8, 1905.
32 *New York Herald,* April 8, 1905; *Harper's Bazar,* September 26, 1906, p. 796; Onde Manners, *Poor Cousins* (New York: Coward-McCann, Geoheagan, 1972), p. 139.
33 JGPS to Mother, April 30, 1905, CU.
34 *New York Times,* July 20, 1905.
35 *New York Evening Telegram,* April 11, 1905; *Jewish Independent,* December 1906.
36 William E. Alberts, *Christianity and Crisis,* August 15, 1883, p. 309, quoted in *AIMS Newsletter,* March–April 1984, p. 5; Dorothy Thompson, *The Chartists* (New York: Pantheon Books, 1984), p. 183.
37 *New York Press,* April 7, 1905.
38 Rose Harriet Pastor to JGPS, April 26, 1905, Tam.
39 JGPS to Mother, May 22, 1905, CU.
40 JGPS to brother Anson, May 29, 1905, Tam.
41 *Dallas Sunday Times Herald,* April 30, 1905.
42 *New York Times,* April 7, 1905.
43 AB, pp. 121–22.

IV. Matrimony: Rags to Riches

1 *New York Sun,* July 18, 1905.
2 *New York Times,* July 19, 1905.
3 Zunser, "Jewish Literary Scene," pp. 290–93. Reference to Rose's aunt is dubious since according to RPS's unfinished autobiography her aunt arrived in the United States well after her wedding. Hattie Mayer was later better known as the novelist Anzia Yezierska, her real name. She had been called Hattie Mayer on her arrival with her family at Ellis Island. Immigration employees often gave such simpler names to immigrants, who were helpless in the matter. *Biography of Anzia Yezierska: A Writer's Life,* by her daughter Louise Levitas was published by Rutgers University Press in 1988.
4 AB, pp. 121–22. Eliakum Zunser was born in Vilna in 1836. He studied at a Yeshiva for a few years but was otherwise self-educated. As a youth he became a *Badchen* (bard) entertaining at festivities with impromptu doggerel in Yiddish. In 1889 he settled in New York. His poems and songs of social significance brought him international fame.
5 Ida Cohen Selavan to the authors, June 13, 1983.
6 *New York Times,* July 20, 1905.
7 AB, pp. 124–25.
8 AB, p. 127.
9 JGPS to Mother, n.d., CU.
10 Lease, CU, signed June 6, 1905, for August 1905 to September 1908.
11 Lillian Baynes Griffin, "Mrs. J. G. Phelps Stokes at Home," *Harper's Bazar* 40 (September 1906): 794–99.
12 *Independent,* November 16, 1905, pp. 1169–70.
13 *Annals of American Academy of Political and Social Science* 37 (January–May 1906): 165–75.
14 Griffin, "Mrs. J. G. Phelps Stokes at Home," pp. 94–99.

15 AB, p. 131.

16 AB, p. 134.

17 Ferdinand Lundberg, *Imperial Hearst* (New York: Modern Library, 1936), pp. 102–4.

18 AB, p. 127.

19 JGPS to Lillian Wald, November 1905, Wald Papers, CU.

20 AB, p. 136.

21 AB, pp. 134–39.

22 J. Stitt Wilson to RPS, August 26, 1906, Tam.

23 OTD to RPS, September 5, 1915, Yale ("The first clause in Pegram's will is a request that I will suitably mark the grave of our child, Rosemary. I think I can do this unobtrusively and without making a gloomy spot on your lovely island").

24 JGPS to Mother, August, December 1906, CU.

25 RPS to Helena Frank, December 21, 1906, CU.

26 Alex Kaun, *Maxim Gorky and His Russia* (New York: Jonathan Cape, 1931), pp. 569–80.

27 Patrick Renshaw, "Pastor-Stokes Marriage and the American Left, 1905–25," *Quarterly Journal of New York State Historical Association* 62 (October 1981): 423.

28 *New York Times,* December 17, 1909.

29 *New York American,* December 15, 1906.

30 *New York Tribune,* December 15, 1906.

31 New York City Department of Bridges to RPS, 1906, Yale.

32 Mari Jo Buhle, "Women and the Socialist Party, 1901–14," *Radical America* 4 (February 1970): 38.

33 Kipnis, *American Socialist Movement,* p. 62.

34 May Woods Simon, "Why Every Woman Should Be a Socialist," *Socialist Woman* 1 (June 1907): 2.

35 Lidia Parce, "What Is the Woman Question?" *Progressive Woman* 2 (March 1909): 3–5.

36 Eugene V. Debs, "Letter to a Socialist Woman," *Socialist Woman* 1 (February 1908): 10.

37 *New York Evening Call,* June 9, 1908.

38 RPS, "What Women Most Lack," *Socialist Woman* 1 (October 1907): cover and p. 2.

39 Cover picture of RPS, *Progressive Woman* 3 (February 1910).

40 Extracts from Stokes Records, 2:122–23, CU.

41 Hebe (pseud.), "Words to Our Comrades at the National Convention," *Socialist Woman* 1 (May 1908): 3.

42 John Spargo, "Woman and the Socialist Movement," *International Socialist Review* 8 (1908): 449–53.

V. In the Movement

1 *Socialism: Its Moral Passion, Intellectual Power and Noble Deeds* (Oakland Calif.: Ruskin Club, 1904).

2 Ellis E. Carr to JGPS, February 20, 1907; JGPS to Carr, May 14, 1907, CU.

3 *New York Evening Telegram,* March 19, 1906.

4 Morris Hillquit, *Loose Leaves from a Busy Life* (New York: Rand School Press, 1934), p. 57. Hillquit, a labor lawyer, was a leader of the SP based in New York. He is generally regarded as a centrist. He was eventually replaced by Norman Thomas.

5 David A. Shannon, *The Socialist Party of America* (New York: Macmillan, 1955), pp. 55–56.

6 *New York Times,* June 4, 1905. Thomas Wentworth Higginson, a Unitarian minister and an abolitionist, commanded the first American regular army regiment of freed slaves. Charlotte Perkins Gilman was well known as a feminist and reformer. Clarence S. Darrow was the country's most prominent lawyer.

7 Shannon, *Socialist Party,* p. 54; *New York Times,* June 4, 1905.

8 The National Civic Federation brought together the organized employers, headed by August Belmont as president, and the AFL, headed by Samuel Gompers, vice-president, as an avowed instrument of class collaboration and antisocialism. See Foner, *History of the Labor Movement in the United States,* 2:384–87.

9 OTD to RPS, July 28, 1906, September 1906, Yale.

10 AB, p. 198.

11 *Chicago Tribune,* January 17, 1907; *New York Press,* January 20, 1907.

12 Quoted in Allen F. Davis, *American Heroine, The Life and Legend of Jane Addams* (New York: Oxford University Press, 1973), p. 266.

13 *New York Times,* January 20, 1907.

14 *New York Press,* January 20, 1907; *New York Evening Telegram,* January 19, 1907; *New York Sun,* January 20, 1907.

15 AB, p. 191.

16 *Brooklyn Citizen,* January 25, 1907.

17 *New York Times,* August 4, 1912.

18 *Boston American,* December 27, 1908.

19 *Milwaukee Sentinel,* June 22, 1907.

20 *New York Evening World,* November 15, 1909.

21 *Poughkeepsie Press,* undated clipping, Tam.

22 *New York Times,* July 15, 1908.

23 Ibid., July 21, 1908.

24 Ibid., October 23, 1910.

25 Edwin Markham to RPS, August 26, 1908, Tam.

26 RPS to JGPS, August 26, 1908, Tam.

27 Bernard J. Brommel, *Eugene V. Debs: Spokesman for Labor and Socialism* (Chicago: Charles H. Kerr, 1978), p. 101.

28 *New York Times,* October 15, 1908.

29 *Trenton Evening Times,* October 17, 1908.

30 *Brooklyn Times,* December 29, 1908.

31 *New York Sun,* December 28, 1908.

32 RPS to unknown, March 1909, Tam.

33 Shannon, *Socialist Party,* pp. 63–66; William English Walling, *Socialism as It Is* (New York: Macmillan, 1915), pp. 119–20, 316–22.

34 Patrick Henshaw, *The Wobblies* (Garden City, N.Y.: Doubleday, 1967).

35 Nick Salvatore, *Eugene V. Debs: Citizen and Socialist* (Urbana: University of Illinois Press, 1982), pp. 244–45.

36 JGPS to William G. Williams, 1910, CU.

37 Richard Drinnon, *Rebel in Paradise* (Chicago: University of Chicago Press, 1961), pp. 128–29.

38 E. G. Flynn to RPS, n.d., Yale.

39 *New York Times,* October 22, 1909.

40 Ibid., June 1, 1909.

41 Shannon, *Socialist Party,* pp. 50–53.

42 *Autobiography of W. E. B. Du Bois* (New York: International Publishers, 1968), pp. 138, 249–51, 254–56; *New York Times,* March 1, 2, 1909; Herbert Aptheker, ed., *Annotated Bibliography of the Published Writings of W. E. B. Du Bois* (Millwood, N.Y.: Kraus-Thompson, 1973), p. 509.

VI. On the Picket Line

1 Anne Traubel to RPS, September 30, October 5, 1909, Tam.

2 Rockwell Kent, *It's Me, O Lord* (New York: Dodd, Mead, 1955), p. 193. Permission to quote granted courtesy of the Rockwell Kent Legacies. A teasing suspicion is that among the heterogeneous group of radicals entertained by the Stokeses during the Kents' stay at Caritas was the elusive Matthew Schmidt who (according to Frank Bohn in a letter to John M. Whitcomb) may have spent the winter of 1909–10 "hiding out" at the island. (Frank Bohn was a founder and leader of the IWW.) Schmidt was arrested in 1915 and accused of the tragic 1910 bombing of the Los Angeles *Times.* He served a long prison term for the offense. Rockwell Kent confirmed in a 1963 letter to Whitcomb that a big man, with blond hair and a lone blue eye, did indeed visit the Stokeses that winter and may have been Schmidt. The description, however, also fits "Big Bill" Haywood, a comrade of Rose and Graham.

3 Ibid., p. 194.

4 Ibid., p. 195.

5 Elizabeth Gurley Flynn, *The Rebel Girl* (New York: International Publishers, 1973), pp. 115–16.

6 Christopher Lasch, *The Agony of the American Left* (New York: Knopf, 1969), pp. 423–44.

7 Kipnis, *American Socialist Movement,* pp. 391–420.

8 RPS to Anna S. Walling, September 17, 1912, Walling Papers, Yale.

9 RPS to Max Lieber, April 17, 1933, Tam.

10 AB, p. 22 (revised p. 180).

11 Fragment of autobiography of JGPS, CU.

12 AB, pp. 189–94.

13 *Greenwich* (Conn.) *Press,* September 15, 1911.

14 *New York Times,* January 2, 1910.

15 Cecyle S. Neidle, *American Immigrant Women* (Boston: Twayne, 1975), p. 181.

16 Eleanor Flexner, *Century of Struggle* (New York: Atheneum, 1974), pp. 241–42, 245, 252.

17 Louis Levine, *The Women's Garment Workers: A History of the International Ladies Garment Workers Union* (New York: B. W. Huebsch, 1924), p. 154; *New York Times,* December 6, 1909.

18 *New York Times,* December 1, 1909.

19 *New York Press,* December 17, 1909.

20 *New York Times,* December 17, 1909.

21 Philip S. Foner, *Women and the American Labor Movement* (New York: Free Press, 1979), p. 365.

22 *New York Times,* December 17, 1909.

23 Levine, *Women's Garment Workers,* pp. 163–67.

24 RPS, "Notes from Mrs. Stokes's memoirs regarding the waiters' strike," unnumbered pages, Yale.

25 Matthew Josephson, *Union House, Union Bar* (New York: Random House, 1956), pp. 97–99.

26 *New York Times,* May 20, 1912.

27 *New York Herald,* June 11, 1912.

28 AB, unnumbered pages.

29 Charles Recht to RPS, June 1912, Tam.

30 RPS to *New York Times,* July 3, 1912.

31 *New York Times,* July 14, 1912.

32 W. E. D. Stokes to RPS, June 24, 1912, Tam.

33 RPS to Anna Strunsky Walling, January 21, 1911, Yale.

34 JGPS to Mother, 1908, CU.

35 *New York Times,* September 25, 1912.

36 RPS to Comrade Ells, October 1916, Tam.

37 *New York Call,* January 13, 1913.

38 *New York Times,* October 12, 1983.

39 RPS Diary, January 6, 1913, Yale.

40 Ibid., January 7, 1913.

41 Ibid., January 11, 1913.

42 *New York Call,* January 11, 12, 1913.

43 RPS Diary, January 13, 1913, Yale.

44 Foner, *Women and the American Labor Movement,* p. 365.

45 RPS Diary, January 14, 1913, Yale.

46 Foner, *History of the Labor Movement,* 5:258–59.

47 *New York Times,* April 19, 1913.

VII. On the Campus

1 RPS Diary, March 17, 1913, Yale.

2 Ibid., March 20, 1913.

3 Maurice Pastor to RPS, December 29, 1912; Cecil Pastor to RPS, November 18, 1913; Rose Goldstaub to RPS, November 20, 1913; Lillian Pastor to RPS, October 15, 1913, all in Tam.

4 Alexander Berkman of *Good Earth* to RPS, January 20, 1913, Yale.

5 *Portsmouth Daily Times,* August 21, 1913.

6 *Lima Republican Gazette,* August 24, 1913; *Cleveland Leader,* August 24, 1913.

7   Flynn, *Rebel Girl,* pp. 167–70.
8   *Universal Jewish Encyclopedia* (New York: KTAV Publishing House, 1969), 10:67; *Hoboken Socialist,* December 27, 1913.
9   Daniel Aaron, *Writers on the Left* (New York: Oxford University Press, 1977), p. 25.
10 RPS to Anna S. Walling, September 1912, Walling Papers, Yale.
11 *Universal Jewish Encyclopedia,* 10:213.
12 Miriam Bloch to RPS, n.d. 1916, Tam.
13 *Chautauqua Daily,* July 15, 1913.
14 *Boston Post,* August 13, 1913.
15 Leroy Scott, "The Natural Development of the Intercollegiate Socialist Society," unidentified tearsheet, reel 2696, xix:10, Tam.
16 Ellen Hayes to RPS, December 30, 1913, Tam.
17 Harry W. Laidler to RPS, November 11, 12, 17, 19, 1913, Tam.
18 JGPS to ISS, n.d., CU.
19 Durant Drake to RPS, November 1913, Yale.
20 Scott, "Natural Development of the Intercollegiate Socialist Society."
21 *Survey* 31(January 1914): 191–94.
22 Aunt Mary (Mary R. Sanford) to RPS, December 9, 1913, Tam.
23 Lippmann's speech to first ISS conference, December 30, 1913, is reported in Ronald Steel, *Walter Lippmann and the American Century* (Boston: Little, Brown, 1980), p. 40.
24 *New York Tribune,* December 31, 1913; ISS press release, New York, December 31, 1913, Tam.
25 Scott Nearing to RPS, January 11, 1914, Tam.
26 RPS to JGPS, February 10, 1914, Tam.
27 Margaret Darkow to RPS, February 13, 1914, Tam.
28 *New York Call,* February 20, 1914.
29 *Newtown Circuit* (Newtown Centre, Mass.), February 27, 1914.
30 Richard M. Vaughn to RPS, February 23, 1914; RPS to Richard M. Vaughn, February 1914, Tam.
31 RPS to *Boston Post,* February 25, 1914.
32 RPS to JGPS, March 10, 1914, Tam.
33 Lyman P. Powell to JGPS, March 12, 1914, CU.
34 Foster Boswell to RPS, March 20, December 31, 1914, Tam.
35 *New York Call,* March 20, 1914.
36 OTD to RPS, October 17, 1915, Yale.
37 OTD to JGPS, May 23, 1914, Tam.
38 RPS to JGPS, May 26, 1914, Tam.
39 JGPS to RPS, June 2, 1914, Tam.
40 OTD to RPS, June 12, 1914, Yale.
41 Joanna F. Cooke to RPS, August 22, 1914, Tam.
42 OTD to RPS, August 2, 1914, Yale.
43 Caro Lloyd Strobell to RPS, 1915, Tam.
44 AB, pp. 225–28.
45 AB, p. 223.

46 Advertisement in unidentified Dover, New Jersey, newspaper, December 20, 1915, Yale.
47 Kate Barnard to RPS, January 5, 1916, Yale.
48 Nathalie B. Ells to RPS, January 20, 1916, Tam.
49 Robert W. Dunn to RPS, March 8, 1916, Yale.
50 Evelyn Kessel to RPS, n.d., Yale.
51 Statement to ISS, April 1915, Tam.
52 JGPS to F. H. Giddings, n.d., CU.
53 Harry Rogoff, *An East Side Epic: The Life and Works of Meyer London* (New York: Vanguard Press, 1930).
54 JGPS to Socialist Headquarters, October 1916, CU.
55 RPS to Comrade Ells, October 1916, Tam.
56 Nathalie Ells to RPS, November 14, 1916, Tam.
57 RPS to Laidler, November 23, 1916, Tam.
58 Charles L. Raper to Harry W. Laidler, November 30, 1916, CU.
59 RPS to Laidler, n.d., 1916, Tam.
60 RPS to Laidler, quoted in AB, pp. 227–28.
61 JGPS to Laidler, January 25, 1917, CU.
62 JGPS to RPS, December 7, 1916, Tam.
63 Elizabeth Gilman to RPS, December 26, 1916, Tam.

VIII. On the Feminist Front

1 RPS to Maxim Lieber, April 17, 1933, Tam.
2 Ibid.
3 Ibid.; AB, p. 188 (2d draft).
4 RPS to Maxim Lieber, April 17, 1933, Tam.
5 Samuel Ornitz to RPS, December 17, 1923, December 1, 1932, Yale.
6 Earl Browder to Ornitz, July 30, 1934; Ornitz to Browder, August 6, 1934, Yale.
7 Irving Howe, *World of Our Fathers* (New York: Harcourt Brace Jovanovich, 1976), p. 267; James Weinstein, *The Decline of Socialism in America, 1912–1925* (New York: Random House, 1969), p. 57.
8 RPS to Maxim Lieber, April 17, 1933, including note to Samuel Ornitz, Tam.
9 Mari Jo Buhle, *Women and American Socialism, 1870–1920* (Urbana: University of Illinois Press, 1983), pp. 129–31.
10 Judith Schwarz, *Radical Feminists of Heterodoxy* (Lebanon, N.H.: New Victoria Publishers, 1982), pp. 11, 13, 18, 24–25, 31–32, 77.
11 Marie Jenny Howe to RPS, n.d., Tam.
12 Rheta Childe Dorr, *A Woman of Fifty* (New York: Funk and Wagnalls, 1924), p. 448; Schwarz, *Radical Feminists*, pp. 7–8.
13 Schwarz, *Radical Feminists*, pp. 41, 47, 54, 61, 77, 79.
14 Ibid.
15 Sara Josephine Baker, *Fighting for Life* (New York: Macmillan, 1939), pp. 182–83.
16 Dorr, *Woman of Fifty*, p. 448.
17 Flynn, *Rebel Girl*, pp. 279–80.

18 Baker, *Fighting for Life,* p. 183.

19 *New York Call,* February 18, 1914.

20 *New York Times,* February 18, 1914.

21 Schwarz, *Radical Feminists,* p. 32; Flynn, *Rebel Girl,* p. 280.

22 Inez Haynes Irwin to RPS, April 22, 1931, Yale.

23 Elizabeth Griffith, *In Her Own Right* (New York: Oxford University Press, 1984), pp. 111, 122–23, 138.

24 Ellen Carol Du Bois, ed., *Elizabeth Cady Stanton and Susan Anthony, Correspondence, Writing, Speeches* (New York: Schocken Books, 1981), pp. 139–45.

25 Barbara Sinclair Deckard, *The Women's Movement* (New York: Harper & Row, 1975), pp. 2, 268–69; Flexner, *Century of Struggle,* p. 248.

26 Flexner, *Century of Struggle,* pp. 249–50.

27 Harriot Stanton Blatch and Alma Lutz, *Challenging Years: Memoirs of Harriot Stanton Blatch* (New York: Putnam, 1940), pp. 92–94.

28 Kipnis, *American Socialist Movement,* p. 264.

29 Barbara Mayer Wertheimer, *We Were There* (New York: Pantheon Books, 1977), p. 282.

30 Ella Reeve Bloor, *We Are Many* (New York: International Publishers, 1940), p. 92.

31 *New York Tribune,* March 29, 1906.

32 *Syracuse Journal,* October 19, 1906; RPS to *Boston Post,* n.d., probably 1913, clipping, Tam.

33 Barbara Sinclair Deckard, *Women's Movement* (New York: Harper & Row, 1975), p. 272.

34 James William Leonard, ed., *Woman's Who's Who of America: Biographical Dictionary of Contemporary Women of the United States and Canada* (New York: American Commonwealth Co., 1914), p. 787.

35 *New York Times,* December 1, 1909.

36 George Strobell to RPS, December 13, 1913, Tam.

37 *Springfield* (Ohio) *Daily Republican,* November 13, 1913; Boston Equal Suffrage Association to RPS, October 15, 1914, Tam.

38 *New York Call,* June 18–19, 1915; RPS to *New York Call,* June 1915, carbon copy on reel 2697, no. 68, Tam.

39 Women's Peace party to RPS, February 23, 1915, Tam.

40 Lasch, *Agony of the American Left,* pp. 423–24.

41 Women's Peace party to RPS, March 15, 1916, Tam.

42 Emma Goldman and Arturo Giovanitti to RPS, May 29, 1916, Tam.

43 RPS to Women's Peace party, March 17, 1917, Tam; *New York Times,* March 18, 1917.

44 Madeline Gray, *Margaret Sanger: A Biography of the Champion of Birth Control* (New York: Richard Marek, 1979), p. 106.

45 Charles Van Doren, ed., *Webster's American Biographies* (Springfield, Mass.: G. and C. Merriam Co., 1975), p. 1163.

46 *Columbia Encyclopedia,* p. 222.

47 Emma Goldman, *Living My Life* (New York: Knopf, 1931), p. 570.

48 *Woman Rebel* was a newspaper written and published by Margaret Sanger in 1914. Because of it she was subjected to government harassment, and it was suspended after nine issues.

49 Gray, *Margaret Sanger,* p. 68.

50 *NAW,* p. 464; National Birth Control League to RPS, February 17, 1916, Yale.

51 James Wesley Reed, *From Private Vice to Public Virtue* (New York: Basic Books, 1978), 105.

52 "Why Race Suicide with Advancing Civilization?" *Arena,* 4 (February 1909): 189–92.

53 Margaret Sanger, *My Fight for Birth Control* (New York: Farrar and Rinehart, 1931), pp. 123–25.

54 Ibid., p. 125.

55 *Louisville Herald,* February 13, 1916.

56 Linda Gordon, *Woman's Body, Woman's Right* (New York: Grossman, 1976), p. 232.

57 *New York Herald,* April 20, 1916.

58 *New York Sun,* May 6, 1916.

59 *New York Herald,* May 6, 1916.

60 *New York Times,* May 6, 1916.

61 Jessie Ashley to RPS, n.d., 1916, Yale.

62 *Boston Post,* May 6, 1916.

63 Goldman, *Living My Life,* pp. 570–71.

64 Anson P. Stokes to RPS, May 21, 1916, Yale.

65 RPS to Anson P. Stokes (copy), May 29, 1916, Yale.

66 Anson P. Stokes to RPS, June (1?), 1916, Yale.

67 RPS to Anson P. Stokes, June 6, 1916, Tam.

68 Sundry letters requesting birth control information: January 27, 1916, June 14, 1916, October 27, 1916, December 4, 1916, Tam.

69 Percival Meigs, Jr., to RPS, June 16, 1916, Tam.

70 Associated Charities of Columbia, S.C., to RPS, December 13, 1916, Tam.

71 *Baltimore News,* April 22, 1916.

72 *New York Call,* February 6, 1916.

73 Ibid., February 8, 1916.

74 Deckard, *Women's Movement,* p. 436.

75 Mari Jo Buhle, *Women and American Socialism, 1870–1920* (Urbana: University of Illinois Press, 1983), pp. 319–21.

IX. The Pen as Weapon

1 RPS to Upton Sinclair, March 23, 1911, Lilly Library, Indiana University, Bloomington.

2 Charles Leinenweber, "Socialists in the Streets," *Science and Society* 41 (Summer 1947): 107.

3 Philip Russ to RPS, October 31, 1927, Tam.

4 RPS to Lincoln Steffens, February 2, 1909, February 4, 1910, Lincoln Steffens Papers, CU.

5 Daniel Kiefer to Benjamin Huebsch, January 24, 1921, Tam.

6 Daniel Kiefer to RPS, January 24, 1921, Tam.

7 Simon Gould to John Whitcomb, January 8, 1959, Yale.

8 Diary, January 15, 1913, Yale.

9 JGPS Papers, CU.

10 *Chicago Record Herald,* February 16, 1915.

11 *Literary Digest,* June 25, 1921, p. 69; Daniel Aaron, *Writers on the Left* (New York: Oxford University Press, 1977), p. 62.

12 Upton Sinclair to RPS, August 31, September 17, 1914, Tam.

13 *Independent,* January 9, 1908, p. 86.

14 RPS to Upton Sinclair, April 2, 1911, Lilly Library, Indiana University, Bloomington.

15 *Books and Authors,* March 1917, unidentified clipping, Yale.

16 *New York American,* October 1, 1913.

17 Winthrop Ames to Miss Kirkpatrick, n.d., Yale.

18 *New York Times,* August 29, 1916.

19 *New York Call,* May 26, 1914.

20 *New York Sun,* May 29, 1914.

21 *New York Tribune,* May 18, 1915; *New York Telegram,* May 8, 1915; *Drama News,* May 15, 1915; *New York Press,* May 7, 1915; *Brooklyn Daily Eagle,* May 7, 1915.

22 OTD to RPS, December 9, 1913, Yale.

23 RPS to "Dear Comrade," December 9, 1916, Tam.

24 John Spargo to RPS, January 15, 1917, Yale.

25 *Philadelphia Press,* March 11, 1917.

26 *New York Call,* May 7, 1915.

27 Robert A. Rosenstone, *Romantic Revolutionary* (1975; rpt. New York: Vintage, 1978), pp. 99–117; Rebecca Zarier, *Art for the Masses, 1911–17* (New Haven: Yale University Press, 1985).

28 Samuel Ornitz to RPS, December 17, 1918, Tam.

29 Carl Beck to RPS, December 20, 1915, Tam.

30 *Motion Picture World,* July 14, 1914.

31 RPS to Alice Blaché, August 14, 1916, Tam.

32 Alice Blaché to RPS, October 27, 1916, Tam.

33 Bert Adler to RPS, November 24, December 6, 1916, Tam.

34 Interviews with Richard Pastor (nephew of RPS) and Anne Williams Feinberg (friend of RPS).

35 Laura P. Elliot to RPS, n.d. (1915), Tam.

36 Mince Parker to RPS, March 16, 1917, Tam.

37 *New York Evening Globe,* March 18, 1917.

38 *New York Herald,* February 8, 1917.

39 RPS to Mrs. Leight, November 2, 1917, Tam.

X. The Great War

1 The account of the Quinlan case is based on a summary prepared by RPS, Tam.

2 Charles E. Russell to RPS, November 28, 1915, Tam.

3 *New York Times,* August 11, 1914.

4 AB, p. 232.

5 Quoted in George Seldes, comp., *The Great Quotations* (New York: Lyle Stuart, 1960), p. 752.

6 Quoted in William Z. Foster, *History of the Communist Party of the United States* (New York: International Publishers, 1952), p. 128.

7 Shannon, *Socialist Party,* pp. 83–84; Weinstein, *Decline of Socialism in America,* pp. 119–20.

8 Joanna F. Cooke to RPS, August 13, 1914, Tam.

9 Agnes D. Warbasse to RPS, n.d., 1915, Tam.

10 Henry Ford to RPS (telegram), November 28, 1915, Yale.

11 RPS to Henry Ford, November 29, 1915, Yale.

12 JGPS to W. E. D. Stokes, January 14, 1916; to "Socialist Comrade," March 1916, CU.

13 M. MacNeille Dixon to JGPS, February 16, 1917, CU.

14 RPS to Women's Peace party, March 17, 1917, Tam; *New York Times,* March 18, 1917.

15 Robert Dwight Reynolds, Jr., "The Millionaire Socialists: James Graham Phelps Stokes and His Circle of Friends" (Ph.D. dissertation, University of South Carolina, 1974).

16 Shannon, *Socialist Party,* pp. 95–98.

17 *New York Call,* April 13, 1917.

18 RPS and JGPS to Local Stamford Socialist party, July 9, 1917, CU.

19 Leroy Scott to JGPS, April 30, 1917; Charles E. Russell to JGPS, April 28, 1917, both in CU.

20 RPS to Eugene Victor Debs, July 22, 1916, Indiana State University, Microfilm Corporation of America, copy at Tam.

21 Ray Ginger, *The Bending Cross* (1944; rpt. New York: Russell and Russell, 1969), p. 346.

22 *New York Times,* July 3, 1917.

23 Shannon, *Socialist Party,* p. 101.

24 Ibid., p. 101.

25 Harry W. Laidler to JGPS, November 28, 1917, CU.

26 RPS, "A Confession," *Century,* November 1917, pp. 457–59.

27 Renshaw, "Pastor-Stokes Marriage," p. 425.

28 Rose Strunsky to RPS, October 31, 1913, Tam.

29 Diary, March 27, 1915, Yale.

30 Joanna Cooke to RPS, May 10, 1926, Tam.

XI. *"Espionage"*

All notes from the National Archives (NA) are as follows:

The Old German (OG) files of the Bureau of Investigation contain several files relating to Rose Pastor Stokes and her husband, James Graham Phelps Stokes. All are on Microcopy 1085.

The main file on RPS, OG 160093 (roll 556), contains reports, correspondence, news clippings, and court documents relating to *U.S.* v. *Rose Pastor Stokes*.

The Department of Justice case files also contain information on RPS. Her main file, covering the years 1918–21 and consisting of two sections and an envelope, is 9-19-1775, Box 802. Files mentioning her are 202600-2734-Box 3060, concerning her 1923 trial in Michigan, and 197009, Serial 18 Box 2899. The Bureau of Investigation (BI) later became the FBI.

1 W. E. D. Stokes, *The Right to Be Well Born: Horse Breeding in Relation to Eugenics* (N.p.: Privately printed, 1917), pp. 74, 81–82, 175. It is available in NYPL.

2 Solon De Leon, ed., *American Labor Who's Who* (New York: Hanford Press, 1925), p. 177; Flynn, *Rebel Girl*, pp. 240, 250.

3 OG, 160093 microcopy 1085, NA.

4 AB, p. 235.

5 *New York World,* November 4, 1917.

6 AB, pp. 237, 239.

7 Box 802, NA.

8 Department of State to A. Bruce Bielaski, February 18, 1918, OG, 160093 microcopy 1085, NA.

9 Anna M. Kelly to RPS, February 1, 1918, Tam.

10 *New York Call,* January 10, 1918.

11 OG, 160093 microcopy 1085, NA.

12 W. E. D. Stokes to Charles Warren, March 4, 1918, Box 802, NA.

13 Annette Moore to RPS, May 13, 1918, Tam.

14 *New York Times,* March 18, 1918.

15 RPS to *Kansas City Star,* March 19, 1918.

16 Box 802, NA.

17 *New York Times,* March 25, 1918.

18 OG, 160093 microcopy 1085, NA.

19 Ibid.

20 *Kansas City Star,* March 25, 1918.

21 Ibid.

22 OG, 160093 microcopy 1085, NA.

23 W. E. D. Stokes to Charles Warren, March 24, 1918, Box 802, NA.

24 *New York Times,* June 20, 1918.

25 W. E. D. Stokes to assistant attorney general, April 13, 1918, Box 802, NA.

26 *New York Times,* May 22, 1918.

27 Ibid., May 25, 1918.

28 Ibid., May 28, 1918.

29 Earl Wayland Brown to Senator William E. Borah, n.d. 1918, Tam.

30 *New York Times,* June 1, 1918.

31 Quoted in Granville Hicks, *John Reed* (New York: Macmillan, 1936), p. 310.

32 Quoted in *Literary Digest* 57 (June 15, 1918): 13.

33 Abraham Sarasohn to RPS, May 26, 1918, Tam.

34 RPS to Abraham Sarasohn, May 28, 1918, Sarasohn Collection, CU.

35 RPS to Anna Strunsky Walling, June 10, 1918, A. S. Walling Papers, Yale.

36 BI agent to Department of Justice, July 10, 1918, OG.

37 *New York Times,* July 20, 1918.

38 OTD to RPS, June 6, 1918, Yale; OTD to RPS, June 29, 1918, Tam; RPS to OTD, July 14, 1918, Tam.

39 RPS to Flora Raugh, July 25, 1918, Tam.

40 Clarence Darrow, *The Story of My Life* (New York: Scribner's, 1934), p. 69.

41 *New York Times,* June 17, 1918.

42 BI agent to Department of Justice, August 11, 1918, Box 802, NA.

43 *New York Times,* September 10, 13, 1918.

44 Ibid., September 13, 1918.

45 Ibid., September 23, 1918.

46 E. V. Debs to RPS, December 5, 1918, Yale.

47 *New York Times,*September 13, 1918.

48 RPS to Mrs. Richard Hogan, June 10, 1918, Tam.

49 RPS to Charles Drake, October 14, 1918, Tam.

50 Salvatore, *Eugene V. Debs,* pp. 278–79.

51 Reported by BI agent, OG, microcopy 1085, NA.

52 RPS to Anna Strunsky Walling, June 15, 1918, Yale.

XII. *"A Dangerous Woman"*

1 Philip S. Foner, *The Bolshevik Revolution: Its Impact on American Radicals, Liberals, and Labor* (New York: International Publishers, 1967), p. 23.

2 *New York Call,* August 1, 1918.

3 OTD to RPS, January 1, 1919, Yale.

4 Theodore Draper, *The Roots of American Communism* (New York: Viking Press, 1957), pp. 144–47; Emmet Larkin, *James Larkin: Irish Labour Leader, 1876–1947* (Cambridge, Mass.: MIT Press, 1965), pp. 229–31.

5 Helen Stokes to RPS, February 1917, Tam.

6 *New York Times,* February 17, 1919.

7 Henry W. Youmans to RPS, March 11, 1919, Tam; Salvatore, *Eugene V. Debs*, p. 321; Mabel D. Curry to RPS, January 3, February 6, May 16, 1919, Yale.

8 David Karsner, *Debs: His Authorized Life and Letters from Woodstock Prison to Atlanta* (New York: Boni and Liveright, 1919), pp. 28–29.

9 JGPS to Upton Sinclair, May 19, 1919, Lilly Library, Indiana University, Bloomington.

10 People's Playhouse circular letter, May 18, 1919, Yale.

11 Samuel Ornitz to RPS, December 11, 1932, Yale.

12 Norman Springer to RPS, May 19, 1919, Tam.

13 RPS to E. V. Debs, April 30, 1919, microfilm at Tam.

14 Theodore Debs to RPS, May 11, 1919, Tam.

15 Mabel D. Curry to RPS, January 3, 1919, Yale.

16 Lusk Committee, *Revolutionary Radicalism,* 4 vols. (Albany: New York State Senate, 1920), 1:725–26. Morris Hillquit in *Loose Leaves from a Busy Life* summarized the role of the Lusk Committee and others of that type: "The Overman Committee of the United States Senate and the Lusk Committee of the New York Legislature were busy securing 'evidence' from all corners of the world to build up a fantastic theory of a myste-

rious, powerful, and dangerous movement in the United States to overthrow our government and to hoist the red flag of Communist revolution on the national Capitol. Red baiting and heresy hunting became the fashion" (p. 249).

17 Laura Stephens Suggett to RPS, May 19, 1919, Sinclair Papers, Lilly Library.

18 RPS to Upton Sinclair, May 24, 1919, July 11, 1919, ibid.

19 RPS to Upton Sinclair, July 23, 1919, ibid.

20 RPS to Upton Sinclair, n.d., ibid.

21 Upton Sinclair to JGPS, June 19, 1919, CU; JGPS to Upton Sinclair, June 26, 1919, Lilly Library.

22 Upton Sinclair to JGPS, July 1, 1919, CU.

23 Nathalie Ells to RPS, June 21, 1919, Tam. Tom Mooney and Warren Billings were convicted in 1916 following a Preparedness Day explosion. Though their innocence was proved, they were given life sentences. They were fully pardoned in 1939 after serving twenty-three years.

24 Lusk Committee, *Revolutionary Radicalism,* 1:24.

25 *New York Times,* June 21, 1919.

26 Ibid., June 23, 1919.

27 RPS to OTD, June 16, 1919, Yale.

28 Shannon, *Socialist Party,* pp. 146–49; Hicks, *John Reed,* pp. 361–62.

29 *New York Times,* September 5, 1919.

30 Ibid., November 17, 1919.

31 Ibid., November 21, 22, 1919.

32 Text of *Novy Mir* speech not available; sent to Hoover with letter of transmittal by BI agent, January 22, 1920, Box 802, NA.

33 *New York Times,* December 20, 1919.

34 Ibid., January 22, 1920.

35 Ibid., January 24, February 14, 1920.

36 Ibid., February 19, 1920.

37 JGPS to Hector Munro-Ferguson, February 27, 1920, CU.

38 *Izvestia,* May 14, 1921.

39 *New York Times,* March 10, 1920.

40 RPS to Theodore Debs, March 22, 1920, microfilm, Tam.

41 Woodrow Wilson to A. Mitchell Palmer, Woodrow Wilson Papers, ser. 2, Manuscript Department, Library of Congress.

XIII. Troubles

1 OTD to JGPS, June 21, 1920, Tam.

2 OTD to RPS, n.d., probably summer 1920, Yale.

3 JGPS to RPS, August 10, 13, 20, September 28, 1920, Tam.

4 RPS to JGPS, October 19, 1920, Yale.

5 Anna Webb to RPS, November 9, 1920, Tam.

6 Lincoln Steffens to Daniel Kiefer, quoted by Kiefer in letter to RPS, November 13, 1920, Tam.

7   Harry Laidler to RPS, October 9, 1920, Tam.

8   JGPS to RPS, November 15, 1920, Tam; OTD to RPS, December 4, 1920, Yale.

9   Two unsigned letters to RPS, ca. December 1920, Yale.

10 AB (undated, unpaged notes at Yale on reel 573 II 6C, folder 14).

11 *New York World,* January 23, 1921.

12 RPS to Cornell Ridderhof, January 25, 1921, CU.

13 Daniel Kiefer to RPS, February 25, 1920, Tam.

14 Daniel Kiefer to B. W. Huebsch, January 24, 1921; Huebsch to Kiefer, February 1, 1921, Tam.

15 Daniel Kiefer to RPS, January 24, 1921, Tam.

16 RPS to Daniel Kiefer, March 3, 11, 1921, Tam.

17 Adam Clayton Powell to RPS, March 23, 1921, Tam.

18 Marc D. Naison, *Communists in Harlem during the Depression* (New York: Grove Press, 1985), p. 8.

19 George H. English to R. P. Stewart, ca. 1921), OG, Box 1085, NA.

20 *New York Times,* September 12, 1921.

21 Justus J. Fernel to Department of Justice, September 22, 1921, NA.

22 Melech Epstein, *The Jew and Communism, 1919–1941* (New York: Trade Union Sponsoring Committee, 1959), pp. 20, 75; *New York Times,* August 15, 1921.

23 OTD to RPS, November 3, 1921, Yale.

24 *New York Times,* November 17, 19, 1921.

25 JGPS to RPS, January 3, December 19, 1921, Yale.

26 JGPS to RPS, December 27, 1921, Yale.

27 RPS to JGPS, December 29, 1921, Yale.

28 RPS to the MacInneses, December 29, 1921, Yale.

29 JGPS to RPS, January 21, 1922, Yale.

30 JGPS to RPS, January 31, 1922, Yale.

31 Jeanette Pearl to RPS, January 16, 1922, Tam.

32 Elmer Allison to RPS, February 2, 1922, Tam.

33 Lincoln Steffens quoted in Daniel Kiefer to RPS, January 27, 1922, Tam.

34 Ginger, *Bending Cross,* pp. 433, 447.

35 Quoted in ibid., p. 451.

XIV. The Red, Red Rose

1   Claude McKay, *A Long Way from Home* (1937; rpt. New York: Arno Press, 1969), pp. 141–67.

2   From minority report of "Sasha" (RPS), Fourth Congress, CI, December 1922, Yale.

3   Samuel Spewack to RPS, April 4, 1923, Yale. Max Eastman was not as reliable as Spewack thought. His course of development was from ardent socialist to communist to Trotskyist to supporter of Joseph McCarthy. See William L. O'Neill, *The Last Romantic* (New York: Oxford University Press, 1978), p. xviii.

4   McKay, *A Long Way from Home,* p. 160.

5 Solon De Leon to RPS, January 12, 1923, Tam; RPS's reply is written on the bottom of De Leon's letter.

6 Helen Stokes to RPS, April 11, 1923, Tam.

7 Helena Louisa Stokes to RPS, January 12, 1923, Tam.

8 RPS to OTD, September 20, 1923, Yale.

9 Kahlil Gibran to RPS, December 11, 1918, Yale.

10 Jean Gibran and Kahlil Gibran, *Kahlil Gibran: His Life and World* (Boston: New York Graphic Society, 1974), p. 331.

11 RPS to OTD, October 10, 1923, January 29, 1924, Yale.

12 RPS to OTD, September 24, 1923, Yale.

13 OTD to RPS, December 25, 1923, Yale.

14 RPS to *New York Times,* December 15, 1923.

15 Rebecca to RPS, July 12, 1923, Yale.

16 *Buffalo Morning Express,* November 5, 1923.

17 John Ballam to RPS, September 12, 1923, Yale.

18 Samuel Ornitz to RPS, December 17, 1923, Yale.

19 *New York Times,* February 11, 1924.

20 RPS to OTD, April 19, 1924, Yale.

21 OTD to RPS, June 6, 1924, Yale.

22 *New York Times,* June 19, 1924.

23 OTD to RPS, n.d., autumn 1924, Yale.

24 Upton Sinclair to RPS, June 7, 1924, Yale.

25 JGPS to RPS, November 6, 1924, Tam.

26 Quoted in Lusk Committee, *Revolutionary Radicalism,* 2:1435.

27 V. I. Lenin, *A Letter to American Workers* (New York: International Publishers, 1934), pp. 21–22.

28 Jeanette Pearl to Central Executive Committee, Workers Party, November 10, 1924, Yale.

29 RPS to C. E. Ruthenberg, November 22, 1924, Yale.

30 JGPS to RPS, February 12, 1925, Yale.

31 RPS to JGPS, February 11, 1925, Yale.

XV. Divorce: From Riches to Rags

1 RPS to JGPS, February 11, 1925, Yale.

2 RPS to OTD, February 11, 1925, Yale.

3 RPS to JGPS, February 18, 1925, Yale.

4 JGPS to RPS, n.d. (ca. February 19, 1925), Yale.

5 RPS to JGPS, March 6, 1925, Yale.

6 RPS to JGPS, March 16, 1925, Yale.

7 JGPS to RPS, n.d. (ca. March 20, 1925), Yale.

8 *New York Times,* March 5, 1925.

9 RPS to JGPS, May 23, 1925, Yale.

10 Helen Stokes to RPS, May 24, 1925, Yale.

11 RPS to George H. Gilman, June 1, 1925, Yale; Gilman to RPS, June 2, July 8, 1925, Yale.

12 RPS to Helen Stokes, June 7, 1925 (copy, no signature); Helen Stokes to RPS, June 10, 1925; RPS to Helen Stokes, July 7, 1925, all in Yale.

13 RPS to C. E. Ruthenberg, June 18, 1925, Yale.

14 RPS to Organization Committee of the Workers party, August 5, 1925, Tam.

15 Julius Hammer to RPS, August 11, 1925; RPS to Julius Hammer, August 16, 1925, both in Yale.

16 JGPS to Mother, October 13, 1925, Yale.

17 Charles Recht to RPS, November 1, 1925, Yale.

18 *New York Times,* October 18, 19, 1925.

19 Minnie F. Corder to RPS, October 19, 1925, Yale.

20 Eugene V. Debs to RPS, October 19, 1925, Yale.

21 RPS to Eugene V. Debs, October 22, 1925, Yale; Debs to RPS, October 27, 1925, microfilm, Yale.

22 RPS to Anna S. Walling, October 28, 1925, Yale.

23 OTD to RPS, December 7, 1925, in the authors' possession.

24 *Collier's,* February 13, 1926.

25 OTD to RPS, December 21, 1925; RPS to OTD, ca. December 1925, both in the authors' possession.

26 RPS to JGPS, March 2, 1926, Yale.

27 RPS to JGPS, March 12, 1926, Yale.

28 JGPS to RPS, March 25, 1926, Yale.

29 RPS to JGPS, March 26, 1926, Yale.

30 E. P. Behringer to Anna Pastor, March 31, 1926, Yale.

31 RPS to E. P. Behringer, April 1, 1926, Yale.

32 RPS to OTD, May 10, 1926, Yale.

33 RPS to Joanna Cooke, May 10, 1926, Tam.

34 Irving Grossman to RPS, June 30?, 1926; RPS to Irving Grossman, July 8, 1926, both in Yale.

35 RPS to OTD, September 2, 1926, Yale.

36 See letters of Rose Marie Macgonnell, March 22, 1930, April 27, 1931, and others, n.d., Yale.

37 RPS to OTD, ca. October 12, 1926, Yale.

38 Eugene Lyons to John Whitcomb, January 8, 1958, JMW.

39 RPS to Jeanette Pearl, ca. December 1926, Yale.

40 *New York Times,* April 18, 1926.

41 A. Bittelman to RPS, August 12, 1926; RPS to A. Bittelman, August 16, 1926, both in Yale.

42 A. Bittelman to RPS, September 16, 1926, Yale; ibid., October 23, 1926, JMW.

43 RPS to A. Bittelman, n.d. (ca. 1926), Yale.

44 Fiorello H. La Guardia to RPS, February 1, 1927, Yale.

45 Globus Press to RPS, April 16, 1928, Yale.

46 Joanna Cooke to RPS, n.d., Tam.

47 Jerome Romain to RPS, June 11, 1928; RPS to Romain, July 10, 1928, both in Yale.
48 RPS to Bernard Pastor, July 11, 1928, Yale.
49 RPS to Jerome Romain, October 17, 1928, Yale.
50 RPS to Jerome Romain, July 18, 1928, Yale.
51 See William F. Dunne, *Gastonia* (New York: Workers Library Publishers, 1929).
52 OTD to RPS, April 26, 1929, in the authors' possession.

XVI. *Last Years*

1 JGPS to Mother, July 17, 1929, CU. We were shown the meditation room by Lettice Stokes on July 28, 1983.
2 *Daily Worker,* December 12, 16, 1929.
3 OTD to RPS, March 2, 1930, Yale.
4 OTD to RPS, March 8, 1930, in the authors' possession.
5 *New York Evening Post,* March 20, 1930; *New York Journal,* March 20, 1930; *New York World Telegram,* October 19, 1932.
6 Lillian Wald to RPS, March 28, 1930, Yale.
7 Cecelia Razovsky Davidson to RPS, April 6, 1930, Yale.
8 Herbert Benjamin to RPS, April 14, 1930, Yale; E. G. Flynn to Mary Heaton Vorse, May 6, 1930, Archives of Labor History and Urban Affairs, Wayne State University, Detroit, Mich.
9 OTD to RPS, May 8, 1930, in the authors' possession.
10 Flora Raugh to RPS, May 21, 1930, Yale.
11 Oswald Garrison Villard to RPS, June 17, 1930, Yale.
12 Anne Williams Feinberg to John Whitcomb, June 30, 1975, JMW; authors' telephone interview with Feinberg; RPS to Adelaide Schulkind Frank, January 30, 1931, Schlesinger Library, Radcliffe College, Cambridge, Mass.
13 OTD to Hans Holfelder, July 14, 1930, Yale.
14 Grace Hutchins to RPS, November 9, 1930, Yale.
15 RPS to Grace Hutchins, November 11, 1930, Yale.
16 OTD to RPS, January 18, 1931, Tam.
17 RPS to Adelaide Schulkind Frank, January 30, 1931, Schlesinger Library, Radcliffe College.
18 Germinal Romain to RPS, January 6, 1931 (erroneously dated January 6, 1930); RPS to Jerome Romain, written on a scrap of paper, undated, unsigned, and unaddressed.
19 RPS to Lillian Wald, February 9, 1931, Wald Papers, CU.
20 Anne Williams to Jerome Romain, n.d., 1931, Tam.
21 RPS to Jerome Romain, April 11, 1931, Yale.
22 RPS to Adelaide Schulkind Frank, May 29, 1931, Schlesinger Library, Radcliffe College.
23 RPS to Jerome Romain, May 2, 1931, Yale.
24 RPS to Anne Williams, n.d., Tam.
25 RPS to William Donner, December 21, 1932, Tam.

26   Hans Holfelder to RPS, November 13, 1931, Tam.

27   Leonard Abbott to RPS, January 6, 1932, Tam.

28   RPS to Jerome Romain, January 2, 1932, Yale.

29   Romain to RPS, n.d., Yale.

30   Clara Renner to RPS, n.d.; RPS to Renner, January 3, 1932, both in Yale.

31   Bella Spewack to RPS, January 6, 1932, Tam.

32   RPS to OTD, January 27, 1932, Yale.

33   Benjamin DeCasseres to RPS, August 10, 1932.

34   Anna W. Shannon, "Afterword" to Fielding Burke [Olive Dargan], *Call Home the Heart* (1932; rpt. Old Westbury, N.Y.: Feminist Press, 1983), pp. 442–46.

35   Dr. Linder to RPS, May 25, 1932, Yale.

36   Paula Jacobi to RPS, October 3, 1932, Yale; Schwarz, *Radical Feminists,* p. 79.

37   June Burr to RPS, January 20, 1933, Yale.

38   RPS to Jeanette Pearl, August 23, 1932, Yale.

39   OTD to RPS, August 1, 1932, Yale.

40   RPS to "Jerry Boy," September 2, 1932, Yale.

41   RPS to Hans Holfelder, December 28, 1932, Yale.

42   RPS, entries in memo book, January 8–March 20, 1933, Yale.

43   OTD to RPS, February 13, 1933, Yale.

44   RPS to Anne Williams (from Frankfurt), n.d., Tam.

45   RPS to Jerome Romain, February 23, 1933, Yale.

46   RPS to Anne Williams, March 15, 1933, Tam.

47   RPS to Joseph Brodsky, March 18, 1933, Yale.

48   RPS to *New York Times,* April 29, 1933.

49   RPS to Joseph Brodsky, April 19, 1933, Yale.

50   Anne Williams Feinberg telephone interview with the authors, January 27, 1984.

51   OTD to RPS, May 27, 1933, Yale.

52   Clara Renner to Jerome Romain, April 17, 1933, Yale.

53   RPS to Joseph Brodsky, n.d. (May?) 1933, Yale.

54   RPS, review of *Violette of Pere Lachaise, Intercollegiate Socialist* 4 (February–March 1916): 30.

55   RPS to OTD (cable), June 21, 1933, Yale.

56   *New York World Telegram,* June 20, 1933.

57   Hans Holfelder to Jerome Romain, July 15, 1933, Yale. In response to a query to the International Tracing Service, Arolsen, West Germany, we were informed that they had no information about Dr. Holfelder (November 8, 1985).

58   Jerome Romain's memo, n.d., Yale.

59   OTD to Jerome Romain, June 22, 1933, Yale.

60   Romain to OTD, June 26, 1933, Yale.

61   OTD to RPS, May 27, 1933, Yale. The text of the poem given here with its title "To Rose Pastor" is taken from Olive Dargan's letter to RPS, May 27, 1933. The poem was published in a revised text titled "Testament to Her—A Gentle Crusader," in Olive Tilford Dargan, *The Spotted Hawk* (Winston-Salem: John F. Blair, 1958), p. 84.

Afterword

1 Samuel Ornitz to Joseph A. Margolies, December 30, 1933, Yale.
2 V. J. Jerome to Samuel Ornitz, May 6, 1934, Yale.
3 Earl Browder to Samuel Ornitz, July 30, 1934; Ornitz to Browder, August 6, 1934, both in Yale.
4 Samuel Ornitz to V. J. Jerome, February 25, 1935, Yale.
5 Joseph A. Margolies to V. J. Jerome, December 14, 1935, Yale.
6 OTD to V. J. Jerome, quoted in Jerome to Covici, February 1, 1937, Yale.
7 Pascal Covici to V. J. Jerome, February 8, 1937, Yale.
8 John Whitcomb to Alice Jerome, April 30, 1967, JMW.
9 Elizabeth Gurley Flynn, in *Worker,* June 23, 1946.

Bibliography

Books

Aaron, Daniel. *Writers on the Left*. 1961. Reprint. New York: Oxford University Press, 1977.

Addams, Jane. *Twenty Years at Hull House*. New York: Macmillan, 1945.

Aptheker, Herbert. *Annotated Bibliography of the Published Writings of W. E. B. Du Bois*. Millwood, N.Y.: Kraus-Thompson, 1973.

Baker, Sara Josephine. *Fighting for Life*. New York: Macmillan, 1939.

Barringer, Emily Dunning. *Bowery to Bellevue*. New York: Norton, 1950.

Birmingham, Stephen. *The Rest of Us*. Boston: Little, Brown, 1984.

Blatch, Harriot Stanton, and Alma Lutz. *Challenging Years: The Memoirs of Harriot Stanton Blatch*. New York: Putnam, 1940.

Bloor, Ella Reeve. *We Are Many*. New York: International Publishers, 1940.

Bourne, Randolph S. *War and the Intellectuals*. New York: Harper & Row, 1964.

Boyer, Richard O., and Herbert M. Morais. *Labor's Untold Story*. New York: Cameron Associates, 1955.

Brommel, Bernard J. *Eugene V. Debs: Spokesman for Labor and Socialism*. Chicago: Charles H. Kerr, 1978.

Buhle, Mari Jo. *Women and American Socialism, 1870–1920*. Urbana: University of Illinois Press, 1983.

Burke, Fielding. See Dargan, Olive Tilford.

Chafee, Zechariah. *The Blessings of Liberty*. Philadelphia: Lippincott, 1956.

Concise Dictionary of American Biography. 2d ed. New York: Scribners, 1977.

Dargan, Olive Tilford. *The Spotted Hawk*. Winston-Salem: John F. Blair, 1958.

———. *Call Home the Heart* (Fielding Burke, pseud.) 1932. Reprint. Old Westbury, N.Y.: Feminist Press, 1983.

Darrow, Clarence. *Story of My Life*. New York: Scribners, 1934.

Davis, Allen F. *The Legend of Jane Addams*. New York: Oxford University Press, 1980.

Deckard, Barbara Sinclair. *The Women's Movement*. New York: Harper & Row, 1975.

Degler, Carl. *At Odds: Women and the Family in America*. New York: Oxford University Press, 1980.

De Leon, Solon, ed. *The American Labor Who's Who*. New York: Hanford Press, 1925.

Dorr, Rheta Childe. *A Woman of Fifty*. New York: Funk and Wagnalls, 1924.

Douglas, Emily. *Margaret Sanger: Pioneer of the Future*. New York: Holt, Rinehart, and Winston, 1970.

Draper, Theodore. *The Roots of American Communism*. New York: Viking Press, 1957.

Drinnon, Richard. *Rebel in Paradise*. Chicago: University of Chicago Press, 1961.

Dubofsky, Melvyn. *When Workers Organize*. Amherst: University of Massachusetts Press, 1968.

Du Bois, Carol, ed. *Elizabeth Cady Stanton, Susan B. Anthony Correspondence, Writings, Speeches*. New York: Schocken Books, 1981.

Epstein, Melech. *The Jew and Communism, 1919–1941*. New York: Trade Union Sponsoring Committee, 1959.

Falk, Candace. *Love, Anarchy, and Emma Goldman*. New York: Holt, Rinehart, and Winston, 1984.

Feldstein, Stanley. *The Land That I Show You*. Garden City, N.Y.: Doubleday, 1979.

Ferree, Myra Marx, and Beth B. Hess. *Controversy and Coalition*. Boston: Twayne, 1985.

Fishbein, Leslie. *Rebels in Bohemia: The Radicals and The Masses*. Chapel Hill: University of North Carolina Press, 1982.

Flexner, Eleanor. *Century of Struggle*. New York: Atheneum, 1974.

Flynn, Elizabeth Gurley. *The Rebel Girl*. New York: International Publishers, 1973.

Foner, Philip S. *The Bolshevik Revolution: Its Impact on American Radicals, Liberals, and Labor*. New York: International Publishers, 1967.

———. *History of the Labor Movement in the United States*. 8 vols. New York: International Publishers, 1947–88.

———. *May Day*. New York: International Publishers, 1986.

———. *Women and the American Labor Movement*. New York: Free Press, 1979.

Foner, Philip S., and Sally S. Miller, eds. *Kate Richards O'Hare: Selected Writings and Speeches*. Baton Rouge: Louisiana State University Press, 1982.

Foster, William Z. *History of the Communist Party of the United States*. New York: International Publishers, 1952.

Freeman, Joseph. *An American Testament*. New York: Farrar and Rinehart, 1936.

Fried, Albert, ed. *Socialism in America*. Garden City, N.Y.: Anchor Books, 1970.

Gartner, Lloyd P. *History of the Jews of Cleveland*. Cleveland: Western Reserve Historical Society and Jewish Theological Seminary of America, 1978.

Gibran, Jean, and Kahlil Gibran. *Kahlil Gibran: His Life and World*. Boston: New York Graphic Society, 1974.

Ginger, Ray. *The Bending Cross*. 1944. Reprint. New York: Russell and Russell, 1969.

Gitlow, Benjamin. *I Confess*. 1939. Reprint. New York: Dutton, 1940.

Goldman, Emma. *Living My Life*. New York: Knopf, 1931.

Gordon, Linda. *Woman's Body, Woman's Rights*. New York: Grossman, 1976.

Gray, Madeline. *Margaret Sanger: A Biography of the Champion of Birth Control*. New York: Richard Marek, 1979.

Griffith, Elizabeth. *In Her Own Right*. New York: Oxford University Press, 1984.

Haywood, Harry. *Black Bolshevik*. Chicago: Liberator Press, 1978.

Hicks, Granville. *John Reed*. New York: Macmillan, 1936.

Hillquit, Morris. *Loose Leaves from a Busy Life*. New York: Rand School Press, 1934.

Horn, Max. *The Intercollegiate Socialist Society*. Boulder, Colo.: Westview Press, 1979.

Howe, Irving. *World of Our Fathers*. New York: Harcourt Brace Jovanovich, 1976.

Howe, Irving, and Lewis Coser. *The American Communist Party*. Boston: Beacon Press, 1957.

Hutchins, Grace. *Women Who Work*. New York: International Publishers, 1934.

James, Edward T., ed. *Notable American Women*. Cambridge, Mass.: Belknap Press of Harvard University Press, 1971.

Josephson, Mathew. *Union House, Union Bar*. New York: Random House, 1956.

Karsner, David. *Debs: His Authorized Life and Letters from Woodstock Prison to Atlanta*. New York: Boni and Liveright, 1919.

Kaun, Alex. *Maxim Gorky and His Russia*. New York: Jonathan Cape, 1931.

Kent, Rockwell. *It's Me, O Lord*. New York: Dodd, Mead, 1955.

Kipnis, Ira. *The American Socialist Movement, 1897–1912*. New York: Monthly Review Press, 1972.

Laidler, Harry W. *Socialism in Thought and Action*. New York: Macmillan, 1920.

Larkin, Emmet. *James Larkin: Irish Labour Leader, 1876–1947*. Cambridge, Mass.: MIT Press, 1965.

Lasch, Christopher. *The Agony of the American Left*. New York: Knopf, 1969.

Lenin, V. I. *Imperialism*. New York: International Publishers, 1939.

Levine, Louis. *The Women's Garment Workers: A History of the International Ladies Garment Workers Union*. New York: B. W. Huebsch, 1924.

Liptzin, Sol. *Eliakum Zunser*. New York: Behrman House, 1950.

Lundberg, Ferdinand. *Imperial Hearst*. New York: Modern Library, 1936.

Lusk Committee. *Revolutionary Radicalism*. 4 vols. Albany: New York State Senate, 1920.

Manners, Ande. *Poor Cousins*. New York: Coward-McCann, Geoheagan, 1972.

Marcus, Jacob Rader, ed. *The American Jewish Woman: A Documentary History*. New York: American Jewish Archives, 1981.

McKay, Claude. *A Long Way from Home*. 1937. Reprint. New York: Arno Press, 1969.

Mereto, Joseph J. *The Red Conspiracy*. New York: National Historical Society, 1920.

Millet, Kate. *Sexual Politics*. Garden City, N.Y.: Doubleday, 1970.

Naison, Mark D. *Communists in Harlem during the Depression*. New York: Grove Press, 1985.

Nearing, Scott. *The Making of a Radical*. New York: Harper & Row, 1972.

Neidle, Cecyle S. *American Immigrant Women*. Boston: Twayne, 1975.

O'Neill, William L. *The Last Romantic*. New York: Oxford University Press, 1978.

Ornitz, Samuel B. *Haunch, Paunch and Jowl*. New York: Boni and Liveright, 1923.

Reed, James Wesley. *From Private Vice to Public Virtue*. New York: Basic Books, 1978.

Reed, John. *Ten Days That Shook the World*. New York: International Publishers, 1934.

Reeve, Carl. *The Life and Times of Daniel De Leon*. Atlantic Highlands, N.J.: Humanities Press, 1972.

Reeve, Carl, and Ann Barton. *James Connolly and the United States*. Atlantic Highlands, N.J.: Humanities Press, 1978.

Rogoff, Harry. *An East Side Epic: Life and Work of Meyer London*. New York: Vanguard Press, 1930.

Rosenstone, Robert A. *Romantic Revolutionary.* 1975. Reprint. New York: Vintage, 1978.

Salvatore, Nick. *Eugene V. Debs: Citizen and Socialist.* Urbana: University of Illinois Press, 1982.

Sanger, Margaret. *An Autobiography.* 1938. Reprint. New York: Dover, 1971.

———. *My Fight for Birth Control.* New York: Farrar and Rinehart, 1931.

Scheuer, Jeffrey. *Legacy of Light.* New York: University Settlement, n.d.

Schwarz, Judith. *Radical Feminists of Heterodoxy.* Lebanon, N.H.: New Victoria Publishers, 1982.

Shannon, David A. *The Socialist Party of America.* New York: Macmillan, 1955.

Shustko, Beatrice. *The Edgies.* New York: Educational Alliance, n.d.

Steel, Ronald. *Walter Lippmann and the American Century.* Boston: Little, Brown, 1980.

Steffens, Lincoln. *Autobiography.* New York: Harcourt, Brace, 1931.

Stokes, Rose Pastor. *The Woman Who Wouldn't and Other Plays.* New York: Putnam, 1916.

Tax, Meredith. *Rivington Street.* New York: Morrow, 1982.

Thompson, Dorothy. *The Chartists.* New York: Pantheon Books, 1984.

Van Doren, Charles, ed. *Webster's American Biographies.* Springfield, Mass.: G. C. Merriam Co., 1975.

Vorse, Mary Heaton. *Reminiscences.* New York: Farrar and Rinehart, 1935.

Walling, William English. *Socialism as It Is.* New York: Macmillan, 1915.

Weinstein, James. *The Decline of Socialism in America, 1912–1925.* New York: Random House, 1969.

Weisbord, Vera Buch. *A Radical Life.* Bloomington: Indiana University Press, 1977.

Werthheimer, Barbara Mayer. *We Were There.* New York: Pantheon Books, 1977.

Wexler, Alice. *Emma Goldman: An Intimate Life.* New York: Pantheon Books, 1984.

Whitney, R. M. *Reds in America.* New York: Beckwith Press, 1924.

Yezierska, Anzia. *Red Ribbon on a White Horse.* New York: Boni and Liveright, 1920.

———. *Salome of the Tenements.* New York: Brazilier, 1925.

Young, Art. *His Life and Times.* New York: Sheridan House, 1939.

Zarier, Rebecca. *Art for the Masses, 1911–17.* New Haven: Yale University Art Gallery, 1985.

Articles, Dissertations, and Pamphlets

Buhle, Mari Jo. "Women and the Socialist Party, 1901–14." *Radical America* 4 (February 1970): 36–57.

Debs, Eugene Victor. "A Graceful Tribute to the Socialist Woman." *Socialist Woman* 12 (May 1908): 3.

Dunne, William F. "Gastonia: Citadel of the Class Struggle in the New South." Workers Library Publishers, 1929.

Griffin, Lillian Baynes. "Mrs. J. G. Phelps Stokes at Home." *Harper's Bazar* 40 (September 1906): 794–99.

Lathrop, V. Terrell. "Short Biographical Sketch of Olive T. Dargan." Manuscript. Pack Memorial Library, Asheville, N.C.

Leinenweber, Charles. "Socialists in the Street." *Science and Society* 41 (Summer 1947): 107.

Parce, Lida. "What Is the Woman Question?" *Progressive Woman* 2 (March 1909): 3–4.

Renshaw, Patrick. "Pastor-Stokes Marriage and the American Left, 1905–25," *Quarterly Journal of the New York State Historical Association* 62 (October 1981): 415–38.

Reynolds, Robert D. Jr. "The Millionaire Socialists: James Graham Phelps Stokes and His Circle of Friends." Ph.D. dissertation, University of South Carolina, 1974.

Schofield, Ann. "Rebel Girl and Union Maid: The Woman Question in the Journals of the AFL and IWW, 1905–20." *Feminist Studies,* Summer 1983, pp. 335–58.

Scudder, Vida D. "Woman and Socialism." *Yale Review* 3 (April 1914): 459.

Sharp, Kathleen Ann. "Rose Pastor Stokes: Radical Champion of the American Working Class, 1879–1933." Ph.D. dissertation, Duke University, 1979.

Sholten, Pat. "Militant Women for Economic Justice." Ph.D. dissertation, Indiana University, 1979.

Sklar, Kathryn Kish. "Hull House in the 1890s: A Community of Women." *Signs* 10 (Summer 1985): 658–77.

Spargo, John. "Women and the Socialist Movement." *International Socialist Review* 8 (February 1908): 449.

Stokes, Rose Pastor. "The Condition of Working Women from the Working Woman's Viewpoint." *Annals of the American Academy of Political and Social Science* 37 (January–May 1906): 165–75.

———. "A Confession." *Century,* December 1917, pp. 457–59.

———. "A Converted Yankee." *Young Worker,* August 1923, p. 15.

———. "From Poverty to Protest: Excerpts from Her Autobiography." *Jewish Currents,* June 1983, pp. 23–28.

———. "The Long Day." *Independent,* November 16, 1905, pp. 1169–70.

———. "Poem." *Literary Digest,* June 25, 1921, p. 69.

———. "Two Sketches." *Young Worker,* May 1922, p. 4.

———. "Woolworth Girl." *Forum,* May 24, 1928, p. 794.

Tamarkin, Stanley. "Rose Pastor Stokes: The Portrait of a Radical Woman, 1905–19." Ph.D. dissertation, Yale University, 1983.

Zunser, Miriam Shomer. "The Jewish Literary Scene in New York at the Beginning of the Century." *YIVO Annual of Jewish Social Science* 8 (1952): 290–93.

Index